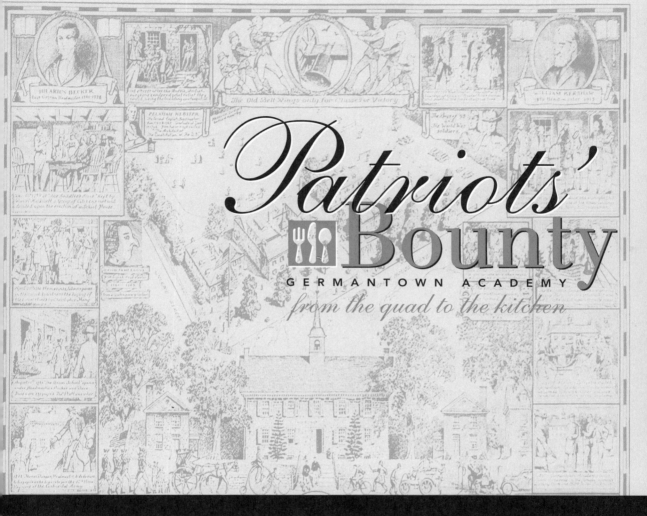

Patriots' Bounty

GERMANTOWN ACADEMY

from the quad to the kitchen

GERMANTOWN ACADEMY — Founded December 6~ A.D. 1759

Germantown Academy Parents' Committee
Fort Washington, Pennsylvania

By Citizens of Germantown and Vicinity as The — Germantown Union School. Chartered 1784
as The Public School of Germantown. Used as — a Hospital after the Battle of Oct. 4th 1777.
Offered to The Continental Congress as — a Place for its meetings . . .

The Germantown Academy Parents' Committee gratefully acknowledges those who came before us who laid the foundation to support the faculty and administration as they strived for academic excellence. To our current parents, whose boundless energy and commitment continues to support the GA legacy. To the next generation of parent leaders, who will continue the tradition of standing behind those who educate future generations. To the past, present, and future of the Germantown Academy community we dedicate this book.

Patriots' Bounty

GERMANTOWN ACADEMY

from the quad to the kitchen

First Printing   May 2010   3,000

Copyright © Germantown Academy 2010. All Rights Reserved

ISBN: 978-0-578-04793-5

www.germantownacademy.net

Copies of Patriots' Bounty may be purchased at www.germantownacademy.net/cookbookorder and order forms are located in the back of the cookbook.

This book, or any portion thereof, may not be reproduced in any form without the written permission from Germantown Academy — 340 Morris Road, Fort Washington, PA 19034

WIMMER
COOKBOOKS

A CONSOLIDATED GRAPHICS COMPANY

800.548.2537   wimmerco.com

Mmmm... I can smell the confections cooking now.

When the Parents' Committee decided to take on this 250th Celebration project , I was more than delighted. From what I hear, this cookbook is not simply a "cookbook" cookbook, but a skillful blending of history and photography and anecdotes and recipes. Food + History, two of my favorites, in a book-my third favorite! This sugar smells even sweeter. Could there be a better time to be a part of GA? Could there be a more opportune time to thank the Parents' Committee for making GA our neighborhood cafe?

From Our Town, to Night of a Thousand Dreams; from the Book Fair to the Sneaker Drive; from the Consignment Shop to Bingo, communal spirit is alive and well when the Parents' Committee is present. I cherish and rely on the close relationship the administration has with Executive Committee. Our relationship serves as a model to other independent schools in our area because GA's Parents' Committee sees problems and offers solutions, keeps a watchful eye for what best serves the good of the whole community, assists by raising funds for the operating budget, and serves as admissions ambassadors to those who are eager to know more about our school, its history and its people.

To have this project reflect true GA creativity and sophistication, as well as their own high standards, the Parents' Committee asked two of their most ambitious and hardworking, Kim Sloane '84 and Deborah Westrum and their committee of colleagues, to take it on. How did they do? Well the "proof is always in the pudding." Read on and you will agree with me that their recipe for success includes the basic ingredients of hard work mixed with good ideas, both lovingly seasoned with a dash of the past, a sprinkle of red, blue and black, and more than a pinch of Patriot pride.

I could not be more proud of or grateful to them and the 300+ plus recipe authors who contributed to the book. Feeling hungry for a Patriot dish? Try a few of these out, read a bit of history, study the photos, then get on the computer and order more copies for family and friends. If you crave a GA keepsake, well, here's one that really "cooks."

Bon Appetit,

James W. Connor 1760

Head of School

Patriots' Bounty Committee

Patriots' Bounty, from the Quad to the Kitchen, has been lovingly produced by the Germantown Academy Parents' Committee to provide families and friends of our school an opportunity to share with each other family recipes, as well as a wealth of information on Germantown Academy's 250 years of rich history. All proceeds from the sale of Patriots' Bounty will be used to support the educational mission of Germantown Academy.

Germantown Academy is a Pre-K through 12th grade independent, non denominational, co-educational, college preparatory day school founded in 1759. There are presently 1,100 students enrolled. The campus is located in Fort Washington, Pennsylvania on 120 acres. Germantown Academy prides itself in offering a strong curriculum for students of all religions, race, social and economic backgrounds who desire to be challenged in a welcoming and supportive environment.

Chairpersons: Kim Flannery Sloane '84, Debbie Westrum

Historical Editors: Lisa Van Blarcom Butler '82, Amy Korman, Kim Flannery Sloane '84

Cover & Layout: Loren Sciascia

Illustrator: Aina Roman

Coordinator: Laura Korman

Committee Members:

Jamie Aronow
Lisa Van Blarcom Butler '82
Kim Forbes
Becky Bown Harobin '88
Kris Henry
Janet Binswanger Israel '79

Maria Kiley
Cheryl Koons
Marcy Kramp
Carol Momjian
Tara Karr Schwartz '84

Madeline Lamm Specter '79
Laurel Stack
Kathie Vit
Peg Wellington
Sue Zaharchuk

We would like to acknowledge and thank a few very special people that without their commitment, dedication and knowledge, this special book would never have been completed.

Sandy Budinsky
Jim Connor 1760
Heather Durkin
Roger Eastlake '59
Tony Garvan 1760
Eileen Hill 1760

Lauren Kelly
Julie Moore
Susan Stratton McGinnis '78
Kathleen Oberkircher '76
Edwin Probert 1760
Marian Ramirez

Val Rodowicz
Gabrielle Russomagno
Joanne Finkelstein Schell '91
Barbara Hitschler Serrill '68
Carla Zighelboim

Sponsors

The *Patriots' Bounty* committee would like to express our sincerest thanks to the many local establishments' owners and chefs that supported us in our efforts to make this special and unique cookbook a reality. Thank you for helping us celebrate this tremendous milestone in Germantown Academy's history.

Alison two

Beginnings

Blue Bell Inn

Bridget's, A Modern Steakhouse

Broad Axe Tavern

Culinary Concepts

Dettera Restaurant-Wine Bar

From The Boot

Jarrettown Hotel-Italian Restaurant

KC's Alley

MaGerk's Pub & Grill

Meriwether Godsey

Rich's Deli

Ristorante San Marco

Sara's Sweets

Savona Restaurant

Shanachie Irish Pub

Scoogi's Classic Italian Restaurant

The Painted Truffle

Trax Café

Zakes Cakes & Cafe

Recipe: LOWER SCHOOL

INGREDIENTS:
380 Students (tender and of varying sizes and shapes)
60 Faculty and Staff (aged and of varying experiences and interests)
1 New Head Chef!

PRE-HEAT THE ENTIRE SCHOOL HOUSE
Slowly combine the following seasonings to the main ingredients. **KNOWLEDGE...**
... that you can't say "you can't play!"
... of how to read many chapter books from the Library!
... of how to write cursive!
... of how to trust, to be responsible and to show kindness!
... of how to make good choices!
... about the real diversity of the world and the people around you!
... of how to be a good sport as well as an artist!
... that mighty oak trees do grow from little acorns!
... of how to sing all of the verses of "The Alma Mater!"
... that if you preserve, you WILL see "the fruits!"

NO SUBSTITUTIONS PLEASE. Bake for approximately seven years. Mixture should detach easily and be ready for Middle School consumption!

Cannie C. Shafer
Head, Lower School

Recipe: MIDDLE SCHOOL

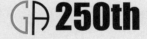

• Mix 250 bright, uninhibited eleven to fourteen year olds with thirty-five creative, dedicated teachers.
• Add one infinitely patient administrative assistant.
• Bring this potent mixture to a rolling boil.
• Gently separate parents and set aside for later.
• Pour while warm into a large new Middle School building and add energy, intellect, emotion and spirit.
• Blend thoroughly.
• Add heaping spoonfuls of athletic and artistic opportunity.
• Layer in a trip to Williamsburg, a sprinkling of music, the magic of memoir, and the thrill of stacking the cups.
• Sprinkle in a generous serving of community service, add spicy student council meetings, rollicking Play Days, magical musicals, and endless pizza parties.
• Add a pinch or two of salt and pepper from the beard of the highly seasoned head chef.
• Cover with grated science fair research...and hope for the best.

Simmer gently for three years.

Deliver piping hot to the Upper School!

Richard House
Head, Middle School

Recipe: UPPER SCHOOL

GA 250th

INGREDIENTS: 486 Students (diverse assortment)
85 Faculty & Staff (well seasoned)
7 Houses (vigorous and carefully mixed)
1 Head of School (freshly picked)
SELECTED ITEMS FOR ADDITIONAL FLAVOR:
1 'GA beats PC - it's easy as 123' button
1 pair opaque shorts, just added to GA gear
2 chairs from the 'awkward date tables' recently bought for the Common Room
1 GA Tie and 1 White Dress to commemorate the new Graduation Dress
1 Graduation Tassel (*secret ingredient!) to commemorate the longing of some for a return to cap and gowns
1 Philadelphia Magazine honoring GA's Belfry as the best theater program in the area
DIRECTIONS:
• Churn the main ingredients well but carefully so as not to injure the US Building we're still holding onto in anticipation of a bigger, more modern facility!
• Sprinkle the items for additional flavor carefully as some are sweet and others quite spicy.
• Bring it all to a 4-year boil before presenting the perfectly cooked product to wonderful colleges and universities across the globe to taste!

Rich Schellhas
Head, Upper School

TABLE OF CONTENTS

APPETIZERS. . . . . page 9

BREADS AND BRUNCH. . . . . page 35

SOUPS AND SALADS. . . . . page 67

PASTA. . . . . page 95

ENTRÉES . . . . page 123

VEGETABLES AND SIDES . . . . page 189

DESSERTS. page 213

GA'S NEIGHBORHOOD. . . . . page 271

INDEX . . . . page 292

FAVORITE RECIPES / NOTES:

_____

_____

_____

_____

_____

_____

_____

_____

_____

_____

_____

_____

_____

_____

_____

_____

_____

_____

_____

_____

_____

_____

_____

_____

_____

mid the amazing events as a nation was born—a few short years after the Liberty Bell was hung outside Independence Hall, before Jefferson penned the Declaration of Independence and Washington encamped at Valley Forge—Germantown Academy was founded. The leading citizens of Germantown, a 6,000-acre parcel of land deeded from William Penn to Daniel Francis Pastorius, were determined that their sons would have a fine classical education.

On December 6, 1759, the men convened at the charming Green Tree Tavern on Germantown Road, and having set their goal, they set out to find a suitable site for the school. Over the next 18 months, the group collected subscriptions and purchased land, and GA opened its doors on August 11th, 1761, near Market Square on Bensell's Lane (later renamed School House Lane), in the Germantown section of Philadelphia. Known originally as the Union School of Germantown, the school was later dubbed "Germantown Academy" by the local newspaper, the *Pennsylvania Gazette*.

GA opened its doors with two headmasters — English-speaking James David Dove, who was a controversial figure with his tyrant ways, and German-speaking Hilarious Becker, a gentleman who led with kindness and encouragement. This dual-headmaster format did not suit the GA Board of Trustees, so they let Dove go. In 1784, the school was granted a charter as the "Public School of Germantown," which is still GA's corporate title today. Its English master at the time, Peletiah Webster, was a champion for education, and wrote a guide used by the delegates of the Constitutional Convention of 1787.

In 1793, with Yellow Fever epidemic in the city of Philadelphia, President George Washington and his cabinet elected to flee to the hills of Germantown, where they convened at Germantown Academy.

When Thomas Dungan, Washington's paymaster in the war, became headmaster at GA, Washington entrusted him with educating his adopted step-son, George Washington Parke Custis, here.

However, the Academy wasn't quite ready to navigate the heady waters of co-ed education. Despite the school's first recorded alumnae being Katherine Harchey in the 1780s, no other women had been officially enrolled in the school until 1831, when headmaster A. Bronson Alcott (father of Louisa May Alcott) registered 19 girls as students. But the co-ed experiment failed, and GA continued as boys-only for the next 125 years. As Philadelphia grew and eventually encroached on the school's campus on School House Lane, an exciting gift was offered by Philadelphia Bulletin owner Robert McLean in December 1958: 160 acres in Fort Washington, a beautiful expanse that included meadows, woods, and portions of the Wissahickon Creek.

CRABMEAT COCKTAIL

3 tablespoons lime juice
2 tablespoons orange juice
2 tablespoons heavy cream
1½ tablespoons Dijon mustard
1 tablespoon horseradish
1 teaspoon Tabasco sauce

1 pound jumbo lump crabmeat, cleaned
¼ cup chopped scallion
¼ cup chopped fresh cilantro
¼ cup sliced fresh chives
½ cup chopped red tomato

In a large bowl, whisk together lime juice, orange juice, cream, mustard, horseradish and Tabasco. Add crabmeat, scallion, cilantro, chives and tomato. Mix until blended. Chill at least 1 hour. Serve chilled in stemware.

SERVES 4 TO 6

Begley Family

FRESH FISHCAKES

2 pounds halibut, or any white flaky fish or salmon
½ pound potatoes, boiled, peeled and coarsely mashed
1 small onion, finely chopped
½ cup mayonnaise
3 large eggs

1 teaspoon Dijon mustard
¼ cup chopped fresh dill
½ teaspoon salt
½ teaspoon black pepper
½ cup bread crumbs
Olive oil for frying

Poach or steam fish; cool and break apart. Combine fish with mashed potato and onion. Add mayonnaise to moisten. Mix in eggs, mustard, dill, salt and pepper. Add bread crumbs to hold mixture together. Use a teaspoon to form mixture into small patties.

Heat olive oil. Drop patties into hot oil and fry on each side; pat dry.

MAKES 32 CAKES

Cheryl Binswanger

Fishcakes are better made a day ahead. Fry a day ahead and reheat for service if desired, or refrigerate and fry for service. Delicious served with tartar sauce or caper mayonnaise.

The Union School, Germantown Academy's original name, opened with 131 students—70 German and 61 English. The first masters were Hilarius Becker for the German School and David James Dove for the English school. Although under the same roof, integrated it was not. Dove was fired as English Headmaster after many complaints, such as charging students too much for firewood to take the chill off the high ceilinged rooms.

Lemon Caper Mayonnaise

1 cup mayonnaise
Zest and juice of 1 lemon
2 tablespoons capers

Combine all ingredients.
Serve with crab cakes.

Maryland Crab Cakes

1 tablespoon finely chopped
    shallot
2 tablespoons finely chopped
    celery
1 tablespoon olive oil
2 large eggs
¾ cup mayonnaise
1 tablespoon chopped fresh dill
1 teaspoon lemon zest

½ tablespoon Dijon mustard
½ teaspoon Old Bay seasoning
1 pound backfin crabmeat, picked
    over
¾ cup panko bread crumbs, or as
    needed
½ teaspoon salt
½ teaspoon black pepper
Oil for cooking

Preheat oven to 350 degrees. Sauté shallot and celery in olive oil until softened; cool. In a mixing bowl, whip together eggs, mayonnaise, dill, lemon zest, mustard and Old Bay seasoning. Gently mix in crabmeat. Slowly add bread crumbs until mixture holds together; not all crumbs may be needed. Season mixture with salt and pepper.

Using a tablespoon, portion mixture into 2 inch diameter patties. Sear crab cakes until brown on both sides in oil in a skillet. Transfer to oven and bake 10 minutes or until crab cakes finish cooking. Serve with cocktail sauce or Lemon Caper Mayonnaise (recipe in sidebar).

MAKES 30 MINI CRAB CAKES   *Culinary Concepts, Inc.*

Ann's Clam Pie

2 (10 ounce) cans minced clams
    with juice
2 teaspoons lemon juice
1 stick butter
1 medium onion, chopped
½ green bell pepper, chopped
2 cloves garlic, minced

½ bunch fresh parsley, chopped
2 teaspoons oregano
¾ cup seasoned bread crumbs
1 drop Tabasco sauce
¼ teaspoon black pepper
Parmesan cheese

Preheat oven to 350 degrees. Heat undrained clams and lemon juice in a covered saucepan over low heat for 15 minutes. In a separate pan, combine butter, onion, bell pepper, garlic, parsley and oregano and sauté until golden. Stir in bread crumbs, Tabasco and black pepper. Add mixture to saucepan with clams and simmer briefly or until mixture is an oatmeal consistency.

Pour mixture into a pie pan. Sprinkle with Parmesan cheese. Bake for 10 to 15 minutes. If freezing, freeze before baking.

SERVES 12   *Eileen Hill*

CHILLED SPICED SHRIMP

1 cup water
1 cup white vinegar
2 tablespoons crushed garlic
2 tablespoons Old Bay seasoning
1 teaspoon black pepper

1 teaspoon crushed red pepper
 flakes
2 pounds shrimp, peeled or
 unpeeled

Combine all ingredients except shrimp in a saucepan. Bring to a boil. Add shrimp and toss until all shrimp are pink. Remove from pan, discard liquid and chill. If needed, peel shrimp before serving.

MAKES 40 SHRIMP,
DEPENDING ON SIZE OF SHRIMP   *Virginia Menno*

BBQ SCALLOPS

1 pound large sea scallops
1 pound sliced bacon

1 (16 ounce) bottle BBQ sauce of
 choice

Preheat oven to 400 degrees. Rinse scallops and cut each into quarters. Cut each bacon strip in half or thirds. Wrap each scallop piece with a bacon piece and secure with a toothpick. Coat wrapped scallops with BBQ sauce and place in a single layer in a glass baking dish.

Bake for 15 minutes or until scallops are cooked through and bacon is crisp. For extra crisp bacon, scallops can be broiled for a couple minutes on each side. Serve hot from the oven.

MAKES 24 PIECES,
DEPENDING ON SIZE OF SCALLOP   *Kathie Vit*

*Very large scallops can be cut into eighths for bite-size appetizers,
however, wrapping bacon is a bit more tedious.*

On December 6th, 1759, the following men met at the house of Daniel Mackinett for the purpose of establishing a school in Germantown:

Christopher Meng—Builder

Christopher Sauer—Printer & publisher

Baltus Reser—Prosperous Tanner

Daniel Mackinett—Owner of the Green Tree Tavern

John Jones—Master Tanner

Charles Bensell—Medical Doctor

Daniel Endt—Business Man

Joseph Galloway—Leading Lawyer of Philadelphia and assistant to Benjamin Franklin.

*I*n 1793, Yellow Fever struck Philadelphia, but missed Germantown, which immediately became a refuge for anyone who could afford it. Population doubled in ten years. Our Trustees wrote a letter (now in the Library of Congress) offering the school to President Washington who was temporarily residing next door. Washington declined, but enrolled his adopted son George Washington Curtis as a student.

SHRIMP PIZZA WEDGES

1½ cups water
8 ounces medium shrimp, unpeeled
2 teaspoons lemon juice
8 ounces cream cheese
1 cup shredded Cheddar cheese
4 scallions, chopped
2 jalapeño peppers, seeded and chopped (optional)
2 cloves garlic, minced
1 teaspoon cumin
1 teaspoon chili powder
2 tablespoons chopped fresh cilantro
9 (10 inch) flour tortillas
1 pint grape tomatoes, sliced

Bring water to a boil. Add shrimp and cook until pink; drain and rinse with cold water. Peel and devein cooled shrimp. Combine shrimp and lemon juice and refrigerate for 30 minutes.

Combine shrimp, cream cheese, Cheddar cheese, scallion, jalapeño, garlic, cumin, chili powder and cilantro in a food processor. Process until smooth.

When ready to bake, preheat oven to 350 degrees. Place tortillas on baking sheets. Spread about ¼ cup of mixture on each tortilla. Top with tomato slices. Bake for 8 to 10 minutes or until edges are brown. Cut each into 8 wedges and serve hot or at room temperature.

MAKES 72 PIECES   *Ginny Lovitz*

HELEN JUSTICE'S ROSEMARY NUTS

6 tablespoons butter
1 pound whole pecans
1 tablespoon dried rosemary
1 tablespoon lemon and pepper seasoning salt
¼ teaspoon Tabasco sauce

Preheat oven to 350 degrees. Melt butter in a 9x13 inch baking dish. Stir in pecans, rosemary, seasoning salt and Tabasco. Bake for 15 minutes. Cool pecans on paper towels to absorb excess butter.

MAKES 1 POUND   *Pamela Adams Chamberlain*

Makes a wonderful holiday gift. Nuts freeze well; rewarm to freshen if frozen for a long period of time. Nuts stay crispier if cooled on brown paper.

Pan Fried Spring Rolls

1 tablespoon olive oil
3 large eggs, beaten
5 cups water
½ teaspoon salt
½ cup dried Chinese mushrooms
1 cup shredded carrot
2 cups shredded cabbage

8 ounces shrimp, peeled,
   deveined and minced (1 cup)
1 cup mung bean vermicelli
1 (400 gram) package spring roll
   wrappers (about 25)
½ tablespoon all-purpose flour,
   dissolved in 1 tablespoon
   water
Canola oil for frying

Warm olive oil in a nonstick skillet over medium to high heat. Add egg to skillet and cook. Cool egg and break into small pieces; set aside.

Bring 5 cups water to a boil over high heat. Add salt. Add mushrooms and carrot. When mixture returns to a boil, add cabbage and cook 1 minute. Drain and immediately cool vegetables in ice water. When cool, drain and squeeze out as much water as possible. Place vegetables in a large mixing bowl. Add shredded egg, shrimp, mung bean vermicelli; set filling aside.

Carefully separate spring roll wrappers. Spoon 2 tablespoons filling onto a corner of each wrapper. Roll up, tuck in both sides and finish rolling, using dissolved flour to glue final corner to roll.

Add 2 tablespoons canola oil to a nonstick 10 inch skillet over medium heat. Arrange 7 rolls at a time in skillet and fry until golden on one side. Turn rolls, add another tablespoon oil and fry until golden. Drain on paper towels. Serve with Dipping Sauce (recipe in sidebar).

MAKES 25 SPRING ROLLS   *She Xiashong*

Dipping Sauce

½ tablespoon Chinese
   cooking wine
1 tablespoon soy sauce
1 tablespoon sesame oil
½ teaspoon salt
¼ teaspoon white pepper
½ teaspoon cornstarch
2 teaspoons minced fresh
   ginger
2 tablespoons minced
   scallion

Combine all sauce ingredients and mix well.

*Well worth the effort! A wonderful rainy
day activity that can be served to your family and friends.*

The coffee house events are run by the *Frequency* music club, which is comprised of around 15-20 Upper School students from all grades. The club sets up the student center three or four times a year to host student and faculty performances. The setting has an informal feel, not unlike that of a neighborhood coffee house (hence the name "coffee house"), which enables novice and veteran performers of all grades to showcase their talents in a supportive environment. Over the years, students have performed music on their own, in groups, acoustically, a cappella, and with full bands. We've even had students do brief stand-up comedy routines and read poetry. The coffee houses are just one example of the kinds of things *Frequency's* members run — they also host visiting musicians periodically, publish a magazine and host weekly meetings focused on music and popular culture.

Artichoke Nibbles

2 (12 ounce) jars marinated artichokes
1 small onion, chopped
1 clove garlic, chopped
4 large eggs
¼ cup bread crumbs

8 ounces Cheddar cheese, shredded
2 tablespoons parsley
Tabasco sauce to taste
Salt and pepper to taste

Preheat oven to 350 degrees. Drain the marinade from one jar of artichokes into a skillet. Chop both jars of artichokes; set aside. Add onion and garlic to skillet with marinade and sauté until brown.

Beat eggs with a fork in a bowl. Add chopped artichokes, sautéed onion mixture, bread crumbs, cheese, parsley, Tabasco and salt and pepper. Transfer mixture to a greased 9 inch square baking pan. Bake for 35 minutes. Cut into bite size morsels.

MAKES 48 BITE SIZE PIECES   *Joan Paltenstein*

Southern Hush Puppies

2 cups cornmeal
1 cup flour
½ teaspoon salt
3 tablespoons sugar
3 large eggs
½ cup milk

2 cups shredded Cheddar cheese
2 jalapeño peppers, seeded and chopped
1 (17 ounce) can creamed corn
1 large onion, chopped
Vegetable oil

Preheat oven to 375 degrees. Combine cornmeal, flour, salt and sugar in a large bowl. Beat eggs in a separate bowl. Mix in milk. Add mixture to dry ingredients and stir until moistened. Mix in cheese, jalapeño, corn and onion; do not over stir.

Pour oil to 2 inches in depth in a small Dutch oven and heat to 375 degrees. Carefully drop batter by rounded teaspoons into oil. Fry a few at a time until golden brown; drain on paper towel.

SERVES 36 TO 40   *Kevin Israel*

A very traditional southern dish! Make larger hush puppies and serve as a side dish with fish, seafood or chicken.

FALAFEL

1 (15 ounce) can chickpeas, well
  drained
1 onion, chopped
½ cup chopped fresh parsley
2 cloves garlic, chopped
1 large egg
2 teaspoons ground cumin
1 teaspoon ground coriander

1 teaspoon salt
Dash of black pepper
1 pinch cayenne pepper
1 teaspoon lemon juice
1 teaspoon baking powder
¼ cup flour
Olive oil for frying

Mash chickpeas in a large bowl until thick and pasty; do not use a blender as the consistency will be too thin. In a blender, process onion, parsley and garlic until smooth. Stir into mashed chickpeas.

In a small bowl, combine egg, cumin, coriander, salt, pepper, cayenne, lemon juice and baking powder. Stir mixture into chickpea mixture. Cover with plastic wrap and refrigerate for 1 hour.

Stir in flour to help when forming falafel. Using a spoon or your hand, form a half-dollar sized falafel or form into balls and smooth the surface. Heat 1 inch of oil in a large skillet over medium-high heat. Fry patties in hot oil until brown on both sides. Serve with pita chips and tahini sauce or yogurt and dill sauce.

MAKES 30 TO 40 FALAFEL,
SERVES 10 TO 14

Abeer Karzoun

COCKTAIL ASPARAGUS

20 extra thin slices white bread,
  crusts trimmed
3 ounces blue cheese
8 ounces cream cheese

1 large egg
20 asparagus spears, cooked
2 sticks butter, melted

Flatten bread slices. Blend blue cheese, cream cheese and egg. Spread mixture over flattened bread. Roll an asparagus spear in each bread slice. Dip rolls in butter and place on a baking sheet. Freeze until firm.

When ready to bake, preheat oven to 400 degrees. Cut each roll into thirds. Bake for 15 minutes.

MAKES 60 PIECES

Kris Henry

HUMMUS

2 (15 ounce) cans chickpeas,
  drained with juice
  reserved
Juice of 3 lemons
4 cloves garlic, crushed, or
  to taste
½ cup olive oil
3 to 4 tablespoons tahini
Salt to taste

Place drained chickpeas in a zip-top plastic bag. Seal and mash chickpeas with a rolling pin; transfer to a large bowl. Add lemon juice, garlic, olive oil, tahini and salt and mix well. Transfer mixture to blender, a little at a time, adding some of reserved chickpea juice between additions. Blend until smooth. Refrigerate 1 to 2 hours. Serve with pita bread or pita chips.

SERVES 10 TO 12

Barbara Azarik

*Try adding spinach, bell
peppers, sun-dried tomatoes or
pine nuts for a variation.*

The son of the first German Headmaster of the Germantown Academy, Hilary Becker, was Mayor of Philadelphia from 1796-1798.

BAKED BRIE WITH PESTO AND SUN-DRIED TOMATOES

1 (16 ounce) container refrigerated large biscuit dough
1 small jar sun-dried tomatoes in oil, or reconstituted if dried

5 ounces pesto
1 (8 inch) wheel Brie cheese

Preheat oven to 350 degrees. Roll biscuit dough into 1 large ball, then flatten with a rolling pin. Dust surface with flour, if needed, to prevent dough from sticking. Chop tomatoes and spread about half over center of dough. Spread 1 to 2 tablespoons pesto on both sides of Brie and place cheese in center of dough. Sprinkle remaining tomatoes over Brie.

Wrap dough around Brie and gather dough on the top. Tie gathered dough with dental floss in a bow. Trim excess dough and transfer to a baking sheet. Bake for 15 minutes or until golden brown. Cool for 10 minutes before serving with crackers.

SERVES 10 TO 15

Robin Crastnopol

STUFFED MUSHROOMS

1 pound large mushrooms (16 to 20), stems removed and reserved
1 cup finely chopped pecans
3 tablespoons chopped fresh parsley
4 tablespoons butter, softened

1 clove garlic, crushed
¼ teaspoon dried thyme
½ teaspoon salt
Black pepper to taste
A few drops of Worcestershire sauce
½ cup heavy cream

Preheat oven to 350 degrees. Place mushroom caps in a shallow baking dish. Finely chop reserved stems. Mix chopped mushrooms with pecans, parsley, butter, garlic, thyme, salt, pepper and Worcestershire sauce. Heap mixture into mushroom caps. Pour cream over caps. Bake for 20 minutes, basting twice with cream in dish.

MAKES 16 TO 20 MUSHROOMS   *Jack and Sue Pickering*

This recipe originally appeared in the 1981 GA cookbook, contributed by Jack and Sue Pickering.

FRIED RAVIOLI

Olive oil for frying
1 cup buttermilk
2 cups Italian style bread crumbs
1 (24 count) package frozen mini
   cheese ravioli, thawed

¼ cup freshly grated Parmesan
   cheese
1 (16 ounce) jar marinara sauce,
   heated

Add olive oil to a large skillet to a depth of 2 inches. Heat over medium heat to 325 degrees. While oil heats, place buttermilk and bread crumbs in separate shallow bowls.

Dip each ravioli into buttermilk, allowing excess milk to drip back into bowl, then dredge in bread crumbs. Place on a baking sheet while breading remaining ravioli.

Working in batches, fry ravioli in hot oil for 3 minutes or until golden brown. Transfer ravioli with a slotted spoon to paper towels to drain. Sprinkle with Parmesan cheese. Serve with warm marinara sauce for dipping.

MAKES 24 PIECES
Katie and Meg Westrum

WILD MUSHROOM PIZZA

1 pound crimini mushrooms, sliced
1 tablespoon chopped garlic
2 tablespoons olive oil
1 teaspoon ground thyme

Frozen or prepackaged nan bread
6 ounces fontina or Swiss cheese,
   shredded

Preheat oven to 400 degrees. Sauté mushrooms and garlic in olive oil over high heat until well browned. Stir in thyme. Sprinkle mushroom mixture evenly over nan bread. Sprinkle with cheese. Bake for 5 to 8 minutes or until edges are brown. Cut into wedges and serve.

MAKES 16 PIECES
David Lovitz

Shiitake or any other wild mushrooms and fresh thyme can be substituted for even more flavor. Truffle oil adds an exotic flavor. Add your favorite ingredients to the nan bread and bake — always tasty with a very crisp crust.

"*At the core of a school are the strengths that enable it to not only endure, but also to thrive. As Germantown Academy faces its 250th anniversary it recognizes that its traditions, character and relationships form that solid core. In the best and in the worst of times, it is critical for a school to call upon its core values, reinforce its mission and to stimulate continued progress toward reaching its aspirations.*"

Cannie Shafer

"GA has been fabulous for our family. This school has the ability to allow each child to find their own niche. I know this because each of my children is incredibly different and they have all thrived here. When the faculty sees someone with talent they encourage them to investigate and develop their interests. Volunteering is a good way to help support this environment, but also to express my appreciation."

Parent Volunteer

CHEESE TORTE

1 pound Cheddar cheese, shredded
1 cup chopped pecans
½ cup mayonnaise
1 bunch scallions, finely chopped
16 ounces cream cheese, divided

6 teaspoons apricot jam
1 teaspoon nutmeg
1 (10 ounce) package frozen chopped spinach, thawed and drained

Combine Cheddar cheese, pecans, mayonnaise and scallion. Spread half of mixture into a loaf pan lined with plastic wrap.

Mix 8 ounces cream cheese with jam and nutmeg. Spread mixture over first layer in loaf pan. Mix remaining 8 ounces cream cheese with spinach and spread over apricot mixture. Top with remaining Cheddar cheese mixture. Fold plastic wrap over top and refrigerate overnight.

To serve, uncover and invert onto a serving plate. Remove pan and plastic wrap. Serve with crackers or bread.

SERVES 15 TO 20   *Maryann Sickles Watson*

CAROL'S MINIATURE QUICHES

1 stick butter, softened
3 ounces cream cheese, softened
1 cup unsifted flour
½ teaspoon salt

1 cup shredded Swiss cheese
1 large egg, lightly beaten
½ cup milk

Preheat oven to 350 degrees. Cream together butter and cream cheese. Work in flour and salt. Chill if dough is soft. Roll dough into 24 balls and press each into a greased small muffin cup.

Fill pastry shells with cheese. Combine egg and milk and dribble mixture over cheese. Bake for 30 minutes. Serve warm.

MAKES 24   *Carol Buckley*

These can be made ahead and frozen on a baking sheet after baking. Transfer to a plastic bag when frozen. When ready to serve, heat frozen quiches; quiches will be soggy if thawed before baking.

Herbed Goat Cheese Tarts with Caramelized Onions

1 teaspoon butter
1 cup thinly sliced yellow onion
1 (10x15 inch) sheet puff pastry
¾ cup goat cheese, softened

1 teaspoon minced fresh rosemary
½ teaspoon salt
¼ teaspoon black pepper

Preheat oven to 325 degrees. Melt butter in a medium skillet over medium heat. Add onion and sauté, stirring often, for 15 to 20 minutes or until nicely caramelized; do not burn onion or allow to cook too quickly. Cool to room temperature.

While onion caramelizes, cut 1½ inch rounds out of pastry with a cutter. Lay rounds at least ½ inch apart on greased or parchment paper-lined baking sheets with shallow edges.

Mix goat cheese with rosemary, salt and pepper. Top each round with ½ to ¾ teaspoon goat cheese mixture. Add several pieces of caramelized onion to each. Bake for 8 to 12 minutes or until puffed and nicely browned; do not overbake.

MAKES 60 TARTS

Meriwether Godsey

The Kast's Bacon Hors D'oeuvre

Slices of bacon

Brown sugar

Preheat oven to 200 to 250 degrees. Arrange bacon slices in a shallow pan. Cover generously with brown sugar. Bake for 1 to 2 hours, basting occasionally and turning once. Drain bacon on paper towel, then transfer to wax paper. When cool and crisp, break in half.

SERVINGS VARY

Bud Kast

This was a faculty favorite while Bud and Angela were at GA.
Delicious and easy!

Although GA is the oldest nonsectarian school in the country, student attendance in chapel was mandatory for almost 200 years. The few surviving chapel benches are now located in the Athletic Hall of Fame. The school has even retained the original pulpit.

At a faculty meeting at the old campus, not very long before the move to the new, a well-known faculty member of that still all male school stood up and expressed grave concern about all of the trees on the new campus. When asked why he was worried, he responded in front of all of his colleagues, "Just imagine what boys and girls will do together behind all of those trees!"

CHEESY SPINACH SQUARES

2 (8 ounce) containers refrigerated crescent roll dough
½ cup mayonnaise
½ cup sour cream
1 (1 ounce) envelope dry vegetable soup and dip mix
1 (10 ounce) package frozen chopped spinach, thawed and drained

1 (14 ounce) can artichoke hearts, drained and chopped
4 ounces feta cheese, crumbled
¼ teaspoon garlic powder
¼ cup freshly grated Parmesan cheese

Preheat oven to 375 degrees. Unroll 1 package crescent dough across one end of a jelly roll pan, placing the longest side of the dough across the width of the pan. Repeat with remaining container of dough, filling pan. Seal perforations with fingers and press sides up edge of pan to form a crust. Bake for 10 to 12 minutes or until golden brown.

Combine mayonnaise, sour cream and soup mix and blend well. Add spinach, artichoke, feta and garlic powder. Spread spinach mixture evenly over crust. Sprinkle Parmesan cheese on top. Bake 10 to 12 minutes longer or until heated. Cut into 24 squares and serve.

MAKES 24 SQUARES   *Kim Dunham*

MOPSY'S CHEESE BALL

1 pound sharp cheese, shredded
1 cup flour

1 stick butter, chilled
1 teaspoon Worcestershire sauce

Preheat oven to 350 degrees. Combine all ingredients and mix well. Roll dough into 1 inch balls. Bake for 10 minutes or until edges begin to brown.

MAKES ABOUT 30 BALLS   *Betsy Duryea and Cornie Walton*

Recipe freezes and doubles well.

ARMENIAN SAUSAGES/LULEH KABOB

2½ pounds combination of lean
  ground beef and lamb
1 tablespoon tomato paste
4 ounces tomato sauce
1 cup bread crumbs
¼ cup evaporated milk
1 teaspoon ground cumin

¼ cup minced fresh parsley
1 tablespoon dried minced onion
1 teaspoon salt
1 teaspoon freshly ground black
  pepper
Chopped onion and parsley for
  garnish

Preheat oven to 400 degrees. Combine all ingredients except garnishes.
Using moistened hands, form mixture into 4 inch long sausage shapes.
Place kabobs in a shallow 9x13 inch baking dish. Bake for 20 minutes. Re-
move from oven.

Preheat a grill. Grill kabobs for 15 minutes, turning once. Garnish with onion
and parsley. Enjoy with pita bread.

MAKES 14 SAUSAGES   *Barbara Azarik*

*This recipe was delicious and an
interesting variation of Kabob.
We make Arabic Kabab all the
time, and would never think to
bake it before barbequing. With
the bread crumbs the patties
formed really well for an excellent uniform presentation and
uniform cooking time. Taste was
great as well. Best looking kabobs
I ever saw.*

BRIE AND APPLE APPETIZERS

1 loaf French bread, cut into
  ½ inch slices
1 (4 inch) wheel Brie cheese, rind
  removed

4 tablespoons butter, melted
½ cup firmly packed brown sugar
⅓ cup chopped walnuts
2 large green apples, thinly sliced

Preheat oven to 350 degrees. Toast bread slices on a baking sheet until
lightly browned. Cut Brie cheese into ¼ inch thick slices. Mix butter, brown
sugar and walnuts. Top each bread slice with a piece of cheese and an
apple slice, then top with walnut mixture. Bake for 5 minutes or until cheese
is melted; be careful that cheese does not burn.

SERVES 8 TO 10   *Pamela Metro*

Brie in log form is easier to slice than a wheel of cheese.

Hot Corn Queso

1 (14 ounce) can whole kernel corn, drained

2 (4 ounce) cans chopped green chiles

½ cup chopped red bell pepper

1 cup shredded Monterey Jack cheese

2 tablespoons chopped jalapeño pepper

½ cup mayonnaise

4 ounces cream cheese, softened

½ cup grated Parmesan cheese

3 tablespoons sliced black olives

Preheat oven to 350 degrees. Combine all ingredients and pour into a 1½ quart baking dish, or similar size dish. Bake, uncovered, for 30 minutes. Serve with tortilla scoop chips.

SERVES 10 TO 12

Sue McGinnis

Flour Tortillas

2 cups flour
½ to 2 teaspoons salt
1 teaspoon baking powder

3 tablespoons vegetable shortening or butter
½ cup boiling water

Combine flour, salt and baking powder in a food processor. Mix for 1 second. Add shortening and process for a few seconds or until mixture resembles meal. With processor running, slowly drizzle in boiling water. The ideal dough will not be sticky but will not quite form a ball. If dough is sticky, add extra flour until dough is soft. If dough is not soft to the touch, add a little more hot water. Remove dough from the processor and knead for a few minutes or until completely smooth.

Tear off enough dough to make a tortilla, about a 2 inch piece. Work dough into a smooth ball; place on a plate and continue making balls with remaining dough. Cover dough balls loosely with plastic wrap and let rest for at least 30 minutes, or refrigerate for a few hours. Letting the dough rest will make the dough easier to roll out.

Lightly flour a flat surface. Roll out dough balls, working hard to keep the tortillas round. Heat a heavy skillet over medium-high heat. Add a tortilla to the skillet. The tortilla may puff as it cooks. If it puffs a lot, simply press down so that tortilla browns more evenly. Once brown, turn over and cook on other side. Repeat with other tortillas.

MAKES ABOUT 10 TORTILLAS

Marian Ramirez

*Similar to pancakes, the first tortilla cooked may not be the best.
Don't judge your success until the second or third. The amount of water used
will vary according to how moist the flour is. If tortillas turn out too crispy,
be careful to stop adding water before the dough gets sticky. The dough
should definitely be soft right after adding the water.*

PEPPERONI CANAPÉS

8 ounces cream cheese, softened
1 (10¾ ounce) can condensed
cream of celery or mushroom
soup

1 pound deli size pepperoni,
chopped into small bits
1 package party rye bread

Preheat oven to 425 degrees. Blend cream cheese, soup and pepperoni. Spread mixture on bread slices and place on a baking sheet. Bake for 10 to 15 minutes. Serve hot.

MAKES 25 PIECES

Mindy McGrath

PATRIOTS' PARTY COCKTAIL MEATBALLS

3 large eggs
1 pound ground veal
1 pound ground pork
1 pound ground beef
2 teaspoons salt
Dash of black pepper
¼ teaspoon garlic powder, plus a
dash for sauce
1 small bunch parsley, minced

3 tablespoons Parmesan cheese
1 medium onion, chopped
Olive oil
2 cups tomato paste
1 cup water
1 (8 ounce) can whole tomatoes
¼ teaspoon sugar
1 bay leaf
Pinch of basil

Beat eggs in a bowl. Add ground meats, salt, pepper, garlic powder, parsley and Parmesan cheese. Shape mixture into small balls by hand or using a melon scoop.

Sauté onion in olive oil in a skillet. Add meatballs to skillet and brown. Stir in tomato paste and water. Press whole tomatoes through a sieve or food mill and add to skillet. Add a dash of garlic powder, salt and pepper to taste, sugar, bay leaf and basil. Simmer for at least 3 hours.

MAKES 125 MEATBALLS

Parents' Committee

*Meatballs can be frozen after cooking. Thaw overnight and reheat for 1 hour.
This was a popular appetizer at the Patriots' Party in the 1970's and 1980's.*

NOTES:

BUFFALO CHICKEN DIP

1 package boneless, skinless chicken breast tenders
8 ounces Ranch salad dressing
8 ounces cream cheese
6 ounces Buffalo wing sauce
8 ounces Cheddar cheese, shredded

Preheat oven to 350 degrees. Boil or roast chicken until fully cooked. Shred meat into bite-size pieces. Combine dressing, cream cheese and hot pepper sauce in a saucepan and heat until cheese melts. Add Cheddar cheese and chicken and mix. Pour mixture into a 10 inch round baking dish, or similar size dish. Bake for 35 minutes. Serve warm with tortilla chips.

SERVES 10 TO 15

Betty Grabfelder

MEXICAN MEATBALLS

1 pound lean ground beef
1 medium onion, chopped
1 large egg
⅓ cup dry plain bread crumbs
¼ cup milk
¼ teaspoon salt
¼ teaspoon cumin
⅛ teaspoon black pepper
1½ cups thick and chunky salsa
2 medium scallions, thinly sliced (optional)

Preheat oven to 400 degrees. Mix all ingredients except salsa and scallion. Shape mixture into thirty 1 inch balls. Place balls in an ungreased 9x13 inch pan. Bake, uncovered, for 15 minutes or until a meat thermometer reaches 160 degrees when inserted into meatballs.

Transfer meatballs to a 2 quart saucepan. Add salsa and heat to a boil, stirring occasionally. Reduce heat, cover and simmer 15 minutes or until hot. Sprinkle with scallion and serve hot.

MAKES 30 MEATBALLS

Linda Robins

This dish works great as a "help yourself" appetizer. Transfer baked meatballs with salsa to a crockpot and cook until heated.

GIN CHEESE

15 ounces English Cheddar
    cheese, room temperature
5 ounces blue cheese, room
    temperature
8 ounces cream cheese, softened

1 stick butter, softened
1 teaspoon grated onion
1 teaspoon soy sauce
¼ cup gin
¾ cup chopped olives

Blend all cheeses and butter thoroughly with a mixer. Mix in onion, soy sauce and gin. Stir in olives using a spoon. Refrigerate to allow flavors to blend; flavors are best after 1 week. Serve with crackers.

SERVES 24

Charley Muir

GAME DAY WINGS

3 pounds chicken wings
Seasoned salt, such as Jane's
    Krazy Mixed-Up Salt, to taste

1 (12 ounce) bottle Buffalo wing
    sauce

Heat a grill to high. Line a 12x17 inch baking pan with nonstick foil and spray foil with cooking spray. Discard wing tips and cut each remaining wing into 2 sections. Arrange wing sections in a single layer on prepared pan. Season wings with seasoned salt.

Grill wings over high heat for 10 minutes. Turn wings, season again if desired, and cook 10 minutes longer. Brush wings with wing sauce and grill another 10 minutes. Turn, brush with sauce and cook 10 minutes more. Remove wings to a serving dish.

SERVES 10
(MAKES ABOUT 50 WINGS)

Cameron Vit

Wings will be crispy! Always great served with celery and blue cheese dip.
Wings can also be made with your favorite teriyaki or BBQ sauce.

*H*ave you looked closely at GA's excellent reproduction of Charles Wilson Peale's 1779 painting, "Washington at Princeton?" The original work of art features in its background Nassau Hall of Princeton University. In GA's reproduction, the original school building is in the background. Although the historical battle in Germantown was unsuccessful, General Washington would still stand proud today as GA celebrates its 250th birthday.

Buy precooked chicken strips at the market, such as Southwestern or Honey Roasted. Buy satay/peanut sauce in the Oriental section of the market; shake bottle thoroughly to mix well. Thread chicken onto toothpicks or skewers and arrange on a microwavesafe dish. Cover with a damp paper towel and microwave on full power for about 2 minutes. Serve chicken strips with satay sauce on the side.

CHICKEN SATAY WITH SPICY PEANUT SAUCE

Chicken

1¼ pounds boneless, skinless chicken breast or tenderloins
2 tablespoons sesame oil
2 tablespoons corn or olive oil
¼ cup dry sherry
¼ cup soy sauce
2 tablespoons lemon juice
1½ teaspoons minced garlic
1½ teaspoons minced ginger
¼ teaspoon sage
¼ to ½ teaspoon black pepper
Dash of Tabasco sauce

Cut chicken into ½x3 inch strips. Combine oils, sherry, soy sauce, lemon juice, garlic, ginger, sage, pepper and Tabasco in a plastic zip-top bag. Add chicken and marinate in refrigerator for 1 to 12 hours; the longer, the more flavor.

When ready to cook, preheat oven to 375 degrees. Thread chicken onto wooden toothpicks or skewers and arrange on baking sheets. Bake for 5 to 10 minutes or until cooked. Serve hot with a bowl of Satay Sauce (recipe below) for dipping.

Satay Sauce

4 teaspoons corn or olive oil
2 teaspoons sesame oil
½ cup minced red onion
2 tablespoons minced garlic
1 teaspoon minced fresh ginger
1 tablespoon firmly packed brown sugar
Dash of Tabasco sauce
⅓ cup peanut butter, smooth or chunky
½ teaspoon ground coriander
3 tablespoons ketchup
3 tablespoons soy sauce
1 tablespoon lemon or lime juice
½ teaspoon black pepper

Heat corn and sesame oils in a small saucepan. Add onion, garlic and ginger and sauté over medium heat until softened. Stir in brown sugar until dissolved. Remove from heat and add Tabasco, peanut butter, coriander, ketchup, soy sauce, citrus juice and black pepper. For a smoother sauce, combine in a blender. Serve at room temperature.

MAKES 50 PIECES   *Nan Ballay*

Sauce can be prepared ahead and refrigerated until needed.
Sauce will thicken and/or separate if stored in refrigerator.
Just mix in a small amount of hot water at a time to regain desired thickness.
Substitute meat of your choice, scallops, shrimp for the chicken.
Seasonings can be adjusted as needed.

BEEF AND BROCCOLI WONTONS

1¼ pounds flank steak
2¼ teaspoons sesame oil
1 teaspoon chopped garlic
1 tablespoon chopped scallion
1½ cups steamed broccoli, finely
    chopped

¼ cup black bean sauce
50 wonton wrappers
2 large eggs, beaten
Peanut or sesame oil for frying

Preheat a grill. Season and grill steak to medium rare; cool and finely chop.

Heat sesame oil in a pan. Add garlic and scallion and sauté until softened. Remove from heat and mix with chopped steak and broccoli. Toss in black bean sauce.

Spoon 1½ teaspoons of steak mixture into the center of each wrapper. Gather sides into a bundle. Use beaten egg as glue to hold bundle together.

Heat peanut or sesame oil. Fry wontons in hot oil until golden brown, turning to promote even browning. Pat dry on paper towels.

MAKES 50 WONTONS   *Jill Garrett*

COCKTAIL PIZZAS

1 pound crumbled hot sausage,
    cooked and drained
1 cup chopped onion
½ cup shredded sharp cheese
½ cup grated Parmesan cheese
1½ teaspoons dried oregano

1 teaspoon garlic salt
1 (8 ounce) can tomato sauce
1 (6 ounce) can tomato paste
3 (8 ounce) containers refrigerated
    flaky biscuit dough

Preheat oven to 425 degrees. Combine all ingredients except biscuit dough. Separate biscuits into individual biscuits, or press each container of dough into one pizza crust round, resulting in 3 rounds total. Place dough rounds on baking sheets. Spread sausage mixture evenly over dough. Bake for 10 minutes.

MAKES 36 PIECES   *Kevin Israel*

Use any pizza topping you like. After topping is added, pizzas can be frozen and pulled out as a last minute hors d'oeuvre or snack; also great for kids' lunches.

Camping trips, Chinatown, and Forest Fest are highlights of the fifth-grade year in Lower School. Fifth grade is also a time to reflect on the journey through GA. One student saw it in this kind of way:

Top 5 reasons you know when you're halfway through Germantown Academy:

5. When your closet is filled with stained and small GA blazers

4. When you know the difference between crew length and no-show socks

3. When you actually know the words to the Alma Mater

2. When you've witnessed a Red Team victory on Field Day

1. And the number one reason how you know when you are halfway through GA is... When you hope that the second half of your schooling goes even slower than the first half, because you really love GA!

Fifth Grade, 2009

British troops, with their Hessian mercenaries, were camped in Germantown. As the occupation wore on, the enemy troops entertained themselves by setting up organized cricket matches on the level grounds around the Union School. They also took pot shots at the weather vane on the belfry of the school. Under Howe's direction, the British troops behaved in a manner more in keeping with a military encampment than as a strong-arming occupation force.

SHRIMP RÉMOULADE

2 cloves garlic, minced
⅓ cup prepared mustard
2 tablespoons horseradish
2 tablespoons chili sauce
2 tablespoons paprika
¾ teaspoon cayenne pepper

1 teaspoon salt (optional)
⅓ cup tarragon vinegar
½ cup olive oil
½ cup chopped scallion
1 to 1½ pounds shrimp, cooked, peeled and deveined

Combine all ingredients except shrimp in a food processor and process until smooth. Marinate cooked shrimp in mixture for at least 3 hours. Drain shrimp, reserving marinade. Serve shrimp on lettuce with reserved marinade on the side for dipping.

SERVES 6 TO 8   *Kathy Schlesinger*

WONTON BASKETS

1 (50 count) package wonton wraps (found in produce department)
1 pound sausage
1½ cups shredded Monterey Jack cheese

1½ cups shredded Cheddar cheese
1 (2¼ ounce) can sliced black olives, drained
½ cup finely chopped red bell pepper
1 cup Ranch salad dressing

Preheat oven to 350 degrees. Press single wonton wraps into greased mini muffin cups to form baskets. Spray baskets with cooking spray. Bake for 6 minutes.

Cook and crumble sausage; drain. Mix together cooked sausage with cheeses, olives, bell pepper and dressing. Spoon mixture into wonton baskets. At this point, baskets may be frozen until ready to serve.

When ready to serve, preheat oven to 400 degrees. Bake for 5 minutes.

MAKES 50 BASKETS   *Mary Louise Ross*

Ground beef or chicken can be substituted for the sausage.

SCARBOROUGH FAIR DIP

2 teaspoons minced fresh parsley
1 teaspoon sage
1 teaspoon rosemary
1 teaspoon thyme
1 small clove garlic, finely minced
    (optional)

8 ounces fresh goat cheese,
    softened
4 ounces cream cheese, softened
Lemon juice to taste
Salt and pepper to taste
3 to 4 sun-dried tomatoes, minced

Combine parsley, sage, rosemary, thyme and garlic in a food processor.
Pulse to blend. Add goat cheese, cream cheese, lemon juice and salt and
pepper and blend until smooth. Mix in sun-dried tomatoes. Refrigerate
for several hours to blend flavors. Serve with pita chips or on French bread
slices.

MAKES 1 PINT   *Anita Franchetti*

BACON CHEDDAR SMASH-UPS

8 slices bacon, chopped
4 ounces Cheddar cheese,
    shredded
1 medium onion, chopped

5 tablespoons mayonnaise
1 teaspoon Worcestershire sauce
¼ teaspoon mustard
6 English muffins, split into halves

Preheat oven to 350 degrees. Mix together all ingredients except English
muffins. Spread mixture on muffin halves. Cut each muffin half into quarters.
Bake for 10 to 12 minutes.

MAKES 48 PIECES   *Jody Kyle*

*These can be frozen until needed before cutting into quarters; they
actually cut better when frozen. Anita Franchetti makes a similar version
with almonds and Pepperidge Farm sandwich bread. These can be cut
into strips and frozen, then baked when needed.*

Greek Salad Salsa

8 ounces feta cheese

1 large tomato, seeded and chopped

3 scallions, thinly sliced

½ cucumber, peeled, seeded and chopped

½ cup sliced black olives

¼ cup chopped fresh flat-leaf parsley

2 tablespoons minced fresh oregano

2 tablespoons chopped fresh dill

Juice of ½ lemon

½ cup olive oil

Salt and pepper to taste

Combine all ingredients. Cover and refrigerate for 2 hours before serving. Serve with toasted pita chips.

MAKES 1 QUART

Maryann Watson

Mexican Layer Dip

8 ounces cream cheese, softened

1 pint sour cream

1 (1 ounce) envelope dry taco seasoning

Chopped lettuce

Chopped tomato

Shredded cheese, such as taco cheese

Chopped black olives

Combine cream cheese, sour cream and taco seasoning. Spread mixture in the bottom of a serving dish. Top with layers of lettuce, tomato, cheese and olives. Serve with scoop-style corn chips.

Peggy Jones

Cocktail Jalapeños

25 medium jalapeño peppers

8 ounces cream cheese, softened

3 cups shredded Cheddar cheese

1½ teaspoons Worcestershire sauce

4 slices bacon, cooked and crumbled

Preheat oven to 400 degrees. Cut jalapeño peppers in half and remove seeds and membranes. Cook in boiling water for 10 minutes; drain.

Combine cream cheese, Cheddar cheese and Worcestershire sauce until blended. Spoon a heaping teaspoon of mixture into each pepper half. Sprinkle with bacon and place on a baking sheet. Bake for 5 minutes or until cheese melts.

MAKES 50 PIECES

Kris Henry

Even the most sensitive taste buds will like these.
Boiling the jalapeños takes the sting out!

BLACK BEAN SALSA

1 (15 ounce) can black beans, drained

1½ cups canned corn, drained

2 medium tomatoes, chopped, juice reserved

1 green bell pepper, chopped

1 red bell pepper, chopped

½ cup minced red onion

1 to 2 jalapeños, seeded and diced

½ cup freshly squeezed lime juice

½ cup olive oil

⅓ cup chopped fresh cilantro

1 teaspoon salt

½ teaspoon cumin

½ teaspoon cayenne pepper

Combine all ingredients in a bowl. Cover and refrigerate for a few hours before serving.

SERVES 8 TO 10

Gretchen Murray

HOT SWISS BACON DIP

8 ounces cream cheese, softened

½ cup mayonnaise

4 ounces Swiss cheese, shredded

3 to 4 tablespoons sliced scallion, some green reserved for topping

8 slices bacon, cooked and crumbled

Mix cream cheese, mayonnaise, Swiss cheese and scallion. Spoon mixture into a pie pan. Sprinkle bacon and reserved scallion on top. Microwave on high for 4 minutes. Serve with crackers or bread.

SERVES 6

Sue Patterson

For a lighter version, use light cream cheese and mayonnaise and turkey bacon.

GA-PC Day has become more than just a day when boys and girls compete on the athletic fields. It is a day when the alumni of both schools gather to renew old friendships, gain new acquaintances, and celebrate school spirit.

Guacamole

2 avocados, peeled and mashed
¼ cup diced red onion
½ cup seeded and chopped tomato
½ jalapeño pepper, seeded and chopped
1 tablespoon chopped fresh cilantro
Juice of 1 lime
½ teaspoon salt

Combine all ingredients.

MAKES 1 PINT

Pamela Metro

Salsa de Casa Cody

2 jalapeño peppers, stemmed and seeded
1½ to 2 cups fresh cilantro, washed and spun dry, large stems removed
½ large sweet or yellow onion, coarsely chopped (about 1 cup)
2 (14 ounce) cans Mexican-style stewed tomatoes, drained

1 (8 ounce) can tomato sauce
1 tablespoon lemon juice
½ teaspoon onion powder
1 to 2 tablespoons firmly packed brown sugar, or to taste
2 ripe avocados, peeled and diced
Salt and pepper to taste

Process jalapeños in a food processor. Add cilantro, onion and drained tomatoes. Pour mixture into a large glass bowl. Add tomato sauce, lemon juice, onion powder, brown sugar, avocado and salt and pepper. Mix with a wooden or plastic spoon. Taste and adjust seasoning as needed. Refrigerate until chilled.

MAKES 1 QUART

Judy Cody

Reuben Dip

1 (14 ounce) can sauerkraut, well drained
1 (10 ounce) package corned beef, shredded

8 ounces Swiss cheese, shredded
1 cup mayonnaise

Preheat oven to 350 degrees. Combine all ingredients and spoon into a deep dish pie pan or quiche pan. Bake for 35 to 40 minutes. Serve with cocktail rye bread or crackers.

SERVES 15

Jennifer Shirakawa

Lightly brush rye bread with olive oil and broil or toast for crispy bread.

SPINACH AND ARTICHOKE DIP

1 (14 ounce) can artichoke hearts, drained and finely chopped
1 (10 ounce) package frozen chopped spinach, thawed and drained

¾ cup grated Parmesan cheese
¾ cup light mayonnaise
½ cup shredded mozzarella cheese
½ teaspoon garlic powder

Preheat oven to 350 degrees. Combine all ingredients. Spoon mixture into a 9 inch quiche dish or pie pan. Bake for 20 minutes. Serve with French bread or crackers.

MAKES 2 ³/₄ CUPS   *Robin Markovitz*

MANGO SALSA

2 mangoes, peeled and cut into chunks
1 bunch scallions, white part only, sliced
1 jalapeño pepper, seeded and finely diced

1 bunch cilantro, or to taste, chopped
Juice of 2 limes
1 clove garlic, crushed

Combine all ingredients in a bowl.

MAKES 1 PINT   *Claire Verden*

SEQUOIA'S SALMON SPREAD

1 (11 ounce) can salmon, drained
8 ounces regular or light cream cheese
1 tablespoon minced onion

1 tablespoon lemon juice
1 teaspoon horseradish
1 teaspoon prepared mustard

Combine all ingredients with a fork in a medium bowl, mixing thoroughly. Cover bowl with plastic wrap and refrigerate for about 1 hour or longer. Transfer dip to a serving dish. Serve with crackers.

SERVES 12 TO 16   *Hank Korth*

NOTES:

In the fall of 1958, a ...ies of very emotional trustee ...etings ensued. GA's 200th ...niversary was approach-...g and several alumni leaders ...gged the Board to keep their ...hool in Germantown. Then, ...rustee Frank Deacon (for whom ...ur football stadium is named), highly respected by proponents on both sides of the question, spoke: "The handwriting is on the wall," he said, "and if we do not risk this opportunity to move we might soon be out of existence." GA's "purpose is education," he reasoned, not "preserving historical monu-ments." That carried the day. A number of trustee resignations followed.

BAKED VIDALIA ONION DIP

2 large Vidalia onions, cut into chunks
1½ cups shredded Parmesan cheese, divided

1 cup mayonnaise
1 cup sour cream
2½ teaspoons fresh dill, divided

Preheat oven to 325 degrees. Process onion in a food processor and transfer to a bowl. Mix in 1 cup cheese. Add mayonnaise, sour cream and 2 teaspoons dill. Spread mixture in two 9 inch pie pans. Sprinkle remaining cheese and dill on top. Bake for 40 to 45 minutes. Serve warm with crackers.

SERVES 10 TO 15

Betty Grabfelder

CLASSIC SWISS FONDUE

1 clove garlic, halved
2 teaspoons cornstarch
2 tablespoons Kirsch liqueur
1 cup dry white wine
1 teaspoon lemon juice

2 cups shredded Gruyère cheese
2 cups shredded Emmentaler cheese
Dash of white pepper
Pinch of ground nutmeg

Dippers

Cubed French bread
Sliced apple or pear

Steamed broccoli

Rub inside of a fondue pot with cut surface of garlic. In a small bowl, dis-solve cornstarch in Kirsch and set aside near stove. Pour wine and lemon juice into fondue pot and cook on stovetop over medium heat until bubbly. Reduce heat to low and gradually stir in cheeses with a wooden spoon. Blend in cornstarch mixture and continue to cook, stirring, for 2 to 3 minutes or until mixture is thick and smooth; do not allow fondue to boil. Season with white pepper and nutmeg. Place fondue pot on the stand and light a heat source. Serve immediately with choice of dippers.

SERVES 4

Carin Levin

A similar liqueur can be substituted for the Kirsch.

Breads & Brunch

In the years following World War II, as more Philadelphians migrated to the suburbs, it was clear that Germantown Academy families were going with them. At the same time, the area around GA was so heavily populated that the school could no longer expand.

But there was no plan until the late 1950s for the school itself to relocate: As Judge Jerome A. O'Neill '28, who wrote about GA's move out of Germantown in *The Miracle of Fort Washington*, noted: "Although we were touched by the winds of change, the Trustees entertained no thought about moving the school. We knew more playing fields and recreational areas were needed if we were to remain competitive, but we were also aware of our financial plight." In Germantown, there was also competition from Penn Charter and Germantown Friends School, which, at the time, were outpacing GA.

Fortunately, GA had a group of trustees who were determined not to let the school fall behind the times. The events of late 1958 and early 1959 were momentous, and at times, contentious. While one faction of the board was dead-set against moving their historic school, another, lead by headmaster Donald Miller had learned that 26 acres of land in Fort Washington was available to a school willing to move to Fort Washington and serve both boys and girls, by a generous family named the McLeans. Trustee Donald Beard and Charter Trustee Robert Bast 1760 (who is today a past president of the board and patriarch of many GA students) helped broker the transaction, with the McLeans eventually increasing their gift to 160 acres of pastoral farmland.

During the highly charged meetings about the possible move, trustee Frank Deacon finally summed up the situation: "The handwriting is on the wall," he noted, "and if we do not risk this opportunity to move, we might soon be out of existence." That idea carried a majority of votes, and on December 6th, 1958, the 199th anniversary of the founding of the school, the board met in the same room at the historic Green Tree Tavern where the school's first leaders had convened in 1759, and agreed to make the move. (Some trustees subsequently resigned because of their strong opposition.)

The sale of the Germantown campus and construction of the new GA took years, and debts piled up. Without the contributions of trustees such as Robert L. McNeil, Jr. '32 and Edwin Lavino 1760, the new campus might never have been completed. Finally, in 1965, with debts settled and buildings complete, the entire campus was thriving, and the "miracle" was complete.

STRAWBERRY-BANANA-BLUEBERRY BREAD

1½ cups flour
¾ teaspoon cinnamon
½ teaspoon baking soda
¼ teaspoon nutmeg
¼ teaspoon salt
1 heaping cup whole strawberries

2 large eggs, beaten
1 cup sugar
½ cup whole blueberries
½ cup mashed bananas
¼ cup canola oil

Preheat oven to 350 degrees. Combine flour, cinnamon, baking soda, nutmeg and salt in a bowl. In a separate bowl, mash strawberries. Mix in egg, sugar, blueberries, banana and oil. Add mixture to dry ingredients and stir until combined. Pour batter into a greased 9x5 inch loaf pan. Bake for 45 to 55 minutes or until a toothpick inserted in the center comes out clean. Cool in pan for a few minutes, then remove to a wire rack to cool completely.

Lisa Butler

PUMPKIN BREAD PERFECTION

3½ cups all-purpose flour
2 teaspoons baking soda
1 teaspoon ground nutmeg
1 tablespoon ground cinnamon
1 teaspoon salt
3 cups sugar
1 cup vegetable oil

⅔ cup water
4 large eggs, well beaten
1 teaspoon vanilla extract
1 (16 ounce) can solid pack
   pumpkin (not pie filling)
1 cup coarsely chopped pecans
   (optional)
1 cup raisins (optional)

Preheat oven to 350 degrees. Sift together flour, baking soda, nutmeg, cinnamon and salt in a medium bowl. In a large bowl, mix sugar, oil and water. Stir in dry ingredients. Add eggs, vanilla and pumpkin and mix to combine; do not overbeat. Fold in pecans and raisins. Divide batter equally into three 8 or 9 inch greased loaf pans. Bake for about 45 minutes or until a toothpick inserted in the center comes out clean.

Kelli and Jennifer Stack

To make pumpkin muffins, fill 24 regular size muffin cups almost full with batter. Bake at 350 degrees for about 20 to 24 minutes.

In December of 1958, one year before the Bicentennial of the Academy, the Board Trustees voted to accept the offer of Robert McLean of 160 acres of rolling meadow and woodland, through which flows the Wissahickon Creek, in Fort Washington. Here we have had an opportunity to create buildings and playing fields for more than double the number of students we could accommodate in Germantown on our original seven acres. It was agreed that in order to serve the whole community, the Academy should enroll both boys and girls as had been done in earlier years.

In September 1965, through the generous efforts of the Trustees and Friends of the Academy the move from Germantown to Fort Washington was completed.

The formal vote occurred on December 6, 1958, the 199th Anniversary of the founding of the School, at the Green Tree Inn on Germantown Avenue in the same room in which the founders of the school had met on December 6, 1759 to draw up and sign the original charter. A plaque hangs today on the side of that building commemorating the unique symmetry of these two historical events.

CHOCOLATE CHIP KAMISH BREAD

1½ cups sugar
1 cup corn oil
4 large eggs
1 teaspoon vanilla extract

1 teaspoon baking powder
3½ cups all-purpose flour
1 (12 ounce) package chocolate chips

Preheat oven to 350 degrees. Combine all ingredients in order listed, mixing after each ingredient is added. Form dough into 4 loaves and place on greased or nonstick baking sheets. Bake for 25 minutes or until golden on top. Cut bread into ½ inch slices and arrange on their sides on baking sheets. Bake for 10 to 12 minutes longer.

MAKES 2 TO 3 DOZEN SLICES   *Jamie Aronow*

GRISWOLDS' BANANA BREAD

1 large egg
1 cup sugar
1 stick butter
3 ripe bananas, mashed by hand

1½ cups flour
1 teaspoon baking soda
1 teaspoon salt

Preheat oven to 350 degrees. Beat egg in a bowl. Blend in sugar and butter. Mix in mashed banana. Add flour, baking soda and salt and mix well until smooth. Pour batter in a large greased loaf pan, or 2 small loaf pans. Bake for 1 hour for a large pan or 45 minutes for smaller pans, or until a toothpick inserted in the center comes out clean.

MAKES 1 LARGE LOAF PAN,
OR 2 SMALL PANS   *Lori Griswold*

Ashley Isaacs Ganz makes a similar recipe but folds in 6 ounces chocolate chips. Sometimes she uses a tube pan rather than loaf pans.

Zucchini Bread

3 cups flour
1 teaspoon salt
1 teaspoon baking soda
1 tablespoon cinnamon
½ teaspoon ground cloves
¼ teaspoon baking powder

3 large eggs, lightly beaten
2 cups plus 2 tablespoons
    granulated sugar, divided
1 tablespoon vanilla extract
1 cup vegetable oil
3 cups grated zucchini

Preheat oven to 350 degrees. Mix together flour, salt, baking soda, cinnamon, cloves and baking powder; set aside. In a mixing bowl, combine eggs, 2 cups sugar, vanilla and oil. Stir in zucchini. Add dry ingredients and mix well. Pour batter into two greased 9x5 inch loaf pans. Sprinkle with remaining 2 tablespoons sugar. Bake for 1 hour.

MAKES 2 LARGE LOAVES

June Davis

Not Just Banana Bread

2 large eggs
½ cup sugar
⅓ cup olive oil or melted butter
¼ cup orange juice
2 or 3 very ripe bananas
1 cup whole wheat flour

1 cup oats
¾ cup raisins
¾ cup dried cranberries
½ cup crushed walnuts
2 teaspoons baking soda
1 teaspoon kosher salt

Preheat oven to 350 degrees. Mix eggs, sugar, oil and orange juice in a large bowl. Add bananas and blend with a masher. Using a wooden spoon, stir in flour, oats, raisins, cranberries, walnuts, baking soda and salt. Pour batter into a bread pan. Bake for 35 to 45 minutes or until golden brown on top. If bread still seems wet in the center but the top is done, turn down oven or turn off and let bread finish baking with residual heat.

Kim Frisbie

Bananas that are so over-ripe that you think they should be discarded are perfect for this recipe. For a really great, moist loaf, add blueberries when in season. Use butter instead of olive oil for a richer taste. I could make this recipe everyday and it would still run out — it goes that fast!

*J*udge Jerome A. (Jerry) O'Neill, Class of '28, was president of the Board of Trustees when the school began the move from Germantown to Fort Washington in 1960. His never say die spirit as he raised money, courted contractors, and encouraged faculty, staff, and trustees through those following 6 years of uncertainty personified the Academy's hard won confidence that it could dream big dreams and then make them come true. That's the real "Miracle of Fort Washington," a school community that can think it up and get it done, a school community that thrives on challenge and renewal, a school community that stores within its cultural memory the portrait of a Common Pleas Judge who loved children and who loved a school and who loved to share those passions with colleagues and strangers who had the means and the skills to unite the two forever.

LEMON BREAD

1½ cups flour
1 teaspoon baking powder
¼ teaspoon salt
6 tablespoons butter
1 cup sugar
2 large eggs, beaten

Zest of 1 lemon
3 tablespoons freshly-squeezed lemon juice, or 1 teaspoon lemon extract
½ cup milk

Preheat oven to 350 degrees. Sift together flour, baking powder and salt; set aside. Cream butter and sugar in a mixing bowl. Add egg, lemon zest and lemon juice. Add dry ingredients alternately with milk. Pour batter into a greased 9x5x3 inch loaf pan. Bake for 45 minutes. Remove from oven and immediately pour glaze over loaf. Let stand in pan 20 minutes before removing.

Glaze

½ cup sugar

Juice of 1 lemon

Combine glaze ingredients and mix well.

MAKES 1 LARGE LOAF

Becky Harobin

DR. J'S SWEET PLUM BREAD

3 large eggs
2 cups sugar
2 cups self-rising flour
1 cup oil

1 teaspoon ground cloves
1 teaspoon cinnamon
1 cup nuts, chopped
2 (4 ounce) jars plum baby food

Preheat oven to 350 degrees. Combine all ingredients in a large bowl and stir until smooth. Pour batter into 4 greased 3x5 inch loaf pans. Bake for 30 to 45 minutes. Pour glaze over top of loaves when removed from oven.

Glaze

1 cup confectioners' sugar

Juice of 1 lemon

Combine glaze ingredients while bread is baking.

MAKES 4 SMALL LOAVES

Heather Foley

Be sure to use self-rising flour. If you do not have self-rising flour, add 1 teaspoon of baking soda to all-purpose flour. This moist spiced bread recipe has been popular in many GA families since the 1970's.

CHALLAH BREAD

2½ cups warm water, divided
2 (¼ ounce) packages active dry
    yeast
1 stick butter, melted and cooled

⅓ cup sugar
3 large eggs
2 teaspoons salt
6½ to 7½ cups bread flour, divided

In a small bowl, combine ½ cup warm water and yeast; let stand for 5 minutes.

In a large bowl, combine remaining 2 cups warm water, cooled butter, sugar, eggs and salt. Beat with an electric mixer on low speed until smooth. Beat in yeast mixture. Gradually beat in 5 cups flour until mixture is smooth. Beat in enough of remaining flour to make a soft dough.

Turn out dough on a lightly floured surface. Knead for 6 to 8 minutes or until dough is smooth and elastic. Place dough in a lightly greased bowl, turning dough to grease top. Cover and let stand in a warm (85 degrees), draft-free place for 1 hour or until doubled in size.

Divide dough into 3 equal portions. Divide each portion into 3 equal portions. Roll each portion into a 14 inch long rope. Pinch 3 ropes together at one end to seal and braid. Repeat with remaining dough. Place braids in 3 lightly greased 9x5 inch loaf pans. Cover and let rise in a warm place for 1 hour.

Preheat oven to 350 degrees. Bake for 30 to 35 minutes or until loaf sounds hollow when tapped. Cover bread with foil if necessary to prevent excess burning while baking. Cool in pans 10 minutes before removing to wire racks to cool.

MAKES 3 LOAVES

Catherine Bown Signorello

"The Schoolhouse was expected to be, as they often were in early days, the chief building, a kind of Town Hall... the town could not boast of any public building, and this fact seems to explain the desire to make the completion of the building so important and necessary."

SWEET POTATO MINI MUFFINS

1 stick butter
1¼ cups sugar
2 large eggs
1¼ cups canned sweet potatoes,
    mashed (16 ounce can)
1½ cups flour

2 teaspoons baking powder
1 teaspoon cinnamon
¼ teaspoon nutmeg
¼ teaspoon salt
1 cup milk
½ cup chopped raisins

Preheat oven to 400 degrees. Cream together butter and sugar. Add eggs and mix well. Blend in sweet potatoes. Sift together flour, baking powder, cinnamon, nutmeg and salt. Add dry ingredients alternately with milk to creamed mixture; do not overmix. Fold in raisins. Pour batter into 48 greased mini muffin cups. Bake for about 20 minutes.

MAKES 48 MINI MUFFINS   *Barbara Cipolloni*

BLUEBERRY MUFFINS

1 tablespoon butter, softened
¾ cup sugar
1 large egg, beaten
½ cup milk
1½ cups flour

2 teaspoons baking powder
2 teaspoons cinnamon
1 teaspoon salt
1 cup blueberries, tossed with a
    little flour

Preheat oven to 375 degrees. Cream together butter and sugar. Mix in egg and milk. Sift together flour, baking powder, cinnamon and salt and add to creamed mixture. Stir in blueberries. Divide batter equally among 10 to 12 greased or paper-lined muffin cups, depending on desired muffin size. Bake for about 25 minutes. Serve warm with butter.

MAKES 10 TO 12 MUFFINS   *Wendy Bender*

Samantha Jordan makes a Hickory Farm version of this yummy muffin, adding 1 teaspoon lemon zest and sprinkling with sugar before baking.

ORANGE MARMALADE MUFFINS

6 tablespoons butter, softened
¾ cup sugar
2 large eggs
1 tablespoon orange zest
¾ cup heavy cream

2 tablespoons Grand Marnier® or
    other orange liqueur
2 cups all-purpose flour
1 tablespoon baking powder
¼ teaspoon salt
¼ cup orange marmalade

Preheat oven to 400 degrees. Cream butter and sugar with an electric mixer until smooth. Add eggs, one at a time, beating well after each addition. Add zest, cream and liqueur and beat until combined.

In a separate bowl, stir together flour, baking powder and salt. Add dry ingredients to creamed mixture and gently beat until flour just disappears. Spoon 1 generous tablespoon batter into each of 12 greased or paper-lined muffin cups and smooth to cover bottom. Place 1 teaspoon marmalade in the center of batter and top with another tablespoon batter to cover. Bake for 20 minutes or until tops are golden and slightly cracked.

MAKES 12 MUFFINS   *Cynthia Eastlake*

Mini chocolate chips can be substituted for the orange marmalade.

Students are introduced to the Harkness method in 9th grade and their confidence increases as their skills evolve. Their ability to think critically sharpens. Encouraged to speak up, to contribute and to question, they learn to trust in the process and to respect their peers. They also learn to come prepared. Harkness teachers are participants in classroom discussions, guiding students without lecturing. Parents sometimes wonder if this means the teacher isn't teaching, when in fact the teacher is demonstrating to the student how to learn, rather than just what to learn. Harkness teachers excel at asking questions that excite inquiry. The more students want to know, the more they learn.

Each day scores of GA Upper School students and their teachers gather around the large oval tables that dominate their English, Modern Language and History classrooms where the table is not so much a piece of furniture as a state of mind.

"This table has a personality. It definitely adds to the intimate atmosphere of this room. The kids find their comfort zone, which is good, since there is absolutely no place to hide."

"Sitting around an oval table where everyone can look each other in the eye creates a unique classroom dynamic. Exchanging ideas, challenging assumptions and sharing knowledge, students participate in their own learning through active discussion. Awareness deepens during these long running conversations."

PUMPKIN CHIP MUFFINS

1 cup vegetable oil
4 large eggs
⅔ cup milk
2½ cups canned pumpkin (2 cans)
3½ cups flour
2 teaspoons baking soda
1½ teaspoons salt
½ teaspoon cinnamon
1 teaspoon nutmeg
3 cups sugar
1 (12 ounce) package chocolate chips

Preheat oven to 350 degrees. Combine oil, eggs, milk and pumpkin in a bowl. In a separate large bowl mix together flour, baking soda, salt, cinnamon, nutmeg and sugar. Add liquid ingredients to dry ingredients and mix well by hand. Fold in chocolate chips. Pour batter into greased muffin cups. Bake for 20 minutes.

MAKES 4 DOZEN MUFFINS   *Mary Anne Van Blarcom*

BANANA CHOCOLATE CHIP MUFFINS

1 stick margarine, softened
1¼ cups sugar
1 large egg
3 ripe bananas
½ tablespoon instant espresso, dissolved in 1 tablespoon hot water
1 teaspoon vanilla extract
2¼ cups flour
¼ teaspoon salt
1 teaspoon baking powder
1 teaspoon baking soda
1 cup semisweet chocolate chips

Preheat oven to 350 degrees. Blend margarine and sugar in a food processor until combined. Add egg, bananas, dissolved espresso and vanilla. Process for 2 minutes. Add flour, salt, baking powder and baking soda and blend just until flour disappears. Mix in chocolate chips with a wooden spoon. Scoop batter into 24 paper-lined muffin cups. Bake for 22 minutes.

MAKES 24 MUFFINS   *Judy Cody*

To make these a tiny bit healthier, substitute whole wheat flour for up to half of the regular flour. Very quick and easy for a Sunday afternoon bake; freeze for kids' snacks during the week.

CAROL'S CARROT CAKE MUFFINS

1½ cups canola oil
4 large eggs
2 cups sugar
2 cups flour
2 teaspoons baking powder
1½ teaspoons baking soda
1 teaspoon salt

2 teaspoons cinnamon
2 cups shredded carrot
1 (8 ounce) can crushed pineapple, drained
¾ cup golden raisins
½ cup chopped walnuts (optional)

Preheat oven to 350 degrees. Beat oil and eggs in a large bowl with an electric mixer until well blended. Add sugar and mix well. In a separate bowl, sift together flour, baking powder, baking soda, salt and cinnamon. Add dry ingredients to batter. Stir in carrot, pineapple, raisins and walnuts by hand. Pour batter into greased or paper-lined muffin tins. Bake for 20 minutes or until a cake tester comes out clean. Cool completely on a wire rack before icing. Keep refrigerated until 10 minutes before serving.

Cream Cheese Icing

1 stick butter, softened
8 ounces cream cheese, softened (Philadelphia brand preferred)

1 teaspoon vanilla extract
1 cup 10X confectioners' sugar, sifted

Cream butter, cream cheese and vanilla in a large bowl until blended with an electric mixer. Add sugar and mix until creamy. Spread over cooled muffins.

SERVES 10 OR MORE   *Carol Leone*

This cake recipe can be baked many different ways, always at 350 degrees. For a 10 inch Bundt or 9x13 inch pan, bake 1 hour; for a 9x5 inch loaf pan, 35 to 40 minutes; a mini muffin pan, 13 minutes. Grease all pans unless using paper liners. One of my favorite ways to make this cake is by making mini muffins and hand piping the icing onto each muffin using a star tip. It's a great presentation, especially for special events. The extra effort, although painful, is well worth it!

Doctor Kershaw, beloved principal, dear friend, we owe to you more than we can ever hope to repay. Through our eleven years of school life you have been our instructor and guide, our advisor and helper. In our troubles we have sought you and you have aided us. You have taken a personal interest in each one of us, not only in our school life, but in our life out of school. At all times you have given us that personal touch which has been so strengthening and stimulating. You have protected us by your loving care and by your guidance we have gained a solid foundation for the forming of strong characters.

Gordon Smyth, Valedictory Speech, 1932

Students are attracted to Germantown Academy for many reasons: the strength of the programs; emphasis in our classes on the individual; the academic achievements of many GA students; the beauty of our campus; the excellent facilities and the rave review of parents and friends. But the reason students stay here is our superb faculty.

DRIED FRUIT CREAM SCONES

2 cups flour
1 tablespoon baking powder
½ teaspoon salt
½ cup sugar

½ cup dried fruit, chopped
   (Craisins, any flavor)
½ cup golden raisins, chopped
1¼ cups heavy cream

Preheat oven to 425 degrees. Combine flour, baking powder, salt and sugar in a bowl and stir with a fork. Add dried fruit and raisins and stir to mix with dry ingredients to keep fruit from clumping together. Using a fork, stir in cream and mix until dough holds together in a sticky rough mass. Drop spoonfuls in a rounded shape onto an ungreased baking sheet. Drizzle with glaze. Bake for 15 minutes or until golden.

Glaze

3 tablespoons butter

2 tablespoons sugar

For glaze, melt butter, then stir in sugar.

MAKES 12 SCONES

Cynthia Eastlake

GRANDMOM McGEEHAN'S SCONES

4 tablespoons butter, softened or
   melted
1 cup sugar
2 large eggs, beaten with a fork
1¾ cups buttermilk

3 cups flour
1 tablespoon baking powder
1 teaspoon baking soda
1 teaspoon salt
1½ cups raisins

Preheat oven to 350 degrees. Cream butter and sugar. Mix in eggs and buttermilk. Beat in flour, baking powder, baking soda and salt. Fold in raisins. Spoon batter into a greased and floured 9x5 inch loaf pan. Bake for 70 minutes or until a toothpick inserted in the center comes out clean. Slice and serve.

MAKES 1 LOAF   *Lori Andress on behalf of Jim and Vince McGeehan*

Using a scone pan will cut baking time to 30 minutes.
Three to four small loaf pans can also be used.

CRANBERRY ORANGE SCONES

2 cups all-purpose flour
¼ cup sugar
1 tablespoon baking powder
½ teaspoon salt
1 stick cold unsalted butter, cut
    into small pieces

½ cup dried cranberries
1 large egg
½ cup heavy cream
Zest of 1 orange

Preheat oven to 350 degrees. Combine flour, sugar, baking powder and salt in a food processor and pulse to mix. Add butter and pulse until pea-size crumbs form. Transfer mixture to a large bowl and stir in cranberries.

In a small bowl, whisk together egg, cream and zest until blended, then add to flour mixture. Using a fork, stir to form large, moist clumps of dough. Turn dough out onto a lightly floured surface and press by hand until dough comes together. Roll dough into a 10 inch round, about ¾ inch thick, flouring as needed. Cut into 8 equal wedges. Press each wedge into a lightly greased scone pan, or place wedges 1 inch apart on a parchment paper-lined baking sheet. Bake for 25 minutes or until scones are golden. Cool on a wire rack for 10 minutes before serving.

MAKES 8 SCONES   *Julie Moore*

Ann Casey suggests a similar recipe but adds ½ cup chopped walnuts and then before baking, brushes the tops of the scones with cream or milk and sprinkles them with a mixture of cinnamon, sugar and a bit of allspice.

THE GEORGE WASHINGTON TELESCOPE

During the American Revolution, Anthony Morris, the owner of the Highlands, a large estate in Whitemarsh, loaned General George Washington a telescope. When Washington had it in his possession, the telescope was already 100 years old. Washington returned the telescope to Morris who, after the Revolution, found himself bankrupt. In an effort to recoup, he sold many of his possessions including the telescope. Eventually it became the property of Dr. William Leibert, an enthusiastic supporter of Germantown Academy. Leibert donated the telescope to the school. The telescope became outdated and was soon replaced with a newer model. The George Washington telescope was then placed in a vault at Germantown Savings Bank where it remained for most of the 20th century. It was re-discovered when the school moved to Fort Washington and is preserved as one of Germantown Academy's historical treasures.

GERMANTOWN ACADEMY HONOR CODE

The spirit of the Germantown Academy Honor Code is expressed in this pledge made by all students:

As a member of the GA community, I maintain a high level of respect and integrity. I uphold the Honor Code in letter and spirit. I do not lie, cheat, steal, vandalize, or commit forgery. I take action to restore trust and integrity to the community whenever I become aware of the commission of an honor offense. I make this pledge in the spirit of honor and trust.

Instances of lying, cheating (including plagiarism), stealing, vandalism, and forgery are considered infractions of the Honor Code.

As trust is the foundation of community, the Honor Code lies at the heart of the school. While the school maintains an Honor Council to consider individual infractions, upholding the Honor Code is the work of all students and teachers.

STICKY BUNS

1½ sticks unsalted butter, softened
1 cup lightly packed light brown sugar, divided
½ cup coarsely chopped pecans

2 (8 ounce) packages crescent rolls
2 tablespoons unsalted butter, melted and cooled, divided
1 tablespoon cinnamon
1 cup raisins

Preheat oven to 400 degrees. Place a 12 cup standard muffin tin on a sheet of parchment paper. Combine softened butter and ⅓ cup brown sugar with an electric mixer. Place a rounded tablespoon of mixture in each of the 12 muffin cups. Distribute pecans evenly on top.

Lightly flour a wooden board or stone surface. Unfold crescent dough on floured surface and seal perforations, leaving dough sheets intact. Brush melted butter over dough. Sprinkle each sheet with ⅓ cup brown sugar, ½ tablespoon cinnamon and ½ cup raisins. Starting with end nearest you, roll up each dough sheet tightly jelly roll-style, finishing with each roll seam-side down. Trim and discard about ½ inch from each end. Slice each roll into 6 each pieces. Place each piece, spiral-side up, in a muffin cup.

Bake for 25 to 30 minutes or until the buns are golden to dark brown on top and firm to the touch. Allow to cool for 5 minutes only, then invert onto parchment paper, easing the filling and pecans out onto the buns with a spoon. Cool completely or eat warm with vanilla ice cream.

MAKES 12 STICKY BUNS   *Kim Sloane*

COFFEE CAKE

Crumb Mixture

¾ cup sugar
2 tablespoons cinnamon

3 tablespoons ground walnuts

Batter

2 sticks butter, softened
2 cups sugar
2 teaspoons vanilla extract
½ teaspoon salt

4 large eggs
3 cups flour
2 teaspoons baking soda
1 pint sour cream

Preheat oven to 350 degrees. Combine all crumb mixture ingredients; set aside.

For batter, cream butter with an electric mixer. Gradually mix in sugar and vanilla. Add salt and eggs and beat at high speed. Sift together flour and baking soda and add to batter alternately with sour cream. Pour half of batter into a greased 9x13 inch baking pan. Sprinkle with half of crumb mixture and cut through batter with a knife. Top with remaining batter and sprinkle with remaining crumb mixture. Cut through batter again.

Bake for about 50 minutes.

Linda Baron

An endowment fund in honor of former Headmaster Edward R. Kast, was established in the Spring of 1986 to enable Germantown Academy to attract and retain the highest quality faculty by providing the means for teachers to grow professionally. Each year, the income from the fund is placed in a separate account to be awarded in grants to those faculty members submitting the best proposals.

The Patrick family makes a similar recipe, but adds 1 cup chopped nuts and ½ cup raisins. They also bake the cake in a 10 inch tube pan or 12 inch Bundt pan for 1 hour.

Considerations of what to wear
as school attire had to be met
when GA went co-ed in the
1960's. One decision hinged
around what the GA girl should
wear. Using the templates
of other girls' schools, the
natural choice was the Scottish
Highland kilt with knee socks.
GA mother, Bea Lippincott,
journeyed to the fabric district
in Manhattan where she found a
non-clan tartan that incorporated
the GA colors. The dress code
for boys remained the same.
Lower School boys wore white
polo shirts and khaki trousers or
shorts. Upper School boys wore
jackets and ties of their choice.

KATIE'S FAVORITE APPLE CAKE

10 to 12 apples, peeled and diced
   into 1 inch pieces
4 teaspoons plus 2 cups sugar,
   divided
2 teaspoons cinnamon
4 large eggs
¾ cup oil
½ cup orange juice
1½ teaspoons vanilla extract
   (no substitutions)
3 cups flour
1 tablespoon baking powder
1 teaspoon salt
1 teaspoon ground cloves

Preheat oven to 350 degrees. Place diced apple in a very large bowl. Combine 4 teaspoons sugar and cinnamon. Sprinkle mixture over apple and toss to coat. In a separate bowl, beat eggs. Add remaining 2 cups sugar, then oil, orange juice and vanilla. In another bowl, combine flour, baking powder, salt and cloves. Add dry ingredients to batter and blend well. Add apple mixture.

Pour batter into a greased 9x13 inch baking pan or two 8x11 inch glass baking dishes. Bake for 1 hour or until golden brown on top and a knife inserted in center comes out relatively clean.

This was a fall favorite I usually made my childrens' unsuspecting classmates help me pick the apples from our orchard…We always saved the peels for the horses and sheep.

MAKES 1 OR 2 CAKES *Kim Frisbie*

CHRISTMAS MORNING CHOCOLATE CHIP CAKE

1 stick butter or margarine,
   softened
1 cup plus ½ cup sugar, divided
2 large eggs
1 cup sour cream, regular or fat
   free
1 teaspoon vanilla extract
2 cups flour
1½ teaspoons baking powder
1 teaspoon baking soda
1 teaspoon cinnamon
1½ cups chocolate chips

Preheat oven to 350 degrees. Cream butter, 1 cup sugar and eggs. Add sour cream and vanilla. In a separate bowl, sift together flour, baking powder and baking soda. Add dry ingredients to batter and beat until mixed. Pour half of batter into a greased 9x13 inch pan.

In a separate bowl, mix remaining ½ cup sugar with cinnamon and chocolate chips. Spoon half of mixture over batter in pan. Pour remaining batter on top and sprinkle with remaining chocolate mixture. Press chocolate mixture into batter until topping is moistened to keep topping from flaking off after baking. Bake for 30 minutes.

Debbie Stamm

Apple Streusel Coffee Cake

Streusel

1¼ cups firmly packed brown
    sugar
¾ cup flour

1 stick cold butter, cut into small
    pieces
2 teaspoons cinnamon

Batter

3¼ cups flour
1½ teaspoons baking powder
¾ teaspoon baking soda
1½ sticks butter, softened
1¼ cups sugar

3 large eggs
2 teaspoons vanilla extract
16 ounces plain yogurt
2 Granny Smith apples, peeled
    and thinly sliced

Preheat oven to 350 degrees. Combine all streusel ingredients mixture will
be lumpy; set aside.

For batter, mix flour, baking powder and baking soda in a bowl; set aside. In
a large bowl, cream softened butter and sugar. Beat in eggs one at a time.
Add vanilla and yogurt. Beat in dry ingredients until blended.

Spoon 3 cups of batter into a greased and floured 14 cup Bundt pan. Sprinkle with ¼ cup streusel. Top with sliced apple and sprinkle with another ½
cup streusel. Pour remaining batter over apple and smooth top. Sprinkle
with remaining streusel and pat down.

Bake for 50 to 60 minutes. Cool before removing from pan.

SERVES 16   *Karin Foreman*

Swedish Pancakes

3 large eggs
2 cups milk, divided
1 cup flour
6 tablespoons butter, melted
1 tablespoon sugar

½ teaspoon vanilla extract
½ teaspoon salt
Confectioners' sugar, fruit, jam or
    Nutella (optional)

Mix eggs and 1 cup milk in a large mixing bowl. Add flour and mix until
smooth. Add remaining 1 cup milk, butter, sugar, vanilla and salt. Heat
a pan over medium heat. Pour ⅓ cup batter into hot pan. After about 3
minutes or when mixture is solid, flip pancake and cook about 2 minutes
longer. Serve warm with optional topping, if desired.

SERVES 3 TO 4   *Cigdem, Richard, Emma and Kevin Knebel*

Fast Facts about Germantown Academy

- The oldest non-sectarian day school in the United States
- Approximately 1,115 students
- 120 acre campus
- Students come from over 100 different communities
- More than 65% of faculty have advanced degrees
- The average tenure for faculty members is 15 years
- 100% college placement
- 21 AP Courses
- 37 teams in Middle School Sports
- 46 teams in Upper School Sports
- 56 student clubs and organiza-tion

The last old school celebration was held on April 27, 1935. This was a celebration of the first 175 years of Germantown Academy. The school presented a pageant, "The Making of a Great Tradition." The pageant was performed on the old school playground; a large seating area was erected allowing for 1,500 seats! The cast was comprised of current students and alumni. The pageant depicted the following ten episodes of important events at the Academy from 1758 through 1935:

1. The Founding of the School, 1759
2. Laying the Corner Stones, 1760
3. The First Meeting of the Trustees, 1761
4. Opening of the School, 1761
5. Master Dove is Dismissed, 1763
6. The War at Germantown, 1777
7. The Bell is Hung, 1784
8. The Building is Offered for the Use of Congress, 1793
9. Lafayette Visits the Academy, 1825
10. William Kershaw, Past Headmaster

After the curtains were drawn, and in the custom we now repeat, the cast and audience sang the Alma Mater!

BRYNNE'S BLUEBERRY BUCKLE

Batter

4 tablespoons butter, softened
¾ cup sugar
1 large egg
1 teaspoon vanilla extract
2 cups sifted all-purpose flour

2 teaspoons baking powder
½ teaspoon salt
½ cup milk
2 cups fresh or frozen blueberries, rinsed

Topping

4 tablespoons butter, softened
½ cup sugar

⅓ cup all-purpose flour
½ teaspoon cinnamon

Preheat oven to 375 degrees. Cream butter and sugar. Add egg and vanilla and beat well. In a medium bowl, sift together flour, baking powder and salt. Add dry ingredients to batter alternately with milk and beat until smooth. Gently fold in blueberries. Pour batter into a greased 9 inch square baking pan.

Combine all topping ingredients and blend well to form crumbs. Sprinkle topping over batter. Bake for 35 minutes.

SERVES 10

Pamela and Brynne DiDonato

CHOCOLATE BANANA PANCAKES

½ cup white flour
½ cup whole wheat flour
2 teaspoons baking powder
¼ teaspoon cinnamon
Pinch of salt
1½ teaspoons granulated sugar
1½ teaspoons firmly packed
   brown sugar

1 large egg
1 teaspoon vanilla extract
1 tablespoon vegetable oil
1 scant cup milk
½ cup chocolate chips
2 ripe bananas, sliced

Combine flours, baking powder, cinnamon, salt and sugars in a large bowl. Add egg, vanilla, oil and milk and mix until smooth. Stir in chocolate chips. Spray cooking spray on a preheated griddle. Pour batter in ½ cup portions onto griddle. Top each pancake with several banana slices. Flip pancakes when bubbles appear on surface; cook until browned. Serve warm with butter and syrup.

SERVES 4

Pamela Metro

ORANGE BRUNCH PANCAKES

3 cups baking mix, such as
    Bisquick
3 cups dry quick oats
3 tablespoons granulated sugar
3 tablespoons firmly packed
    brown sugar

2 tablespoons orange zest
6 large eggs
3 cups milk
½ cup orange juice
1 teaspoon vanilla extract

Combine baking mix, oats, sugars and orange zest in a large bowl. In a separate bowl, beat together eggs, milk, orange juice and vanilla. Add liquid mixture to dry ingredients and mix quickly. Use ¼ cup batter for each pancake. The batter can be made a day ahead.

MAKES 24 PANCAKES

Susan Weeks

JEFF'S WONDERFUL WAFFLES

¾ cup all-purpose flour
¼ cup cornstarch
½ teaspoon baking powder
¼ teaspoon baking soda
½ teaspoon salt

1 cup whole milk or buttermilk
⅓ cup vegetable oil
1 large egg
1½ teaspoons sugar
¾ teaspoon vanilla extract

Combine flour, cornstarch, baking powder, baking soda and salt in a medium bowl; mix well. Add milk, oil, egg, sugar and vanilla and mix well. Let batter stand for 30 minutes. Measure out 1 cup batter for each waffle. Pour batter onto a preheated waffle iron. When done, serve immediately with butter and syrup.

SERVES 3 TO 4

Jeffrey Honickman

Do not use nonstick spray on the waffle iron;
the oil in the batter will allow the waffle to release easily.

RINGING OF THE BELL

Back in Germantown, the bell tolled to signal the beginning of class each morning, to celebrate important events such as a visit from General Lafayette, and to tell people the hour of the day. The tradition of ringing the bell followed the belfry to the new campus. The bell continues to ring as the school celebrates momentous occasions.

Since the move to Fort Washington, Germantown Academy has embellished its well-deserved reputation as an innovative, entrepreneurial school. We were the first historically single sex school in the greater Philadelphia area to become co-educational, the first to develop a school-wide counseling program, to offer creative curricular options such as the Upper School Academy Scholars Program, to provide institutional "community service" via the founding of the Community Partnership School, and, most recently, to see and begin to use the counseling, social, and leadership advantages embedded in a day school "house system."

CHOCOLATE CHIP PANCAKES

2 large eggs
2 cups milk
¼ cup canola oil
2 cups all-purpose flour
2 tablespoons sugar

2 teaspoons baking powder
1 teaspoon baking soda
1 teaspoon salt
¾ cup chocolate chips

Preheat griddle. Beat eggs in a large mixing bowl. Add all remaining ingredients and beat until smooth. Scooping from bottom of bowl, ladle batter onto hot griddle. When pancake puffs and fills with bubbles, flip and cook another 1 to 2 minutes. Serve with butter, syrup or whipped cream.

MAKES 12 TO 16 PANCAKES   *Joe Korth*

WHOLE WHEAT BUTTERMILK PANCAKES

¾ cup unbleached flour
¾ cup whole wheat flour
3 tablespoons sugar
¼ teaspoon salt
2½ teaspoons baking powder
1 teaspoon baking soda
1 tablespoon maple syrup

1 large egg
1 cup buttermilk
¾ cup low fat milk
2½ tablespoons canola oil
Splash of vanilla extract
1 cup berries

Combine flours, sugar, salt, baking powder and baking soda in a mixing bowl. Add syrup, egg, buttermilk, milk, oil and vanilla and mix. Ladle batter onto a hot griddle and sprinkle with berries. Cover berries with an additional 1 tablespoon batter. Cook until batter bubbles. Flip and cook on other side.

SERVES 4   *Ellen McMichael-Reaume*

If you do not have buttermilk, make it by adding 1 tablespoon white vinegar to 1 cup of milk and let stand 5 minutes.

PANNEKOEKEN (GERMAN PANCAKE)

Batter

6 large eggs
1 cup flour
2 tablespoons sugar

1 teaspoon salt
1 cup milk
2 tablespoons butter

Toppings

Butter
1 cup confectioners' sugar
Fresh berries

Lemon wedges, squeezed over
   top
Sautéed Apples (recipe in sidebar)
   with cinnamon ice cream

Preheat oven to 400 degrees. Beat eggs. Blend in flour, sugar, salt and milk. Place a 10 inch nonstick skillet with upright sides in oven with butter until melted. Swirl pan and pour batter into pan. Bake for 15 minutes. Reduce oven temperature to 325 degrees and bake for 40 minutes or until lightly browned. Pancake will rise, doubling in size, then deflate after leaving oven.

Garnish with your choice of toppings.

SERVES 6   *Cheryl Koons*

SAUTÉED APPLES

1 teaspoon butter
2 apples, sliced
1 teaspoon cinnamon
2 teaspoons sugar

Melt butter in a skillet. Add apple slices, cinnamon and sugar and sauté for 10 minutes.

CRÊPES

1½ cups all-purpose flour
1 tablespoon sugar
½ teaspoon baking powder
½ teaspoon salt

2 cups milk
2 tablespoons butter, melted
½ teaspoon vanilla extract
2 large eggs

Preheat a skillet over medium heat. Sift together flour, sugar, baking powder and salt in a large bowl. Stir in milk, butter, vanilla and eggs and mix until smooth. Lightly oil pan. Pour ¼ cup batter into pan and tilt pan in a circular motion so batter evenly coats surface. Cook 2 minutes or until the bottom is light brown. Loosen crêpe with a spatula, turn and cook on other side. Remove to a plate and stack as crêpes finish cooking. Serve topped with fresh fruit or chocolate sauce, or dusted with confectioners' sugar.

MAKES ABOUT 12 CRÊPES   *Chanda Patel*

CHILES AND CHEESE CORNBREAD

1 cup cornmeal
1 cup flour, sifted
¼ cup sugar
1 tablespoon baking powder
1 teaspoon salt
¼ cup oil
1 large egg, beaten
1 cup milk
1 (4½ ounce) can chopped chiles
1 cup shredded Cheddar cheese

Preheat oven to 425 degrees. Combine cornmeal, flour, sugar, baking powder and salt in a bowl. In a separate bowl, mix together oil, egg and milk. Mix liquid mixture with dry ingredients. Stir in chiles and cheese. Pour batter into a greased 9 inch square pan. Bake for 25 minutes.

Carolyn Moatz

GRANDMA'S SPOONBREAD

4 cups milk
1 cup yellow or white cornmeal
4 tablespoons butter
½ teaspoon salt
½ teaspoon baking powder
1 to 2 tablespoons sugar
4 large eggs, separated

Preheat oven to 350 degrees. Bring milk to a boil in a large saucepan. While milk is heating, slowly stir in cornmeal and continue to mix until a little thick and no lumps. Add butter, salt, baking powder and sugar. Remove from heat and let stand about 5 minutes.

Beat egg yolks and stir into batter. Beat egg whites until stiff. Fold whites into batter. Pour batter into a well greased 9x13 inch baking dish. Bake for 45 minutes or until set and golden brown. The spoonbread will have a moist, custard-like consistency when done.

SERVES 6 TO 8   *Carol and Harold Saunders*

Spoonbread, a pudding-like cornbread, is intended to be served piping hot from the oven. It has to be eaten with a spoon because of its soft and creamy texture. It works as a side dish with chicken or pork and vegetables; as a main dish with a green salad; use instead of crackers or bread with soup or chili, or as part of a brunch. The classic topping is lots of butter, but variations include guava jelly, herring roe or bacon on top.

CRÈME BRÛLEE FRENCH TOAST

1 stick unsalted butter
1 cup firmly packed light or dark
   brown sugar
2 tablespoons pure maple syrup
1 loaf challah bread, with or
   without raisins

4 large eggs
1½ cups half & half
1 to 2 teaspoons vanilla or
   orange extract
½ teaspoon cinnamon

Melt butter with brown sugar and maple syrup in a small saucepan over medium heat, stirring until smooth. Pour mixture into a baking dish, or melt in microwave directly in baking dish, and spread to coat entire bottom. Cut six to eight 1 inch thick slices of challah and arrange in a single layer in the baking dish, squeezing them slightly if needed to fit.

In a bowl, whisk together eggs, half & half, vanilla and cinnamon until well combined. Pour mixture evenly over the bread. Cover and refrigerate overnight.

When ready to bake, preheat oven to 350 degrees and bring dish to room temperature. Bake, uncovered, for 30 minutes or until toast is puffed and edges are pale and golden. Serve immediately.

SERVES 6 TO 8

Gwen Riesenberg

When the school moved to Fort Washington arrangements were made for the existing class stones to be taken to the new campus. In 1964, Louis Baldino carefully removed the 43 stones and repaired the walls at old Germantown Academy for the sum of $847. The well-established ivy remained planted around the main building in Philadelphia.

Milk can be substituted for the half & half and less brown sugar can be used, if desired. Other thickly sliced bread can be used for the challah. Try adding chopped nuts or raisins before baking or top with fruit before serving.

Do you remember

. . . decorating the Moose's antlers, located in the old George Washington lobby, with everything from tinsel and lights to missing underwear?

. . . the girl's bathroom (gossip central) shared a door that was not soundproof with the faculty conference room?

Cinnamon French Toast Bake

12 slices cinnamon bread
1 (12 ounce) can evaporated milk
2 large eggs
4 egg whites
½ cup firmly packed brown sugar
1 teaspoon vanilla extract
½ teaspoon cinnamon

Arrange 6 slices bread in a greased 9x13 inch baking pan. Whisk together milk, eggs, egg whites, brown sugar, vanilla and cinnamon in a bowl. Pour up to one-third of mixture over bread. Arrange remaining bread slices in a second layer. Pour remaining egg mixture over the top. Cover and refrigerate 1 hour or more.

When ready to bake, preheat oven to 350 degrees. Bake, uncovered, for 30 minutes or until lightly browned. Serve drizzled with melted butter and sprinkled with sugar with syrup on the side, if desired.

SERVES 8   *Janet Lorraine*

Blintze Soufflé

16 to 24 frozen blintzes
2 sticks butter or margarine, melted
8 large eggs, lightly beaten
½ cup sugar
2 teaspoons vanilla extract
½ teaspoon salt
1 cup orange juice
1 pint sour cream

Preheat oven to 350 degrees. Arrange blintzes in a 9x13 inch baking dish. Mix all remaining ingredients and pour over blintzes. Bake for 1 hour.

SERVES 10 TO 12   *Eve Rose*

For a sweet taste, use fruit-filled blintzes or serve topped with fruit pie filling.

LEEK AND MUSHROOM FRITTATA

3 pounds fresh mushrooms, sliced
2 bunches leeks
4 ounces Jarlsberg or Swiss
   cheese, shredded
¼ cup grated Parmesan cheese

19 large eggs
1 pint heavy cream
½ teaspoon salt
½ teaspoon pepper
2 tablespoons butter

Preheat oven to 350 degrees. Sear mushrooms in a hot pan; cool completely. Trim away top two-thirds of green from the leeks. Slice leeks in half lengthwise and wash well in a large bowl of water. Drain leeks and cut into ¼ inch slices. Mix leek slices with cooled mushrooms; set aside. Mix cheeses in a bowl; set aside. In a separate bowl, beat eggs with cream, salt and pepper; set aside.

Heat a 14 inch nonstick oven-proof pan, or two 8 inch pans, over medium heat. Add butter until melted. Add half the egg mixture, stir and allow mixture to set. Layer mushroom/leek mixture and then cheese mixture on top. Pour remaining egg mixture over cheese. Transfer to oven and bake for 25 minutes or until the internal temperature is 150 degrees. To serve, invert onto a serving tray and cut into wedges.

Janet Israel

MARE'S FRIED MATZOH

5 pieces matzoh
3 large eggs
1 tablespoon water

Vegetable oil
Salt

Crush matzoh over a colander into quarter-size pieces or smaller. Run warm water over broken matzoh until all pieces are soaked; set aside to soak. Beat eggs with 1 tablespoon water in a large mixing bowl. Heat a large skillet over medium heat with ¼ inch vegetable oil in bottom. Add wet matzoh to egg mixture and stir thoroughly, making sure matzoh is saturated with egg. When oil is hot, drop matzoh mixture into oil, creating pancakes about 6 inches in diameter. Fry until light brown and a little crispy on each side. Transfer fried matzoh to a plate, sprinkle with salt and enjoy.

MAKES 5 LARGE PIECES

Larry Altman

Some like to add chopped onion to the mixture.

THE BRAUN LECTURE HALL

Mr. W. F. Harold Braun, a member of the class of 1905 and one of GA's most beloved supporters, gave generously to GA during those early years on the new campus. Of his many gifts, the one that is best known now, The Braun Study Hall, is actually just the bottom floor of the two-story amphitheater in the Middle and Upper Schools. That impressive room seated over 100 and was completely equipped for large-scale lectures, including those in science that required fire and water. The room was used by former teacher, Mr. Peter Biggs, for a cross discipline lecture series, class meetings and for Driver's Ed classes. The Braun Lecture Hall was mainly used for Upper School study halls prior to 1980 when every free period was a study hall for all freshman and sophomores, and for all juniors except those on Dean's list!

This popular breakfast recipe was submitted by 7 different people! Here are some variations to try:

The Best Middle School Advisory Breakfast: Use a lasagna pan and double the recipe. Remove from oven and rush straight to school while still warm!

Caren Levin

Baked Breakfast: Butter one side of the bread and skip the salt. Bake covered for 30 minutes, then uncover and bake another 15 minutes.

Kelly Dalsemer

Texas Egg Casserole: Try using spicy or sage sausage and potato bread. You can also mix in or substitute pepper jack cheese, skip the salt and bake, covered, except for the last 15 minutes.

Michele Stambaugh

Breakfast Casserole: Use 2 cups cubed ham instead of sausage or substitute Swiss cheese. Reduce salt to ½ teaspoon.

Liz Kaufman

Mom's Egg Casserole: Use 4 cups croutons instead of bread for extra crunch and flavor.

Kim Whittaker Morris

Egg Poof: Just before baking, sprinkle 2 cups corn flakes or Rice Chex on top and drizzle with 4 tablespoons melted butter.

Heather Johnston Foley

MISS ELLIE'S BREAKFAST CASSEROLE

1 pound sausage or bacon
6 large eggs
2 cups milk
1 teaspoon salt
1 teaspoon dry mustard
6 to 8 slices bread, cubed
1 to 1½ cups shredded Cheddar cheese

Pull sausage apart with fingers into skillet and cook until done. Drain grease, using a small amount of fat to grease a 9x13 inch baking pan. If using bacon, cook and use bacon grease to coat pan. Chop cooked bacon with a knife.

Beat eggs until frothy. Add milk, salt and mustard and beat 1 minute longer. Layer bread cubes, sausage or bacon and cheese, in order listed, in prepared baking dish. Pour egg mixture on top. Cover with plastic wrap and refrigerate overnight.

When ready to bake, preheat oven to 350 degrees. Bake for 40 to 45 minutes.

SERVES 8 TO 10   *Ken Patrick*

TEXAS BACON

Round buttery crackers   Milk
Thick cut bacon

Preheat oven to 350 degrees. Crumble crackers, using about 2 crackers for every slice of bacon. Dip bacon in milk, then dredge through cracker crumbs. Bake for 10 minutes on each side.

YIELD VARIES   *Megan Brogan*

Spinach Quiche

1 (10 ounce) package frozen
   chopped spinach
1 cup cottage cheese
½ teaspoon nutmeg
2 large eggs, lightly beaten

Salt and pepper to taste
1 onion, diced
1 (9 inch) pie crust, baked
1 cup shredded Cheddar cheese
Parmesan cheese

Preheat oven to 350 degrees. Cook spinach slightly; drain and transfer to a bowl. Mix in cottage cheese, nutmeg, egg and salt and pepper. Sauté onion and add to spinach mixture. Spoon half of mixture into baked pie crust. Sprinkle with ½ cup Cheddar cheese. Repeat layers. Sprinkle Parmesan cheese on top. Bake for 35 minutes or until set.

Julie Moore

Hash Brown Egg Bake

4 cups frozen hash browns,
   thawed
4 tablespoons butter, melted
6 ounces sharp Cheddar cheese,
   shredded
4 ounces mozzarella cheese,
   shredded
4 ounces grated Parmesan cheese

1 zucchini, peeled and chopped,
   or 4 to 6 ounces chopped
   mushrooms
2 large eggs
½ cup milk
Salt and pepper to taste
¼ teaspoon dried dill, or
   1 teaspoon fresh

Preheat oven to 425 degrees. Place hash browns in an 8 inch square baking dish or a 9 inch pie pan. Press hash browns with a paper towel to absorb some of the moisture. Drizzle butter on top and bake for 25 minutes. Remove from oven and reduce temperature to 350 degrees.

Combine all cheeses and zucchini or mushrooms in a bowl and toss to mix. Add mixture to hash browns. Beat eggs with milk and salt and pepper and pour over cheese mixture. Sprinkle with dill.

Bake for 30 minutes or until golden and bubbly around the edges. Let stand about 5 minutes before serving.

Julie Rink

This egg casserole has a delicious hash brown crust. Use whatever cheeses you like. Mushrooms and zucchini work well, but other veggies can also be used. To give the crust more flavor, try adding 1 teaspoon salt and sautéed chopped onion to the hash browns.

CRUSTLESS ZUCCHINI QUICHE

3 cups thinly sliced zucchini (2 medium)
1 small onion or 2 scallions, chopped
½ cup vegetable oil
½ cup baking mix, such as Bisquick
½ cup grated Parmesan cheese
½ cup shredded Swiss cheese
4 large eggs, beaten
½ teaspoon black pepper
½ teaspoon fresh rosemary
½ teaspoon salt

Preheat oven to 350 degrees. Combine all ingredients until well coated. Pour mixture into a lightly greased 10 inch quiche or pie pan. Bake for 30 minutes or until golden brown.

Quiche can be prepared a day ahead and refrigerated until ready to bake. Add sliced beefsteak tomatoes to top of quiche before baking for extra color and flavor.

SERVES 6

Nancy Jones

POTATO CRUST BROCCOLI QUICHE

4 medium potatoes
1 teaspoon vegetable oil
Salt and pepper
1 small head broccoli, cut into bite-size pieces
1 cup milk
2 large eggs
Pinch of garlic powder
½ teaspoon oregano
1½ cups shredded extra sharp cheese

Preheat oven to 350 degrees. Peel and shred potatoes into a colander. Rinse potatoes and drain well. Transfer to a mixing bowl. Add oil and a pinch of salt. Mix with fingertips making sure all potatoes are lightly coated. Press mixture into a lightly greased 9 inch glass pie dish to form a crust. Bake for 10 minutes. Remove crust from oven and arrange broccoli evenly on top.

In a bowl, whisk together milk, eggs, garlic powder, oregano and salt and pepper to taste. Stir in cheese. Pour mixture over crust. Bake for 30 minutes longer or until eggs test done when a toothpick inserted in the center comes out clean. Remove from oven and let stand 10 to 15 minutes before serving.

SERVES 6

Chanda Patel

QUICK QUICHE LORRAINE

1 (9 inch) frozen pie crust
2 slices Swiss cheese
6 slices bacon, cooked crisp and crumbled
2 scallions, chopped

Filling

1½ cups heavy cream
3 large eggs
½ teaspoon salt
¼ teaspoon black pepper
½ teaspoon sugar
¼ teaspoon red pepper flakes

Preheat oven to 425 degrees. Place pie crust in a glass pie dish. Place cheese, bacon and scallion in bottom of crust. Whisk together all filling ingredients and pour into crust. Bake for 20 minutes or until top is light brown. Reduce oven temperature to 350 degrees and bake for 25 minutes longer. Remove from oven and let stand 5 to 10 minutes before serving.

SERVES 6

Debbie Westrum

TOMATO CRAB QUICHE

2 tablespoons minced scallion
3 tablespoons butter
¼ pound fresh shrimp or crab,
    cooked
2 pinches black pepper, divided
2 tablespoons Madeira wine

3 large eggs
1 cup heavy cream
¼ teaspoon salt
1 (9 inch) pie crust, partially baked
1 large tomato, sliced
¼ cup shredded Gruyère cheese

Preheat oven to 375 degrees. Sauté scallion in butter for 2 minutes. Add seafood and stir 1 minute. Add a pinch of black pepper and wine, increase heat and boil for a moment; allow to cool slightly.

In a bowl, beat eggs with cream, salt and a pinch of pepper. Gradually stir egg mixture into cooled seafood mixture. Pour mixture into partially baked pie crust. Top with tomato slices and sprinkle with cheese. Bake in top third of the oven for 30 to 45 minutes or until set and done.

SERVES 6   *Kris Henry*

NETHERLANDS' CHEESE PIE

4 large eggs
2 cups light cream, scalded and
    cooled slightly
½ teaspoon salt
Freshly ground black pepper
    to taste

Pinch of nutmeg
Pinch of cayenne pepper
1 cup shredded Gouda cheese
1 (9 inch) pie crust

Preheat oven to 450 degrees. Beat eggs. Gradually stir in cream. Mix in salt, pepper, nutmeg, cayenne pepper and cheese. Pour mixture into pie crust. Bake for 12 minutes. Reduce oven temperature to 300 degrees and bake 35 minutes longer or until set. Cool for 15 minutes before serving.

SERVES 6   *Ruth Honig*

To scald cream, heat, stirring constantly, until tiny bubbles form; do not boil.

First graders enter the magic world of McLean Hall for new and exciting adventures. The year is divided into various reading themes that present the students with numerous activities to enhance these themes. While reading about animals, the children visit the Elmwood Zoo and follow the Iditarod Sled Race. While reading about food, the students prepare breakfast (fruit salad and pancakes) at school.

THE FOUNDING PLAQUE

In the mid-nineteenth century, Germantown Academy placed a plaque by its main entrance, proudly indicating its inception year of 1760. When the school moved to Fort Washington, the earlier date of 1759 became the official birth year of the school. This plaque memorializes the groundbreaking of the schoolhouse.

REUBEN QUICHE

3 tablespoons caraway seeds
½ (15 ounce) package refrigerated pie crust dough
1 tablespoon Dijon mustard
8 large eggs
1 cup whole milk
1¼ cups heavy cream
1 teaspoon ground nutmeg
½ teaspoon salt
½ teaspoon black pepper
½ cup chopped onion
2 teaspoons chopped shallot
2 tablespoons unsalted butter
5 ounces corned beef, shredded
1 cup shredded Swiss or Jarlsberg cheese
4 ounces sauerkraut, well drained

Preheat oven to 350 degrees. Toast caraway seeds in oven for 5 to 10 minutes or until fragrant. Roll out pie dough with caraway seeds sprinkled on top. Transfer crust dough to a 9 or 10 inch pie pan. Press foil onto dough and add rice or pie weights on top of foil. Bake for 10 minutes. Remove rice or pie weights and foil.

Spread a thin layer of mustard over crust. Beat eggs in a bowl. Add milk, cream, nutmeg, salt and pepper. Sauté onion and shallot in butter until translucent, then add to egg mixture.

Layer corned beef, cheese and sauerkraut in pie crust. Pour egg batter on top. Place quiche on a baking sheet while baking in case of spillage. Bake for 35 minutes or until golden and a thin knife inserted in the center comes out clean.

SERVES 6

Janet Israel

A unique take on quiche!

ULTIMATE CREAMED DRIED BEEF

1 medium onion, diced
4 tablespoons butter, plus extra for sautéing
1 cup quartered button mushrooms
1 (14 ounce) can artichoke bottoms (not hearts), halved and sliced
¼ cup flour
1 teaspoon paprika
1 (8 ounce) package dried beef
2 cups milk, warmed
4 English muffins
8 thick slices tomato
8 slices provolone cheese

In a skillet large enough to hold entire recipe, sauté onion in butter; set onion aside in a bowl. In same skillet, sauté mushrooms, adding artichoke about halfway through; add to onion in bowl. In same skillet, melt 4 tablespoons butter. Stir in flour and paprika. Cook, stirring constantly, until roux turns slightly brown. Add beef and stir until roux coats beef. Stir in sautéed vegetables. Add milk, a little at a time, stirring until mixture gains an even consistency each time. Once all milk has been added, bring mixture to a simmer, stirring often. Simmer for 3 to 4 minutes or until sauce thickens. Remove from heat and let stand.

Split English muffins and toast. Top each half with a slice of tomato and a slice of cheese. Broil until cheese melts. To serve, spoon dried beef mixture over each muffin half and enjoy.

SERVES 4

George Coates

Most butchers sell fresh dried beef. Try fresh rather than the packaged version from the supermarket. The cost is about the same and it's much tastier! An elegant alternative to regular creamed dried beef.

TRIPLET FRUIT SMOOTHIE

4 cups orange juice
1 banana, sliced
1½ cups frozen mixed berries
1 (6 or 8 ounce) yogurt, any flavor

Blend all ingredients on high for 30 seconds.

Fruit smoothie with triple fruit that I hand to my triplet high-schoolers as they rush out the door in the morning.

SERVES 4

Becky Bown Thomas

TROPICAL FRUIT SMOOTHIE

1 mango, peeled and seeded
1 papaya, peeled and seeded
½ cup fresh raspberries
¾ cup orange juice
Ice cubes (optional)

Place mango, papaya, raspberries and orange juice in a blender and process until smooth, adjusting amount of juice used for desired consistency. For a frozen smoothie, add a few ice cubes or use frozen fruit.

For healthier option add 1½ teaspoons psyllium husks.

SERVES 2

Catherine Bown Signorello

GA VS. PC CROSS COUNTRY APPLES

½ cup sugar
⅛ teaspoon ground cloves
1½ teaspoons cinnamon
4 teaspoons cornstarch

7-8 apples, mixed varieties, peeled and sliced
½ cup dried fruit, such as golden raisins, dried cranberries or cherries

In a large microwave-safe bowl, mix together sugar, cloves, cinnamon and cornstarch. Add apple and mix until coated. Add dried fruit and mix again. Cover with wax paper and microwave on high for 4 minutes. Stir thoroughly and microwave 5 minutes longer. Stir thoroughly again and serve immediately (or reheat in the cross country tailgate tent in a chafing dish.)

SERVES 6 TO 8

Michael and Andrew Schlesinger

GARLIC CHEESE GRITS

5 cups water
1 teaspoon salt
1¼ cups dry quick-cooking grits
4 ounces sharp Cheddar cheese, shredded
4 ounces Monterey Jack cheese, shredded

2 cloves garlic, crushed, or to taste
½ cup half & half
1 tablespoon butter
¼ teaspoon black pepper

Bring water with salt to a boil in a medium saucepan over medium-high heat. Gradually whisk in grits and return to a boil. Reduce heat to medium-low and simmer, stirring occasionally, for 10 minutes or until thickened. Stir in cheeses, garlic, half & half, butter and pepper until cheese is melted and mixture is blended. Serve immediately.

SERVES 6 TO 8

Peg Wellington

Stone ground grits may be substituted. Increase liquid to 6 cups and increase cooking time to 50 minutes. Omit garlic for plain cheese grits. Recipe can be made ahead and kept warm in a crockpot until serving time.

RAW "OATMEAL"

1 apple, shredded
1 banana, chopped
Small handful shredded coconut
¼ cup chopped almonds
¼ cup sunflower seeds or flax
  seeds

Splash of almond milk or coconut
  water
1 teaspoon honey
Dash of cinnamon or nutmeg

Combine all ingredients in a large bowl. Enjoy!

Catherine Bown Signorello

GRANOLA

3 cups rolled oats (not instant)
1 to 2 cups walnuts, chopped
¾ cup shredded sweetened
  coconut
¼ cup plus 2 tablespoons firmly
  packed dark brown sugar

¼ cup plus 2 tablespoons real
  maple syrup
¼ cup vegetable oil
½ teaspoon salt
1 cup raisins

Preheat oven to 300 degrees. In a large bowl, combine oats, walnuts, coconut and brown sugar. In a separate bowl, combine maple syrup, oil and salt. Add syrup mixture to oat mixture and blend. Spread mixture onto 2 large sheet pans with shallow sides. Bake for 1 hour or more, stirring every 15 minutes to achieve an even color. Remove from oven and cool on paper. Add raisins and mix until evenly distributed. Store in an airtight container.

SERVES 14 (½ CUP SERVINGS)   *Charlotte Baker Dean*

This is a very versatile recipe. You may substitute pecans or almonds for the walnuts. Try uncooked multi-grain hot cereal instead of the oats. Any chopped dried fruit can be used instead of the raisins. Add ⅓ cup wheat germ for extra nutrition. This is great as a snack or as a topping for ice cream.

MANGO LASSI
(YOGURT AND MANGO SHAKE)

½ cup ice
1 cup plain yogurt
½ cup mango pulp
2 to 3 teaspoons sugar
Pinch of salt

Crush ice in a blender. Add all remaining ingredients and blend for 45 seconds. Pour the lassi into a tall glass. Sip it with a straw!

SERVES 2

Savita Joshi

PEANUT BUTTER SMOOTHIE

1 banana, cut into chunks
¼ cup peanut butter
1 cup milk
½ cup plain or vanilla yogurt
1 tablespoon honey
1 tablespoon ground
  flaxseed, or wheat germ
  or soy protein powder
5 ice cubes

Combine all ingredients in a blender and blend until smooth.

SERVES 2

Becky Harobin

*L*et the flag, the bell and the song call us to our duty now, the duty to do all that we can to preserve and enlarge GA's legacy as a place where talented people go and make good things happen. If we perform that duty then we will find that miracles don't just happen in storybooks and in dreams, but in the everyday, with our eyes wide open and our challenges fully embraced. The trustees who brought GA to Fort Washington learned that lesson. Let us preserve their miracle even as we build our own.

PUMPKIN SEED TRAIL MIX

1½ teaspoons oil
1 cup pumpkin seeds
2½ tablespoons maple syrup
½ to ¾ teaspoon cinnamon
¾ teaspoon nutmeg

½ teaspoon allspice
½ teaspoon salt
1¼ cups dried cranberries or cherries

Preheat oven to 300 degrees. Use oil to lightly grease a baking sheet. Spread pumpkin seeds evenly on sheet. Roast 20 minutes or until almost dry. Transfer seeds to a bowl and mix in syrup until well coated. Combine cinnamon, nutmeg, allspice and salt and sprinkle over seeds. Transfer seeds back to baking sheet. Roast 15 minutes or until dry. Cool 30 minutes. Mix seeds with dried fruit.

Cheryl Koons

ENERGY BOOST BARS

1 (8 ounce) bag almonds
¼ cup sesame seeds
1½ cups quick-cooking oats
½ cup dried cranberries

1 cup dried blueberries
⅔ cup maple syrup
1 teaspoon cinnamon

Preheat oven to 275 degrees. Grind almonds in a food processor until they resemble coarse meal. Transfer ground almonds to a large bowl. Mix in remaining ingredients and stir well. Using wet fingers, press mixture into a lightly greased 9 inch square pan. Bake for 1 hour. Cool thoroughly in pan. Slice into bars.

MAKES 20 SMALL BARS

Becky Harobin

These bars are perfect to send in as a Lower School morning snack.
Save the crumbs from cutting to toss on yogurt.

Soups & Salads

ermantown Academy's original home, built in 1760, included a beautiful bell tower topped with a crown-shaped finial at its peak, signifying that Pennsylvania at the time was a member in good standing of the British Empire.

Unfortunately, for the next 12 years, the belfry stood empty-having a bell forged in London was so costly that it took more than a decade to amass the necessary funds. In 1772, money in hand, trustee Thomas Wharton set off to England to have GA's bell cast at the same foundry in Whitechapel where the Liberty Bell had been made. When the bell was ready, it was sent to Philadelphia aboard the tea ship ***Polly***. But the ship was turned away from port.

Finally, at war's end, the bell came back and was installed in 1784. However, the bell was not melodic, and rang with more of a clunk than a proper peal, so it was locally altered and re-installed. Its familiar E-flat ring helped students keep track of time (who occasionally conspired to ring the bell to try to end the school day early).

When GA moved to Fort Washington, another belfry was erected, and a new bell was cast. But legend has it that trustees quietly switched the bell, and that the old 18th century bell still hangs above our current campus.

Other longtime symbols important to GA history include the school flag, the seal and the Alma Mater. The flag has its roots in GA's cricket-playing days-an original GA flag was too similar to GA's competitors at Philly Cricket Club, so a new red, blue and black flag was designed, which is still used to lead the school's kids in a parade to Field Day. The seal inspires students with the phrase, "By persevering we shall see the fruits," and shows a divine hand watering flowers. By placing the sun and the fruits on the seal, the school announced its duty to continue God's work of fostering. This theme is also seen in GA's Alma Mater, written in 1900, unites students and alumni with these old-fashioned but still true sentiments: *Then whate'er betide us, we will together stand, By one bond united, one common impulse grand*. The song combines sentimentality with a fight song and signifies a student's sentimental attachment to the school that nourished them.

A charming GA tradition that continues today was started in 1885. That year, graduating class presented a commemorative stone engraved with "GA" and the year, 1885. Successive alumni followed suit and for the next 46 years, at the old campus in Germantown, beautifully carved stones, often designed with an ivy motif, were presented as a living memorial to the students' time at school.

In 1931, the annual class stone presentation ceased, a victim of changing times and the Great Depression. In 1964, all of the historic class stones were moved to the Fort Washington campus, and in 1980, the tradition was revived, with that class presenting the first stone in 49 years. With the upcoming construction of the Campus Master Plan, the stones that had been displayed on the exterior walls of the Braun Study Hall and the Arts Center will be incorporated in some way into the new Middle/Upper School building that is set to open in September 2011. Once in place, the stones will again be an inspiring presence for current GA students anxiously awaiting their own graduation year to be mounted.

CREOLE SPICE SOUP

1 pound ground beef
1 large onion, finely chopped
8 cups water
1 (28 ounce) can diced tomatoes, undrained
1 (14½ ounce) can diced tomatoes, undrained
3 cups peeled and cubed potatoes
2 (11 ounce) cans condensed Italian tomato soup, undiluted
1 tablespoon Cajun seasoning
1 tablespoon chili powder

1 tablespoon Creole seasoning
1 tablespoon dried red pepper flakes
1 cup sliced carrots
1 cup chopped green bell pepper
1 cup frozen peas
3 stalks celery, finely chopped
4 cubes chicken bouillon
3 tablespoons dried parsley
2 tablespoons minced garlic
1 bay leaf

Cook beef over medium heat in a soup pot or Dutch oven. Add onion and continue to cook until meat is no longer pink; drain. Add all remaining ingredients and bring to a boil. Reduce heat and simmer, uncovered, for 45 minutes or until vegetables are tender. Discard bay leaf before serving.

SERVES 12 TO 15   *Laurel Stack*

If your grocery store does not carry Italian tomato soup, use regular condensed tomato soup and add 1 teaspoon Italian seasoning. Creole seasoning generally consists of salt, cayenne pepper, onion powder and paprika. Cajun seasoning can contain a spicy blend of salt, peppers, onion powder, garlic powder and paprika. Both are used to add "kick" to soup recipes.

THE ALMA MATER

Hail, Our Alma Mater, to

Germantown we sing,

Cherished are the mem'ries

which 'round they old walls

cling.

May thy glorious spirit ever stay

thy loyal ones

And lead us on to victory, tho'

foes unnumbered come.

Then whate'er betide us, we will

together stand,

By one bond untied, one com-

mon impulse grand.

Call us then together, while we

raise our voices high,

And fling defiance to our foes —

thy spirit cannot die.

J. Helffenstein Mason '1900

The basements of buildings at Oxford and Cambridge Universities were kept dry because ivy had been planted at the ground level of these structures: ivy absorbs ground water, thus reducing cellar dampness. Metaphorically: in that ivy is a symbol of good faith ... Traditionally: the Ivy League and ivy-covered walls became both associated with academia and represented a preeminent educational experience. Since colonial times Germantown Academy was considered an outstanding school associated with schools of the Ivy League.

CHEESE TORTELLINI SOUP

1 tablespoon butter
4 cloves garlic, minced
2 (14 ounce) cans chicken broth
1 (9 ounce) package fresh cheese
  tortellini
4 tablespoons grated Parmesan
  cheese, divided

1 (14 ounce) can stewed tomatoes
½ bunch fresh spinach, cleaned
  and stemmed, or prewashed
  packaged spinach
6 fresh basil leaves, chopped

Melt butter in a large heavy saucepan. Add garlic and sauté for 2 minutes. Stir in broth and tortellini and bring to a boil. Reduce heat to a simmer. Stir in 2 tablespoons Parmesan cheese. Add tomatoes, spinach and basil. Simmer 2 minutes longer. Top individual portions with remaining Parmesan cheese.

SERVES 4   *Kathy Oberkircher*

CHEDDAR CHICKEN CHOWDER

4 slices bacon
1 pound chicken, cubed
1 cup chopped onion
1 cup chopped red bell pepper
2 cloves garlic, minced
4½ cups chicken broth
1¾ cups peeled and diced potato
  (about 6 small)

2¼ cups frozen whole kernel corn
½ cup all-purpose flour
2 cups 2% milk
1 to 1½ cups shredded Cheddar
  cheese
½ teaspoon salt
¼ teaspoon black pepper

Cook bacon in a 5½ quart Dutch oven coated with cooking spray. Remove bacon, crumble and set aside. Add chicken, onion, bell pepper and garlic to Dutch oven and sauté in pan drippings for 5 minutes. Add broth and potato and bring to a boil. Reduce heat and simmer, covered, for 20 minutes or until potato is tender. Stir in corn.

Place flour in a bowl. Gradually add milk and whisk until blended. Add mixture to soup. Cook over medium heat for 15 to 30 minutes or until thickened, stirring frequently. Stir in cheese and season with salt and pepper. Sprinkle bacon on individual servings.

SERVES 6 TO 8   *Stacy Palmer*

White Bean, Pasta and Sun-Dried Tomato Soup

1 cup dried white beans, such as
   Great Northern or cannellini,
   rinsed and picked through
½ cup olive oil
2 cups finely diced yellow onion
2 medium carrots, diced
½ cup diced fresh fennel
4 cloves garlic, minced
¾ teaspoon dried red pepper
   flakes

2 bay leaves
7 to 8 cups chicken broth, divided
4 to 8 ounces dry bow-tie pasta
   (farfalle)
½ cup sun-dried tomatoes packed
   in oil, drained and finely diced
Salt to taste
Freshly grated Parmesan cheese
   to taste

Soak beans overnight in enough water to cover by 3 inches. Drain beans thoroughly.

Heat olive oil in a large heavy pot over medium heat. Add onion, carrot, fennel, garlic, pepper flakes and bay leaves. Reduce heat to low and cook, covered and stirring occasionally, for 15 minutes or until onion is tender.

Add beans and 7 cups broth. Increase heat and bring to a boil. Reduce heat and simmer, partially covered, for 75 minutes or until beans are tender. At this point, soup can be covered and refrigerated for a day; return to a simmer when ready to proceed.

Add pasta and tomatoes to soup. Simmer, partially covered, for 15 minutes or until pasta is very tender. Add up to 1 cup broth if soup is thick. Taste and season as needed with salt. Discard bay leaves. Top individual servings with Parmesan cheese.

SERVES 4   *Chris McDade*

The presentation of the class stone at graduation has become part of a tradition whose origins pre-date the Academy itself. In the main, the stones have ivy motif because in former times each graduating class planted an ivy vine on Ivy Day to celebrate its' tenure at GA; at this time, they dedicated a stone plaque to commemorate the occasion

Celery can be substituted for the fennel. To quick-soak beans, place beans in pot with enough water to cover by 3 inches. Bring to a boil, then remove from heat.

Class Trees

1990 Sweetgum

1991 Sycamore

1992 Saw Tooth Oak

1993 Japanese Scholar

1994 Pin Oak

1995 London Plane

1996 Tulip Poplar

1997 Maple

1998 Maple

1999 Dwyck Beech

2000 Purple Weeping Beech

2001 Catalpa

2002 Holmgren Elm

2003 Kryptomaria

2004 Red Oak

2005 Hornbeam

2006 Hardy Rubber

2007 Tri-color Beech

2008 Horse Chestnut

Hearty Michigan Bean and Sausage Soup

1⅓ cups dried navy beans
1 pound beef kielbasa, cubed
2 cups coarsely chopped onion
2 cups coarsely chopped celery
2 cups coarsely chopped carrot
1 (28 ounce) can plum tomatoes, cut up
2 quarts chicken broth
2½ teaspoons dried thyme, crushed
2 bay leaves
Salt and pepper to taste

Combine beans and 6 cups water in a covered container. Soak overnight in refrigerator. Drain beans and set aside.

In a large Dutch oven, cook sausage over medium heat for 5 to 10 minutes. Remove sausage from pot and set aside. Add onion, celery and carrot to pot and cook, covered, in pan drippings for 8 to 10 minutes or until vegetables are crisp-tender.

Add beans, sausage, tomatoes, broth, thyme and bay leaves to pot. Bring to a boil. Reduce heat and simmer, covered, for 2 ½ hours. Discard bay leaves. Adjust seasoning to taste with salt and pepper.

SERVES 8 TO 10

Ralph Wellington

Minestra (Escarole and Bean Soup)

6 tablespoons extra virgin olive oil
4 to 6 cloves garlic, crushed
7 ounces sliced Canadian bacon, chopped
1 medium onion, chopped
2 pounds escarole, washed and coarsely chopped
1 (14 ounce) can cannellini beans, drained
1 quart chicken broth
2 pinches ground nutmeg, or freshly grated
Coarse salt and pepper to taste
Shaved Parmigiano-Reggiano cheese for topping

Heat olive oil in a large, deep heavy pot over medium heat. Add garlic and Canadian bacon and sauté 3 minutes. Add onion and cook 1 to 2 minutes longer.

Add escarole and cook until wilted down to fit all in the pot. Add beans, broth and nutmeg. Season with salt and pepper. Cook over medium to medium-high heat for 12 minutes or until greens are no longer bitter. Serve with Parmigiano-Reggiano for topping and with bread and red wine.

SERVES 4 TO 6

Lillian Heyse

Mushroom Barley Soup

3 tablespoons butter
1 cup chopped carrot
2 teaspoons minced garlic
1 pound mushrooms, sliced
3 quarts chicken broth
1 teaspoon salt
½ teaspoon black pepper
⅛ teaspoon nutmeg
1 teaspoon dried thyme
1 cup pearl barley

Melt butter in a large stockpot. Add carrot and garlic and sauté until tender but not browned. Add mushrooms and cook until softened. Stir in broth, salt, pepper, nutmeg, thyme and barley. Bring to a boil. Simmer 2 hours or until barley is tender. If soup becomes too thick while cooking, add more broth.

MAKES 3½ QUARTS
Karin Foreman

Vegetarian Chili

¼ cup olive oil
1 large onion, coarsely chopped
3 cloves garlic, minced
1 (12 ounce) package frozen soy protein crumbles
1 (28 ounce) can diced tomatoes
1 large green bell pepper, coarsely chopped
2 teaspoons cayenne pepper or red chile powder, or to taste
2 teaspoons ground cumin
1 teaspoon dried oregano, crushed
2 bay leaves
Salt and pepper to taste
2 (15 ounce) cans red kidney beans, undrained
Sour cream and shredded Cheddar cheese for topping

Heat olive oil in a large stew pot over medium heat. Add onion and garlic and sauté 10 minutes or until golden brown. Stir in protein crumbles, tomatoes, bell pepper, cayenne, cumin, oregano, bay leaves and salt and pepper. Bring to a simmer. Reduce heat to low and simmer, covered, for about 30 minutes, stirring as needed.

Taste and adjust seasonings as needed. Add undrained kidney beans and cook, uncovered, for 20 minutes. Remove bay leaves before servings. Serve in soup bowls with sour cream and Cheddar cheese on the side for toppings.

SERVES 6
Hamish Patel

This recipe can also be used as a vegetarian Bolognese sauce served over cooked pasta shells.

Above all of the concerts, cities, landmarks, and activities, it was the people of Poland that really made the experience. I have never met people that were more interested in learning about us and America. I remember Mr. Kemp saying 'when you meet a friend in Poland, you will have a friend for life,' but it is only now that I realize how true his statement was. Already I have sent many e-mails to kids from the other choir in both Warsaw and Krakow. Overall, after discussing situations about Poland with the students in Polish schools, I realized how privileged we are to live in America, and I think that is one of the most important lessons to be learned from this trip.

A 2009 GA Graduate

GREEK LENTIL SOUP

½ cup olive oil
1 medium onion, finely chopped
1 pound lentils, washed and
    picked through
1 cup chopped celery
1 cup chopped carrot
3 cloves garlic, chopped

1 teaspoon sea salt
¼ teaspoon black pepper
1 cup tomato sauce
1 to 2 bay leaves
2 tablespoons red wine vinegar
    (optional)

Heat olive oil in a large pot. Add onion and sauté. Add lentils, celery, carrot, garlic, salt, pepper, tomato sauce and bay leaves. Add enough water to cover ingredients. Bring to a boil. Reduce heat and simmer, covered, for 1 to 2 hours or until tender. Add more water, or beef or chicken broth, if needed while cooking. Remove bay leaves and stir in vinegar before serving.

SERVES 6 TO 8   *Sophia Papadakes Frangakis*

KINDERGARTEN VEGETABLE SOUP

2 to 3 tablespoons butter or
    olive oil
3 to 5 cloves garlic, chopped
½ large onion, chopped
2 to 3 stalks celery, chopped
2 carrots, chopped
1 sweet potato, diced

1 stalk broccoli, chopped
1 zucchini, chopped
4 cups chicken or vegetable broth
¼ to ½ cup dry orzo pasta or
    pasta of choice
Salt to taste

Heat butter in a large soup pot. Add garlic and onion and sauté over medium-low heat until softened. Add celery and stir to coat with butter. Add carrot, potato, broccoli and zucchini and stir to coat. Cook until vegetables start to soften. Add broth and bring to a low boil. Stir in pasta. Season with salt and simmer on low heat until vegetables and pasta are tender. Enjoy with freshly baked bread.

SERVES 8 TO 10   *Melanie Warwick*

Children love to help by washing the vegetables, peeling the onion and garlic and chopping cut up pieces into smaller bits.

MINESTRONE SOUP

⅓ cup olive or salad oil
4 tablespoons butter or margarine
2 large carrots, diced
2 large stalks celery, diced
2 medium potatoes, diced
1 large onion, diced
½ pound green beans, cut into
    1 inch pieces
½ small head green cabbage,
    coarsely chopped
4 (14 ounce) cans beef broth

1 (14½ ounce) cans tomatoes,
    undrained
1 teaspoon dried oregano
2 medium zucchini, diced
1 (15 to 19 ounce) can white
    kidney beans
1 (15 to 19 ounce) can red kidney
    beans
1 (10 ounce) package frozen
    chopped spinach
½ cup grated Parmesan or
    Romano cheese

Heat oil and butter in an 8 quart Dutch oven over high heat. Add carrot, celery, potato, onion and green beans and cook until lightly browned. Add cabbage, broth, tomatoes with liquid and oregano. Bring to a boil. Reduce to low heat and simmer, covered, for 15 minutes. Add zucchini, cover and simmer 15 minutes longer or until vegetables are tender. Stir in all kidney beans and frozen spinach and cook over medium heat, stirring occasionally, until heated through. Sprinkle cheese on individual servings.

SERVES 10   *Jolene DeFusco*

OYSTER AND BRIE CHEESE SOUP

2 pints oysters, reserving liquid
4 tablespoons butter
¼ cup flour
4 cloves garlic, chopped
1 bunch scallions, chopped
½ cup chopped onion

1 pint heavy cream
1 large wedge Brie cheese, rind
    removed, chopped
1 pint half & half
Salt and pepper to taste
¼ cup chopped fresh parsley

Place oysters with liquid in a 4 quart pot and simmer over medium heat until oysters curl. Remove from heat and set aside.

Melt butter in a large soup pot over medium-low heat. Slowly blend in flour and cook, stirring constantly, until roux is light tan in color. Add garlic, scallion and onion and sauté until softened. Stir in cream and cheese. Cook and stir until cheese melts. Add oysters and liquid and reduce heat to a simmer. Add half & half and cook over low heat for 5 minutes, stirring occasionally. Season with salt and pepper and garnish with parsley.

SERVES 6 TO 8   *Peg Wellington*

"Instead of being run by authority from the top down, GA is run on mutual respect."

Tony Garvan

Increasing demand for admission, growing curricular needs, and expanding technologies begged for a more defined and dedicated space for GA's Middle School. In September, 1996, a new multi-level facility was added to the existing Middle School space. The Alter Middle School now offers a light infused Commons which supported the administration's desire to "move" sixth graders into the Middle School. The class of 2003 became the first sixth grade in the Academy's history to become Middle Schoolers!

PEG'S LOUISIANA
SHRIMP AND CORN CHOWDER

14 tablespoons butter, divided
¾ cup flour
6 (10 ounce) cans diced tomatoes
  with green chiles
6 (10 ounce) packages frozen
  white corn in butter sauce
½ teaspoon salt

1 teaspoon black pepper
2 tablespoons butter
4 cloves garlic, minced
2 pounds raw fresh or frozen
  shrimp, peeled and deveined
4 cups half & half, or as needed

Melt 12 tablespoons butter in a large non-reactive Dutch oven over medium-low heat. Slowly mix in flour. Cook, stirring constantly, until roux reaches a medium golden brown color. Stir tomatoes into roux and cook, uncovered, for 5 minutes or until mixture reaches a thick stew consistency. Add frozen corn and stir until all ingredients are heated through. Season with salt and pepper.

While soup heats, melt remaining 2 tablespoons butter in a skillet over medium heat. Add garlic and sauté until lightly browned; do not overcook. Add shrimp and sauté until pink. Add shrimp to heated soup and cook 10 to 15 minutes. Refrigerate at least 8 hours.

Reheat on low. Stir in half & half, adding more if needed to reach desired consistency. Adjust seasoning with salt and pepper.

SERVES 8 TO 10

Peg Wellington

ASPARAGUS SOUP

4 to 8 tablespoons unsalted butter
2 large onions, quartered
4 to 8 large cloves garlic, sliced
1½ quarts chicken broth
3 pounds or more asparagus,
    tough ends discarded, several
    tips reserved for garnish
1 cup chopped fresh parsley,
    stems removed

2 medium carrots, chopped
1 cup sliced mushrooms (optional)
8 to 10 fresh large basil leaves
1 tablespoon dried tarragon
1 teaspoon salt
1 teaspoon black pepper
Pinch of cayenne pepper, or a few
    dashes Tabasco sauce
Parmesan cheese

Melt butter in a large heavy saucepan over low heat. Add onion and garlic and cook, uncovered, until softened. Add broth and bring to a boil. Add asparagus, parsley, carrot, mushrooms, basil, tarragon, salt, pepper and cayenne. Reduce heat and simmer, covered, for 50 minutes or until vegetables are tender. Remove from heat and cool.

Purée cooled soup with a stick blender, or purée solids in a blender or food processor and return to saucepan. Cook until heated. Garnish individual servings with asparagus tips and Parmesan cheese.

SERVES 6 TO 8 *Kathy Wyszomierski*

PUMPKIN PEAR SOUP

3 ripe pears, peeled and thinly
    sliced
¼ cup chopped onion
2 tablespoons butter, melted
2 cups canned solid pumpkin pack
2 (14½ ounce) cans chicken broth
½ cup water

¼ cup Chablis or other dry white
    wine
¼ teaspoon salt
1 (3 inch) cinnamon stick
⅓ cup half & half
Sour cream and scallion strips for
    garnish

Sauté pear and onion in butter in a large skillet over medium heat until tender. Place knife blade attachment in a food processor. Add pear mixture and pumpkin and process until smooth. Transfer mixture to a large saucepan. Add broth, water, wine, salt and cinnamon stick. Bring to a boil. Reduce heat and simmer, uncovered, for 20 minutes. Remove cinnamon stick. Stir in half & half and heat thoroughly; do not boil. Garnish individual servings as desired.

SERVES 4 TO 6 *Janice Connor*

The oldest uninterrupted schoolboy football rivalry in the United States is held every autumn between Germantown Academy and Penn Charter. "The Game" has been played more times than the annual Army vs. Navy or Harvard vs. Yale football rivalries. The competition now extends beyond football to fall sports for boys and girls, including soccer, field hockey, cross country, tennis and water polo.

ROASTED JERUSALEM ARTICHOKES

Peel and slice Jerusalem artichokes and place on a baking sheet. Drizzle with olive oil and sprinkle with salt. Roast at 450 degrees until cooked through.

CAULIFLOWER VICHYSSOISE

2-4 tablespoons unsalted butter
2 leeks, lower white part only, chopped
1 shallot, finely chopped
1 head cauliflower, chopped
¼ cup dry white wine
4 to 6 cups chicken or vegetable broth

Heavy cream to taste
Fresh lemon juice to taste
Salt and pepper to taste
Bias-cut chives and roasted Jerusalem artichoke hearts (see sidebar) for garnish

Melt butter over medium-low heat in a saucepan. Add leek and shallot and sauté until translucent. Add cauliflower and sauté for 3 to 4 minutes. Deglaze pan with wine and cook until liquid evaporates. Add enough broth to just barely cover all the vegetables. Simmer until cauliflower is cooked through, being careful to not overcook.

Purée mixture with a stick blender, or purée in a blender and return to pan. Warm soup over medium heat. Stir in cream, lemon juice and salt and pepper. Serve warm garnished with chives and artichoke hearts.

SERVES 8 TO 10

Kate Connor

The lemon juice helps to make the taste cleaner and cut through some of the cream so it does not coat the tongue. Only a small amount is needed to brighten the flavors but not have the soup taste lemony.

SQUASH AND CASHEW SOUP

1 teaspoon canola oil
1 medium onion, coarsely
   chopped
1 cup raw cashews
1 (2½ to 3½ pound) acorn or
   butternut squash, peeled and
   coarsely chopped

3½ cups chicken or vegetable
   broth
¾ cup buttermilk
⅛ teaspoon white pepper
¼ cup dry sherry (optional)

Heat canola oil in a large soup pot. Add onion and cashews and sauté 4 to 5 minutes or until onion is softened and translucent. Add squash and broth. Simmer, covered, for 40 to 45 minutes or until squash is tender.

Transfer mixture to a food processor or blender and purée. Return purée to pot. Whisk in buttermilk, pepper and sherry. Cook 5 minutes or until heated through. Serve immediately.

SERVES 8   *Julia Blumenreich*

HEALTHY ROASTED BUTTERNUT SQUASH SOUP

1 (4 pound) butternut squash,
   peeled and cubed
2 Granny Smith apples, peeled
   and cubed
2 onions, cubed
3 cloves garlic, whole

½ teaspoon chili powder, or to
   taste
Salt and pepper to taste
¼ cup extra virgin olive oil
5 cups chicken broth
Snipped fresh chives for garnish
Sour cream for garnish (optional)

Preheat oven to 350 degrees. Toss squash, apple, onion and garlic with chili powder, salt and pepper and olive oil. Transfer mixture to a roasting pan. Bake for 40 minutes or until vegetables are very tender. In 2 batches, purée mixture with some of broth in a food processor or blender. Pour purée into a saucepan. Add any remaining broth to pan. Cook until heated. Garnish with chives and sour cream.

SERVES 4   *Kris Henry*

For curried squash soup, add curry powder. Add less broth for a thicker soup.
Add heavy cream for a richer soup.

During the final month of their GA experience, seniors complete the off campus Senior Project. Developed to give graduating seniors a memorable opportunity to apply their competence and confidence, the Senior Project asks students to explore a topic of their own choosing or learn something completely new. They keep a daily journal of their experience and present a final speech to the faculty to share their newfound insight. Some seniors travel abroad to study another country's ecosystem. Others job-shadow a business executive in a field they are considering as a future career. Still others engage in service projects or create works of art. The GA Senior Project is designed to satisfy the inner explorer, the sophisticated learner, the mature individual each student has become.

Even before the move to Fort Washington 50 years ago, Germantown Academy could boast of a series of "firsts." It was GA mathematics teacher George Hartley Deacon who, in 1887, founded the Inter-Academic League, the oldest school boy league in the country. The Upper School Belfry Club, established seven years later, is the country's oldest organized drama group. Field Day dates to 1876 and spurred the development of the GA flag, the first of its kind among schools in this area and likely in the nation.

Butternut Squash and Heirloom Apple Soup

1 (3 to 4 pound) butternut squash, peeled and quartered
1½ pounds Vidalia onion, peeled and halved
4 to 5 tart apples of choice, peeled and left whole
2 tablespoons olive oil
Salt and pepper to taste

10 cups chicken broth
2 tablespoons chopped fresh sage
1 tablespoon chopped fresh thyme
2 tablespoons unsalted butter, cut into small pieces
Heavy cream
Molasses (optional, but preferred)

Preheat oven to 400 degrees. Place squash, onion and whole apples on a baking pan. Drizzle with olive oil and generously season with salt and pepper. Roast for 1 hour or until a knife goes through each with little resistance. Turn the vegetables and apples once or twice while roasting. Cool, then chop vegetables and apple into 1 to 2 inch pieces, discarding apple cores. Transfer chopped mixture to a large pot.

Add broth, sage and thyme. Bring to a simmer. Cover and simmer for 45 minutes. Add butter and purée with a stick blender, or purée in small batches in a food processor while gradually adding butter to batches. Heat to rewarm soup, if needed. Serve with a generous splash of cream and a drizzle of molasses.

MAKES 4 QUARTS

Neal Gauger

GAZPACHO

2 (14½ ounce) cans stewed
    tomatoes
2 large cucumbers, cut into chunks
2 large red bell peppers, cut into
    chunks
2 clove garlic
2 tablespoons balsamic vinegar

1 tablespoon olive oil
½ teaspoon dried basil
1 teaspoon salt
¼ teaspoon pepper
¼ teaspoon Tabasco sauce
    (optional)
Croutons

Blend all ingredients except croutons in batches in a blender. Combine
batches in a container and refrigerate until chilled. Serve cold with croutons.

S E R V E S   6   T O   8

Beth Snyder

GOODMAN GAZPACHO

2 (46 ounce) cans V-8 vegetable
    juice
1 (46 ounce) can tomato juice
5 stalks celery, finely chopped
2 cucumbers, peeled, seeded and
    finely chopped
2 large white onions, finely
    chopped
3 scallions, finely chopped
2 red bell peppers, finely chopped

2 yellow bell peppers, finely
    chopped
3 tomatoes, seeded and finely
    chopped
Large handful of fresh green
    beans, finely chopped
1 tablespoon fresh lemon juice
Dash of Tabasco sauce
Salt and pepper to taste

Mix juices in a large soup pot. Add all vegetables, lemon juice and Tabasco.
Season with salt and pepper. Chill well. Serve cold.

S E R V E S   1 2   T O   1 4

Judi Goodman

*Soup will keep for days in refrigerator. Adjust ingredient quantities
according to taste. Take the time to chop all vegetables by hand — they will
stay crisper. My son called this "liquid salad!"*

I can't pinpoint a single accomplishment that stands out during the four years, only the larger accomplishment of graduating feeling as if I'd truly learned and grown. When I entered high school, I had no concept of the kind of learning I would do - learn the laws of motion in physics, read the opera Carmen in French, deeply analyze *A Passage to India*, take calculus, come to grasp 800 years in European history. I entered high school knowing that I wanted to do well, but I left with a love of learning and a sense that teachers had imparted great knowledge. To look back on the ninth grade version of myself and the ninth grade versions of my peers is to realize how much we've grown since entering high school. I left GA with the sense that I had matured academically, socially, and as a person, and that feels like the greatest accomplishment of all.

GA Graduate 2008

Cold Avocado Soup

1 large or 2 small ripe avocados
2¼ cups chicken broth, divided
1 teaspoon curry powder
¾ teaspoon salt
⅛ teaspoon white pepper

½ cup heavy cream
4 thin avocado slices for garnish, sprinkled with lemon juice to prevent browning

Blend avocado with 1 cup broth, curry powder, salt and pepper in a blender. Transfer to an enamel pot. Add remaining broth to pot and bring to a boil. Refrigerate until cooled.

Stir in cream and refrigerate until ready to serve. Float an avocado slice on individual servings for garnish.

SERVES 4

Debbie Westrum

Chilled Blueberry Soup

5 cups fresh blueberries
4 cups water
4 whole cloves
1 (2 inch) cinnamon stick
⅔ cup honey
Juice of 1 lemon

3 tablespoons Crème de Cassis (black currant liqueur)
1 tablespoon blueberry vinegar
Plain yogurt, sour cream and orange zest for garnish (optional)

Combine blueberries, water, cloves and cinnamon stick in a large pot. Bring to a boil. Stir in honey. Reduce heat and simmer, partially covered, for 15 minutes or until blueberries are very tender. Cool.

Remove cinnamon stick. Strain soup through a sieve. Stir in lemon juice, Crème de Cassis and vinegar. Refrigerate at least 6 hours before serving. Garnish as desired.

SERVES 8 TO 10

Linda Catherwood

If blueberry vinegar is hard to find, substitute a light colored vinegar, such as raspberry vinegar.

CHARLENE'S COMPOSED SALAD

Spicy Caramelized Pecans

¼ cup pecans
½ teaspoon canola oil

1 tablespoon sugar
⅛ teaspoon cayenne pepper

Sherry Vinaigrette

1½ tablespoons canola oil
1½ teaspoons sherry vinegar

Dash of salt
¼ teaspoon freshly ground black pepper

Salad

1 medium Golden Delicious apple
1½ teaspoons lemon juice
4 cups salad greens, preferably white center of curly endive or escarole

1 ounce semi-dry or hard goat cheese, crumbled into ½ inch pieces

Place pecans in a skillet and barely cover with water. Bring to a simmer over high heat, then drain immediately. Return pecans to skillet. Add oil, sugar and cayenne. Cook over medium to high heat, stirring, until pecans brown and mixture caramelizes. Transfer to a plate to cool.

For vinaigrette, mix all ingredients in a salad bowl; set aside.

To prepare salad, halve and core apple, then cut into ½ inch slices. Mix apple with lemon juice to prevent browning. When ready to serve, toss greens with vinaigrette in salad bowl. Arrange greens on individual plates. Place apple slices on top and sprinkle with crumbled goat cheese and pecans. Serve immediately.

SERVES 4

Charlene Curtis

Children learn by example, and we find ways to bring Upper and Middle School students into the lives of Lower School students whenever possible. Older students become mentors and role models as they come to the Lower School for the "KTK" (Kids Teaching Kids) science program, the "Espanol Para Los Ninos" program, or simply to read together or work on community service projects. Our older students embody the Germantown Academy spirit of hard work, respect, and independence-Lower School students undoubtedly benefit from being in their presence. Naturally, the advantages work both ways.

The school day was very short in the early 1900s. The older boys were dismissed at 1:30 in the afternoon and the younger boys even earlier. Lunch was sold and served by the janitor in his own house!

The History of Germantown Academy

SARAH'S SALAD

1 (15 ounce) can chickpeas, drained
1 cucumber, unpeeled and chopped to size of chickpeas
½ red onion, chopped
½ cup coarsely chopped flat-leaf parsley
1 orange, peeled and chopped
1 medium Fuji apple, chopped
Pinch of cinnamon
Olive oil and pomegranate vinaigrette

Combine all ingredients except vinaigrette in a salad bowl and mix. Drizzle vinaigrette over salad. Great served with shrimp.

SERVES 6   *Tina Rodowicz*

THAI SESAME NOODLE SALAD

Sauce

¼ cup sesame oil
¼ cup chunky peanut butter
2 tablespoons red wine vinegar
½ cup apple juice
6 tablespoons soy sauce
1 tablespoon sugar
1 clove garlic, crushed
½ teaspoon dried red pepper flakes

Salad

1 pound dry spaghetti, cooked al dente and drained
3 scallions, chopped
1 red bell pepper, chopped
1 green bell pepper, chopped
1 cucumber, chopped
1 carrot, chopped

Mix all sauce ingredients.

Combine all salad ingredients in a large bowl. Pour dressing over salad and mix.

SERVES A LOT!   *Becky Harobin*

Vary vegetables as desired. Chicken or shrimp can be added to make a meal.

SNOW PEA SALAD

Salad

2 cups snow peas
2 large red bell peppers, sliced
    into rings

8 ounces fresh mushrooms, sliced
Dressing (see sidebar)
Toasted sesame seeds (optional)

Blanch snow peas in boiling water for 1 to 2 minutes. Drain and immediately rinse with cold running water to stop cooking; cool. Transfer snow peas with pepper rings and mushrooms to a salad bowl.

Just before serving, toss salad with dressing. Sprinkle sesame seeds on top and serve.

SERVES 6 TO 8

Cheryl Ross

DRESSING

⅓ cup walnut oil
2 tablespoons champagne
    vinegar or white vinegar
1 tablespoon sugar
1 tablespoon lemon juice

Combine all dressing ingredients in a small container.

CRUNCHY ROMAINE TOSS

Dressing

1 cup vegetable oil
½ cup sugar
½ cup wine vinegar

1 tablespoon soy sauce
Salt and pepper to taste

Salad

1 cup chopped walnuts
1 (3 ounce) package ramen
    noodles, flavor packet
    discarded, broken into pieces

4 tablespoons unsalted butter
1 head romaine lettuce, shredded
1 bunch broccoli, chopped
4 scallions, chopped

Whisk together all dressing ingredients.

For salad, brown walnuts and ramen noodles in butter; cool on paper towel. Mix walnuts, noodles, lettuce, broccoli and scallion in a salad bowl. Pour 1 cup dressing over salad and mix.

SERVES 4 TO 6

Lori Greenberg Cagnoli

AUNT ASHLY AND UNCLE DAN'S CAESAR DRESSING

1 teaspoon mustard
1 teaspoon chopped garlic
1 tablespoon lemon juice
1 teaspoon anchovy paste
2 teaspoons Worcestershire
    sauce
3 tablespoons freshly grated
    Parmesan cheese
¼ cup extra virgin olive oil
Salt and pepper to taste

Whisk together all ingredients. Pour desired amount of dressing over romaine lettuce and mix in your favorite croutons.

MAKES ABOUT
½ CUP DRESSING

Liz Berger

The Board of Trustees announced the purchase of the Alburger property in 1915. The house situated on that property was built in 1763 by David James Dove, the first English master at the Academy. George Washington occupied the house while he was President of the United States during the yellow fever outbreak in Philadelphia, 1793. Several meetings of Congress were also held in this building, which was later called Kershaw Hall in honor of Headmaster Kershaw.

Bok Choy Salad

Dressing
6 tablespoons soy sauce
1 cup sugar

1 cup olive oil
⅔ cup rice wine vinegar

Salad
2 heads bok choy, chopped, or baby bok choy
2 (3 ounce) packages ramen noodles, broken into pieces

2 (3½ ounce) packages sliced almonds
1 to 2 (3½ ounce) packages sunflower seeds
2 bunches scallions, chopped

Mix all dressing ingredients.

Combine all salad ingredients in a salad bowl. Drizzle dressing over salad and toss well. Salad is best if dressing is allowed to soak into salad a little before serving.

SERVES 8 TO 10

Stephanie Goldman Wolfer

Cucumber Raita

2 cups plain yogurt
½ English cucumber, shredded with or without peel and squeezed dry
½ medium tomato, finely chopped
Hot green chile pepper, finely chopped, to taste (optional)

¼ teaspoon ground cumin
Salt to taste
10 leaves fresh mint, finely chopped
5 sprigs fresh cilantro, chopped

Beat yogurt well in a bowl. Add cucumber, tomato, chile pepper, cumin, salt, mint and cilantro and mix well. Serve chilled with Indian roti bread or nan and rice.

SERVES 4 TO 6

Rini Shah

Serve with any Indian meal or rice, or as a dip with tortilla chips.
A regular cucumber can be substituted for the English cucumber.

KACHUMBER

2 carrots, shredded or finely chopped
1 medium tomato, finely diced
1 medium onion, finely diced
1 teaspoon finely chopped fresh cilantro
2 hot green chile peppers, chopped (optional)

2 tablespoons coarsely ground peanuts
2 teaspoons lemon juice
¼ teaspoon salt, or to taste
1 teaspoon sugar, or to taste
½ teaspoon ground cumin

Mix all ingredients in a bowl. Refrigerate until ready to serve. Serve as a salad or a dip, or as a spread for wraps or sandwiches.

Savita Joshi

ORZO FETA SALAD

Vinaigrette

¼ cup red wine vinegar
2 tablespoons freshly squeezed lemon juice

1 teaspoon honey
½ cup olive oil

Salad

6 cups chicken broth or water
1 pound dry orzo
2 cups grape tomatoes
1 (7 ounce) package feta cheese

1 cup fresh basil
1 cup chopped scallion
Salt and pepper to taste
½ cup pine nuts, toasted

Whisk together all vinaigrette ingredients. Cover and chill.

For salad, bring broth to a boil. Stir in orzo and cook until tender. Drain and toss until cool. Mix tomatoes, feta, basil and scallion into orzo. Add vinaigrette and season with salt and pepper. Let stand at room temperature to allow flavors to blend. Add pine nuts just before serving.

SERVES 10 TO 12

Megan Judson

Great for large parties. Use a disposable foil tray for quick clean-up.

DRESSING

1 cup salad oil
⅓ cup wine vinegar
Reserved artichoke juice from marinated artichokes
½ teaspoon powdered mustard
½ teaspoon garlic powder
1 teaspoon sugar
½ teaspoon salad herbs
Salt and pepper to taste

Combine all ingredients.

SALAD MADE BY MANY

1 pound fresh mushrooms, thinly sliced
2 (6 ounce) jars marinated artichoke hearts, juice reserved
Dressing (see sidebar)
2 pounds cooked chicken or turkey breast, diced
2 pounds cooked ham, diced
2 pounds Cheddar cheese, shredded
2 pounds bacon, cooked and crumbled
1 dozen large eggs, hard cooked and grated
3 to 4 ripe avocados, peeled and diced
1 (7¾ ounce) can pitted black olives, thinly sliced
2 bunches radishes, thinly sliced
2 bunches scallions, thinly sliced
1½ pints cherry tomatoes, halved
5 to 6 heads lettuce, preferable mixed greens, torn into bite-size pieces

Marinate mushrooms and artichokes in dressing for 3 to 4 hours.

When ready to serve, combine chicken, ham, cheese, bacon, egg, avocado, olives, radish, scallion, cherry tomatoes and lettuce in a very large wooden bowl. Add mushroom, artichoke and dressing mixture and toss to mix.

SERVES 24 TO 30   *Sally Beil*

BROCCOLI SALAD

½ cup canola oil
3 tablespoons red wine vinegar
¼ cup sugar
1 (3 ounce) package beef ramen noodles, broken into pieces, seasoning packet reserved
1 (12 ounce) package broccoli slaw

Combine canola oil, vinegar, sugar and seasoning packet from noodles in a salad bowl. Mix in broccoli slaw. Top with broken noodles and toss to mix.

SERVES 6 TO 8   *Ellen Perlmutter*

Dressing may be enough for 2 packages of slaw. Roasted chicken can be added for a main course. Sunflower seeds or slivered almonds can also be added.

CHICKEN WALDORF SALAD

2 medium-size red apples,
    coarsely chopped (2 cups)
½ cup or more mayonnaise or
    salad dressing
2 medium stalks celery, chopped

8 to 10 ounces chicken tenders,
    cooked and cubed
½ cup coarsely chopped walnuts
⅓ to ½ cup golden raisins
Salt to taste

Mix apple with mayonnaise in a large salad bowl. Add celery. Mix in chicken. Add walnuts and raisins and mix. If needed, add more mayonnaise to coat all ingredients. Season with salt and chill about 1 hour. Serve on salad greens, if desired.

SERVES 4

Jane Beadle

WHITE BEAN SALAD

2 cups dried great Northern beans
2 bay leaves
1½ teaspoons salt
1 small red onion, chopped
½ cup chopped fresh flat-leaf
    parsley

6 tablespoons olive oil
5 tablespoons fresh lemon juice
1 teaspoon ground cumin
½ teaspoon cayenne pepper
Salt and pepper to taste

Place beans in a large saucepan and cover with water 2 inches above beans. Soak beans overnight.

The next day, drain beans and cover again with water 2 inches above beans. Add bay leaves and bring to a boil. Reduce heat to medium-low and simmer 30 minutes. Add salt and simmer 15 minutes or until tender. Drain beans and discard bay leaves. Add onion and parsley to beans.

In a bowl, whisk together oil, lemon juice, cumin and cayenne pepper. Season with salt and pepper. Pour dressing over beans and toss to combine.

SERVES 8

Cheryl Koons

For a shortcut, use canned cannellini beans. Drain beans, omit bay leaves and salt, and begin with combining of beans, onion and parsley.

Jim Connor remembers that when he became Head of School in the early 1990's, the only fax machine in the area was at Rich's Deli. If a fax came in for the school Rich would call the office and someone would walk over to Rich's to retrieve. Oh, how things have changed!

One hundred and twenty five years ago, in 1884, yearly tuition was $100 for the Academic Department; $75 for the Primary Department and First and Second Forms; $50 for 3rd and 4th Forms.

FRANCHETTI FAMILY CHICKEN SALAD

Dressing

⅓ cup olive oil
¼ cup red wine vinegar
¼ cup lemon juice
1 tablespoon sugar

1 teaspoon salt
½ teaspoon freshly ground black pepper
1 clove garlic, crushed

Salad

Mixed salad greens, such as romaine, red or green leaf lettuce or Bibb
1½ cups cooked and cubed chicken (about 2 chicken breast halves)
⅓ cup diced red bell pepper
1 small jar marinated artichoke hearts, quartered

1 (2¼ ounce) can small black olives, or ¼ cup pitted kalamata olives
Cherry or grape tomatoes, halved
1 avocado, peeled and cubed
Toasted pine nuts
Crumbled blue cheese or feta cheese

Combine all dressing ingredients in a small jar with a lid and refrigerate. Remove garlic before pouring dressing over salad.

Layer salad ingredients in order listed in a large salad bowl. Pour dressing over salad and toss to mix.

SERVES 3 TO 4   *Anita Franchetti*

To prevent avocado from browning, leave a small amount of dressing in jar after adding to salad. Add diced avocado to jar and toss gently to cover. Add avocado to salad last. Salad can be prepared earlier in the day; add dressing and toss just prior to serving.

Summer Pasta Salad

1 (8 ounce) package tri-color or
    whole grain rotini pasta
1 tablespoon vegetable oil
1 (6 ounce) jar marinated artichoke
    hearts, juice reserved
½ cup Italian salad dressing
2 tablespoons cider vinegar

1 cup mayonnaise
Salt and pepper to taste
½ cup chopped broccoli, cooked
½ cup frozen peas, thawed
10 cherry tomatoes, halved
½ cup halved black olives

Cook pasta according to package directions, adding vegetable oil to cooking water; drain well. Place cooked pasta in a large mixing bowl. Drain juice from artichokes over pasta. Cut artichokes hearts into quarters and add to pasta. Add dressing and mix gently.

In a small bowl, combine vinegar and mayonnaise. Season mixture with salt and pepper and pour over salad. Gently mix in broccoli, peas, tomatoes and olives. Refrigerate overnight to allow flavors to blend. Mix gently before serving.

SERVES 6

Holly Stauber

Creamy Potato Salad

2¾ pounds Red Bliss potatoes
    (about 6)
¾ cup diced celery
1½ cups diced onion
4 large eggs, hard-cooked
1 cup mayonnaise-type salad
    dressing

⅓ cup milk
1 teaspoon salt
¼ teaspoon black pepper
1 tablespoon sugar
Paprika for garnish

Cook potatoes in boiling water until tender; drain. Peel cooled potatoes and dice. Rinse diced potatoes in a colander with cold water; drain. Transfer potatoes to a large bowl. Add celery and onion to potatoes. Chop 3 eggs and add to salad, reserving fourth egg for garnish.

Combine salad dressing, milk, salt, pepper and sugar and mix well. Add dressing mixture to salad and mix. Slice remaining egg and place on top of salad. Garnish with a dusting of paprika.

SERVES 6 TO 8

Cindy Smith

Mom's Pixie Salad Dressing

½ cup sugar or Splenda
    sweetener
½ cup natural applesauce
½ cup reduced-fat
    mayonnaise
¼ cup ketchup
2 teaspoons prepared yellow
    mustard
Salt and pepper to taste

Mix all ingredients in a blender. Refrigerate 2 hours to allow flavors to blend.

Serve over a garden salad made with iceberg and romaine.

MAKES 2 CUPS

Violet Sible

LEAS HALL

Leas Hall opened early in the 1960s as the Kindergarten Building and was followed by the opening of McLean Hall in the spring of 1964 as additional space for the Lower School. In September 1999, the Abramson Lower School added additional classrooms as well as music and science facilities that served the needs of pre-k through fifth grade students.

GRAHAM'S GRADUATION TORTELLINI SALAD

Sun-Dried Tomato Pesto

½ stick pepperoni, cut into small pieces

3 tablespoons Dijon mustard

4 cloves garlic, minced

1 (7 ounce) jar sun-dried tomatoes packed in oil

1½ cups olive oil

2 tablespoons lemon juice

Salt and pepper to taste

Salad

2 pounds cheese tortellini, cooked and drained

2 ripe medium tomatoes, chopped

1 yellow bell pepper, chopped

½ cup chopped pepperoni

½ cup chopped fresh parsley

3 tablespoons chopped fresh basil

Place pepperoni, mustard, garlic and tomatoes with oil in a food processor. Process until smooth. With machine running, add olive oil in a thin, steady stream through the feed tube. Process until smooth. Season with lemon juice and salt and pepper.

To assemble salad, combine tortellini, tomato, bell pepper and pepperoni in a large mixing bowl. Add pesto and toss to coat. Sprinkle parsley and basil on top.

SERVES 8 TO 10 *Lynne Kaltman*

SPRING PASTA SALAD

1 pound dry penne pasta

1½ pounds asparagus

8 ounces fresh mozzarella cheese, cubed

1 bunch scallions, sliced

24 cherry tomatoes, sliced

½ cup pine nuts, lightly toasted

1 large handful chopped fresh basil

Juice and zest of 1 lemon

½ cup olive oil

Salt and pepper to taste

Cook pasta until al dente; drain and cool. Meanwhile, blanch asparagus in boiling water for 3 minutes. Drain and rinse immediately to stop cooking process. Cool and diagonally slice asparagus.

Combine pasta, asparagus, mozzarella, scallion, tomato slices, pine nuts and basil. Add lemon juice and zest and olive oil and gently toss to mix. Season with salt and pepper.

SERVES 8 *Linda Weber*

BLACK BEAN AND RICE SALAD

2 (14½ ounce) cans chicken broth
½ cup water
1 (16 ounce) package long grain rice
2 bay leaves
2 (15 ounce) cans black beans, drained and rinsed

2 red bell peppers, diced
1 green bell peppers, diced
1 medium-size red onion, diced
1 medium bunch fresh cilantro, chopped, some leaves reserved for garnish
Dressing (see sidebar)

Bring broth and water to a boil in a large heavy saucepan. Add rice and bay leaves and bring back to a boil. Reduce heat to low. Cover and cook until liquid is absorbed.

Transfer rice to a large bowl, discard bay leaves. Mix in beans, all bell peppers, onion and cilantro. Pour dressing over salad and mix to combine. Refrigerate at least 4 hours before serving. Garnish with cilantro leaves.

SERVES 10 TO 12 *Ralph Wellington*

DRESSING

½ cup olive oil
2 tablespoons orange juice
2 tablespoons red wine vinegar
2 teaspoons ground cumin
1 teaspoon chili powder

Mix all dressing ingredients in a separate bowl.

AMISH COLE SLAW

4 cups finely shredded green cabbage
1 cup chopped Vidalia onion

¼ to ½ cup Splenda sweetener, or to taste

Dressing

1 tablespoon Splenda sweetener
1 teaspoon celery seed

1 teaspoon salt
2 tablespoons light olive oil

Place cabbage and onion in a large mixing bowl. Sprinkle Splenda on top.

Combine all dressing ingredients in a small saucepan and bring to a boil. Cook for 3 minutes; cool. Pour cooled dressing over salad and mix. Refrigerate until chilled.

SERVES 12 *Jodi Bohr*

STRAWBERRY AND MANGO SALAD

Salad

2 (10 ounce) packages mesclun greens
1 mango, peeled and sliced
8 ounces strawberries, sliced

¾ cup dried sweetened cranberries
½ cup pine nuts
½ cup crumbled feta cheese

Dressing

⅓ cup balsamic vinegar
¼ cup sugar

¾ cup olive oil

Combine all salad ingredients in a serving bowl.

Whisk together all dressing ingredients. Just before serving, pour dressing over salad and toss to mix. Serve immediately.

SERVES 8   *Myra Petras*

SUMMER RICE SALAD

2 cups cooked rice, brown, white or combination
1 cup cherry tomatoes, quartered
⅓ cup chopped red onion or scallion
1 (2¼ ounce) can sliced black olives, drained
3 tablespoons cider vinegar
2 tablespoons canola or olive oil

2 tablespoons chopped fresh cilantro or parsley
1 tablespoon sugar
½ teaspoon black pepper
½ teaspoon salt, or to taste
2 tablespoons orange juice
Juice of ½ lime
2 tablespoons Italian salad dressing

Combine rice, tomato, onion and olives in a large bowl.

In a small bowl, whisk together vinegar, oil, cilantro, sugar, pepper, salt, orange juice, lime juice and salad dressing. Mix well and pour over rice mixture. Chill for several hours. Serve on lettuce leaves.

SERVES 4 TO 6   *Betty Grant*

Any ingredients may be increased or decreased to taste. Other vegetables, such as diced cucumber, shredded carrot or corn may be added. Increase amount of rice and salad dressing if adding extra vegetables.

Spiced Fresh Fruit Salad

2 oranges, peeled and cut
    into ½ inch pieces
2 cups fresh pineapple chunks,
    cut into ½ inch pieces

½ cup orange juice
¼ cup confectioners' sugar
¼ teaspoon cinnamon
2 bananas

Combine oranges, pineapple, orange juice, confectioners' sugar and cinnamon in a mixing bowl. Refrigerate at least 1 hour, stirring occasionally.

When ready to serve, peel and slice bananas into the salad. Stir gently to mix and serve immediately.

SERVES 8 TO 10

Cheryl Ross

Mandarin Orange Salad

Dressing

½ cup vegetable oil
2 tablespoons sugar
2 tablespoons parsley

1 teaspoon salt
¼ cup white vinegar
Dash of black pepper

Salad

½ head red leaf lettuce, torn into
    pieces
½ head romaine lettuce, torn into
    pieces
½ head green leaf lettuce, torn
    into pieces

½ cup chopped celery
4 scallions, chopped
1 (11 ounce) can Mandarin orange
    slices, drained
½ cup sliced almonds
3 tablespoons sugar

Whisk together all dressing ingredients and chill for 1 hour.

For salad, combine all lettuce, celery, scallion and orange slices in a salad bowl. Stir almonds and sugar in a skillet over low heat until browned; cool.

When ready to serve, pour dressing over salad and toss to mix.

SERVES 6 TO 10

Laura Korman
Stephanie Wolfer

Spinach and Strawberry Salad

6 tablespoons sugar
1 cup sliced almonds
    (candied)
2 (10 ounce) packages
    spinach
2½ pints strawberries, sliced

Stir almonds and sugar in a skillet over low heat until browned; cool.

Combine spinach, strawberries and candied almonds in a salad bowl. Just before serving, pour dressing (see below) over salad and toss to mix.

Great salad at Christmas dinner.

Dressing

1 tablespoon poppy seeds
2 tablespoons sesame seeds
¼ teaspoon paprika
½ cup champagne vinegar
½ cup olive oil
½ cup sugar

Mix all dressing ingredients. Chill several hours or overnight.

SERVES 12

Tara Schwartz

The performing arts department contributes to the overall purpose and objectives of Germantown Academy by providing strong academic and extracurricular programs in music, drama and media arts. The performing arts department provides a foundation in music to all students in prek through 8th grade through the general music courses and choral and instrumental ensembles in Lower and Middle School. In the Upper School, students are required to fulfil one credit in the arts. This may be realized in the performing arts or in the visual arts. In the performing arts students may choose from a variety of music ensembles, music theory, drama electives, courses in film and video, MIDI and recording arts. Extracurricular activities are offered in all three disciplines.

GERMAN POTATO SALAD

5 pounds red potatoes
½ teaspoon salt

1 medium-size yellow onion, diced

Dressing

½ cup boiling water
½ cup vegetable oil
½ cup white vinegar

1 teaspoon black pepper
Pinch of sugar

Cook potatoes in boiling water until they start to soften. Potatoes are probably done when skins start to come off and a butter knife can be inserted into one of the larger potatoes. Drain potatoes and cool a couple hours. Peel and slice cooled potatoes and sprinkle with salt. Add onion, but do not mix yet.

To prepare dressing, pour ½ cup boiling water into a measuring cup or a small plastic container with a snap-tight lid. Add oil, vinegar, pepper and sugar. Close lid and shake very briefly. Pour dressing over salad and mix well.

SERVES 10 TO 12

Christopher Horner

This recipe came to my family through my grandmother, Christine Hagedorn (nee Schadwinkel), who immigrated to the United States from Germany in the late 1920's. Many members of my mother's family make their own variations. The salad is better the next day. It's also good when freshly made if you can slice the potatoes while they are still warm.

*C*asting female roles became a whole lot easier once Germantown Academy went co-ed in the 20th century, but the Belfry Club, GA's Upper School theater program, was founded in 1894 by GA grad Frank J. Palmer. Palmer named the club for the school's iconic belfry tower, where, legend has it, he convened his first troupe of actors on the old campus. And Palmer was so devoted to the dramatic arts at GA that he stayed on as the Belfry Club's artistic director for the next 30 years. His work has had such a lasting effect that every GA student now has the chance to perform and hone their public speaking skills during their time at school. Starting with the Pre-Kindergarten's Mother Goose Show, moving through 3rd grade's African Dance performance and the 4th grade's drama of England's King Henry the 8th, students are well-prepared to take the stage for the Middle School musical, held every January, and then the Belfry Club.

The Belfry Club's light has shown brightly over the past several years, with the brightest spotlight coming when Germantown Academy was named Philadelphia Magazine's Best High School Theater Program in 2009. The cast of Thoroughly Modern Millie (2009) took home seven Philadelphia area CAPPIE awards, in the school's first time competing against other high school theater programs. In 2010, the Belfry Club honored the school's historical 250th year by putting on Oscar Wilde's "An Ideal Husband" - in the round! The show was selected because it was written the year the Belfry Club was founded, 1894.

Music, too, is a valued part of GA culture. Instrument instruction is available for even the youngest students, and GA students form an impressive Lower School Orchestra. Students from the Lower School forms its chorus, which is heard every December at the always-adorable Holiday Program, and the 5th grade produces an annual Forest Fest play which features standout performers and original songs.

In 2009, the Singing Patriots hosted the First High School of Krakow, Poland Choir in three outstanding concerts, including the Global Youth Concert in Germantown. This show featured not only the Singing Patriots and the choir from Krakow, it also included the melodious voices of the Greater Philadelphia/Youth Mass Choir. Every other year, the Singing Patriots take a journey across the globe to perform in a different foreign country where the sound of music reaches across all languages.

All grades, from Lower School through Upper School, participate in studio art classes and study art history, and examples of painting, photography and sculpture made by students can be seen in GA's Art Center and on walls throughout the school.

Chicken with Fresh Herbs and Tomatoes on Linguini

1 tablespoon olive oil
1 medium onion, finely chopped
1 red or green bell pepper, finely chopped
8 ounces mushrooms, sliced
3 boneless, skinless chicken breasts, cut into ½ inch cubes
⅓ cup red wine
1 (28 ounce) can crushed tomatoes in purée

1 clove garlic, minced
1 teaspoon sugar
Salt and pepper to taste
1 pound dry linguini pasta
2 tablespoons chopped fresh basil
1 tablespoon chopped fresh parsley
1 tablespoon chopped fresh sage
Parmesan cheese

Heat oil in a large nonstick skillet. Add onion, bell pepper and mushrooms and sauté over medium heat for 6 to 7 minutes or until softened, stirring occasionally. Add chicken and sauté until no longer pink. Add wine and bring to a boil; allow to boil for 2 minutes. Add tomatoes, garlic, sugar and salt and pepper. Cover and continue to cook for 15 minutes or until chicken is tender.

When sauce is almost finished cooking, cook pasta in boiling water until just tender; drain.

Meanwhile, add basil, parsley and sage to sauce and continue to simmer 5 minutes longer. Toss pasta with sauce and garnish with Parmesan cheese. Serve immediately.

SERVES 6 TO 8

Cheryl Ross

The combination of outstanding on-campus facilities and our proximity to the Philadelphia cultural scene makes our fine arts program a haven for the imagination. The program includes drawing, sculpture, photography, painting, digital media, art history, and architecture, all of which provide progressively more challenging and diverse experiences for students at every grade level. The most accomplished and committed art students can aspire to be part of the Honors Art Program and exhibit their work in the Honors Art Gallery.

Simply delicious!

Music and theatre are part of a long-standing GA tradition and reinforce the curriculum by enhancing learning in many academic disciplines. Music is a "language" our Lower and Middle School experiences frequently, through singing, playing instruments, and eventually joining choir, band, or string ensemble. Our Upper School instrumental and vocal ensembles perform for GA and the surrounding community. Some, such as the Singing Patriots, travel long distances to share their gifts with National or European audiences.

PENNE AND CHICKEN DIJON

4 chicken breasts, cut into 1 inch pieces
Salt and pepper to taste
1 stick butter
2 cups heavy cream
1 pound dry penne pasta

½ cup Dijon mustard
3 tablespoons chopped fresh parsley
2 tablespoons chopped fresh chives

Season chicken with salt and pepper. Melt butter in a skillet. Add chicken and sauté 3 minutes; set aside. Blend cream into skillet. Bring to a boil. Reduce heat and simmer 5 minutes.

Meanwhile, cook pasta until tender; drain.

Add mustard to cream sauce. Stir in chicken and simmer 5 minutes. Pour sauce over pasta. Garnish with parsley and chives.

SERVES 6 TO 8   *Sarah Andrews*

CHICKEN NAPOLITANO

¼ cup flour
½ teaspoon garlic powder
1 pound raw boneless, skinless chicken breast tenders, cut into chunks
3 to 4 tablespoons olive oil
2 (14½ ounce) cans stewed tomatoes

8 ounces fresh or canned mushrooms, sliced
½ cup chicken broth
½ teaspoon dried thyme
1 pound dry fettuccine pasta
Parmesan cheese

Combine flour and garlic powder in a gallon-size zip-top bag. Add chicken and toss to coat well. Heat oil in a skillet over medium-high heat. Add chicken pieces and sauté 3 to 5 minutes or until done. Add tomatoes, mushrooms, broth and thyme. Bring to a boil. Reduce heat and simmer for at least 15 minutes. The sauce can be made up to a day ahead for best flavor.

When ready to serve, cook pasta until tender; drain. Serve sauce over hot fettuccine. Top with Parmesan cheese.

SERVES 4   *Beth Napolitano*

I was given a version of this recipe when I was first married. It has been modified over the years and has become a family favorite for birthday dinners.

Chicken Tetrazzini

1 pound dry fettuccini pasta,
    broken into thirds
6 tablespoons butter
¼ cup flour
2 cups chicken broth
¾ cup half & half or light cream
3 tablespoons sherry (optional)
1 tablespoon dried parsley, or 2 to
    3 tablespoons chopped fresh
1 teaspoon salt

¼ teaspoon nutmeg
¼ teaspoon cayenne pepper
4 cups or more cooked and
    chopped chicken
    (2 to 3 large breasts)
Sautéed sliced mushrooms
    (optional)
Sautéed bell pepper (optional)
¾ cup grated or shredded
    Parmesan cheese

Preheat oven to 350 degrees. Cook pasta in boiling water until al dente; do not overcook as it will be cooked again. Drain and set aside.

Melt butter in a Dutch oven or large saucepan. Stir in flour with a flat whisk until smooth to make a roux. Add broth and cook over medium-low heat, stirring almost constantly until sauce thickens. Remove from heat. Stir in half & half, sherry, parsley, salt, nutmeg and cayenne pepper.

Toss chicken, sauce and pasta together. Add sautéed mushrooms and bell pepper, if using. Turn mixture into a 9x13 inch baking pan. Top with cheese. Bake for 30 minutes and serve immediately.

SERVES 10 TO 12   *Ken Patrick*

Whole Wheat Pasta with Brie and Fresh Tomatoes

1 pound dry whole wheat pasta
6 large plum tomatoes, chopped
1 cup fresh basil, chopped
1½ tablespoons roasted garlic

6 ounces Brie cheese, rind
    discarded, chopped
¼ cup extra virgin olive oil
½ cup Parmesan cheese

Cook pasta in boiling water until tender; drain.

Meanwhile, mix tomatoes, basil and garlic in a bowl. Add Brie cheese. Mix in olive oil. Add hot pasta and toss until Brie melts. Top with Parmesan cheese.

SERVES 4   *Carol Begley*

The George Washington Portrait

The portrait of General George Washington came into the possession of Germantown Academy in the early twentieth century. At that time, the school was undergoing a revitalization program that included creating a colonial ambience for the campus. One of the buildings, Washington-Kershaw Hall, had been a private dwelling where Washington met his cabinet. Washington-Kershaw Hall served as a temporary meeting place for officials as they avoided the Yellow Fever epidemic of 1793. Washington-Kershaw Hall later became a GA Administration building, and the George Washington portrait was part of its interior design. This portrait is currently displayed in the office of Head of School James Connor.

The portrait is a copy of an original done by Gilbert Stuart who was the recognized "Father of American Portraiture." He painted over 100 likenesses of Washington!

We believe that the performing arts are an integral part of the human spirit. Throughout history, in every corner of the world, the performing arts have reflected every aspect of our existence. They have provided a means for expressing life's inner most feelings; they have been a joy, a comfort, a call to battle, an adjunct to religion.

CHICKEN OR TURKEY TETRAZZINI FOR A CROWD

15 to 18 chicken breasts
1 pound spaghetti, broken into thirds

3 pounds fresh mushrooms, sliced
½ cup chopped celery
Parmesan cheese

Sauce

2 sticks butter
¾ cup flour
4½ cups chicken broth

3½ cups milk
1 cup light cream

Preheat oven to 350 degrees. Cook chicken until done; cut into bite-size pieces. Cook spaghetti in boiling water until tender; drain. Sauté mushrooms and celery.

For sauce, melt butter in a saucepan. Stir in flour until smooth and bubbly. Whisk in broth and bring to a boil and cook 2 minutes. Stir in milk and cream.

Combine sauce with chicken, pasta and sautéed vegetables. Divide mixture between 2 large oblong casserole dishes. Sprinkle with cheese. Bake for 45 to 60 minutes.

SERVES A CROWD   *Barbara Karr*

ROTINI WITH BROCCOLI

2 large cloves garlic, finely chopped
2 tablespoons olive oil
1 tablespoon butter
1 tomato, cut into ½ inch cubes
½ teaspoon crushed red pepper flakes (optional)
½ teaspoon salt
¼ teaspoon black pepper

3 cups boiling water
8 ounces dry penne, rotini or ziti pasta
1½ pounds broccoli, cut into bite-size florets
½ cup heavy cream
Grated Romano or Parmesan cheese

Sauté garlic in olive oil and butter in a 10 inch skillet for 30 seconds. Stir in tomato, pepper flakes, salt and pepper. Cook and stir for 1 minute. Add 3 cups boiling water and pasta and cook for at least the amount of time suggested in package directions. After 3 minutes, arrange broccoli evenly over pasta. Cover and simmer for remaining time or until broccoli is tender and pasta is al dente. Stir in cream and heat 30 seconds. Toss and serve immediately with cheese.

SERVES 4   *Diane Hall*

Amazing Fusilli with Lemon and Arugula

2 tablespoons butter
1 tablespoon extra virgin olive oil
2 tablespoons minced garlic
2 cups heavy cream
Juice of 2 lemons
Kosher salt and freshly ground
    black pepper to taste
1 tablespoon salt

1 pound dry fusilli pasta
8 ounces baby arugula, or
    2 bunches regular arugula
    with stems removed and
    leaves cut into thirds
½ cup freshly grated Parmesan
    cheese
2 tomatoes, diced

Heat butter and olive oil in a medium saucepan over medium heat. Add garlic and cook for 1 minute. Stir in cream, lemon juice and salt and pepper. Bring to a boil. Reduce heat and simmer for 15 to 20 minutes or until it starts to thicken.

Bring a large pot of water to a boil. Add 1 tablespoon salt and pasta and cook for 12 minutes or until al dente, stirring occasionally. Drain and return to pot. Immediately add cream mixture to pasta. Cook over medium-low heat for 3 minutes or until pasta has absorbed most of the sauce. Pour hot pasta into a large bowl. Add arugula, cheese and tomatoes and toss well. Adjust seasoning to taste and serve hot.

SERVES 6   *Diane Jeckovich*

Asparagus Linguini

6 ounces dry linguine pasta
1 small onion, chopped
2 cloves garlic, minced
2 tablespoons olive oil
2 teaspoons butter
8 ounces fresh asparagus, cut
    into ½ inch pieces

2 tablespoons white wine or
    chicken broth
2 tablespoons grated Parmesan
    cheese
1 tablespoon lemon juice
Salt and pepper to taste

Cook pasta until tender; drain and return to pot. Sauté onion and garlic in olive oil and butter until tender. Add asparagus and cook 2 minutes or until asparagus is just tender. Add wine and cook and stir for 1 to 2 minutes or until liquid is reduced. Add mixture to drained pasta. Add cheese, lemon juice and salt and pepper. Toss and serve immediately with toasted Italian bread.

SERVES 2 TO 4   *Rose Mary Hoy*

The performing arts, in all their variety, have been constant companions. Through exceptional musical repertoire and theatrical literature, advanced technology and fine sequential teaching materials, we strive to develop the artistic understandings, skills and values of our students. Through the performing arts, we also seek to enhance our students' understanding of themselves and the peoples of the world. Ultimately, our hope is that our students come to appreciate the arts, participating as performers, audience and supporters of the arts throughout their lives.

FETTUCCINE WITH SHRIMP MAGGIORE

1 pound medium to large shrimp, peeled and deveined
2 to 3 tablespoons butter
1 cup tomato sauce with basil
¼ cup dry white wine
1 cup heavy cream
1 teaspoon dried or fresh basil
1 teaspoon dried oregano
¼ teaspoon dried or fresh dill
1 pound fresh fettuccine pasta
Parmesan cheese

Sauté shrimp in butter. Add tomato sauce and wine and simmer 2 to 3 minutes. Add cream, basil, oregano and dill and simmer 2 minutes.

Meanwhile, cook pasta in boiling water until tender; drain. Serve sauce over fettuccine. Top with Parmesan cheese.

SERVES 4   *Anthony Donofrio*

RIGATONI WITH SPINACH AND FETA CHEESE

2 tablespoons olive oil
1 cup chopped onion
5 cloves garlic, minced
1 pound fresh spinach, or
    2 (10 ounce) packages frozen chopped, thawed and well drained
2 (14½ ounce) cans stewed tomatoes
Salt and pepper to taste
1 pound dry pasta
12 ounces feta cheese, crumbled
¼ cup Parmesan cheese

Heat oil in a skillet. Add onion and sauté until softened. Add garlic and sauté 2 minutes longer. Add spinach and tomatoes and sauté 3 minutes or until hot and bubbly. Season with salt and pepper.

Cook pasta in boiling water; drain. Divide pasta among individual dishes. Spoon sauce on top. Sprinkle with feta and Parmesan cheese.

SERVES 4   *Maria Kiley*

Add cooked and chopped chicken breast to the sauce.

ADELA'S HEAVENLY ANGEL HAIR

2 tablespoons olive oil, divided
2 cloves garlic
1 (16 ounce) can cannellini beans, drained

½ teaspoon minced fresh rosemary
1 pound fresh angel hair pasta
4 ounces pancetta, sliced
Zest of 1 lemon

Add 1 tablespoon olive oil to a warm pan. Crush garlic cloves with the flat of a knife and add to oil. Sauté for 2 minutes. Add beans and rosemary and simmer for 5 minutes.

Meanwhile, cook pasta in boiling water; drain, reserving 1 cup cooking water.

Add remaining olive oil to a heated large pan. Add pancetta and sauté until crisp; remove to paper towel to drain, reserving fat in pan. Add drained pasta and ½ cup reserved cooking water to pan. Add lemon zest and beans. Crumble pancetta into pasta and toss well. Serve with Parmesan cheese.

SERVES 4   *Bridget Flynn*

More olive oil can be added to the pasta before serving. The flavor of the raw olive oil can enhance the dish. Fresh sage can be substituted for the rosemary.

*D*uring his tenure as principal from 1877 to 1910, William Kershaw recalled the following:

It used to be the custom for the boys to come together and give the principal and the teachers Christmas gifts. One of my first presents was a microscope. The boys suspected that I had guessed what was coming so decided to play a trick. When I opened the big square package, instead of the expected microscope there was a just a block of wood, which gave me a chance to immediately thank them for such a fine specimen of their heads, made even more realistic by the large crack in the block of wood. The laugh being on them, Jim Pease hastily went out and returned with the microscope.

The History of Germantown Academy

"*It was a year since* the exodus from Germantown. The buildings were completed and the dust had finally settled. Everything seemed new and standardized. Yet, one incongruous element from the old Academy remained: the senior class. We still thought of ourselves as students of the small, intimate boys' school. Yet everywhere our image was challenged by reality. The great hallways, the swollen enrollment, and finally the rustle of plaid skirts belied our faith. …it seemed at times the administration was caught up in the question of just what type of school GA had become. We flourished in the confusion and savored the best qualities of the old GA while skeptically adjusting to those of the new."

Foreword, Ye Primer 1967

TORTELLINI WITH CREAMY HERB SAUCE

1 (9 ounce) package fresh tortellini pasta
2 cloves garlic, minced
3 tablespoons olive oil
2 tablespoons butter
1 teaspoon dried basil, or fresh to taste

1 tablespoon dried parsley, or fresh flat-leaf to taste
¾ cup heavy cream
¼ cup grated Parmesan cheese, plus extra for serving

Cook pasta 2 minutes less than directed on package; drain. Sauté garlic in olive oil in a medium skillet until golden but not brown. Add butter, basil and parsley. Stir in cream and cheese. Gently stir in tortellini. Serve with extra Parmesan cheese on the side.

SERVES 4 *Maria Kiley*

Super quick and simple dinner or side dish. Dry tortellini can be substituted. For a lower fat version, use less sauce — it still tastes great. Also, add some veggies such as broccoli, mushrooms, carrots and spinach.

Ten Minute Tortellini à la Erb with Sausage and Cream

2 tablespoons vegetable oil
1 large onion, chopped
1 (1 pound) package sweet Italian sausage, casings removed
2 (9 ounce) packages fresh tortellini

1 teaspoon salt
2 cups heavy cream
1 cup chicken broth
1 cup grated Parmesan cheese
¼ cup chopped fresh basil

Preheat oven to 350 degrees. Drizzle vegetable oil in a 12 inch skillet over medium-high heat. Add onion and lightly sauté. Crumble sausage into skillet and sauté about 6 minutes or until browned.

Fill a large pot with water and bring to a boil over high heat. Add tortellini and 1 teaspoon salt and cook for 3 minutes; drain. Meanwhile, in a separate bowl, combine cream and broth and lightly whisk.

Mix tortellini, cream mixture and sausage in a greased 12 inch baking dish. Sprinkle with Parmesan cheese and cover with foil. Bake for 10 minutes. Remove from oven and sprinkle with basil and salt to taste.

SERVES 8

Dora Erb

Three Cheese Pasta

1 pound dry pasta, cooked and drained
3 tablespoons butter
1 cup Parmesan cheese

½ cup shredded Swiss cheese
½ cup shredded mozzarella cheese
1 cup heavy cream

Preheat oven to 400 degrees. Toss cooked pasta with butter and place in a 9x13 inch baking dish. Mix three cheeses and sprinkle over pasta. Pour cream over top. Bake for 30 minutes.

SERVES 6 TO 8

Robin Dowzicky

Half & half can be substituted for some of the heavy cream.

"*Tomorrow there will be awarded the diplomas for which we have been striving for so many years. Through those years there has developed among us a bond of friendship that we earnestly hope shall be of lifelong duration.*"

Salutatory, 1931

Shrimp Scampi with Linguini

½ to ¾ cup olive oil
2 large onions, grated
5 cloves garlic, minced
1 large bunch tarragon, chopped
1 teaspoon kosher salt
Freshly ground black pepper to
    taste

42 large shrimp, peeled and
    deveined
Juice of 1 large lemon
6 quarts water
1 pound dry linguini pasta

Heat olive oil in a medium skillet. Add onion and sauté 3 minutes. Add garlic and sauté 1 minute longer. Stir in tarragon, salt and pepper and sauté 1 minute. Remove from heat and allow to cool.

In a large bowl, combine shrimp, lemon juice and cooled mixture. Allow mixture to stand for 30 minutes.

Bring 6 quarts water to a rolling boil in a large stockpot. Generously salt water and add linguini. Cook 10 to 12 minutes or until al dente, stirring occasionally; drain.

Preheat a broiler and line a broiler pan with foil. Place shrimp on foil, spooning onion mixture over each shrimp. Broil for 4 to 5 minutes or until shrimp turn pink. Serve immediately over linguini.

SERVES 6   *Cheryl Koons*

Greek Style Shrimp with Penne

5 tablespoons olive oil, divided
1 tablespoon minced garlic
2 cups peeled whole tomatoes, diced, or 1 (28 ounce) can diced
½ cup dry white wine
¼ cup chopped fresh basil, plus extra for garnish

1 teaspoon dried oregano
Salt and pepper to taste
1½ pounds raw medium/large shrimp, peeled and deveined
⅛ teaspoon dried red pepper flakes
8 ounces crumbled feta cheese
12 to 16 ounces dry penne pasta

Preheat oven to 400 degrees. Heat 2 tablespoons oil in a skillet. Add garlic and cook briefly, stirring often. Add tomato and cook 1 minute. Mix in wine, basil, oregano and salt and pepper. Cook over medium heat for 10 minutes; set aside.

Meanwhile, season shrimp with salt and pepper. Heat remaining 3 tablespoons oil in a large skillet. Add shrimp and cook 1 minute or until shrimp turn red. Sprinkle pepper flakes over shrimp. Spoon shrimp and pan juices into a 9x13 inch baking dish. Sprinkle feta cheese over shrimp and spoon tomato sauce on top. Bake for 10 minutes or until piping hot.

While shrimp bakes, cook pasta in boiling water until tender; drain. Place pasta in a serving dish. Spoon tomato sauce with shrimp over pasta and garnish with extra fresh basil.

SERVES 5 TO 6

Nicole Riter

*M*iddle School students at GA enthusiastically respond to the call to understand the process of learning and to take a more active role in their own education. They make mature decisions that reflect their varied abilities and interest. They are engaged in lively discussion, small group and student-led classes. They take advantage of extracurricular and curriculum related opportunities, finding a multitude of ways to develop their intellects as well as their bodies and spirit-whether they take honors classes in math or foreign language, pursue their passion for sculpting, violin, or basketball; or thrive as community service or student government devotees.

The Academy Chamber Society and the Academy Chorale have established a reputation for musical excellence, compelling programming, and vitality of performance. Rehearsing under the auspices of Germantown Academy and serving as the school's cultural ambassadors to the surrounding communities, these ensembles provide exceptional musical opportunities for those who love good music.

Classic Lasagne

1 pound lean ground beef
1 clove garlic, minced
1 tablespoon dried basil
3½ teaspoons salt, divided
1 (14½ ounce) can tomatoes
2 (6 ounce) cans tomato paste
10 ounces lasagne noodles
3 cups ricotta cheese

½ cup grated Parmesan cheese
2 tablespoons dried parsley
2 large eggs, beaten
2 teaspoons salt
½ teaspoon black pepper
1 pound mozzarella cheese, thinly sliced

Preheat oven to 350 degrees. Brown meat slowly in a skillet; spoon off excess fat. Add garlic, basil, 1½ teaspoons salt, tomatoes and tomato paste. Simmer, uncovered, for 30 minutes, stirring occasionally.

Meanwhile, cook noodles in a large amount of boiling salted water for 10 minutes; drain and rinse. Combine ricotta cheese, Parmesan cheese, parsley, egg, 2 teaspoons salt and pepper.

Arrange half the noodles in a 9x13 inch baking dish. Spread half the cheese mixture over noodles and layer half of mozzarella cheese on top. Spread half of meat sauce over cheese. Repeat layers.

Bake for 30 minutes. Remove from oven and let stand 10 minutes before cutting.

SERVES 12   *Kelly Dalsemer*

If preparing in advance and refrigerating before baking,
add about 15 minutes to baking time.

ITALIAN MEAT LASAGNA

Lean ground meat
2 pounds fresh ricotta cheese
2 cups shredded Locatelli Romano
  cheese, divided
2 large balls lightly salted
  mozzarella cheese, shredded,
  divided

2 large eggs
Salt and pepper to taste
Basil to taste
3 to 4 cups tomato baking sauce,
  divided
6 fresh lasagna pasta sheets

Preheat oven to 350 degrees. Brown meat in a skillet; drain and set aside.

Mix ricotta with half the Romano cheese, half the mozzarella cheese, eggs, salt and pepper, basil and 1 cup tomato sauce.

Add enough tomato sauce to the bottom of a large disposable pan to coat. Layer 2 pasta sheets over sauce. Top with half the ricotta mixture and sprinkle with about half of cooked meat. Add a layer of about half of remaining tomato sauce. Repeat steps. Top with a final layer of pasta sheets and sprinkle with remaining Romano and mozzarella cheese. Bake for 45 minutes.

SERVES 18 TO 20

Kirsten Gambone

Members of the 100 voice Chorale include not only Germantown Academy faculty, staff, parents, and alumni, but also singers from the surrounding community. The Academy Chamber Society, our 50 piece chamber orchestra, numbers among its membership many of the finest amateurs and teaching professionals in the Greater Philadelphia area.

Fresh ingredients and freshly prepared sauce are key for taste. Double layers of pasta at bottom, top and middle are key to keeping lasagna together.

A receipt dated September 22, 1826 records payment of $10 to a gentleman for "ringing the bell of the school to the time agreed for by the Committee To Get The Bell Rung."

I Can't Believe It's Vegetarian Lasagna

Sauce

½ to 1 cup olive oil
2 large eggplants, peeled and cut into cubes
6 cloves garlic, minced
1 green bell pepper, sliced
1 red bell pepper, sliced
8 ounces mushrooms, sliced (optional)
2 red onions, sliced
4 (14½ ounce) cans peeled Italian plum tomatoes
2 (6 ounce) cans tomato paste

2 tablespoons drained capers
2 teaspoons garlic powder
2 teaspoons dried basil
4 teaspoons dried oregano
1 tablespoon salt, or to taste
2 teaspoons freshly ground black pepper
Hot pepper flakes or fresh cayenne peppers to taste (optional)
¼ cup black olives
½ to 1 cup water

Assembly

2 pounds regular or whole wheat lasagna noodles
2 (1 pound) balls whole or skim milk mozzarella, sliced ¼ inch thick

1 (32 ounce) container whole or skim milk ricotta cheese
4 large eggs, hard-cooked, sliced
¼ to ½ cup Parmesan cheese

Add just enough olive oil to a large skillet to cover and heat over medium heat. Add eggplant and cook and stir until lightly browned and softened. Add more oil if needed while cooking. Remove cooked eggplant to a large bowl. In same skillet, add a bit more oil. Stir in garlic, bell peppers and mushrooms and sauté until just starting to soften. Add onion and sauté 5 minutes longer.

Add tomatoes and tomato paste to a large soup pot. Mash tomatoes with a large masher until a thick mixture forms. Turn to low heat. Add sautéed vegetables, capers, garlic powder, basil, oregano, salt, pepper, pepper flakes and olives, stirring after each addition. Simmer about 10 to 20 minutes, stirring occasionally. As mixture thickens, add ½ cup water to allow mixture to cook at a slow pace, adding up to ½ cup more water if needed. Simmer about 1 hour, stirring occasionally to avoid sticking.

While the sauce simmers, cook pasta in a pot of boiling water until al dente. Drain most but not all cooking liquid; set aside.

To assemble, ladle enough sauce into a large lasagna pan to cover the bottom with about a ½ inch thick layer. Add a layer of pasta, creating a wall-to-wall layer of pasta. Ladle on more sauce. Break apart pieces of the mozzarella and place randomly over the top. Scoop ricotta cheese and place throughout the layer, filling in near the mozzarella. Add a few slices of egg; not too many as the egg should be a surprise when eating, so do not over do it. Sprinkle Parmesan cheese on top. Cover with another layer of pasta, arranged in the opposite direction of noodles in last layer. Add a layer of sauce. Continue layering until desired thickness is reached or until the pan if full.

When ready to bake, preheat oven to 350 degrees. Bake for about 45 to 60 minutes or until top is browned.

SERVES 8 TO 10   *Angelo J. Devita*

CROCKPOT LASAGNA

2 pounds ground turkey or beef
1 (32 ounce) container low fat
  ricotta cheese
1 (16 ounce) container low fat
  cottage cheese
2 large eggs

2 tablespoons Italian seasoning
2 (9 ounce) packages oven-ready
  lasagna noodles
1 (32 ounce) jar mushroom and
  garlic spaghetti sauce
Grated Parmesan cheese

Brown turkey in a pan; this can be done up to a day ahead and refrigerated until needed. Combine ricotta cheese, cottage cheese, eggs and Italian seasoning in a large bowl.

Layer lasagna noodles in the bottom of a crockpot. Cover with a layer of browned meat and spaghetti sauce. Add another layer of noodles. Cover with cheese mixture and sauce. Continue layering, alternating meat and cheese mixture layers, repeating layers until crockpot is filled. Make sure top layer is covered with sauce. Cover crockpot. Cook on low heat for about 6 hours. Sprinkle with Parmesan cheese and serve.

SERVES 8 TO 12   *Karen Viola*

For vegetarian lasagna, use frozen meatless protein crumbles instead of turkey.
A bag of chopped spinach can be mixed into the cheese mixture, too.
Instead of ricotta cheese, mozzarella can be substituted.

*T*he Primer (Ye Primer as we know it today) was started by the class of 1895 to contain an account of the Class Day (graduation) exercises which had hitherto been printed in the June issue of the Academy Monthly. It was a modest, paper-covered booklet, tastefully printed and soon became an annual custom. Like other school customs it soon followed college ways in an elaborate leather-bound book of considerable size and profuse illustration, after the manner of the senior record at colleges.

***The History of
Germantown Academy***

REMEMBER:

The ski club trip where nobody got in trouble? (No, you don't!)

The Turner father, son, or grandson who wasn't a great football player? (No, you don't!)

Winter track practice indoors? (No, you don't!)

SPINACH AND CHICKEN ALFREDO LASAGNA

1½ pounds boneless, skinless chicken breast cutlets
2 pinches salt
¼ teaspoon black pepper
¼ teaspoon Italian seasoning
2 (10 ounce) boxes frozen chopped spinach, thawed and drained
1 (15 ounce) container ricotta cheese
1 (16 ounce) jar Alfredo sauce, or homemade (see "Sauces" section)
12 lasagna noodles
Bread crumbs

Preheat oven to 350 degrees. Heat a skillet over medium heat. Spray skillet with cooking spray and add chicken, salt, pepper and Italian seasoning. Cook for 3 to 5 minutes on each side or until golden; cool to room temperature. Cut chicken into bite-size pieces.

Mix spinach, ricotta cheese and chopped chicken in a large mixing bowl; mixture should have a thick consistency.

In a large saucepot, bring 3 cups water to a boil. Spray cooking spray in water for 5 seconds to prevent noodles from sticking. Boil until tender; drain and cool to room temperature.

Arrange a single layer of noodles slightly overlapping in a greased lasagna pan. Spread a thin layer of Alfredo sauce over noodles. Spread chicken mixture over sauce. Repeat layers twice. Pour enough of remaining Alfredo sauce to just cover top layer. Sprinkle with bread crumbs. Bake for 25 to 35 minutes.

SERVES 12 TO 16

Alaiya Duncan

Healthy substitutes:
Ricotta cheese made with skim milk.
Whole wheat noodles and whole wheat bread crumbs.

STUFFED SHELLS

8 ounces spinach, well rinsed and thick stems removed

2 to 3 cloves garlic, minced

1½ cups whole milk ricotta

12 ounces mozzarella cheese, shredded

1 large egg, lightly beaten

1 tablespoon finely minced fresh basil

Salt and pepper to taste

20 jumbo pasta shells

2 teaspoons olive oil

1½ cups homemade or high-quality tomato sauce

½ cup Pecorino Romano cheese

Preheat oven to 375 degrees. Lightly grease a baking dish large enough to hold the shells in a single layer. Place wet spinach in a skillet with a few drops of water. Cover and cook 3 minutes or until leaves are just wilted. Rinse under cold water until cool, drain, squeeze dry and finely chop. Mix spinach with garlic, ricotta, mozzarella, egg, basil and salt and pepper.

Cook pasta according to package directions; drain. Toss shells with olive oil to prevent sticking.

Spoon half of tomato sauce into prepared dish. Fill each shell with a heaping tablespoon of ricotta mixture. Arrange shells in a single layer in dish. Pour remaining sauce over and around the shells. Sprinkle Romano cheese on top. Cover with foil. Bake for 30 to 40 minutes.

MAKES 20 SHELLS

Kim Sloane

Boil more than 20 shells because some always break.

HOMESTYLE BAKED ZITI

1 pound ricotta cheese

1 pound, 4 ounces mozzarella cheese, shredded, divided

8 ounces Locatelli Romano cheese, shredded

Chopped parsley to taste

1 large egg

1 pound dry ziti noodles, cooked and drained

2 (28 ounce) jars spaghetti sauce, or homemade

Preheat oven to 350 degrees. Mix ricotta cheese, 1 pound mozzarella cheese, Romano cheese, parsley and egg in a bowl. Add cooked ziti and spaghetti sauce. Transfer mixture to a 15x11x3 inch baking pan. Sprinkle remaining 4 ounces mozzarella cheese on top. Bake, covered, for 35 to 40 minutes. Uncover and bake 10 minutes longer.

SERVES 10 TO 12

Karen McCurdy

This recipe is great for a crowd. It can be prepared a day ahead and baked just before serving. Add mushrooms or 1 pound cooked lean ground beef or sausage, if desired. The recipe was given to me by an Italian friend. It is a family favorite!

Second Grade is synonymous with dinosaurs! It is a year for eight-year-old paleontologists to "dig" for information on all the dinosaurs they can imagine. They measure the length of T-Rex or Apatosaurus down the hallway, perch themselves inside the mouth of Triceratops at the Academy of Natural Sciences, "stump the expert" with their own tough questions about dinosaurs, and write detailed reports about their dinosaurs-of-choice. It is a journey into a prehistoric world during this historic year at GA.

KYLE SMITH'S MAC 'N CHEESE

1 pound dry elbow macaroni
1 stick butter or margarine
⅓ cup all-purpose flour
2 cups milk
3 cups shredded Cheddar cheese, divided

1 (12 ounce) container small curd cottage cheese
2 large eggs, lightly beaten
1 teaspoon salt
½ cup dry bread crumbs
¼ teaspoon nutmeg

Preheat oven to 350 degrees. Cook pasta according to package directions; drain. Melt butter in a Dutch oven over low heat. Whisk in flour until smooth. Cook 1 minute, whisking constantly. Gradually stir in milk over medium heat until thickened and bubbly. Add 2 cups Cheddar cheese, cottage cheese, egg and salt. Stir in cooked pasta. Spoon mixture to a lightly greased 9x13 inch baking dish. Top with remaining 1 cup Cheddar cheese.

Combine bread crumbs and nutmeg and sprinkle on top. Bake for 25 minutes.

Kyle Smith

GRANDMA BOWES MACARONI AND CHEESE

1 (16 ounce) package elbow macaroni pasta
4 tablespoons butter
3 tablespoons flour
2½ cups milk

½ teaspoon salt, or to taste
½ teaspoon black pepper, or to taste
1 (10 ounce) package white extra sharp or Vermont sharp Cheddar cheese, shredded

Cook macaroni per package directions, drain and set aside. Melt butter over low heat in a saucepan. Whisk in flour to form a paste. Immediately add milk, salt and pepper and increase to medium heat. Cook and stir for a few minutes or until mixture is slightly thickened; do not allow to boil. Reduce heat to low and stir in cheese, cooking until completely melted; remove from heat if sauce is too hot.

Add three-fourths of cooked pasta to an ungreased large casserole dish. Stir in cheese sauce. Add remaining macaroni, if needed, until the sauce is absorbed by the pasta; there will be extra noodles once recipe is complete.

SERVES 10

Kim Forbes

Gourmet Mac 'N Cheese

8 tablespoons unsalted butter, divided
½ cup flour
4 cups half & half
1 cup milk
1 teaspoon black pepper
½ teaspoon red pepper flakes
1 teaspoon garlic powder
½ teaspoon nutmeg
2 cups shredded white Cheddar cheese

2 cups shredded Monterey Jack cheese, divided
2 cups shredded Swiss or Gruyère cheese, divided
1¼ cups grated Romano cheese, divided
1 pound penne pasta
8 ounces applewood smoked bacon, chopped, cooked and drained

Melt 6 tablespoons butter in a large saucepan. Blend in flour and whisk constantly over heat. After 1 minute, slowly add half & half and milk. Stir in black pepper, pepper flakes, garlic powder and nutmeg. Cook, whisking constantly, until bubbling and thickened. Remove from heat and stir in Cheddar cheese, 1 cup Monterey Jack cheese, 1 cup Swiss cheese and 1 cup Romano cheese; set sauce aside. Combine remaining cheese; set aside.

Cook pasta in boiling water until al dente; drain. Mix pasta with remaining 2 tablespoons butter. Stir in cheese sauce and bacon. Pour mixture into a casserole dish and sprinkle remaining cheese on top. Bake for 45 minutes or until browned on top. Transfer to a wire rack to cool for 10 minutes.

SERVES 8 TO 10

Chris Hibbitts

Baked Macaroni and Cheese with Crunchy Crouton Topping

2 cups dry elbow macaroni
2 cups shredded Cheddar cheese
3 to 4 ounces Swiss cheese, shredded
1 teaspoon salt

⅛ teaspoon black pepper
3 cups milk
2 slices white bread, cubed a day ahead to allow to stale
4 tablespoons butter, melted

Preheat oven to 350 degrees. Cook macaroni in boiling water for 7 minutes. Rinse with cold water until cool; drain. Mix macaroni with cheeses, salt and pepper in a bowl. Transfer mixture to a greased 9x13 inch baking dish. Carefully pour milk into dish at one corner. Top with bread cubes and drizzle with melted butter. Bake, uncovered, for 1½ hours.

SERVES 12

Lori Worrell

The Community Partnership School opened in September 2006 and for the 2009-2010 school year served 72 children in pre-kindergarten through fourth grade in North Central Philadelphia. The school will add one grade of 12 students each year, until it serves children from pre-kindergarten through the fifth grade.

Behind the Community Partnership School lies a simple belief: With a top-notch education, the type delivered at the country's best independent schools-inner-city children can achieve at the same level as their more affluent suburban peers. The school's goal is to prepare talented students from North Central Philadelphia so they are ready to attend excellent middle schools once they graduate from CPS. Germantown Academy supplies the school's core curriculum and administrative oversight, while Project H.O.M.E. provides the school's venue as well as social services and support to the families attending the school.

LOBSTER MACARONI AND CHEESE

1 stick butter
2 pounds cooked lobster meat, thawed and drained, if frozen; drained, if canned
3 tablespoons all-purpose flour
1 cup milk
1 cup half & half
¼ teaspoon cayenne pepper

12 ounces extra sharp Cheddar cheese, shredded
6 ounces Gruyère, shredded
6 ounces Asiago, shredded
1 pound dry rigatoni pasta
2 tablespoons olive oil
2 tablespoons salt
½ cup seasoned bread crumbs

Preheat oven to 375 degrees. Melt butter in a large saucepan. Add drained lobster and sauté about 5 minutes over medium-low heat. Remove lobster and set aside. Increase heat to medium-high and blend flour into saucepan drippings. Cook, stirring constantly, for 5 minutes or until mixture is thick and bubbly. Add milk, half & half and cayenne pepper and stir until thick and bubbly; do not allow mixture to come to a full boil or burn. Reduce heat to medium. Slowly stir in all cheeses until melted.

Meanwhile, cook pasta in 4 quarts boiling water with olive oil and salt for 10 minutes or until al dente, stirring occasionally. Remove from heat and drain well.

Mix pasta with cheese sauce in a 2-quart casserole dish. Gently fold in lobster. Sprinkle bread crumbs on top. Bake for 30 minutes.

SERVES 6 TO 8

Paul Oppenheimer

One of my favorite dishes to make and eat! I first enjoyed it at a local restaurant and knew I could make my own version at home. You can successfully use any number of cheese or pasta combinations.

HEARTY HOMEMADE HAM MACARONI AND CHEESE

1 pound penne pasta
2 cups diced ham
2 cups shredded Cheddar cheese
1 (16 ounce) jar low-fat Alfredo
 sauce
2 cups milk

1 cup Parmesan cheese, divided
1 teaspoon dried oregano
1 teaspoon dried thyme
1 teaspoon minced garlic
½ cup panko bread crumbs

Preheat oven to 350 degrees. Cook pasta in boiling water until tender; drain and return to saucepan. Mix in ham, Cheddar cheese, Alfredo sauce, milk, ½ cup Parmesan cheese, oregano, thyme and garlic. Transfer to a 9x13 inch baking dish.

Combine remaining ½ cup Parmesan cheese and bread crumbs and sprinkle on top. Cover with foil. Bake for 40 minutes, removing foil for last 5 minutes of baking to allow for browning.

SERVES 6

Anne Flood

The Community Partnership School also hopes to create a model for partnering other suburban independent schools with community-based programs to bring new educational opportunities to children in low-income urban areas. At the same time, the school seeks to establish a demonstration program illustrating best teaching practices for urban children.

BAKED MACARONI AND CHEESE

1 pound dry elbow macaroni
4 tablespoons butter
5 tablespoons flour
1 teaspoon salt
½ teaspoon white pepper
¾ teaspoon dry mustard
3½ cups skim milk

10 dashes Tabasco sauce
3 cups shredded Cheddar cheese
2½ cups shredded processed
 cheese loaf, or Cheddar
 cheese
5 tablespoons grated Locatelli
 Romano cheese

Preheat oven to 350 degrees. Cook macaroni in boiling water until almost completely cooked; do not overcook as it will cook further in the oven. Drain and transfer to a 9x13 inch casserole dish.

In same saucepan, melt butter over low heat. Stir in flour, salt, pepper and mustard. Increase to medium heat and stir in milk and Tabasco sauce. When completely mixed, slowly blend in cheese. Cook and stir over low heat until cheese is melted and sauce is thickened. Pour half to all of sauce over macaroni. Sprinkle Romano cheese on top and cover with foil. Bake for 20 minutes.

Sandy Naber
Nicole Roman

SERVES 6

WHAT IS 4TH GRADE?

Make a solid cake of mathematics, poetry, language skills, reading and geography.

Include some American History.

Add one slice of Roanoke, one slice of Jamestown, and one chunk of Plymouth Rock.

Mix in a Salem Witch Trial.

Don't forget to sprinkle with other simulations and hands-on experiences to taste.

Make a heady brew of Revolutionary fervour.

Visit the Highlands to gather for a Constitutional Convention.

Throw in a trip to Olde Philadelphia and the National Constitution Center.

DAD'S MACARONI AND CHEESE

4 tablespoons unsalted butter
1 large Vidalia onion, ⅛ inch diced
1 tablespoon minced garlic
3 tablespoons all-purpose flour
4 cups low-fat milk
1 teaspoon paprika
½ teaspoon kosher salt
1 teaspoon freshly ground black pepper
1 cup shredded extra sharp Cheddar cheese
1 cup shredded Wisconsin Asiago cheese
1 cup grated mild Parmesan cheese
1 pound dry elbow macaroni, cooked and drained
2 plum tomatoes, sliced
½ cup bread crumbs
1 tablespoon chopped fresh parsley
1 tablespoon chopped fresh thyme
1 tablespoon chopped fresh chives

Preheat oven to 400 degrees. Melt butter in a large pot over medium heat. Add onion and garlic and cook 2 minutes or until softened. Whisk in flour and cook, stirring constantly, for 3 minutes or until mixture turns light brown. Gradually whisk in milk. Add paprika, salt and pepper. Reduce heat to low and cook, stirring, for 5 minutes or until sauce is thickened. Add all cheeses and stir until melted. Add cooked macaroni and stir until thoroughly coated. Remove from heat and transfer to a greased 12 inch cast-iron skillet, or two 6 inch skillets.

Top with sliced tomatoes and sprinkle with bread crumbs. Bake for 30 minutes or until cheese is bubbling and golden brown. Garnish with fresh herbs.

SERVES 12 SERVINGS   *Nicos Scordis*

GRANDMOTHER'S MEATBALLS AND SAUCE

1 pound ground round or lean ground beef
1 cup bread crumbs
1 tablespoon grated Parmesan cheese
A few shakes black pepper
A few shakes garlic powder
¼ teaspoon salt
2 large eggs
Tomato sauce

Mix all ingredients except tomato sauce and shape into balls. Brown balls in a hot skillet sprayed with cooking spray, turning every few minutes to cook on all sides; meatballs do not have to be cooked through. Place meatballs in a large pot of tomato sauce with a lid and simmer on low for 1 hour to finish cooking meatballs; or cook in a crockpot. Serve over pasta or use for meatball sandwiches.

SERVES 12   *Maria Kiley*

Kathleen's Hearty Meat Sauce

Sauce

1 (29 ounce) can tomato purée or crushed tomatoes
1 (12 ounce) can tomato paste
1 tomato paste can water
1 (14½ ounce) can stewed tomatoes
¼ cup dried parsley
1 tablespoon oregano

½ teaspoon dried red pepper flakes (optional)
3 bay leaves, broken in half
1 (8 ounce) can tomato sauce
Generous sprinkle of fresh or dried basil
Salt and pepper to taste
1½ tablespoons sugar

Meat

1 large onion, chopped
3 cloves garlic, chopped

1½ pounds ground beef
1 pound Italian sausage links

Combine all sauce ingredients in a large stockpot. Stir well and simmer 1 hour.

Meanwhile, sauté onion and garlic in oil, being careful to not burn. Add ground beef and cook until browned; drain. In a separate skillet, cook sausage in an inch of water, piercing skin to release fat; water will evaporate. Slice sausage into bite-size pieces.

Add all meat to sauce in stockpot. Simmer 1 hour. Remove bay leaves. Serve meat sauce over your favorite pasta.

SERVES 12   *Kathleen Rodgers*

What is 4th Grade?

(continued)

Watch it grow Westward with Lewis and Clark.

Decide how much Industrial Revolution to include.

Send it on the Underground Railroad and through the Civil War.

Slowly blend in immigration and strain it at Ellis Island.

Mix in the Statue of Liberty.

Decorate with a personal time-line.

Put in the oven of Germantown Academy

For one school year at nine or ten years old.

Sauce is delicious and is even better the next day.
Make a double batch and freeze half for another meal.

For years, a vital part of the Upper School government and, years later, the Upper School Advisory Council called itself the "Student Faculty Affairs Committee" with very few people recognizing the humor in its name.

Bracciole

(Meatballs and Sausage in Tomato Sauce for Pasta)

Bracciole

½ cup Italian-flavored bread crumbs
½ cup Parmesan cheese
1 tablespoon chopped fresh parsley

12 pieces steak, thinly sliced (ACME sells "chipped steak" that works well)
12 slices prosciutto
12 slices mozzarella cheese

Meatballs and Sausage

1 pound ground beef
1 large egg
¾ cup Italian-flavored bread crumbs

½ cup chopped onion
1 clove garlic, chopped
1 pound hot or sweet Italian sausage

Sauce

1 (28 ounce) can crushed tomatoes
1 (12 ounce) can tomato paste
2 tomato paste cans water

1 (15 ounce) can tomato sauce
1 to 2 cloves garlic, minced
Oregano to taste
Basil to taste

Mix bread crumbs and Parmesan cheese. Mix in parsley. Place a piece of steak on a flat surface and sprinkle with 1 tablespoon bread crumb mixture. Place a slice of prosciutto and a slice of mozzarella lengthwise along the middle of the steak. Roll up steak, starting with the narrow end, keeping the bread crumbs, prosciutto and mozzarella filling inside. Tie roll with a 2 foot length of kitchen string. Repeat with each piece of steak. Brown rolls in a small amount of oil in a large skillet. Arrange browned rolls in a large pot.

Combine all meatball ingredients except sausage and form into 12 to 14 meatballs. Brown balls on all sides in a skillet. Add browned meatballs to bracciole in pot. Cut Italian sausage into 1 inch pieces and cook until browned. Add sausage to other meats in pot.

Add all sauce ingredients to pot of meat. Bring to a boil. Reduce heat to just barely simmering. Cook for 1 hour, stirring occasionally. Serve over your favorite pasta.

SERVES 6 TO 8

Maryanne Boettjer

Bracciole with sauce is fantastic on its own!
It is helpful to remove the string from the bracciole before serving.

ALFREDO SAUCE

1 stick butter
½ pint heavy cream

1 (6 ounce) container Parmesan cheese

Combine all ingredients in a saucepan. Heat over low until smooth.

MAKES 2 CUPS

Laura Korman

SPAGHETTI SAUCE MARINARA

¼ cup olive oil
½ cup chopped onion
1 clove garlic, chopped
1 (6 ounce) can tomato paste
(Contadina)
1 (28 ounce) can tomato purée
(Contadina)

1 (28 ounce) can tomato sauce
(Hunt's)
1 (15 ounce) can tomato sauce
(Hunt's)
1 (15 ounce) can water
2 tablespoons sugar
1½ teaspoons dried basil
1 tablespoon salt

Heat olive oil in a saucepan. Add onion and garlic and sauté until softened. Add tomato paste and cook and stir until onion and garlic absorb paste and turn dark red. Add tomato purée, tomato sauce, water, sugar, basil and salt. Bring to a boil. Reduce heat and simmer for 30 minutes or longer.

SERVES 15

Muffin Oppenheimer

Use brands listed for this recipe.

In the old school, the boys wore suits at graduation until late 1930s. Archival photographs show senior boys wearing caps and gowns in the 1940s and 1950s. When the school moved to Fort Washington in the 1960s, the boys wore gray pants, a school blazer and school tie at graduation. The girls chose their own style of white dress. During the years under Headmaster Bud Kast, the tradition of caps and gowns returned in the 1970s. As typical of change, the class of 2010 will be the first class in many years to return to blue blazers and white dresses for graduation!

Pesto Sauce I

1 cup fresh basil
½ cup fresh parsley or cilantro
¼ cup Parmesan cheese
¼ cup pine nuts, walnuts or
   hazelnuts, or combination

¼ cup extra virgin olive oil
2 cloves garlic
¼ teaspoon salt
½ tablespoon lemon juice
1 tablespoon water

Combine all ingredients in a blender or food processor. Purée to a smooth, thick paste.

MAKES 2 CUPS   *Raju Patel*

Pesto II

2 cups packed basil leaves
½ cup parsley
¾ to 1 cup grated Locatelli
   Romano cheese

4 cloves garlic
½ cup pine nuts
1 cup extra virgin olive oil

Combine all ingredients except oil in a food processor. Blend thoroughly. With processor running, drip in oil.

MAKES 1½ CUPS   *Jennifer Gobora*

Serving suggestions:

Pasta sauce - *You will need to add more oil to thin sauce for the pasta; do this while processor is running.*

Pizza sauce - *Spread half the pesto sauce on top of a store-bought pizza crust. Top with thinly sliced mozzarella cheese. Bake as directed on crust package, or make your own crust.*

Vegetable wraps - *Toss mixed roasted vegetables, such as peppers, mushrooms, red onion, zucchini and eggplant with pesto sauce. Spoon mixture down the center of a tortilla. Top with small pieces of soft goat cheese, wrap and serve. The amount of pesto sauce needed depends on amount of vegetables and taste.*

SUNDAY FOOTBALL VODKA SAUCE

2 tablespoons olive oil
3 tablespoons butter
1 small onion, chopped
1 clove garlic, minced
1 (28 ounce) can plum tomatoes
1 tablespoon chopped fresh basil,
    or 1½ teaspoons dried

⅛ teaspoon dried red pepper
    flakes
½ cup vodka
½ cup heavy cream
3 tablespoons Parmesan cheese

Heat olive oil and butter in a skillet. Add onion and sauté 5 minutes. Add garlic and sauté 1 minute. Add tomatoes, basil, pepper flakes and vodka. Simmer 15 minutes or until sauce is reduced. Add cream and simmer about 5 minutes longer. Add Parmesan cheese.

MAKES 2 CUPS

Kris Henry

Perfect over pasta. Delicious with grilled sausage.

Amidst the confusion caused by the workmen, classes somehow struggled on. … All the class stones from the old school were cemented into place…[they] not the only things transferred from Germantown to the new campus. School spirit was reborn as the student body began to take pride in the new building as it progressed in its construction. The students felt a spirit of pioneering…which enabled them to bear the myriad inconveniences facing them gracefully.

BUTTERNUT SQUASH RISOTTO

4 cups vegetable or chicken broth
3 cups 1 inch cubed butternut
  squash (about 2 large)
3 tablespoons unsalted butter
¾ cup chopped onion
1½ cups Arborio rice

½ cup dry white wine
½ cup freshly grated Parmesan
  cheese
½ teaspoon salt
2 tablespoons chopped fresh
  chives

Heat broth to a simmer. Add squash and cook about 5 minutes. Reduce heat to low and keep warm.

In a separate saucepan, heat 2 tablespoons butter. Add onion and sauté about 3 minutes. Add rice and stir. Add wine and simmer about 3 minutes. Add warm broth, ½ cup at a time, and cook and stir until almost all broth is absorbed before adding more. Continue adding broth until rice is tender. Stir in Parmesan cheese, salt and chives until combined. Add squash and stir. Serve immediately.

SERVES 8   *Kris Henry*

CHAMPAGNE RISOTTO

7 to 8 cups chicken broth
2 tablespoons butter
1 pound mushrooms of choice,
  sliced
Salt and pepper to taste
3 tablespoons olive oil, divided

2 shallots, chopped
2 cups Arborio rice
1 cup champagne
½ cup freshly grated Parmesan
  cheese
Italian parsley for garnish

Heat chicken broth in a saucepan; keep warm. Heat butter in a skillet. Add mushrooms and sauté until brown. Season with salt and pepper.

In a separate large saucepan, heat 2 tablespoons olive oil. Add shallots and sauté. Add rice and stir until grains are well coated. Stir in champagne and cook until liquid is nearly absorbed. Add 1 ladle of warm broth and cook and stir until absorbed. Continue to cook and stir, adding broth 1 ladle at a time, allowing each addition to be absorbed before adding more. After 20 to 25 minutes, the rice should be al dente. Remove from heat and stir in mushrooms and Parmesan cheese. Season with salt and pepper. Drizzle remaining 1 tablespoon olive oil on top. Garnish with parsley.

SERVES 6 TO 8   *Cheryl Koons*

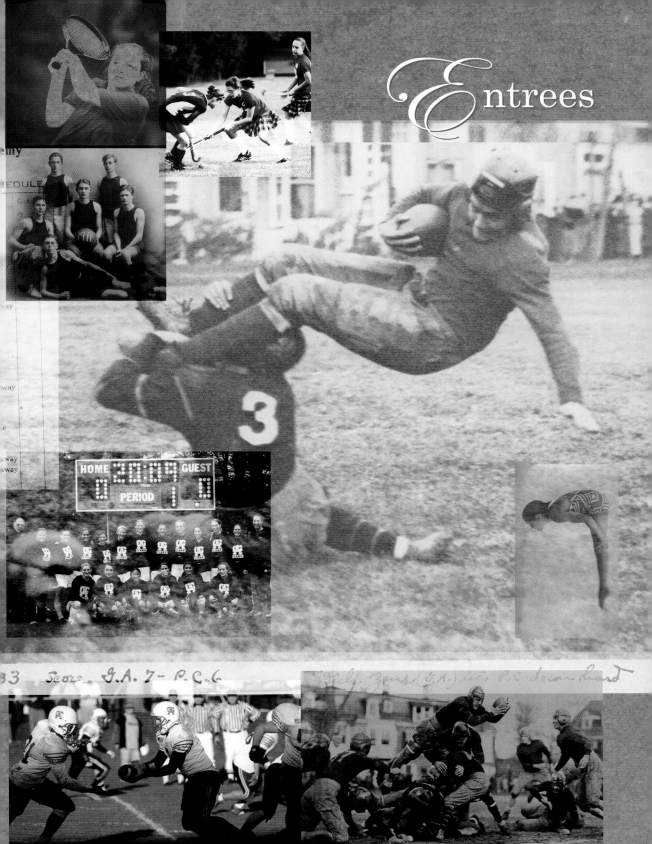

Entrees

Games and fitness have been integral at Germantown Academy since its first days on School House Lane in Germantown. The young men of GA were expected to treat their bodies with the respect that they did their minds, and they did so in a variety of sports ranging from cricket to swimming to bowling.

After classes on the old campus, students played football, cricket (the school's best team), tennis and squash at the nearby Manheim Cricket Club in Germantown, where teams posed on the front steps for pictures and enjoyed the beautiful grass tennis courts. Sports were so popular that GA started its beloved Field Day in spring of 1887, with events divided by age, with variations on the same events still held today: Wheelbarrow, bicycle, and three-legged races. (Alumni were included back in the 19th century, running an 880-yard dash.)

While GA has long enjoyed beating the pants off Episcopal Academy and the Haverford School, no rivalry compares to that between GA and Penn Charter. The first GA-PC Day, also held in 1887, featured a rough-and-tumble rugby match that included a round ball, no helmets and a coach, GA's math teacher George Hartley Deacon, who joined the team on the field to play against PC. Naturally, GA won, 20-6. As the years went on, the game was football, not rugby, and GA-PC Day became so popular that Philadelphia bookies took bets on its outcome. For alumni, it became an ersatz homecoming day, made even more festive with a traditional post-game cocktail party.

The following year, in 1888, the school's first gym, Alumni Hall, was built, filled with of-the-moment workout facilities including a basketball court and indoor track. That same year, Mr. Deacon, a gifted athlete and Penn grad who led GA's athletic program, had the notion that the Philadelphia area needed a formalized league to organize games between its prep schools. And in spring of 1888, GA joined with the Haverford School, Episcopal Academy, the Rugby School and William Penn Charter School to form the Inter-Academic Athletic Association (the Inter-Ac), still going strong today.

GA-PC Day, of course, carries on, with co-ed games, and soccer, cross-country, field hockey, tennis and water polo matches added to the traditional football game. And every Lower School student knows which Field Day team he/she's on—blue or red.

Beef Fillet with Rosemary

1 (6 to 7 pound) fillet of beef
¼ cup kosher salt

3 tablespoons freshly ground
black pepper
¼ cup fresh or dried rosemary

Preheat oven to 450 degrees. Trim fat from beef. Rub meat with salt, pepper and rosemary. Bake for 45 minutes for rare (140 degrees), or to desired degree of doneness. (I prefer 155 degrees for medium, which takes about 60 to 70 minutes.) Tent with foil and allow to rest 15 minutes before carving.

SERVES 12 TO 14

Frank Koons

Steak Au Poivre

4 (1¼ inch thick) strip steaks or
fillets
8 tablespoons whole peppercorns,
very coarsely ground

2 to 3 tablespoons coarse salt
Butter Sauce (recipe below)
8 tablespoons cognac

Sprinkle the bottom of a skillet with salt and heat on high for 10 minutes. Equally divide and press ground peppercorns into each steak. When done heating, place steaks in hot skillet and sear, uncovered, for 2 minutes per side. Reduce to medium heat and cook steaks to desired degree of doneness. Remove steaks from skillet and set aside.

Clean skillet of pan drippings and return to heat. Return steaks to skillet and pour Butter Sauce over steaks. Add cognac to skillet and immediately ignite. Shake pan until flames subside. Simmer 2 minutes and serve.

Butter Sauce

2 sticks butter, melted
4 teaspoons Worcestershire sauce

½ cup freshly squeezed lemon
juice

Combine all sauce ingredients in a small bowl; set aside.

SERVES 4

George Riter

Try accompanying this steak dish with
Oven Roasted Parmesan Vegetables (page 200).

George Deacon, Professor Emeritus of Mathematics of Germantown Academy, at Germantown Academy's 175th anniversary celebration on April 26, 1935, remarked:
The fellowship existing between the Faculty and the students was so remarkable that it's influence extended far beyond Germantown. We know that, because the headmasters of the schools of New England asked Dr. Kershaw if he would please explain to them this feeling of fellowship between the students and the teachers. In my forty years at the Academy this spirit of good will in school and out, has become a part of me, so that when the Recording Angel takes account of my life, I believe he will find written on my heart, the words, "Germantown Academy."

The History of
Germantown Academy

The 1934 football team was one of the greatest in the history of the Academy. The team swept through a schedule of nine games without a defeat. Of all the high schools and prep schools in the city, our school was the only one that could boast of an untied and undefeated eleven, a record and honor in itself. Our last and most important game was played on November 16th at Penn Charter. TEN thousand people attended this game, by far the most exciting game of the season. When the final whistle blew, the score was GA 13- PC 12. The old bell which had rung after every other victory during the year, rang long and hard after the PC game.

MOM'S FAVORITE TOP ROUND ROAST

2 teaspoons freshly ground black pepper
2 teaspoons dry mustard
1 teaspoon dried rosemary
1 teaspoon dried thyme
½ teaspoon allspice
½ teaspoon cayenne pepper
1 to 2 cloves garlic, crushed
2 teaspoons olive oil
4 pounds top round roast (do not trim)

Preheat oven to 325 degrees. Combine all ingredients except meat in a small glass bowl. Rub seasoning mixture evenly into roast. Place roast, fat-side up, on a rack in a shallow roasting pan; do not add water to pan.

Bake, uncovered, for 2½ hours or until internal temperature registers 140 degrees for medium-rare or 155 degrees for medium. Remove from oven, tent with foil and let stand 15 minutes before carving into thin slices.

SERVES 8 TO 10

Kathie Vit

STEAK TERIYAKI

1¼ cups cider vinegar
1¼ cups tomato purée
1 cup pineapple juice
1 cup soy sauce
1 cup firmly packed brown sugar
⅓ cup molasses
¼ teaspoon garlic powder
6 to 8 sirloin or tenderloin steaks

Combine vinegar, tomato purée, pineapple juice, soy sauce, brown sugar, molasses and garlic powder in a saucepan and mix well. Bring to a boil, stirring constantly; cool. Pour cooled marinade over steaks in a shallow dish. Marinate, covered, in refrigerator for 24 hours.

When ready to cook, preheat a hot grill. Drain steaks, reserving marinade. Grill steaks to desired degree of doneness. Heat reserved marinade to a boil. Serve steaks with heated marinade on the side.

SERVES 6 TO 8

Tara Schwartz

This would be great with Thai Sesame Noodle Salad (page 82).

Beef Stroganoff

8 ounces beef sirloin, trimmed and
   cubed
2 tablespoons olive oil
2 cups cooking sherry
Seasoned salt

Dash of black pepper
1 medium onion, sliced
1 cup sliced mushrooms
1 cup low-fat sour cream

Tenderize beef if needed. Brown beef in olive oil for 5 to 7 minutes in a large skillet. Add sherry and cook 5 minutes or until volume is reduced by half. Season to taste with seasoned salt and pepper. Add onion and mushrooms and cook 10 minutes or until vegetables are tender. Season to taste. Stir in sour cream. Serve with brown or wild rice.

SERVES 4

Richard House

Easy Steak Diane

4 (6 ounce) sirloin steaks
1 stick butter, divided
¼ cup chopped shallot
2 tablespoons Worcestershire
   sauce

Salt and freshly ground black
   pepper to taste
Chopped fresh parsley to taste

Place steaks between 2 pieces of wax paper and pound to ⅓ inch thick. Heat 2 tablespoons butter in a small saucepan. Add shallot and cook until lightly browned. Add Worcestershire sauce and heat until bubbling.

Heat remaining 6 tablespoons butter in a 12 inch skillet or chafing dish. When butter starts to brown, add steaks and cook for 3 minutes. Turn steaks and cook 2 to 3 minutes longer or until cooked to desired degree of doneness. Transfer to a serving dish and sprinkle generously with salt and pepper. Drizzle sauce over steaks and sprinkle with parsley.

SERVES 4

Ann Waldman

This recipe was given to me by the chef at the Whitehall Club in Chicago.

"*We are fortunate* as a school to share a big game tradition with The William Penn Charter School. Important games played with well respected rivals provide some of life's most vivid memories. I encourage everyone from both schools to take a moment this weekend to step back, take in the larger perspective, and see that GA-PC Day is a forum for expressing pride in our identities as successful school communities. At GA and at PC, all the students are winners. Now that's a fact that is worth a full day of celebration. "

Jim Connor, Head of School

GRANDMOM'S BARBECUE BEEF

1 pound ground beef
1 large yellow onion, finely diced
½ cup ketchup

1 teaspoon red wine vinegar
1½ teaspoons sugar
2 teaspoons Worcestershire sauce

Brown beef with onion in a large skillet. Add ketchup, vinegar, sugar and Worcestershire sauce. Simmer about 30 minutes, partially covered and stirring frequently. Serve on hamburger rolls.

SERVES 4 TO 5

Liz Berger

KOREAN BEEF SHISH KABOBS

1 tablespoon sesame seeds, toasted
3 cloves garlic, minced
¼ cup light soy sauce
1 teaspoon sugar
1 tablespoon Asian sesame oil

1 teaspoon dried red pepper flakes
1 teaspoon grated or minced ginger
1 pound beef, cubed

Combine all ingredients except beef in a small bowl. Pour marinade mixture over beef in a plastic zip-top bag and refrigerate several hours or overnight.

When ready to cook, preheat a grill. Soak bamboo skewers in water for 10 to 15 minutes. Thread beef onto skewers. Grill over hot coals for 4 to 5 minutes on each side.

SERVES 3 TO 4

Christine McDade

Prepare separate skewers of vegetables such as peppers, cherry tomatoes, onions and mushrooms brushed with olive oil so the meat and vegetables can each cook the correct amount of time. To toast sesame seeds, bake in a toaster oven at 350 degrees until fragrant.

BBQ Beef

2 (26 ounce) bottles ketchup
½ cup sugar
1 teaspoon chili powder
10 whole cloves
1 teaspoon dry mustard
1 teaspoon cinnamon
1 teaspoon allspice
1 clove garlic, whole
2 bay leaves

4 medium onions, chopped
2 tablespoons Worcestershire sauce
1 teaspoon salt
1 teaspoon black pepper
1 teaspoon ground ginger
1 cup distilled vinegar
5 to 6 pounds chuck roast

Preheat oven to 225 degrees. Combine all ingredients except roast in a bowl. Brown roast in a skillet. Transfer meat to a roasting pan and pour seasoning mixture over meat.

Bake for 6 hours or more. Remove cloves, garlic and bay leaves. Separate meat from fat, discarding fat. Pour sauce over meat and leave in pan until ready to serve. Slice and serve on rolls.

SERVES 8 TO 12

Janet Israel

Mimi's Brisket

1 large first-cut brisket
1 (1 ounce) package dry onion soup mix

1 (18 ounce) bottle Sweet Baby Ray's Honey Barbeque Sauce

Preheat oven to 425 degrees. Place brisket in a Dutch oven or a deep casserole dish with a cover. Sprinkle soup mix over meat and pour barbeque sauce on top. Bake, uncovered, for 25 minutes.

Add about 3 cups water or just enough to come halfway up the meat - do not cover the brisket with water. Reduce temperature to 325 degrees and cover pan. Bake 3 hours or until a carving fork goes into meat smoothly but meat does not fall apart. Remove from oven and cool. Slice against the grain and place in a serving dish. Pour gravy from pan over meat.

SERVES 6 TO 8

Alison Tress

I find that brisket is better when covered tightly and frozen after done baking. To serve, thaw in refrigerator and warm slowly. Great with Sylvia's Garlic Kugel (page 211).

The rivalry, still fiercely competitive, has grown over the years. Once known for its male athletic contests, GA - PC Day began including match-ups between the girls field hockey, cross country, girls soccer and girls tennis teams in the 1990's. In 2001 boys water polo was added to the day's events. Girls water polo would follow in 2008. A special Competition Cup, established in 1996, is awarded to the school who achieves overall excellence on GA-PC Day.

With other government officials, Washington and his family lived in Germantown when they were seeking refuge from the Yellow Fever that was raging in the capitol, Philadelphia. Here in the outskirts of the largest English speaking city outside of London, life moved at a slower more relaxed pace. Washington had time to focus on familial matters such as helping to plant a Chestnut tree on the campus of the school where his adopted son, George Washington Parke Curtis was a student. The tree was cut down later because it was well past its prime yet a piece was preserved. The gavel used today by the President of the Board of Trustees was designed and cut from the wood of the original tree!

HEART-WARMING BEEF STEW

⅓ cup flour
2 teaspoons salt, divided
¾ teaspoon black pepper, divided
2¼ pounds stew meat
3 bacon slices, divided
1 cup chopped onion
1 cup sliced carrot
4 cloves garlic, minced
1½ cups dry red wine

1 (14 ounce) can reduced-sodium beef broth
4 cups halved mushrooms
2 tablespoons tomato paste
2 teaspoons chopped fresh thyme
2 bay leaves
1 (16 ounce) package egg noodles, cooked
3 tablespoons chopped fresh parsley

Combine flour, 1 teaspoon salt and ¼ teaspoon black pepper in a large zip-top bag. Add stew meat and shake to coat. Cook half the bacon in a large Dutch oven over medium-high heat until crisp. Remove bacon with a slotted spoon; crumble and set aside. Add half of beef to bacon drippings and brown on all sides; set aside. Repeat with remaining bacon and beef and set aside with other bacon and beef. Add onion, carrot and garlic to pan and sauté 5 minutes. Stir in wine and broth, scraping pan to loosen browned bits. Add bacon, beef, remaining 1 teaspoon salt, remaining ½ teaspoon pepper, mushrooms, tomato paste, thyme and bay leaves. Bring to a boil. Cover, reduce heat and simmer for 45 minutes. Uncover and cook 1 hour longer. Serve over egg noodles garnished with parsley.

SERVES 10

Kris Henry

BEEF STEW IN A SLOW COOKER

1½ pounds stew beef, cubed
2 cups ¼ inch thick sliced carrot
2 cups peeled and diced potato

1 (14½ ounce) can diced tomatoes (optional)
2 to 3 teaspoons beef bouillon
6 to 8 cups water

Brown beef in a pan over medium heat. Transfer beef and pan juices to a 5 or 6 quart slow cooker. Add carrot, potato, tomatoes and bouillon. Add enough water to cover meat and vegetables. Cook on high for 5 hours or until vegetables are tender.

SERVES 6 TO 8

Cheryl Ross

One-half cup chopped onion can be cooked with the beef during browning, or added raw to the slow cooker.

HAMBURGER CASSEROLE

1 stick butter
½ cup chopped onion
8 ounces mushrooms, sliced, or
    1 can sliced
2 pounds ground beef
6 tablespoons burgundy wine
    (optional)

5 tablespoons lemon juice
2 (11 ounce) cans beef consommé
Salt and pepper to taste
4 cups dry medium egg noodles
2 cups sour cream
Fresh parsley

Preheat oven to 350 degrees. Melt butter in a skillet. Add onion and mushrooms and sauté until browned. Add beef and cook and crumble until browned. Add wine, lemon juice, consommé, salt and pepper. Simmer about 5 minutes. Add noodles and cook 10 minutes or until noodles are soft. Stir in sour cream. Transfer to a casserole dish. Bake for 30 minutes or more. Garnish with parsley.

SERVES 6 TO 8

Sara Wolf

SWEET AND SOUR MEATBALLS

Meatballs

½ cup water
1 slice white or wheat bread
2 pounds ground meat, a
    combination of beef, pork
    and veal

1 small onion, finely chopped
1 large egg

Sauce

2 medium onions, coarsely
    chopped
2 tablespoons oil

¼ cup water
1 (16 ounce) can tomato sauce
1 (15 ounce) can cranberry sauce

To make meatballs, pour ½ cup water over bread. Mix saturated bread with ground meat, finely chopped onion and egg. Form mixture into small balls, using gloves if possible.

For the sauce, sauté coarsely chopped onion in oil until brown in a large soup pot over low heat. Add meatballs and ¼ cup water. Cover and cook over low heat for 10 minutes. Add tomato sauce and cranberry sauce and cook at least 1 hour.

SERVES 8

Kathy Schlesinger

The Germantown Academy Parents' Committee is a diverse group of active parents whose objective is the enrichment of the GA community by promotion of communication, cooperation, friendship and understanding among parents, faculty and students. The Committee also helps raise funds for special school projects. The Committee has an Executive Committee, Co-Chairs representing each class, and Standing Committees that are responsible for school-wide activities. All parents are members of the Parents' Committee. It meets monthly in the Parents' Room and ALL parents are welcome. Please join the activities and share your talents.

A blonde Jaspan and brunette
Bauersmith
Brains beauty and youth are
needed to cook with

Drop in one boisterous Wetzel
and one handsome Stahl
So needed to define the boys of
the hall

Add some Fresh French Vieille,
and most most of all
One whole Wyszomierski, the
spelling I can't recall

Now that you have gathered such
a fine chef array
You'll need the ingredients and
we're off and away

A dash of colonial day though it
must be well rested
Add two pounds African Dance
with Folktales (ten years tested)

A teaspoon of multiplication,
division, and fractions
A cupful of Creek and Valley
Green walks to help with digestion

Mix in three Class Babies, Type
to Learn and Time for Kids,
Lockers, Continents, Oceans,
and graph paper grids

LOW-FAT MEDITERRANEAN MEATBALLS

Meatballs

2 yellow onions, coarsely chopped
2 tablespoons lemon juice
2 cups fine-grind bulgur
1½ pounds very lean ground beef
¼ cup pine nuts, finely chopped

2 cloves garlic, minced
1 teaspoon salt
1 teaspoon ground cumin
½ teaspoon cinnamon
½ teaspoon freshly ground black
    pepper

Sauce

2 cups nonfat plain yogurt
¼ cup tahini
2 tablespoons lemon zest

2 teaspoons dry mustard
1 teaspoon salt
¼ cup chopped cilantro

Preheat oven to 350 degrees. Purée chopped onion in a food processor.
Strain onion through a fine-mesh sieve or a colander double-lined with
cheesecloth to extract all juice possible; discard solids. Add lemon juice to
onion juice and enough water to measure 1½ cups liquid. In a large bowl,
combine onion liquid and bulgur and soak for 20 minutes. Add beef, pine
nuts, garlic, salt, cumin, cinnamon and pepper and mix well. Form meat
into small balls. If mixture is too crumbly, add a small amount of water.
Place meatballs on a baking sheet lightly sprayed with olive oil cooking
spray. Spray meatballs lightly on top. Bake for 25 to 30 minutes or until
lightly browned. Serve with sauce.

For sauce, whisk together all ingredients in a small bowl. Cover and refrigerate. Sauce is better if allowed to stand in refrigerator for several hours
before serving.

SERVES 8

Cathy Black

*Great served in pita bread pockets with chopped lettuce and sliced cucumbers and
sauce drizzled on as a dressing. Meatballs can be made ahead and frozen.*

NANNIE'S MEATLOAF

Meatloaf

2 pounds ground beef
1 teaspoon salt
¼ teaspoon black pepper
½ teaspoon dry mustard

2 teaspoons Worcestershire sauce
½ cup chopped onion
¾ cup bread crumbs
1 large egg, beaten

Sauce

1 (8 ounce) can tomato sauce, divided
¼ cup water
2 tablespoons firmly packed brown sugar

2 tablespoons vinegar
1 teaspoon Worcestershire sauce
2 teaspoons dry mustard

Preheat oven to 300 degrees. Combine all meatloaf ingredients; do not overmix or meatloaf will be mushy. Add ½ cup of the tomato sauce to beef mixture. Pack mixture into a large loaf pan or form into a loaf in a 12x8 inch glass baking dish.

For sauce, combine remainder of tomato sauce with water, brown sugar, vinegar, Worcestershire sauce and mustard. Pour sauce over meatloaf.

Bake for 1½ hours or until nicely browned.

Nancy Greenberg Cutler and Margery Miller

MINI MEAT LOAVES

1½ pounds ground beef
3 cups fresh bread crumbs
1 (10½ ounce) can condensed onion soup

6 ounces cheese of choice, cut into cubes

Preheat oven to 400 degrees. Combine beef, bread crumbs and undiluted soup. Spoon mixture into ungreased cupcake cups. Top with cheese cubes. Bake for 15 minutes or until done.

SERVES 6

Kellianne Toland

Ground turkey can be substituted for the beef.
Beef bouillon can be used instead of the onion soup.

"WILD THIRD GRADER SURPRISE" FEEDS SIXTY (continued)

Fifty abbreviations, Capitals and States
But only one Night of Wax Museum to keep down the weight

Stir in Plantations Ridley, Rittenhouse, and Penn
And a just dash of cursive, know when to say when

Now throw them all in the McLean melting pot
And mix, mash, cajole (don't yell), and stir up the lot

To make a third grader, a bright one at that
Needs love, care and patience or else it falls flat

Check in on it often, slow roast, don't rush
The outcome will be 'Wild Third Grader Surprise' with a flaky moist crust

So oven bake for months, we find nine works the best
Savor when done… let fourth grade deal with the mess!

Third Grade, 2009

The Class of 1760 is a small select organization created to recognize non-alumni of Germantown Academy who, because of their outstanding contributions to the Academy, are deemed worthy of being admitted to the Class of 1760, which commemorates the founding of the school. Nominations are solicited from the entire school community.

Meat Loaf with Mushroom Sauce

Meat Loaf

1 tablespoon canola oil
1 large white onion, finely chopped
3 cloves garlic, minced
2 large eggs, beaten
½ teaspoon chopped fresh thyme
1 teaspoon chopped fresh oregano
3 tablespoons whole-grain Dijon mustard
2 tablespoons Worcestershire sauce

½ teaspoon hot pepper sauce
1 cup skim milk
2 pounds lean ground meat, equal parts beef, pork and turkey preferred
⅔ cup crushed saltine crackers
¼ cup minced flat-leaf parsley
2 teaspoons coarse salt
1 teaspoon freshly ground black pepper

Mushroom Sauce

3 tablespoons butter, divided
2 cloves garlic, minced
2 portabello mushrooms, cut into ⅜ inch cubes
1 (16 ounce) can low-sodium chicken broth

1 ounce dried porcini mushrooms, ground to dust in a spice or coffee grinder
1 tablespoon all-purpose flour

Preheat oven to 350 degrees. Heat oil in a skillet over medium-high heat. Add onion and garlic and sauté 5 minutes or until translucent. Remove from heat and cool.

In a mixing bowl, stir together eggs, thyme, oregano, mustard, Worcestershire sauce, pepper sauce and milk. Place ground meat in a separate bowl. Pour egg mixture over meat. Add crackers, parsley, salt, pepper and sautéed onion. Gently mix until well blended.

Form mixture into a loaf on a baking sheet. Bake for 1 hour or until an instant-read thermometer reads 160 degrees. Remove from oven and let rest 5 minutes before slicing. Serve sliced meatloaf with mushroom sauce.

To prepare mushroom sauce, heat 2 tablespoons butter in a skillet. Add garlic and cubed mushrooms and sauté until softened. Bring broth to a boil in a saucepan and cook until reduced by a quarter. Remove from heat and stir in ground dried mushrooms. Dissolve flour in ¼ cup water in a bowl. Add sautéed mushrooms and flour mixture to broth. Return to low heat and stir until broth thickens. Stir in remaining 1 tablespoon butter just before serving.

SERVES 8   *Frances Nicos and Camille Scordis*

TURKEY AND BLACK BEAN CHILI

1 tablespoon extra virgin olive oil
1 cup chopped yellow onion
2 cups combination chopped red and green bell pepper
1 cup diced carrot
1 clove garlic, chopped
1 tablespoon ground cumin
2 tablespoons chili powder

1 pound ground turkey breast
1 (16 ounce) container mild salsa
3 cups chicken broth, regular or reduced-sodium fat-free
2 (16 ounce) cans black beans, drained and rinsed
1 tablespoon tomato paste, regular or low-sodium
1 cup fresh or frozen corn

Heat oil in a saucepan over medium-low heat. Add onion, bell pepper, carrot and garlic and sauté 8 minutes or until vegetables are tender and onion is golden. Sprinkle in cumin and chili powder. Add ground turkey and cook and crumble 5 to 7 minutes or until browned. Add salsa, broth, beans and tomato paste and stir well. Mix in corn. Reduce heat and simmer, uncovered, for 45 minutes or until liquid reduces and chili is thickened.

SERVES 8 TO 10

Liz Berger

GRANDMOTHER'S TURKEY MEATLOAF

1 pound ground turkey
1 tablespoon horseradish
1 tablespoon Worcestershire sauce
1 tablespoon chopped red or green bell pepper

1 tablespoon barbecue sauce or ketchup
1 tablespoon Dijon mustard
1 small onion, chopped
1 large egg
1 slice white bread
¼ cup warm milk

Preheat oven to 350 degrees. Combine all ingredients by hand. Pack mixture into a loaf pan. Bake, uncovered, for 45 minutes.

SERVES 6

Grandmother Clement

Meat mixture can also be shaped into meatballs. For yummy leftovers, heat sliced meatloaf with a can of undiluted tomato soup.

Angela Kast, wife of the legendary Headmaster Bud Kast, used to love to tell the story of Mr. Kast 's return home to Cleveland after his first visit to GA. She said his first words, before even greeting her, were, "no way, absolutely, no way, never!" Needless to say, regardless of his words, Mr. Kast accepted the challenge of becoming GA's headmaster from 1970 to 1986. With the recent move to the new campus, GA was not yet a smooth running machine. In fact, Mr. Cheston Newbold, Director of Admissions in the early 1970s, said he often prayed for local public school strikes come August!

In 1963, the Mother's Committee donated $5,550 to the school from their fundraising efforts. These funds provided the furniture for the new kindergarten building ($3,950), furnishings for the faculty room ($330), and $579 for the Science Department. Six hundred additional dollars were donated to be applied towards other necessary items.

Chili and Angel Hair Pasta

Angel hair pasta
1¾ pound hamburger
1 (10 ounce) bottle Worcestershire sauce
1 (1 ounce) package chili seasoning mix
Salt and pepper to taste
Chili powder to taste
1 (16 ounce) can tomato sauce
1 (8 ounce) can tomato sauce
1 (16 ounce) can dark red kidney beans, drained and rinsed

Fill a 3½ quart saucepan half-full with water and bring to a boil over high heat. Add a 1 inch diameter bundle of pasta and cook 5 minutes. Drain pasta into a large colander, reserving the cooking water in a large mixing bowl. Set aside cooking water and pasta in colander.

Meanwhile, place a 12 inch skillet on stove over medium heat. Add hamburger to skillet and cook and crumble until browned; drain. Reduce heat to low. Sprinkle Worcestershire sauce evenly over meat. Add chili seasoning and stir until evenly mixed. Season with salt and pepper and chili powder. Pour cooked pasta on top of beef. Using a spatula, chop pasta into 1 inch pieces while mixing thoroughly.

Transfer mixture to a 6 quart saucepan. Stir in tomato sauce. Mix in beans, half at a time. Pour in reserved cooking water, adding enough to reach desired thickness. Place over medium-low heat and simmer 20 to 25 minutes. Serve with tortilla chips, shredded cheese and salsa.

SERVES 8 TO 12
Joni Cosgriff

Calico Beans

½ pound bacon
½ pound ground beef
1 large onion, chopped
½ cup ketchup
2 teaspoons prepared mustard
4 teaspoons cider vinegar
¾ cup firmly packed brown sugar
1 (16 ounce) can baked beans
1 (16 ounce) can garbanzo beans, drained
1 (16 ounce) can green lima beans, drained
1 (16 ounce) can red kidney beans, drained

Preheat oven to 350 degrees. Cook bacon in a large pan until crisp; remove bacon, reserving fat in skillet. Crumble bacon and set aside. Add ground beef to bacon fat and cook and crumble until browned. Add onion, ketchup, mustard, vinegar, brown sugar and crumbled bacon. Simmer 5 minutes. Mix all beans together and add to meat sauce. Pour mixture into a roasting pan. Bake for 40 minutes.

SERVES 10 TO 15
Eileen Guers

MARINATED PORK TENDERLOIN

¼ cup soy sauce
2 tablespoons red wine
1 tablespoon honey
1 tablespoon firmly packed light
    or dark brown sugar

2 cloves garlic, minced
½ teaspoon cinnamon
2 scallions, white and green parts,
    chopped
2 to 2½ pounds pork tenderloin

Whisk together all ingredients except pork in a large measuring cup. Pour marinade mixture over pork in a plastic zip-top bag or shallow dish. Marinate in refrigerator overnight.

If cooking on a grill, preheat grill. Remove tenderloin from marinade and pat dry, reserving marinade. Grill over medium heat for 35 to 40 minutes.

To roast in oven, preheat oven to 350 degrees. Remove tenderloin from marinade and pat dry, reserving marinade. Bake for 45 minutes. Remove from oven and let stand about 10 minutes.

While cooking meat, pour marinade into a small saucepan. Gently simmer until sauce reduces and is thickened. To serve, cut tenderloin into 2 inch pieces. Drizzle sauce over sliced meat.

SERVES 6 TO 8

David Oberkircher

REMEMBER:

Students many times secretly snuck into the attic above the Upper and Middle Schools. It is only student graffiti that documents this secret nook and pastime. After a student fell through the attic floor and landed in the library during a senior prank, the "secret" nook no longer exists.

Make the "Have a Party" Potatoes (page 204) to accompany this fabulous pork tenderloin.

We're proud to say that there is no typical Germantown Academy student. One of our distinctive qualities is the rich mixture of talents that flourishes here. We respect and nurture the individuality of our students and teachers. GA students are religiously, racially, and economically diverse. Students come to GA from 90 towns and cities in the Philadelphia metropolitan area. Their academic abilities range from average to extraordinary. But, because we're a college preparatory school, we accept only students we believe will achieve this goal. Many kinds of students come to GA, but almost to a one they possess a willingness to work hard.

FALL DINNER PARTY STUFFED PORK LOIN

Brine
8 cups water
¾ cup sugar
¾ cup kosher salt
2 tablespoons lemon zest

2 tablespoons chopped fresh oregano
2 cloves garlic, crushed
1 (3½ pound) center cut boneless pork loin roast

Stuffing
¾ cup dry jasmine rice
1 (6 ounce) package fresh baby spinach
½ teaspoon salt
½ cup kalamata olives, chopped

1 teaspoon dried red pepper flakes
1 teaspoon lemon zest
2 teaspoons fresh lemon juice
1 tablespoon black pepper

Combine all brine ingredients except pork. Add pork, cover and refrigerate 8 hours.

When ready to bake, preheat oven to 325 degrees. Remove pork from brine. Starting off-center, slice pork lengthwise cutting to, but not through, the other side. Open pork and lay flat on a work surface. Place plastic wrap over the pork and pound to an even thickness; remove plastic.

For stuffing, cook rice according to directions, omitting salt called for in package directions. Add spinach and ½ teaspoon salt to hot rice, stirring until spinach wilts. Stir in olives, pepper flakes, lemon zest and lemon juice. Spread stuffing over pork. Roll up pork like a jelly roll and secure with twine at 2 inch intervals. Rub black pepper over pork and place in a broiler pan. Bake for 1 hour, 20 minutes or until a meat thermometer registers 155 degrees. Remove from oven and let stand 10 minutes before slicing.

SERVES 6
Kris Henry

The flavors are fabulous! A great accompaniment would be
Healthy Roasted Butternut Squash Soup (page 77).

APPLE BACON PORK

4 slices thick-cut bacon
1½ pounds pork tenderloin
1 teaspoon seasoned salt
Coarsely ground black pepper
1½ cups unpeeled diced Granny
   Smith apple

2 tablespoons firmly packed
   brown sugar
2 tablespoons red wine vinegar
1½ cups chicken broth
1 tablespoon flour, dissolved in
   ¼ cup cold water

Fry bacon in a large heavy skillet with a lid until crisp; remove bacon and crumble, reserving pan drippings in skillet. Sprinkle pork with seasoned salt and pepper. Add pork to pan drippings in skillet over medium-high heat. Add bacon and apple to skillet. Whisk together brown sugar and vinegar and add with broth to skillet. Cover skillet and bring to a boil. Reduce heat and simmer for 12 to 15 minutes.

Remove pork, bacon and apple to a serving platter. Bring skillet liquid to a boil and cook until slightly reduced while scraping bottom of skillet. Thicken glaze with flour mixture, adding more if needed. Slice pork and serve with bacon/apple topping and glaze.

SERVES ABOUT 5   *Patrice Machikas*

Pork chops could also be used in this recipe.
Try German Potato Salad (page 94) with this dish.

"*I* give Germantown Academy a lot of kudos for the vision which allows their teachers to take a leadership role beyond the school. What we are doing here in Fort Washington is now being shared all over the US and Canada. It is so forward-thinking of the school that the administration supports continual growth, the sharing of knowledge, and the allowance of intellectual curiosity. Many schools think only of themselves, of what is in it simply for them. But GA seems to sense that increased knowledge effects increased motivation, and that teaching teachers increases the effectiveness of the teaching we do with our own students."

Michael Kemp

CRANBERRY ROAST PORK

1 (4 pound) boneless pork loin,
   tied with kitchen string
Salt and pepper to taste
Olive oil
1 (16 ounce) can whole berry
   cranberry sauce

¼ cup chopped yellow onion
¾ cup orange juice
¼ teaspoon cinnamon
¼ teaspoon ground ginger

Preheat oven to 325 degrees. Rub pork loin with salt and pepper and a little
olive oil. Place pork on a rack in a roasting pan. Bake for 2½ hours; longer if
pork loin exceeds 4 pounds.

Meanwhile, combine cranberry sauce, onion, orange juice, cinnamon and
ginger in a saucepan. Bring to a boil. Reduce heat and simmer 5 minutes.
Halfway through roasting, baste pork every 15 minutes with sauce. When
done roasting, allow pork to rest 10 minutes. Slice pork and serve with
sauce on the side.

SERVES 8

Lynn Gadsden

PORK BARBECUE

4 to 5 pounds Boston butt or
   shoulder roast
1 large onion, chopped
¼ cup firmly packed light brown
   sugar
2 tablespoons dry mustard
¼ teaspoon cayenne pepper

¼ teaspoon black pepper
½ cup cider vinegar
1½ cups water
½ cup ketchup
½ cup Worcestershire sauce
1 teaspoon salt
1 teaspoon celery seed

Preheat oven to 325 degrees. Place pork in a large Dutch oven or roasting
pan. Mix all remaining ingredients and pour over meat. Cover tightly with a lid
or foil. Bake for 4 to 5 hours or until meat is tender and falls apart easily with a
fork. Cool and refrigerate. When hardened, remove fat from top of roast.

To serve, use 2 forks to shred meat. Heat and serve on hamburger buns
with barbecue sauce and cole slaw on the side.

SERVES 10 TO 12

Gretchen Murray

*The pork could be eaten immediately after baking, but chilling
meat allows for fat removal. Leftovers freeze well.*

PHILLY ROAST PORK SANDWICHES

Meat

2½ tablespoons chopped fresh rosemary
3 tablespoons chopped fresh parsley
3 tablespoons chopped fresh garlic

1 tablespoon salt
½ teaspoon freshly cracked black pepper
1 tablespoon olive oil
1 (5 pound) pork loin

Broccoli Rabe

1 pound broccoli rabe
¼ cup olive oil
2 to 3 cloves garlic, crushed

¼ teaspoon dried red pepper flakes

Sandwiches

2 dozen Italian football-shaped rolls

1 pound sharp provolone cheese, sliced

Preheat oven to 350 degrees. Mix all meat ingredients except pork in a medium bowl. Score pork and rub with seasoning mixture. Place pork in a large roasting pan. Bake, covered, for 2 to 2½ hours or until very tender. Cool 15 minutes. Slice pork into ¼ inch slices; meat should crumble slightly.

About 15 minutes before pork is done baking, bring 3 quarts salted water to a boil. Wash broccoli rabe and separate into florets. Trim about an inch from the bottom of the stems. While pork is cooling, boil stems and leaves for about 1½ minutes. Add florets and boil about 5 minutes longer or until tender. Drain, reserving about ½ cup cooking liquid. Heat olive oil in a skillet. Add broccoli rabe, garlic and pepper flakes and sauté over low heat for about 5 minutes. Stir in reserved cooking liquid.

To serve, slice rolls and toast, if desired. Place hot sliced meat in the center of a platter and surround with the broccoli rabe. To assemble sandwiches, place provolone on rolls and add hot meat and broccoli rabe.

MAKES 24 SANDWICHES

Cathy Black

Perfect New Year's Day lunch fare and a big hit at
Super Bowl parties and for chilly crew regattas.

RUSS'S BABY-BACKS WITH COFFEE-BOURBON BARBECUE SAUCE

Barbecue Sauce

1 cup bourbon whiskey
¼ cup vegetable oil
1 cup chopped yellow onion
1 tablespoon Emeril's Essence
2 teaspoons minced garlic
1 jalapeño pepper, stem removed, seeded and minced
1 teaspoon lemon zest
1 cup ketchup
¾ cup brewed strong black coffee

½ cup firmly packed dark brown sugar
¼ cup red wine vinegar
¼ cup freshly squeezed lemon juice
2 tablespoons Worcestershire sauce
2 tablespoons dark molasses
½ teaspoon salt
½ teaspoon black pepper

Dry Rub and Ribs

½ cup firmly packed light brown sugar
3 tablespoons kosher salt
1 tablespoon chili powder
½ teaspoon black pepper

½ teaspoon cayenne pepper
½ teaspoon Old Bay seasoning
½ teaspoon rubbed thyme
5 to 7 pounds baby-back ribs

Braising Liquid

1 cup white wine
2 tablespoons apple cider vinegar
2 tablespoons Worcestershire sauce

1 tablespoon honey
2 cloves garlic, chopped

To make sauce, place bourbon in a small saucepan over medium-high heat. Simmer until reduced to ⅓ cup; be careful not to allow bourbon to boil as it could flame. Remove from heat and cool. In a large saucepan, heat oil over medium-high heat. Add onion and Essence and cook, stirring, for 3 minutes or until softened. Add garlic, jalapeño and lemon zest and cook, stirring, for 30 seconds. Add ketchup, coffee, sugar, vinegar, lemon juice, Worcestershire sauce and molasses. Bring to a simmer, stirring to dissolve sugar. Add bourbon and cook, stirring, for 2 minutes. Simmer for about 15 to 20 minutes. Remove from heat. Purée mixture with a hand-held stick blender on high speed until smooth. Season with salt and pepper.

Combine all dry rub ingredients and mix well; set aside.

Place rib slabs on individual pieces of heavy-duty foil, shiny side down. Sprinkle each side generously with dry rub. Pat dry rub into the meat. Wrap foil around ribs to create a sealed packet. One end of each packet will be used to pour braising liquid into when ready. Refrigerate ribs for at least 1 hour.

Preheat oven to 250 degrees. In a microwave-safe container, combine all braising liquid ingredients. Microwave on high for 1 minute or until hot. Place rib pouches on a baking sheet. Open one end of each foil packet and pour braising liquid into packet. Reseal packets tightly and tilt baking sheet in order to equally distribute liquid. Bake for 2½ hours.

When done baking, remove ribs from foil and place back on baking sheet, being careful not to break the ribs apart as the meat will be very tender. Brush on a coating of sauce and broil for 5 to 7 minutes or until ribs are lightly browned. Brush on more sauce and broil no longer than 5 minutes more, watching ribs carefully to assure even browning. (The sauce has a lot of sugar in it so browning, and burning, can happen quickly if not careful.)

To serve, cut rib slabs into sections and serve with extra sauce on the side.

SERVES 4 TO 6

Russ Kliman

This recipe is worth the time!

GERMANTOWN ACADEMY MISSION STATEMENT *(continued)*

- A curriculum that promotes curiosity, reasoning and questioning, imagination and aesthetics, understanding of others and oneself, clear communications, broad applications of knowledge, and satisfaction in learning;

- Talented teachers who enjoy young people and model for them what it means to be a continuing learner and mature individual;

- Encouragement for students' emerging identities, learning styles, talents and interests;

- Student leadership and service to others;

- Respect for the environment;

- Good sportsmanship, fitness and health;

- Regular evaluation and adjustment of programs to fulfill the school's mission.

Germantown was the first suburban town in the United States. Schools were not new in the mid 1700's but they were very small, usually church related and almost always for boys. Our founders had a different vision: an alliance of German Sectarian and British Friend, a "high school" as we know it today, going beyond the simple reading, writing and arithmetic of the times.

KEVIN'S AMAZING PULLED PIG

Dry Rub
3 tablespoons coarse sea salt
6 tablespoons smoked paprika
2 tablespoons garlic powder

3 tablespoons firmly packed dark brown sugar
2 tablespoons dry mustard

5 to 7 pounds pork shoulder or Boston butt roast

Barbecue Sauce
1¾ cups apple cider vinegar
½ cup ketchup
½ cup firmly packed dark brown sugar
1 cup brown mustard

1 teaspoon cayenne pepper (optional)
1 teaspoon kosher salt
4 cloves garlic, smashed
½ teaspoon black pepper

Cole Slaw
1 head cabbage, chopped
1 red onion, chopped
2 carrots, shredded
1 fresh red chile, sliced (optional)
1½ cups mayonnaise
¼ cup Dijon mustard
Juice of 1 lemon

A few drops hot pepper sauce (optional)
1 teaspoon super fine sugar
2 scallions, chopped
½ teaspoon celery seeds
1½ tablespoons apple cider vinegar

Combine all pork rub ingredients. Rub mixture over pork and refrigerate overnight.

In the morning, preheat oven to 275 degrees. Roast pork 7 to 8 hours or until a meat thermometer reaches 170 degrees. Remove from oven and let rest 15 minutes. Transfer pork to a platter. Separate pork into pieces by pulling apart with 2 forks.

Meanwhile, prepare barbecue sauce. Combine all sauce ingredients in a saucepan. When pork is done roasting, add pan drippings deglazed with 1 cup water to sauce. Simmer sauce; skim fat.

To prepare cole slaw, combine cabbage, onion, carrot, and sliced chile in a large bowl. Mix mayonnaise, mustard, lemon juice, pepper sauce, sugar, scallion, celery seeds and vinegar. Pour dressing mixture over vegetables. Refrigerate until serving.

To serve, pour sauce over pork, or serve on the side, or both. Spoon pork onto rolls and top with cole slaw.

SERVES 6 TO 10

Kevin Haugen

Tuscan-Style Spare Ribs

2 tablespoons extra virgin olive oil
2 tablespoons rosemary leaves
½ tablespoon kosher salt
½ tablespoon fennel seeds
2 teaspoons black pepper
2 teaspoons chopped sage
2 teaspoons chopped thyme
2 teaspoons paprika
1 teaspoon dried red pepper flakes
1 teaspoon ground coriander
½ teaspoon allspice
6 pounds spareribs
3 tablespoons balsamic vinegar

Preheat oven to 325 degrees. Combine all ingredients except ribs and vinegar. Rub seasoning mixture over ribs. Place ribs on a greased baking sheet, meat-side up, and cover. Bake for 2 hours or until tender.

Preheat a grill to medium heat. Brown ribs on grill. Remove from heat, baste with vinegar and let stand 5 minutes before serving.

SERVES 8 TO 10

Chris Hibbitts

Sausage and Bean Casserole

1 pound bulk sweet sausage
½ pound bacon
1 cup chopped celery
1 cup chopped onion
1 (10¾ ounce) can condensed tomato soup plus ¾ can water
1 (6 ounce) can tomato paste plus ¾ can water
¾ cup firmly packed brown sugar
2 tablespoons mustard
1 tablespoon Worcestershire sauce
1 (16 ounce) can green beans, drained
1 (16 ounce) can wax beans, drained
1 (16 ounce) can lima beans, drained
1 (16 ounce) can kidney beans, drained
1 (16 ounce) can chickpeas, drained
1 (16 ounce) can pork and beans, undrained

Preheat oven to 350 degrees. Brown sausage; drain and set aside. Fry bacon; remove bacon and crumble, reserving drippings in pan. Add celery and onion to bacon drippings and sauté until browned.

In a saucepan, mix soup, tomato paste, water, brown sugar, mustard and Worcestershire sauce. Combine all beans and sautéed vegetables in a 4 quart casserole dish. Pour tomato sauce over beans and mix. Stir in sausage and top with crumbled bacon. Bake for 1 hour.

SERVES MANY

Carol Buckley

Oriental Spare Ribs

1½ pounds ribs, any style
2 tablespoons sugar
¼ cup soy sauce
⅛ teaspoon cinnamon
½ cup water

Preheat oven to 350 degrees. Trim any excess fat from ribs. Cut into separate ribs and place in a baking pan. Combine sugar, soy sauce, cinnamon and water and pour over ribs. Bake for 1 hour, turning ribs every 15 minutes.

SERVES 6

Pat Dawe

RACK OF LAMB WITH MINT SAUCE AND COUSCOUS

Lamb

1 (6 rib) lamb rib roast (about 1¾ pounds)
¼ teaspoon salt
2 tablespoons butter or margarine

1 slice white bread, minced into fine crumbs
1 teaspoon chopped fresh parsley
1 tablespoon Dijon mustard

Mint Sauce

¼ cup mint-flavored apple jelly
1 tablespoon white wine vinegar
½ teaspoon salt

2 tablespoons minced fresh parsley

Couscous

½ cup water
½ cup dry couscous
⅓ cup frozen peas, thawed
3 tablespoons dark seedless raisins

¼ teaspoon salt
2 tablespoons slivered almonds, toasted

Preheat oven to 375 degrees. Trim excess fat from lamb. Rub salt over lamb. Place roast on rib bones in a small roasting pan. Insert a meat thermometer into the center of the roast, making sure pointed end does not touch bone. Roast lamb 50 minutes.

Meanwhile, melt butter in a small saucepan over medium-high heat. Add bread crumbs and sauté until golden. Remove from heat and stir in parsley. After lamb has roasted 50 minutes, remove from oven. Spread mustard over top of roast. Sprinkle with bread crumbs and press onto lamb. Roast lamb 15 minutes longer or until thermometer reaches 140 degrees for rare, or to desired degree of doneness.

When roast is almost done, prepare mint sauce. Melt jelly with vinegar and salt. Stir in parsley. Keep warm until serving.

When roast is done, remove to a cutting board and let stand 10 minutes for easier carving. Discard all but 1 tablespoon fat from roasting pan. Add ½ cup water, stirring to loosen brown bits from bottom. Pour drippings mixture from roasting pan into a 2 quart saucepan. Bring to a boil over high heat. Stir in couscous, peas, raisins and salt. Remove from heat, cover and let stand 5 minutes.

To serve, cut off back bones from ribs and cut roast into 1-rib pieces. Arrange lamb on 2 individual dinner plates. Spoon mint sauce over lamb. Arrange couscous on plates with lamb and sprinkle almonds on top.

SERVES 2   *Joy Holmes*

GRILLED LEG OF LAMB

1 cup olive oil
1 teaspoon thyme
1 teaspoon salt
½ teaspoon rosemary
2 teaspoons chopped fresh mint,
  plus extra for garnish

1 cup dry white wine
1 teaspoon oregano
½ teaspoon black pepper
2 cloves garlic, minced
1 (5 to 6 pound) leg of lamb,
  butterflied

Mix all ingredients except lamb until well blended. Pour mixture over lamb. Turn meat in marinade, cover and marinate overnight.

When ready to cook, preheat a grill. Drain lamb, reserving marinade. Grill over medium heat for 30 minutes, basting with marinade every 10 minutes.

To serve, carve lamb into thin slices; meat will be pink. Sprinkle with extra chopped mint.

SERVES 6 TO 8

Sara S. Wolf

RACK OF LAMB PERSILLE

1 rack of lamb
4 tablespoons butter
⅓ cup minced fresh parsley
½ teaspoon minced garlic

¼ teaspoon thyme
Salt and pepper to taste
½ cup fine bread crumbs
1 to 2 tablespoons mustard

Preheat oven to 475 degrees. Trim rack of lamb until only a thin layer of fat remains. Combine butter, parsley, garlic, thyme and salt and pepper in a small pan. Stir over medium heat for 2 to 3 minutes; do not let mixture brown. Remove from heat and mix in bread crumbs; set aside.

Season lamb by rubbing lightly with mustard and salt and pepper. Place lamb in a roasting pan, fat-side up. Roast for 20 minutes. Remove from oven and pat crumb mixture firmly onto browned lamb fat. Roast 15 minutes longer. Transfer lamb to a heated serving platter and let stand 10 minutes before carving. Carve into chops to serve.

SERVES 2

Gloria Pflaumer

Good with béarnaise sauce.

Apricot Couscous

1 package couscous
1 cup chopped dried apricots
1 cup chopped scallion
1 cup chopped fresh
   coriander

Prepare couscous according to package directions and toss with apricots, scallion and coriander.

Preserved Lemons

6 to 8 lemons
2 cups kosher salt

Wash and dry lemons. Cut lemons into quarters starting at the top but being careful to not cut all the way through the bottom. Pack salt into the cuts and press lemons into a sterilized quart jar. Pack lemons as tightly as possible, squeezing juice from remaining lemons into jar. Top with salt and lemon juice, completely covering lemons. Seal with a non-metallic lid. Refrigerate for at least 3 weeks, or up to 6 months. Rinse before using, discarding pulp and seeds.

Lamb Tagine with Apricot Couscous

2 pounds lamb shoulder, cubed
2 tablespoons canola oil
2 cups sliced carrot, cut on bias
2 cups diced onion
4 tablespoons freshly grated
   ginger
3 to 4 cloves garlic, minced
1 cup raisins

2 tablespoons ground cumin
1 tablespoon cinnamon
1 cup kalamata olives
½ cup sliced Preserved Lemons
   (recipe in sidebar)
2 quarts chicken broth
1 tablespoon sugar
Salt and pepper to taste

Brown lamb in oil in a hot casserole pot; remove lamb and set aside. Add carrot, onion and ginger to pot and sauté 5 minutes. Add garlic and sauté 2 minutes longer. Stir in raisins, cumin and cinnamon and mix well. Return lamb to pot and add olives, lemon slices and broth. Bring to a boil. Simmer 2½ hours or until fork tender. Season with sugar and salt and pepper to taste. Serve with Apricot Couscous (recipe in sidebar).

SERVES 6 TO 8   *Cheryl Koons*

Flavorful Veal Stew

2 tablespoons butter
1 to 1¼ tablespoons olive oil
1 clove garlic, finely chopped
1 medium onion, finely chopped
1 to 1½ pounds veal stew meat,
   cut into 1 inch cubes
4 tomatoes, skinned and chopped
½ cup dry white wine

1 tablespoon tomato paste
¾ cup finely chopped Italian
   parsley
1 teaspoon chopped fresh basil
1 red pimento, chopped
2 medium stalks celery, chopped
Salt and pepper to taste

Heat butter and oil in a large heavy saucepan with a lid. Add garlic and onion and cook over low heat until softened but not browned. Add veal cubes and cook briskly until meat is browned. Add tomato, wine, paste, parsley, basil, pimento and celery. Season with salt and pepper and bring to a boil. Reduce heat and cover pan. Simmer 1½ to 2 hours or until veal is tender.

SERVES 4   *Kathy Oberkircher*

This stew is so flavorful you can also spoon it over rice or noodles.
Grab a crusty loaf of bread and go! Beef can be used in place of the veal.
The stew freezes well.

Veal Marsala

1½ pounds veal medallions, thinly sliced
1 cup flour
Salt and pepper to taste
2 to 3 sticks butter, divided
3 to 4 cloves garlic, minced, divided

½ pound Parmesan cheese, shredded (not grated)
1 (750 ml) bottle high quality Marsala wine
1 (15 ounce) can young peas, drained

Preheat oven to 180 degrees. Pound veal medallions until thin to tenderize veal and shorten cooking time. Season flour with salt and pepper. Dredge veal in seasoned flour. Melt 4 to 6 tablespoons butter in a 10 to 12 inch skillet over medium heat. Add about ¼ teaspoon garlic. Add a veal medallion to pan and sauté, turning once, for 1 to 2 minutes per side or until golden brown on both sides. Transfer cooked veal to a large serving platter and keep warm in oven while cooking remaining veal. Sprinkle Parmesan cheese over each medallion. Remove skillet from heat and add about ¼ cup wine. Return skillet to high heat. Add a pinch of minced garlic, a pinch of flour and a pinch of shredded Parmesan cheese to create "junk in the pan." As the wine reduces, the "junk" absorbs flavors to make the dish tasty. Reduce to a syrupy consistency and pour over veal on platter; do not clean skillet. Reduce heat to medium and repeat veal cooking process until all veal is cooked, using more butter and garlic each time.

When all veal is cooked, remove pan from heat. Add ¾ cup wine, 2 tablespoons butter, ¼ teaspoon minced garlic and half the can of peas. Return to high heat and cook 4 to 7 minutes or until reduced to a syrupy consistency, adding 2 to 3 pinches Parmesan cheese while cooking. Pour reduction over medallions. Repeat reduction step, using remaining peas. Lightly sprinkle Parmesan cheese over veal and serve.

SERVES 4 TO 6   *Patrick Williams*

A Look at 6th Grade, 2009

NYC

PAFA

Reading Terminal

Echo Hill

ERB's

Author Study

The Giver, Single Shard, Crispin

Fishing

Human Body Research Project

Transitions

Cinco de Mayo

Miam Monday

An easy dish to make that presents very elegantly.
A first place winner at the "Cedarbrook Country Club Men's Cook-Off."
Always remember to turn flame off when adding alcohol.
Keep lid handy to place over pot in case of a flame up.

LEMON VEAL

1 cup flour
Salt and pepper to taste
1½ to 2 pounds veal scallops, thinly sliced and pounded
1 clove garlic, finely chopped or crushed

3 tablespoons butter, divided
3 tablespoons olive oil
2 lemons
¾ cup chicken broth, divided
2 tablespoons minced fresh parsley

Preheat oven to 350 degrees. Season flour with salt and pepper in a small bag. Dredge veal in seasoned flour to coat. Sauté veal and garlic in a skillet in 1 tablespoon butter and olive oil until golden. Transfer veal to a baking dish; reserving skillet with pan drippings. Slice 1 lemon and arrange slices on veal. Add ½ cup broth and parsley to drippings in skillet, scraping up browned bits in pan. Pour broth over veal; reserving skillet. Bake for 20 minutes.

Add remaining ¼ cup broth to skillet along with juice from remaining lemon. Cook until reduced to a glaze. Remove from heat and swirl in remaining 2 tablespoons butter. Spoon glaze over cooked veal.

SERVES 4 TO 6

Kathy Schlesinger

I only use pepper (no salt) to season the flour and prefer to use low sodium broth. Mushrooms and shallots can be added to the veal. Try Champagne Risotto (page 122) with this recipe.

Portabello Buffalo Burgers with Celery Apple Slaw

Burgers

2 tablespoons plus 2 teaspoons oil, divided
1 medium onion, chopped
10 ounces portabello mushrooms, chopped

½ teaspoon salt
½ teaspoon black pepper
1 pound ground buffalo

Slaw

1 tablespoon mayonnaise
1½ teaspoons cider vinegar
1 teaspoon olive oil
1 teaspoon whole grain mustard

½ teaspoon sugar
Salt and pepper to taste
1 Granny Smith apple, julienne
2 stalks celery, julienne

Heat 2 tablespoons oil in a skillet. Add onion and mushrooms and cook over medium heat until lightly browned and liquid has evaporated. Season with salt and pepper and transfer to a bowl to cool. When cooled, mix in ground buffalo. Form mixture into four 4 inch patties.

Meanwhile, prepare slaw. Combine mayonnaise, vinegar, olive oil, mustard, sugar and salt and pepper. Add apple and celery and toss to mix.

To cook burgers, heat remaining 2 teaspoons oil in skillet over medium heat. Add burger patties and cook, turning once, for about 8 minutes for medium-rare. Serve burgers on buns topped with slaw.

SERVES 4

Cheryl Koons

The annual GA plant sale and book fair that we enjoy today, has been going on since at least the 1940's. In 1963 if you purchased $6.00 worth of plants you received free delivery.

You can adjust the spice in this recipe to taste. As the chili cooks, the spices will become more intense, so adjust amounts accordingly; or add chili powder and cayenne towards the end of the cooking process. This chili freezes well.

STEPHEN'S VENISON CHILI

2 pounds spicy venison sausage, casing removed, or 1¾ pounds ground venison sausage and 4 ounces spicy Italian sausage

1 large onion, diced

1 jalapeño pepper, diced

1 (15½ ounce) can tomato sauce

1 (15½ ounce) can red kidney beans, drained and rinsed

1 (16 ounce) can vegetarian refried beans

2 tablespoons chili powder

Ground cayenne pepper to taste

Brown sausage in a skillet, drain and set aside. In same skillet, brown onion over medium heat for 5 minutes or until golden. Add jalapeño and sauté 1 minute. Transfer meat and sautéed vegetables to a stockpot. Add tomato sauce, kidney beans and refried beans. Bring to a low boil. Reduce heat to a simmer. Stir in chili powder. Simmer, stirring frequently, for at least 4 hours; the longer the chili simmers the more the flavors will blend. The chili is done when the red beans have softened. Add cayenne to taste.

SERVES 8

Stephen Olitsky

Venison is a very lean meat and reaches medium-rare at a much lower temperature than beef. It is best served at medium rare since venison will dry out if over-cooked. The secret to well cooked venison is not to over cook it. Water may need to be added to the pan to prevent the marinade from dying out.

ROAST VENISON LOIN

3 to 4 pounds venison tenderloin

1 head garlic, cloves peeled and crushed

¼ cup fresh thyme

½ cup Barolo red wine

¾ teaspoon black pepper, divided

¼ cup plus 1½ tablespoons extra virgin olive oil, divided

1 tablespoon coarse sea salt

Toss venison with garlic, thyme, wine, ½ teaspoon pepper and ¼ cup oil in a plastic zip-top bag. Marinate in refrigerator overnight. Remove from refrigerator for 30 to 60 minutes before cooking to bring to room temperature.

When ready to cook, preheat oven to 450 degrees; place rack in center of oven. Remove venison from bag, reserving marinade. Sprinkle venison on all sides with salt and remaining ¼ teaspoon pepper. Heat remaining 1½ tablespoons oil in a heavy skillet over medium-high heat. Brown venison in oil on all sides. Pour reserved marinade into a shallow baking pan with a meat rack. Place venison on meat rack. Roast 25 to 30 minutes or until an instant-read thermometer reads 120 to 125 degrees for medium-rare.

SERVES 6

Tamar Olitsky

Salmon in Papillote

3 tablespoons chopped scallion
1 teaspoon peeled and minced
   fresh ginger
1 tablespoon low-sodium soy
   sauce
½ cup mirin
2 tablespoons chopped fresh
   cilantro
1 tablespoon dark sesame oil
4 salmon fillets

Preheat oven to 400 degrees. Whisk together all ingredients except salmon. Place each salmon fillet in the center of a 15 inch square of parchment paper. Top each fillet with a fourth of the mixture. Working with one parchment square at a time, fold opposite 2 edges of paper over the fish several times, then repeat with remaining sides, forming a sealed packet. Repeat with remaining packets.

Place packets on a baking sheet. Bake in center of oven for 15 minutes or until paper starts to brown.

SERVES 4

Cathy Black

Simple Swordfish

1½ pounds swordfish
Salt and pepper
Juice of 1 lime
½ cup mayonnaise
¼ cup soy sauce
½ Vidalia onion, sliced

Preheat a grill to medium-high. Rinse swordfish, pat dry and sprinkle with salt and pepper. Combine lime juice, mayonnaise and soy sauce. Spread one-fourth of mixture over fish. Place fish on grill, sauce-side down, and grill for 3 to 4 minutes. Spread more sauce on top of fish and turn. Place onion slices on fish and top with more sauce, if desired. Grill 5 to 10 minutes or until done.

SERVES 4

Alex Henry

A simple, delicious summer dinner! Serve with coconut rice and a salad. Grilled swordfish is also excellent marinated in Coconut Marinade (page 188)

Poached Salmon with Yogurt Dill Sauce

To poach salmon, place in pan and brush with butter. Sprinkle with ½ teaspoon of dill. Fill pan ¼ full with water. Bake at 400 degrees for 20 minutes.

DILL SAUCE:
½ cup low-fat plain yogurt
2 tablespoons Dijon mustard
¼ cup low-fat or regular
   mayonnaise
2 tablespoons white wine
2 tablespoons chopped fresh
   dill
Salt and pepper to taste
2 tablespoons capers, rinsed,
   or 1 clove garlic, minced

Combine all ingredients.

Cheryl Ross

Arugula Sauce

2 cups mayonnaise
1 bunch arugula
Juice of 1 lemon
Salt and pepper

For sauce, purée mayonnaise with arugula and lemon juice. Season with salt and pepper.

Mustard-Herb Crusted Salmon with Arugula Sauce

¼ cup whole grain mustard
Juice of ½ lemon
2 tablespoons chopped fresh thyme
2 tablespoons chopped fresh parsley
Salt and pepper to taste
¼ cup extra virgin olive oil, plus extra for drizzling
1½ cups panko bread crumbs
1 side of salmon

Preheat oven to 450 degrees. Combine mustard, lemon juice, thyme, parsley, salt and pepper in a bowl. Stir in olive oil and panko. Place salmon on a parchment-lined baking sheet. Drizzle with olive oil. Spread mustard mixture over salmon. Roast for 10 to 15 minutes or until just cooked. Serve salmon with Arugula Sauce (recipe in sidebar).

SERVES 8

Kris Henry

Salmon with Miso-Soy Sauce

¼ cup firmly packed brown sugar
2 tablespoons soy sauce, regular or low sodium
2 tablespoons hot water
2 tablespoons red miso
4 (6 ounce) salmon fillets
1 tablespoon chopped fresh chives

Preheat oven to 400 degrees. Combine brown sugar, soy sauce, hot water and miso with a whisk. Arrange fillets in a shallow baking dish coated with cooking spray or olive oil. Spoon miso mixture evenly over salmon. Bake for 10 minutes. Baste with miso mixture and broil 8 to 10 minutes or until slightly crispy on top. Sprinkle with chives and serve.

SERVES 4

M. Diana Helweg Newton

Miso can be found in the produce section of the grocery store or with soy and dairy products in natural food markets.

MARVELOUS MAHI MAHI WITH CUCUMBER SAUCE

1½ pounds white fish, such as mahi mahi or tilapia

1 tablespoon olive oil, plus extra for brushing

⅓ cup vermouth or white wine

1 English cucumber, peeled, seeded and sliced

½ red onion, sliced

⅓ cup Mustard Vinaigrette (recipe in sidebar)

1 tablespoon butter

Brush fish on both sides with olive oil. Cook fish in olive oil for 2 minutes on each side; remove from pan and keep warm. Add vermouth to pan. Add cucumber and onion and cook over low heat for 5 minutes or until softened. Add fish to pan and pour vinaigrette on top. Bring to a simmer. Remove fish to a serving plate. Add butter to sauce in pan and stir until melted. Pour sauce over fish.

SERVES 4

Nancy Beck

MUSTARD VINAIGRETTE

2 tablespoons white wine vinegar

¼ cup olive oil

1 teaspoon Dijon mustard

Salt and pepper to taste

Pinch of sugar

Whisk together all vinaigrette ingredients.

PANKO ENCRUSTED FISH

½ cup panko bread crumbs

3 fish fillets, such as halibut, flounder or mahi mahi

½ tablespoon butter

2 teaspoons extra virgin olive oil

1 tablespoon Parmesan cheese (optional)

Place panko in a plastic zip-top bag. Add fish and gently shake to lightly coat each fillet. Melt butter with oil in a medium nonstick skillet over medium-high heat. Add fillets and cook until brown on each side, turning when fish turns white around the edges. Cook until fish flakes easily.

SERVES 3

Mazie Minehart Colen

Use the freshest fish possible; best made with fresh-caught flounder.
This recipe can be made with just extra virgin olive oil, but a little bit of butter
adds great flavor. Serve with Summer Squash Casserole (page 195).

Harvey Cedars Bluefish

1 stick butter
½ cup lemon juice
½ cup Worcestershire sauce
6 bluefish fillets

Preheat a grill. Melt butter in a small saucepan. Stir in lemon juice and Worcestershire sauce. Cut 2 large pieces of heavy-duty foil. On each piece, place 2 fillets and cover with one-third of sauce. Seal foil carefully so no sauce is lost. Place packets on hot grill for 10 minutes, turning once.

SERVES 6

Andy Thatcher

Patriot Fish Fillets in Wine

1 (16 ounce) can stewed
    tomatoes, liquid reserved
4 white fish fillets (1 to 1½
    pounds)
½ cup dry white wine or vermouth
1 teaspoon dried basil, or
    1 tablespoon fresh
Black pepper to taste
2 tablespoons grated Parmesan
    cheese
2 tablespoons chopped black
    olives (optional)

Preheat oven to 350 degrees. Pour ¼ cup reserved tomato liquid into a 9x13 inch baking dish. Arrange fish fillets in a single layer in dish. Pour wine over fish. Mash stewed tomatoes and spoon over fillets. Sprinkle with basil, pepper, Parmesan cheese and olives. Cover with foil. Bake for 20 to 25 minutes or until fish flakes when tested with a fork.

SERVES 4

Cheryl Ross

Bluefish in Gin

1½ pounds bluefish fillets
8 tablespoons butter, melted,
    divided
⅓ cup chopped onion
⅓ cup panko bread crumbs
¼ cup chopped tomato
2 teaspoons Crazy Jane's salt
3 ounces gin or vodka

Preheat a broiler. Place fillets in a large shallow pan. Pour 4 tablespoons melted butter over fish. Sprinkle onion, panko, tomato and salt on top. Broil on center rack for 5 minutes or until slightly browned. Remove from oven. Combine gin and remaining 4 tablespoons butter. Pour mixture over fish and ignite. When flame dies down, return to center rack and broil 5 to 10 minutes or until fish flakes.

SERVES 4

Alex Henry

Excellent with Tomato Corn Pie (page 192).

CHILEAN SEA BASS WITH SPINACH, PINE NUTS AND SHALLOTS

1½ to 2 pounds Chilean sea bass
2 teaspoons Dijon mustard
¼ cup chopped fresh Italian
    parsley
2½ tablespoons olive oil, divided
½ teaspoon salt

½ teaspoon black pepper
¼ cup minced shallot
2 pounds fresh spinach
¼ cup golden raisins, soaked in
    water
¼ cup toasted pine nuts

Preheat oven to 425 degrees. Rinse bass and pat dry. Combine mustard, parsley, 1½ tablespoons olive oil, salt and pepper. Spread mixture over fish and place in an oven-proof skillet. Bake for 15 minutes or until fish flakes easily with a fork.

Meanwhile, sauté shallot in remaining 1 tablespoon oil in a skillet until softened. Add spinach and a pinch of salt and pepper. Drain raisins and mix with pine nuts. Add mixture to spinach. Transfer spinach mixture to a plate. Top with sea bass. Serve with a salad and bread.

SERVES 6 TO 8

Kris Henry

VARIATION:

A delicious way to roast Chilean Sea Bass: combine ¼ cup soy sauce, ¼ cup teriyaki sauce, 1 tablespoon sesame oil, a dash of Worcestershire sauce, 1 clove crushed garlic, 1 tablespoon grated ginger, 2 chopped scallions and pineapple juice (optional). Pour mixture over 1½ pounds of fish in a baking dish. Roast at 400 degrees for 20 minutes.

PARENTS' COMMITTEE PECAN FLOUNDER

¼ cup dry white wine
1 tablespoon mustard
2 teaspoons herbes de Provence

⅓ cup finely chopped pecans
⅓ cup olive oil
4 (6 ounce) fillets flounder

Combine all ingredients except flounder. Pour marinade over fillets and marinate for 1 hour.

When ready to cook, preheat oven to 350 degrees. Place a fillet on individual pieces of foil. Spoon 1 tablespoon marinade over each fillet and seal foil tightly around fish. Bake for 20 minutes.

SERVES 4

Bruce Henry

Fresh Tomato and Caper Fish Sauce

1 onion, chopped
2 tablespoons olive oil
Salt and pepper to taste
5 plum tomatoes, seeded
    and coarsely chopped
2 tablespoons capers, rinsed
2 cloves garlic, minced
Pinch of sugar

Sauté onion in olive oil. Add a pinch of salt and pepper. Add tomato, capers, garlic and sugar. Season with salt and pepper. Serve over fish; especially good with tuna.

Tuna Steaks with Mango Chutney

½ cup soy sauce
1 tablespoon honey
1 teaspoon hot pepper flakes
1 teaspoon ground cumin
1 teaspoon turmeric
4 fresh tuna steaks

Combine all ingredients except tuna in a small bowl. Pour marinade mixture over tuna in a shallow dish. Marinate in refrigerator for 1 hour.

When ready to cook, preheat grill. Drain tuna and grill to desired degree of doneness. Serve with Mango Chutney (recipe below).

Mango Chutney

2 mangoes, peeled and chopped
½ red onion, chopped
¼ cup chopped cilantro
¼ cup chopped jalapeño pepper
2 tablespoons fresh lime juice
1 tablespoon balsamic vinegar
1 teaspoon honey

Combine all chutney ingredients. Serve with tuna.

SERVES 4   *Sue McGinnis*

Tequila Mussels

1 stick butter
5 cloves garlic, minced
¾ cup diced tomato
½ cup sliced scallion
½ cup sliced celery
6 jalapeño peppers, sliced with
    seeds in
¼ cup tequila
2 tablespoons fresh lime juice
40 to 60 mussels, soaked in water
    and cleaned
Salt and pepper to taste

Melt butter in a large stockpot. Add garlic and sauté for 1 minute. Mix in tomato. Stir in scallion, celery, jalapeño pepper, tequila and lime juice. Add mussels, cover and simmer until mussels open. Remove mussels to a serving bowl.

Simmer sauce, uncovered, until slightly reduced. Season with salt and pepper. Pour sauce over mussels.

Serve with crusty baguette to dip in sauce with Sangría or Corona and lime on the side.

SERVES 4 TO 6   *Lisa Roth*

Aunt Dona's Shrimp Dinner

1½ sticks margarine, divided
1 teaspoon chopped garlic
1 large red bell pepper, chopped
1 large yellow pepper, chopped
1 bunch scallions, chopped
6 to 8 ounces mushrooms, chopped

Salt and pepper to taste
½ cup white wine
2 pounds large shrimp, peeled, butterflied and deveined
Cooked white rice

Melt 6 tablespoons margarine in a 10 inch deep skillet. Add garlic and sauté 3 minutes. Add 3 tablespoons margarine. Add bell peppers, scallion, mushrooms and salt and pepper and sauté 3 minutes. Add remaining 3 tablespoons margarine. Stir in wine and cook 2 minutes. Add shrimp and sauté 3 to 5 minutes or until shrimp turn pink and opaque. Serve rice on the side with garlic bread and a green salad.

The meal they always come home for!

SERVES 4   *Madeline Lamm Specter*

Fried Soft Shell Crabs

2 large eggs
1 cup milk
½ cup half & half
1 tablespoon Creole mustard
3 dashes Tabasco
3 dashes Worcestershire sauce

1 teaspoon Zatarain's liquid crab boil (optional)
2 cups flour
Salt and pepper to taste
1 dozen small soft shell crabs, cleaned
4 cups oil for frying

Combine eggs, milk, half & half, mustard, Tabasco, Worcestershire and crab boil to create a batter.

Season flour with salt and pepper in a shallow dish. Dredge crabs in seasoned flour, then dip in batter. Place on a plate or pan and refrigerate for 15 minutes.

Heat oil in a deep fryer to at least 325 degrees. Drop crabs in hot oil without crowding. Fry until crabs reach a golden color and begin to float; remove from oil and drain.

SERVES 6   *Cameron Retif*

Serve as a po-boy sandwich on crusty French bread,
or simply with a tomato, basil, and mozzarella salad.

The Lower School physical education department brings you 10 ways to burn 250 calories through activity…

1) 70 minutes of easy walking
2) 17 minutes of swimming
3) 40 minutes of yard work
4) 75 minutes of shopping
5) 30 minutes of bicycling
6) 120 minutes of watching T.V.
7) 31 minutes of stair climbing
8) 22 minutes of jogging
9) 21 minutes of jump roping
10) 53 minutes of fishing

MARYLAND CRAB CAKES

1 pound lump crabmeat
2 tablespoons mayonnaise
1 tablespoon yellow mustard
1 large egg, beaten
1½ cups bread crumbs, panko preferred, plus extra for topping
2 teaspoons Old Bay seasoning, or to taste

Mix all ingredients together and shape into patties. Glaze top of cakes with olive oil and sprinkle extra bread crumbs on top. Broil for 10 minutes or until golden brown.

Sandy Budinsky

CRAB CAKES WITH AVOCADO-TOMATO GARNISH

8 ounces jumbo lump crabmeat
¼ teaspoon freshly ground black pepper
¼ teaspoon dried thyme
1 tablespoon chopped fresh chives
⅛ teaspoon Tabasco sauce, or to taste
¼ teaspoon salt
3 tablespoons mayonnaise
1 large egg
1½ ounces fresh bread crumbs or ¾ cup panko crumbs
2 tablespoons peanut oil

Cut crabmeat pieces in half to yield about 1½ cups. Mix crabmeat with pepper, thyme, chives, Tabasco, salt, mayonnaise and egg and toss gently to blend. Add bread crumbs and toss lightly. Form mixture into 4 patties. Refrigerate at least 20 minutes.

Heat peanut oil in a large skillet. When hot, place patties in a pan and sauté over medium heat for 3 to 4 minutes on each side.

To serve, spoon Avocado-Tomato Garnish onto 4 individual serving plates. Top each with a crab cake and sprinkle with chives.

Avocado-Tomato Garnish

1 ripe tomato, peeled, seeded and coarsely chopped
1 small ripe avocado, peeled and chopped
2 tablespoons red wine vinegar
¼ cup peanut oil or extra virgin olive oil
¼ teaspoon freshly ground black pepper
¼ teaspoon salt
1 tablespoon chopped fresh chives

Combine tomato and avocado in a bowl. Add vinegar, oil, pepper and salt. Sprinkle chives all over before serving.

SERVES 4

Anita Franchetti

The garnish can be made a day ahead and kept covered in the refrigerator. Crab cakes can be made about an hour before serving and held in a 200 degree oven on a baking sheet. Crab cakes can also be made bite size to serve with cocktails.

GREEK SHRIMP SCAMPI

2 pounds (12 to 15 count) shrimp, peeled, butterflied and deveined, tails left intact
5 tablespoons good olive oil
¼ cup dry white wine
3 tablespoons capers (optional)
½ cup crumbled feta
½ cup kalamata olives, chopped
½ cup chopped tomato
Pinch of salt and pepper

1½ sticks unsalted butter, softened
4 cloves garlic, minced
½ cup minced white onion
Zest of ½ lemon
Juice of 1 lemon
1 large egg yolk
½ cup panko bread crumbs
Fresh lemon wedges and parsley for garnish

Preheat oven to 350 degrees. Toss shrimp in olive oil, wine, capers, feta, olives, tomato and salt and pepper. Set aside to marinate.

In a small bowl, mix butter with garlic, onion, lemon zest, lemon juice, egg yolk and panko. Place shrimp in a gratin dish with tails up and pour marinade mixture over shrimp. Top shrimp with butter and bread crumb mixture.

Bake for 12 to 15 minutes. Place under broiler for 1 minute to get brown and bubbly. Sprinkle with parsley and serve with lemon wedges.

SERVES 6   *Kathy Lawlor Riley*

How long was the Brachioraurus?

Was Spinosaurus a carnivore, herbivore, or omnivore?

In what prehistoric period did the raptors live?

If you are curious about the answers to these and other questions about dinosaurs, just ask a GA second grader.

Dinosaur is one of the "hot topics" of the second grade program.

Through a variety of learning experiences, students expand their knowledge of these amazing creatures that roamed the earth millions of years ago.

Shrimp can be prepared ahead and cooked in oven just before serving.

Some easy, delicious ways to grill shrimp or scallops:

Marinate in one of the following...

- BBQ sauce

- Tequila, lime juice and orange juice

- Soy sauce, sesame, pineapple juice and minced garlic

- Mayonnaise, lime juice, lime zest and powdered wasabi

- Mango chutney, lime juice, ginger, garlic and a small amount of olive oil

- Skewer and grill 2 to 3 minutes per side.

ALPHABETIA SHRIMP FLORENTINE

2 (10 ounce) bags fresh spinach
2 pounds medium shrimp, cooked, peeled and deveined
1 stick butter
½ cup flour
3 cups milk
1 cup dry white wine

3 scallions, chopped
1 clove garlic, minced
1 teaspoon black pepper
1 teaspoon salt
1 teaspoon paprika
2 cups shredded Monterey Jack cheese

Preheat oven to 350 degrees. Spread spinach in the bottom of a 9x13 inch casserole dish. Arrange shrimp over spinach.

Melt butter in a saucepan. Whisk in flour until smooth. Add milk, wine, scallion and garlic. Cook, stirring constantly, until bubbly. Add pepper, salt and paprika. Pour sauce over shrimp. Sprinkle cheese on top. Bake, covered, for 30 minutes.

SERVES 8

Joy Holmes

Dish can be assembled ahead and refrigerated until ready to bake.
Add 10 minutes to baking time. Serve with rice, salad and bread. For more flavor,
sauté garlic and a small diced shallot in butter before adding flour.

Mrs. P's Secret Sea Scallops, from the Kitchen of Mrs. Paul

2 pounds fresh sea scallops
Paprika to taste
Salt and pepper to taste
8 slices American cheese

1 pound rice, cooked according to package directions
Lemon wedges for garnish

Preheat a broiler. Slice sea scallops in half and place on a foil-lined baking sheet. Spray top of scallops with nonstick cooking spray. Broil scallops for 10 minutes; drain excess liquid. Turn scallops and spray again with cooking spray. Broil 10 minutes longer; drain excess liquid. Season scallops with paprika, salt and pepper.

Place cheese slices on top of scallops and broil about 1 minute or until cheese melts and turns light brown. Serve over rice and garnish with lemon wedges. Enjoy with Secret Recipe Seafood Sauce (recipe in sidebar).

SERVES 4   *Olga Piszek*

Secret Recipe Seafood Sauce

1 tablespoon Colman's dry mustard
1½ teaspoons water
1 cup mayonnaise
Freshly ground black pepper to taste

Place mustard in a mixing bowl. Stir in water. Mix in mayonnaise. Season with pepper. Mix sauce vigorously, cover and refrigerate until ready to serve.

Nancy's Seafood Fancy

1 pound mushrooms, sliced
4 tablespoons butter
¼ teaspoon curry powder
½ teaspoon Worcestershire sauce
2 cups chicken broth, divided
2 cups light cream
2 to 4 tablespoons flour
3 tablespoons ketchup

3 tablespoons chili sauce
1 pound peeled, deveined and cooked shrimp
1 pound crabmeat
¼ cup sherry
Dash of cayenne pepper
Salt and pepper to taste
½ cup shredded Parmesan cheese

Sauté mushrooms in butter in a large skillet. Stir in curry and Worcestershire sauce. Add 1½ cups chicken broth. Bring to a boil. Reduce heat, cover and simmer 5 minutes. Add cream.

Place flour to a bowl. Slowly stir in remaining ½ cup broth and mix until smooth. Pour mixture into simmering mushrooms. Continue to stir over medium heat for 10 minutes or until thickened. Stir in ketchup and chili sauce. Fold in shrimp and crabmeat. Cook until mixture is just hot.

Stir in sherry and season with cayenne, salt and pepper. Sprinkle Parmesan cheese on top.

SERVES 6 TO 8   *Kris Henry*

Tomato-Mango Salsa for Grilled Scallops

8 to 10 scallops
Olive oil
2 medium tomatoes, seeded and chopped
¾ cup chopped mango
3 tablespoons chopped red onion
2 tablespoons chopped fresh basil
2 tablespoons red wine vinegar
1 tablespoon capers, drained and rinsed

Brush scallops with olive oil and grill or sauté. Mix tomato, mango, onion, basil, vinegar and capers. To serve, spoon salsa over scallops.

SERVES 2

Scallops Wolfeboro

2 tablespoons olive oil
2 scallions, chopped
2 tablespoons minced garlic
2 cups chopped fresh tomato
¾ cup dry red wine
3 tablespoons red wine vinegar
¼ cup chopped fresh parsley
1 tablespoon chopped fresh basil
1 teaspoon salt
1 teaspoon black pepper
¾ pound dry fettuccine pasta
1½ pounds sea scallops, rinsed
¼ cup grated Parmesan cheese

Heat olive oil in a large skillet. Add scallion, garlic, tomato, wine, vinegar, parsley, basil, salt and pepper. Cook for 5 minutes over medium-high heat or until boiling. Reduce to medium-low heat and cook 15 minutes.

Cook pasta according to package directions; drain. While pasta is cooking, add scallops to tomato mixture and cook 5 to 7 minutes or until scallops are done. Add drained pasta to tomato sauce and toss. Sprinkle Parmesan cheese on individual servings.

SERVES 4

Nancy Beck

Hawaiian Fish Stew

2 tablespoons vegetable oil
1 medium-size green bell pepper, cut into 1 inch pieces
1 medium onion, sliced
1¼ pounds halibut or swordfish, cut into 1 inch pieces
½ cup ketchup
3 tablespoons orange juice
2 cloves garlic, minced
1 teaspoon orange zest
¼ teaspoon salt
1 tablespoon chopped fresh parsley for garnish

Heat oil in a 10 inch skillet. Add bell pepper and onion and sauté until onion is transparent. Add fish. Stir in ketchup, orange juice, garlic, orange zest and salt. Stir over medium heat for 10 minutes or until fish is cooked through. Garnish with parsley and serve with rice.

SERVES 6

Pat Dawe

GRILLED ISLAND FISH BURGERS

¼ cup fresh lemon juice
2 tablespoons soy sauce
¼ teaspoon minced garlic
¼ teaspoon black pepper
¼ teaspoon hot pepper sauce
¼ cup olive oil

4 (6 ounce) white fish fillets, such as tilapia, grouper or mahi mahi
4 hamburger buns
Tartar Sauce (recipe in sidebar)
Tomato slices
Lettuce leaves

Combine lemon juice, soy sauce, garlic, black pepper, pepper sauce and olive oil in a plastic zip-top bag. Place fish in mixture and marinate for 1 hour.

When ready to cook, preheat a grill. Drain fish and grill until fish flakes easily. Serve fish on buns with tartar sauce, tomato and lettuce.

SERVES 4   *Andy Thatcher*

FISH TACOS

½ head cabbage, thinly sliced
¼ cup chopped red onion
4 tilapia fillets, or other firm white fish
1 cup bread crumbs, or more if needed
¼ teaspoon chili powder, or to taste

2 large eggs, beaten
Canola oil for frying
1 package small flour or blue corn tortillas
Salsa (recipe in sidebar)
Fish Taco Sauce (recipe in sidebar)

Combine cabbage and onion; set aside.

Cut fish into 1 inch strips, 4 to 5 inches long. Mix bread crumbs and chili powder in a shallow dish. Place beaten egg in a separate dish. Dip fish strips in egg wash, then dredge in bread crumbs. Heat canola oil in a large skillet. Fry fish in hot oil for 3 minutes on each side or until crispy brown; drain.

Warm tortillas in damp paper towel in a microwave for 1 minute. To assemble, place fish on a tortilla. Top with cabbage mixture and sauce and salsa.

SERVES 4   *Peter Keblish*

Canola oil is key to making fish crispy.
Tacos best served with ice cold Coronas!

TARTAR SAUCE

1 cup mayonnaise
1 tablespoon lemon juice
1 tablespoon chopped scallion
1 tablespoon relish
1 tablespoon capers
1 tablespoon chopped fresh parsley
Dash of hot pepper sauce
Salt and pepper to taste

Mix all tartar sauce ingredients until combined.

SALSA

1 cup seeded and chopped tomato
¼ teaspoon hot pepper sauce, or to taste
¼ cup chopped fresh cilantro

Combine all salsa ingredients.

FISH TACO SAUCE

¼ cup sour cream
¼ cup mayonnaise
Juice of ½ lime

Mix all sauce ingredients. Serve at room temperature.

*L*earning to cook begins in pre-kindergarten! The children enjoy sharing recipes and snacks they have prepared, with each other. Parents are invited to sign-up their child to be "chef-of-the-day". The chefs are encouraged to select nutritious food recipes. The children learn organizational skills by actively preparing or assisting in the preparation of snacks and the cooking experience teaches the children to become confident in giving directions for step-by-step preparations. In addition children learn to use kitchen tools, to develop good safety habits, and to recognize food groups. The children are encouraged to taste all snacks as it has been discovered that many children enjoy foods they have never before tasted.

SUMPTUOUS SEAFOOD STEW

¼ cup olive oil
1½ cups chopped onion
2 tablespoons chopped garlic
4 teaspoons dried oregano
1½ teaspoons fennel seeds
2½ cups canned crushed tomatoes
  in liquid
2½ cups bottled clam juice
1 cup dry white wine
2 (6½ ounce) cans chopped clams,
  drained with liquid reserved

1 pound raw shrimp, peeled and
  deveined
6 ounces fresh or canned
  crabmeat
½ pound scallops
½ cup chopped fresh basil
1 tablespoon anchovy paste
Tabasco to taste
Worcestershire sauce to taste
Salt and pepper to taste

Heat olive oil in a large heavy pot over medium heat. Add onion, garlic, oregano and fennel and sauté until onion is tender. Add tomatoes in liquid, clam juice, wine and reserved clam liquid. Bring to a boil and cook 15 minutes or until slightly thickened.

Stir in clams, shrimp, crabmeat and scallops. Simmer 2 minutes. Mix in basil and simmer until seafood is cooked through. Season with anchovy paste and Tabasco, Worcestershire, salt and pepper to taste.

SERVES 6   *Jane Henry*

Any combination of fish can be used.

Joy's Chicken Rosemary

1 (2½ to 3 pound) whole chicken, rinsed
Salt and pepper to taste
8 sprigs fresh rosemary, divided
10 sage leaves, divided
2 bay leaves
1 medium onion, halved
1 clove garlic, halved

¼ cup olive oil
2 bunches scallions, trimmed and cut into 2 inch lengths (2 cups)
1 cup thinly sliced carrot
½ cup thinly sliced celery
6 slices dried porcini mushrooms
2 cups chicken broth, divided

Preheat oven to 450 degrees. Season chicken inside and out with salt and pepper. Stuff cavity with 2 rosemary sprigs, 4 sage leaves, bay leaves, onion and garlic.

Heat oil in a 9x12 inch flameproof pan or ovenproof skillet over medium heat. Add scallion, carrot, celery and mushrooms and cook for 4 minutes or until scallion is wilted. Spread vegetable mixture into an even layer. Place chicken, breast side up, over vegetables. Pour ½ cup broth over chicken. Sprinkle chicken with remaining rosemary and sage.

Roast chicken in oven, basting frequently with enough of remaining chicken broth to keep vegetables moist. Bake for 1 hour or until vegetables and chicken are golden brown.

SERVES 4   *Joy Holmes*

Larger carrot and celery pieces and even halved red potatoes can be added to roasting pan with the chicken and served along side the carved chicken. Quick and easy Thanksgiving any day! Place a turkey breast half, breast side up, in a roasting pan. Brush with melted butter and season with salt and pepper. Place onion, carrot, potato and celery around turkey, if desired. Roast at 450 degrees for 45 minutes. Baste occasionally with cooking juices. Serve with cranberry relish or sauce.

One cannot begin the story of girls at Germantown Academy without first remembering Virginia Belle Day, Class of 1760, our founding Dean of Girls in the Upper School. Miss Day served GA for 31 years, 23 of which were as Dean. The Dean of Girls' position and the Dean of Boys' position have become a part of Fort Washington history as the House System replaced the Dean System and a new Upper School administrative era begins.

Curry Sautéed Chicken with Sweet and Hot Apricots

2 boneless, skinless chicken breasts, halved (4 pieces)
2 tablespoons canola oil
3 cloves garlic, minced
4 tablespoons butter, divided
20 dried apricots, diced

½ cup apricot preserves
1 teaspoon lemon juice
½ teaspoon dried red pepper flakes
Curry powder to taste
Salt and pepper to taste

Place chicken breast pieces in a shallow dish. Brush oil on chicken and spread garlic on top; set aside to marinate while preparing apricots.

Heat 2 tablespoons butter in a skillet. Add apricots and sauté until fruit begins to soften. Stir in preserves, lemon juice and pepper flakes. Cook over low heat for 5 minutes. Remove from pan and set aside. Return pan to heat.

Wipe garlic and excess oil from chicken, leaving a small amount of oil to prevent chicken from sticking. Sear chicken on both sides in hot pan over medium-high heat, using marinade oil if needed to prevent sticking. Sprinkle seared chicken with curry powder. Add remaining 2 tablespoons butter to pan. Reduce heat to low and cook until chicken is cooked through. Season with salt and pepper. Serve chicken with apricot mixture.

SERVES 4
Christine McDade

You may want to make extra apricots - they always go quick!
Orange marmalade can be substituted for the apricot preserves. For quicker even cooking, flatten chicken breasts between sheets of wax paper before cooking.

UNDER THE BLUE MOON SESAME PECAN CHICKEN

2 large cloves garlic, peeled
1 teaspoon salt
1 cup buttermilk
4 boneless, skinless chicken breast halves, flattened slightly with mallet
¾ cup pecans
¾ cup walnuts
½ cup natural sesame seeds

¼ cup flour
1 teaspoon paprika
Salt and pepper to taste
1 tablespoon butter or margarine
1 tablespoon corn oil
¾ cup heavy cream
1 rounded teaspoon Dijon mustard

Crush garlic with 1 teaspoon salt. Add buttermilk. Pour mixture over chicken in a shallow dish and marinate 2 hours or overnight.

Combine pecans, walnuts, sesame seeds, flour, paprika and salt and pepper in a food processor. Pulse on and off until mixture is blended but not too fine. (This amount of breading should be enough for several additional breasts, depending on size.)

Wipe most of the marinade from the chicken. Dredge chicken in nut mixture, pat lightly and refrigerate for several hours with wax paper under and over chicken and between layers.

Melt butter with oil in a skillet until almost smoking. Reduce heat to low. Add chicken and cook 3 to 4 minutes per side or until brown on both sides and firm to the touch. Transfer chicken to a serving platter; drain fat from pan.

Add cream and mustard to pan. Season with salt and pepper, if desired. Cook, whisking occasionally, until mixture thickens. Pour sauce over chicken and serve.

SERVES 4

Serve with Oven Roasted Parmesan Vegetables (page 200).

Though Miss Day's focus was on the girls, boys loved and respected her and sought her presence as well. Her office, always open and rumpled and cluttered with piles of books, papers, and folders, a daily stream of Upper School students looking to change a class, have a quick upbeat conversation or a longer talk about readings of Edith Wharton or Eugene O'Neill, reveal a personal crisis or reflect on college plans, take a nap, have the length of a skirt measured, see pictures of her numerous cats, edit an essay, dream about the distant future, or muse about a budding romance. A television comedy/drama could have been written about the comings and goings in Jinny Day's office. She would have gladly shared the spotlight with every student and teacher in the cast.

*J*inny Day was a Dean straight from central casting. Warmth, cheerfulness, intelligence, humor, humility, an occasional and refreshing hint of zaniness, as detected in the style of her ever present eye-glasses, overlaid her driving sense of purpose. Jinny Day was, at once, easy to be with and impossible to forget. Hers was the perfect personality for pioneering and then establishing a secure feminine presence in GA's dominant male culture.

PATRIOTS' GOLDEN CHICKEN

2 tablespoons olive oil
1 pound boneless, skinless chicken breast, each breast cut into thirds
½ teaspoon salt
½ teaspoon black pepper
1 large yellow onion, thinly sliced
1 cup large pimento-stuffed olives, quartered
2 cloves garlic, thinly sliced
1 pint cherry tomatoes, halved
¾ cup dry white wine
¾ cup chopped fresh flat-leaf parsley
1 cup dry long grain rice, prepared according to package directions

Heat olive oil in a large skillet over medium heat. Season chicken with salt and pepper. Cook chicken in hot oil for 3 minutes per side or until golden brown; transfer chicken to a plate. Add onion to skillet and cook, stirring occasionally, for 5 minutes or until slightly softened. Add olives, garlic and tomatoes and cook and stir for 2 minutes.

Return chicken to skillet. Add wine and bring to a simmer. Cook 4 to 6 minutes or until chicken is cooked through and the sauce is slightly thickened. Stir in parsley.

Divide chicken among individual plates. Spoon sauce over chicken. Serve with rice.

SERVES 4

Robyn and Peter Heckler

WHITE WINE AND LEMON HERBED CHICKEN LEGS

2 tablespoons marjoram
2 tablespoons oregano
2 tablespoons rosemary
12 chicken legs, skin removed
3 tablespoons butter
1 cup dry white wine
¼ to ½ cup lemon juice
Salt and pepper to taste

Place marjoram, oregano and rosemary in a large plastic bag and toss to mix. Add chicken to bag and shake to coat, adding more herbs if needed.

Melt butter in a large pan until foaming. Add chicken legs and sauté until brown. Remove chicken from pan and deglaze pan with wine and lemon juice to loosen herbs. Return chicken to pan and simmer, covered, for 45 to 60 minutes or until cooked through. Season to taste with salt and pepper.

SERVES 6

Susan Sauter

GINGERED PEAR CHICKEN WITH WALNUTS

1½ pounds boneless, skinless chicken breast, cut into chunks

3 tablespoons butter, melted

¼ teaspoon salt

1 (16 ounce) can pear halves, juice reserved

¾ cup ginger ale

¼ cup firmly packed light brown sugar

3 tablespoons soy sauce

2 teaspoons cornstarch

¼ cup water

¼ teaspoon powdered ginger

¾ cup walnuts, coarsely broken

Preheat oven to 350 degrees. Sauté chicken in butter in a skillet over medium heat until brown on both sides. Sprinkle with salt.

Drain pear juice into a measuring cup, adding water if needed to make ¾ cup liquid. Mix pear liquid with ginger ale, brown sugar and soy sauce. Pour mixture over chicken and cook, covered, over medium heat, turning occasionally, for 20 minutes or until chicken is tender. Use a slotted spoon to transfer chicken from skillet to a 8x12 inch baking dish. Cut each pear half into 2 wedges and arrange pears around chicken.

In a small bowl, dissolve cornstarch in water until smooth. Stir in ginger. Pour mixture into pan juices in skillet. Cook and stir 5 minutes or until thick. Pour thickened mixture over chicken and pears. Sprinkle walnuts on top. Bake, uncovered, for 10 to 15 minutes or until very hot.

SERVES 4

Emily Ross

*G*A has been enriched beyond measure by the courage of those female pioneers who took on the challenge of changing the male GA culture and succeeding.

Casserole may be prepared up to 24 hours ahead and refrigerated until ready to bake.

The honor code calls on each of

us to:

• promise to try our hardest not

to lie, cheat or steal

• confront ourselves if we can't

keep our promise

• take responsibility for our ac-

tions if we break our promise

• confront and take responsibil-

ity for others who break their

promise if and when they refuse

to first take responsibility for

their mistake.

The Patriot Winter 1998

DINNER PARTY CHICKEN PAPRIKA

1 cup flour
2½ teaspoons paprika
¼ teaspoon cayenne pepper
¼ teaspoon powdered ginger
¼ teaspoon dried basil
⅛ teaspoon nutmeg
2 teaspoons salt
¼ teaspoon black pepper
10 to 12 boneless, skinless chicken
    pieces

4 tablespoons butter or oil, or as
    needed
1 large clove garlic, minced
2½ cups chicken broth
2 cups sour cream, room
    temperature
2 tablespoons Worcestershire
    sauce
½ cup dry sherry
15 water chestnuts, drained and
    sliced

Preheat oven to 325 degrees. Combine flour, paprika, cayenne pepper, ginger, basil, nutmeg, salt and pepper in a paper bag. Add chicken pieces, a few at a time, and shake; remove and shake off excess. Brown chicken on all sides in butter. Transfer chicken to a large casserole dish; reserving drippings in pan.

Add more butter to pan if needed. Add garlic and sauté 2 minutes. Stir in broth, sour cream, Worcestershire sauce, sherry and water chestnuts. Heat, stirring constantly, without allowing mixture to boil. Pour mixture over chicken. Bake, uncovered, for 1 hour.

SERVES 10 TO 12   *Kris Henry*

Sauce is thin, but delicious! Great dish for a dinner party
served over rice with a green salad on the side.

ABSOLUTELY NO WORK CHICKEN!

1 tablespoon curry powder
2 tablespoons soy sauce
½ cup honey

½ cup Dijon mustard
6 boneless chicken breast halves

Combine all ingredients except chicken. Place chicken in a 9x13 inch baking dish, skin side down. Pour honey mustard mixture over chicken and refrigerate at least 6 hours or overnight.

When ready to bake, preheat oven to 300 degrees. Turn chicken and cover dish with foil. Bake for 30 minutes. Uncover and baste chicken with pan juices. Cook 15 minutes longer. Spoon sauce over chicken to serve.

SERVES 6

Candise McAllister

FIELD DAY CHICKEN

4 tablespoons olive oil, divided
2 cloves garlic, crushed
12 plum tomatoes, quartered
4 pinches of sugar
12 ounces spinach, chopped
4 pinches of nutmeg

4 boneless, skinless chicken
  breasts, cut into pieces
½ cup flour
½ teaspoon salt
¼ teaspoon black pepper
½ cup white wine

Heat 2 tablespoons olive oil in a skillet. Add garlic and tomatoes and sauté over low heat for about 10 minutes. Stir in sugar and transfer mixture to a bowl. Add spinach to pan and cook until wilted. Mix in nutmeg and add spinach to tomato mixture.

Heat 2 tablespoons oil in same pan. Toss chicken pieces with flour in a strainer. Shake off excess flour and add chicken to hot oil. Cook 3 minutes on each side. Season chicken with salt and pepper. Return tomato and spinach mixture to skillet along with wine. Bring to a boil and serve.

SERVES 4

Nancy Beck

Can be prepared ahead and reheated when ready to serve.
Serve with grilled corn or over rice pilaf.

Although the specific details of each year's celebration change, Germantown Academy has a long-standing tradition of honoring its 50th reunion alumni classes by inducting them into the GA Old Guard. Some classes have returned to campus to be a part of graduation ceremonies and other have returned to go to Upper School classes, but all are recognized and honored at the annual Old Guard Luncheon. Held in the spring each year, the luncheon is attended by current Old Guard members - those more senior than the 50th reunion class. So far, all Old Guard inductees are men who went to GA in Germantown. The class of 1968, the first class with women, will also be the first to induct women into the Old Guard in 2018.

Germantown Academy Summer Programs started as a Day Camp in 1969 to meet the summer needs of neighborhood children. Over the next 20 years, school faculty developed other camps in areas such as sports, science, theater, academics, and art. Beginning in 1990, these camps were organized under one name, Germantown Academy Summer Programs. We are pleased to be entering our 41st year of offering campers in the Philadelphia area an opportunity to learn, play, and grow. Through more than 70 camps and courses, we believe we offer the most extensive slate of summer offerings in Montgomery County.

TUSCAN CHICKEN

4 boneless, skinless chicken breasts
Salt and pepper to taste
12 large basil leaves

4 ounces fresh mozzarella cheese, thinly sliced
4 thin slices prosciutto
1 tablespoon extra virgin olive oil

Butterfly-cut chicken without cutting all the way through; unfold like a book on a flat surface. Sprinkle chicken with salt and pepper. Layer basil leaves and mozzarella slices evenly over chicken and fold breast closed. Wrap each breast with a slice of prosciutto and brush with olive oil.

Grill chicken over medium heat for 4 minutes. Turn and cook 4 minutes longer. Turn and cook another 4 minutes or until chicken is done. Serve with your favorite pasta and a green salad.

SERVES 4

Ella Henry

LEMON GARLIC CHICKEN

3 cloves garlic, minced
3 to 4 tablespoons olive oil
6 to 8 boneless chicken breasts, pounded to desired thickness
2 to 3 large eggs, beaten
¾ cup bread crumbs

Juice of 2 lemons
½ cup chicken broth
½ cup white wine
¼ cup grated Parmesan cheese
Garlic powder to taste

Preheat oven to 350 degrees. Sauté garlic in olive oil in a 10 inch skillet. Remove garlic with a slotted spoon and discard. Dip chicken in egg, then dredge in bread crumbs. Add chicken to hot oil in skillet and cook until lightly browned. Transfer chicken to a baking dish.

Sprinkle chicken with lemon juice. Add broth and wine. Sprinkle Parmesan cheese and garlic powder on top. Bake for 1 hour.

SERVES 6 TO 8

Maria Kiley

Very tasty and so easy; one of my favorites! This dish can be made in advance.

MIRIAM'S PORTABELLO MUSHROOM CHICKEN

3 pounds skinless chicken, cut up
Salt and pepper to taste
1 tablespoon olive oil
8 ounces portabello mushrooms, halved
1 large onion, cut into thin wedges

1 (14 ounce) can diced tomatoes, undrained
1 (6 ounce) can tomato paste with Italian seasonings
1 teaspoon crushed sage
½ cup water

Preheat oven to 375 degrees. Season chicken with salt and pepper. Brown chicken in olive oil in a skillet for about 10 minutes. Transfer chicken to a 10x14 inch baking dish. Add mushrooms and onion to skillet and sauté over medium heat for about 5 minutes.

Drain fat. Reduce heat to low and add tomatoes, tomato paste, sage and water. Mix well and spoon over chicken. Bake, uncovered, for 40 to 45 minutes. Serve with orzo.

SERVES 4 TO 6   *Martha Sack*

QUICK AND HEALTHY CHICKEN IN WINE SAUCE

1½ cups white cooking wine
2 bay leaves
1 envelope dry onion soup mix
4 chicken cutlets

8 ounces dry spinach or whole wheat linguini pasta, cooked al dente

Combine wine, bay leaves and soup mix in a bowl; set aside. Sauté chicken over medium to low heat in a pan until just starting to brown. Add soup mixture and bring to a boil. Reduce heat and simmer, uncovered, for 20 minutes or to desired consistency. Serve over hot pasta.

SERVES 4   *Jacqueline Kaiser Zivitz*

For a richer taste and a thicker sauce, dip chicken in egg white and dredge in flour before sautéing. Add flour to sauce to thicken. Dish is excellent cold and freezes well.

DID YOU KNOW…

The first class of students in 1761 included a woman named Catherine Harchy?

In the "old days" there was a pep rally every Friday.

CHICKEN MARBELLA

3½ pounds boneless chicken, cubed
1 head garlic, peeled and chopped
¼ cup dried oregano
½ cup red wine vinegar
½ cup olive oil
1 cup prunes
½ cup green olives
½ cup capers with a hint of juice
6 bay leaves
1 cup firmly packed brown sugar
1 cup white wine

Preheat oven to 350 degrees. Combine chicken, garlic, oregano, vinegar, oil, prunes, olives, capers and bay leaves; marinate in refrigerator overnight.

When ready to cook, preheat oven to 350 degrees. Place chicken mixture in a large casserole dish. Sprinkle brown sugar on top and pour wine around the outside of the chicken. Bake for 30 to 40 minutes. Serve cold, room temperature or hot over couscous.

SERVES 8 TO 10

Betsy Palmer

AUNT GILL'S HOLIDAY CRANBERRY CHICKEN

8 (4 ounce) boneless, skinless chicken breasts or thighs, trimmed of fat
1 envelope dry onion soup mix
1 (16 ounce) can whole cranberry sauce

Preheat oven to 350 degrees. Arrange chicken in a 9x13 inch casserole dish in a single layer. Sprinkle soup mix evenly on top. Stir cranberry sauce in the can to loosen, then spoon evenly over chicken. Bake, uncovered, for 45 minutes.

SERVES 6 TO 8

Jessica Chadwin

Serve with Sweet Potato Casserole (page 201).

ARROZ CON POLLO

2 chicken breasts, split
1 chicken bouillon cube
4 cups water
1 tablespoon oil
3 slices bacon, chopped
1 bunch scallions, chopped
½ onion, chopped
2 red tomatoes, chopped
1 (8 ounce) can peas, drained and
    rinsed, or 8 ounces frozen
    peas

1 (8 ounce) can carrots, drained
    and rinsed, or 2 fresh carrots,
    coarsely chopped
½ teaspoon salt
¼ teaspoon black pepper
¼ teaspoon garlic powder
¼ teaspoon onion salt
2 tablespoons Worcestershire
    sauce
¼ cup soy sauce
2 cups cooked rice

Place chicken, bouillon cube and 4 cups water with a pinch of salt in a pot. Cover and cook over high heat for 30 minutes or until chicken is cooked through and can be pulled apart. Pull chicken off bone in pieces.

Heat oil in a skillet. Add bacon and sauté until bacon is crisp. Add scallion and onion and sauté until onion turns transparent. Add tomato and sauté until the tomato breaks down. Stir in peas and carrots. Add salt, pepper, garlic powder, onion salt, Worcestershire sauce and soy sauce. Simmer slowly, being sure mixture stays moist; add chicken broth if needed to keep mixture from drying out. Add chicken and simmer for 5 minutes. Add rice and simmer 5 minutes longer. Remove from heat. If desired, serve with fried ripe plantains and sliced avocado.

SERVES 4   *Paulina Fernandez*

The Class of 1931 was the last class to present a stone and plant ivy at the school in Germantown. The Class of 1932 chose to plant a tree as a living memorial to their class. With the passage of time, the Depression and the move to Fort Washington the tradition was set aside.

Use rotisserie chicken from the supermarket to cut down on preparation time.

"Every fall when Second Grade begins their unit on insects, the Lower School becomes infested with giant papier mache "Art Bugs"! In art class, second graders get to design their own unique insects first on paper, then with Sculpey clay, and finally, larger-than-life papier mache versions are created. You can catch a glimpse of the bugs creeping around the Lower School office in late fall!"

Lower School Art

AUTUMN CHICKEN

Sauce
2 cups cider
2 tablespoons Dijon mustard
1½ to 2 cups half & half
1 tablespoon cider vinegar
⅛ teaspoon cayenne pepper
¼ teaspoon salt
¼ teaspoon freshly ground black pepper

Chicken
6 boneless chicken breasts
¾ cup flour
1½ teaspoons salt
1½ teaspoons freshly ground black pepper
¼ cup canola oil
¼ cup clarified butter
4 Granny Smith apples, cored and cut into ¼ inch rings

Boil cider in a 2 quart saucepan until reduced to ½ cup, skimming off any solids that rise to the top. Whisk in mustard and enough half & half to result in about 2 cups liquid. Cook over medium-high heat until sauce reduces to desired consistency. Add vinegar, cayenne, salt and pepper and stir well; set aside.

For chicken, preheat oven to 200 degrees. Pound chicken breasts until slightly flattened and trim. Mix flour with salt and pepper in a shallow dish. Dredge chicken in seasoned flour and shake off excess. Mix oil and clarified butter. Add 6 tablespoons of oil mixture to a large skillet over medium heat. Add chicken to skillet and sauté for 5 minutes on each side, turning just once. Remove chicken from skillet and keep warm in oven.

Wipe out skillet. Add remaining oil mixture to skillet. Add apple slices and sauté for 3 to 5 minutes, turning only once.

Warm sauce on low heat while apple slices cook. Place chicken on a serving platter. Pour warm sauce over chicken and top with apple rings.

SERVES 6

Cathy Black

We prepare this dish every year for a family member who has a September birthday. It has become a traditional dish to kick off the change of seasons in our household. Great side dishes are garlic mashed potatoes, green beans and carrot cake for dessert.

CHICKEN ZIGGY

4 boneless chicken breasts, cut
    into pieces
½ onion, chopped
1 stalk celery, chopped
Olive oil or butter for sautéing
8 ounces cream cheese, softened

7 tablespoons butter, melted,
    divided
2 scallions, chopped
2 (8 ounce) containers refrigerator
    crescent rolls
½ cup chopped walnuts

Preheat oven to 350 degrees. Sauté chicken breasts, onion and celery in olive oil or butter. Mix chicken, sautéed vegetables, cream cheese, 4 tablespoons melted butter and scallion for a filling.

Unroll crescent rolls. Press 2 triangles together to form a rectangle on a baking sheet. Repeat with remaining dough, using 2 baking sheets total. Spoon filling evenly among rectangles. Bring together corners above rectangles and pinch edges to seal and form bundles. Brush each bundle with remaining melted butter and sprinkle with walnuts. Bake for 30 minutes or until golden.

SERVES 8

Geri Wysocki

Kids adore this dish. Great for a quick bite before a sports game or trick or treating.

In the 1760's salaries for the first schoolmasters, were 100 pounds ($165 in current currency exchange). Tuition was 40 shillings; if you studied only spelling and reading and skipped writing and arithmetic, it was only 30 shillings.

RED BOOK CASSEROLE

4 pieces boneless, skinless chicken breast

1 (10 ounce) package frozen chopped spinach, cooked and drained

1 (10¾ ounce) can condensed cream of chicken soup

2 cups mayonnaise

1 tablespoon curry powder

1 tablespoon lemon juice

1 cup shredded Cheddar cheese

Preheat oven to 350 degrees. Bake chicken in a baking dish for 30 minutes. Cool, then chop or shred; set aside.

Place spinach in the bottom of a casserole dish. Spread chicken over spinach. Mix soup, mayonnaise, curry powder and lemon juice in a bowl. Spoon mixture over chicken and spread evenly. Top with cheese. Bake for 45 minutes. Serve with rice and a green salad.

SERVES 4 TO 6

Sam Jordan

COMFORT CHICKEN

2 cups chicken broth

6 tablespoons flour

1 teaspoon salt

½ cup sour cream

½ cup grated Parmesan cheese, plus extra for topping

½ cup mayonnaise

1 bunch broccoli, cooked and cut into bite-size pieces

2 boneless, skinless chicken breasts, cooked and cut into bite-size pieces

1 cup cooked rice

Bread crumbs for topping

Preheat oven to 350 degrees. Heat broth in a saucepan. Dissolve flour in a small amount of cold water. Add flour mixture and salt to broth and cook and stir until thickened; cool. Add sour cream, ½ cup Parmesan cheese and mayonnaise to cooled sauce and mix well.

Place broccoli in a casserole dish. Cover with one-third of sauce. Add chicken, then half of remaining sauce. Top with rice and then remaining sauce. Sprinkle with bread crumbs and Parmesan cheese. Bake for 30 minutes.

SERVES 6

Bruce and Ella Henry

A Henry family favorite meal in one!

Barbara's Chicken Divan

4 cups fresh or frozen broccoli
    pieces
4 boneless, skinless chicken breast
    halves, cooked and diced
1 (10¾ ounce) can condensed
    cream of chicken soup

½ cup milk
½ cup shredded Cheddar cheese
2 tablespoons dry bread crumbs
1 tablespoon butter, melted

Preheat oven to 350 degrees. Place broccoli in a shallow 2 quart baking dish. Spread chicken over broccoli. Combine soup and milk and pour over chicken. Sprinkle cheese on top. Mix bread crumbs and butter and sprinkle over cheese. Bake for 30 minutes.

SERVES 6 TO 8

Laura Martin

Chicken Difrancois

1½ to 2 pounds boneless, skinless
    chicken (4 large breasts)
2 (10¾ ounce) cans condensed
    cream of chicken soup
10 ounces regular or light
    mayonnaise

3 (8 ounce) boxes frozen broccoli
    florets
2 cups shredded sharp Cheddar
    cheese
1 (6 ounce) can French fried
    onions

Preheat oven to 350 degrees. Boil chicken in water until cooked; drain and cool. Cut cooled chicken into 1 to 2 inch pieces. Mix soup with mayonnaise for a sauce. Spread a thin layer of sauce in a 9x12 inch casserole dish. Arrange broccoli florets in dish, placing heads to the outside and placing remaining broccoli in the center. Top with a little more sauce. Lay chicken pieces over broccoli layer. Cover chicken and any exposed broccoli with remaining sauce.

Bake for 35 minutes. Remove from oven and spread cheese on top. Return to oven until cheese is melted. Top with fried onions. Bake 1 to 2 minutes longer or until topping is light brown. Cool 5 minutes before serving.

SERVES 4 TO 6

Frank Tornetta

This casserole freezes well, but reserve cheese and
fried onion topping until final cooking. Perfect for a sports team dinner.
Serve with crusty French bread and a light salad.

*D*uring the Great Depression, to avoid increasing tuition and the possibility of pricing many families out of a Germantown Academy education, Headmaster Samuel E. Osbourn organized a giving fund. An appeal was sent to GA alumni for aid and the response was so gratifying that many young men were able to remain in school until graduation. Since that time, the Germantown Academy Annual Fund was established and continues to grow. This community-wide support is of primary importance to this day. It pays for the extra dimension that makes the school even more able to meet the needs and talents of every individual. Gifts to the Annual Fund can be seen in action on campus every day, benefiting our students and ensuring the GA legacy.

COMPANY CHICKEN

1 (10¾ ounce) can condensed
   cream of mushroom or
   celery soup
8 ounces sour cream
1 (7 ounce) package dry
   stuffing mix
6 boneless, skinless chicken
   breast halves

Preheat oven to 350 degrees.
Mix soup and sour cream
in a bowl. Place stuffing in
a separate bowl. Dip each
chicken breast in soup mixture, then roll in stuffing mix.
Place chicken in a 7x11 inch
baking dish. Bake for 45 to 60
minutes.

S E R V E S   6

Kelly Asplundh

*Dish can be prepared ahead and
refrigerated until ready to bake.*

BUCKLEY MARTIN CHICKEN

2 (10¾ ounce) cans condensed
   cream of chicken soup
1 soup can milk
1 (16 ounce) package dry egg
   noodles, cooked al dente and
   drained
4 chicken breasts, cooked and
   diced
1 (6 ounce) can sliced mushrooms,
   drained (optional)
Dry stuffing mix
Melted butter

Preheat oven to 350 degrees. Combine soup and milk. Place cooked
noodles in a bowl and pour soup mixture on top. Mix in chicken and mushrooms. Pour mixture into a casserole dish. Top with stuffing mix. Drizzle with
melted butter. Bake for 30 minutes or until heated through.

S E R V E S   6   T O   8

Katie, Jeff and Will Martin

UNLUCKY CHICKEN

2 cups white rice
2½ cups water
1 teaspoon salt
½ teaspoon black pepper
1 teaspoon curry powder, or to
   taste
1 envelope dry onion soup mix
Flour for dredging
1½ chickens, cut into 12 pieces
   and rinsed
2 (11 ounce) cans golden
   mushroom soup
½ cup milk
¼ cup white wine

Preheat oven to 350 degrees. Pour rice into a greased baking dish large
enough to hold chicken. Stir in water, salt, pepper, curry powder and onion
soup mix. Season dredging flour with salt and pepper to taste in a plastic
bag. Coat chicken in seasoned flour. Arrange chicken, skin side up, in pan.

In a separate bowl, combine golden mushroom soup, milk and wine. Pour
mixture over chicken in pan until floured surface is covered. Cover dish with
foil. Bake for 2 hours. For a crispier topping, remove foil for final 30 minutes
of baking time.

S E R V E S   6

Rich Schellhas

*We call it Unlucky Chicken because it was the only dish my
mother ever cooked. Whenever she entered the kitchen, she was an
unhappy camper, so her wrath was felt far and wide!*

HOT CHICKEN SALAD

4 large chicken breasts
2 large carrots, cut into pieces
Salt and pepper to taste
1-2 dashes tarragon
2½ cups diced celery
1 cup slivered almonds
1 teaspoon black pepper

4 teaspoons grated onion
½ teaspoon Worcestershire sauce
2 cups mayonnaise
1½ (10 ounce) packages frozen
   artichoke hearts
1½ cups shredded sharp Cheddar
   cheese

Preheat oven to 400 degrees. Poach chicken with carrot, salt and pepper to taste and tarragon in boiling water until cooked; drain, discarding carrot. Cool chicken and shred into small pieces. Mix in celery, almonds, 1 teaspoon pepper, onion, Worcestershire sauce and mayonnaise.

Cook artichokes according to package directions; drain. Chop artichokes and add to chicken mixture. Transfer mixture to a greased casserole dish. Top with cheese. Bake for 10 minutes. Reduce heat to 300 degrees and bake 20 minutes longer.

SERVES 8 TO 10   *Diane Doyle*

POTTS CHICKEN CRUNCH

1 pint sour cream
2 tablespoons lemon juice
2 teaspoons Worcestershire sauce
1 teaspoon celery seed
1 teaspoon paprika
½ teaspoon garlic salt

½ teaspoon salt
⅛ teaspoon black pepper
1 (7 ounce) package dry stuffing
   mix
10 boneless, skinless chicken
   breast halves
1 stick butter, melted

Combine sour cream, lemon juice, Worcestershire sauce, celery seed, paprika, garlic salt, salt and pepper in a bowl. Place stuffing mix in a food processor and process into crumbs; transfer to a shallow dish. Dip chicken in sour cream mixture, then dredge in stuffing crumbs until coated. Place chicken in a large casserole dish, rolling breasts if needed to fit chicken in dish. Refrigerate overnight.

When ready to bake, preheat oven to 350 degrees. Pour melted butter over chicken. Bake, uncovered, for 1 hour.

SERVES 10 TO 12   *The Potts Family*

AN "EXPERIMENTAL YEAR" FOR NEW GIRLS' INTERAC_

Given the outstanding success and longevity of the Boy's Inter Academic League, it seemed a logical and practical assumption that our girl athletes would profit from the same kind of organization. After several years of discussion, that is exactly the course that G.A. and other independent area schools decided upon as they inaugurate an "experimental year" for the newly formed girls Inter Academic League, with every confidence that the "experiment" will prove to be a lasting success.

The birth of this new organization is largely the result of the interest and enthusiasm of Phyllis Morrison, GA's former athletic Director.

The Patriot, 1982

"*I* came here 25 years ago for professional reasons, but I have been blessed with personal treasures, as well. I have become a member of an elite faculty; I have made personal friends; and, most importantly, I have found my calling. I was put on this earth to nurture and teach young children. That is how I find meaning in life and make a difference in this world. I say to parents on Meet-the-Teacher Night that, while I am not a wealthy man, I am a rich one. The students I teach are my legacy to the world. They are my points of light around the globe, and they're out there – in Manhattan, Ecuador, or Scotland. There is a little piece

McLean Hall Stuffed Chicken

6 asparagus stalks, tough ends snapped off and discarded
3 ounces Colby-Jack or Swiss cheese
1 cup plain dry bread crumbs
½ cup grated Parmesan cheese
½ cup pine nuts, finely chopped
3 large eggs
6 boneless, skinless chicken breast halves, pounded ¼ inch thick
Salt and pepper to taste
6 ounces pesto sauce
1 cup heavy cream

Preheat oven to 400 degrees. Cook asparagus in boiling water for 1 minute; drain, rinse with cold water and pat dry. Cut stalks into 3 inch lengths.

Cut Colby cheese into 3x½x½ inch sticks; set aside. Combine bread crumbs, Parmesan cheese and pine nuts in a bowl. In a separate bowl, beat eggs. Season chicken with salt and pepper and lay on a flat surface. Place an asparagus piece and a cheese stick next to each other along a long edge of a chicken breast. Roll breast around asparagus and cheese, tuck in ends and secure with a toothpick. Repeat for remaining chicken breasts. Dip each chicken roll in egg, then dredge in bread crumb mixture. Place chicken rolls in a baking dish. Bake for 20 to 25 minutes.

Meanwhile, combine pesto sauce and cream in a small saucepan. Bring to a boil. Cook 2 minutes or until reduced and slightly thickened. Serve pesto sauce over chicken.

SERVES 6

Becky Harobin

Crockpot Chicken Chili

2 (15 ounce) cans great Northern white beans, drained
2 (15 ounce) cans black beans, drained
4 boneless, skinless chicken breasts
1 (16 ounce) jar spicy salsa
1 (14 ounce) can diced tomatoes
1 (8 ounce) package shredded Mexican cheese
Salt and pepper to taste
Chili powder to taste

Place all beans in the bottom of a crockpot. Place raw chicken breasts on beans. Pour salsa and tomatoes over chicken. Cook on high for 4 to 6 hours.

When chicken is cooked through, use 2 forks to shred meat. Sprinkle cheese over chili and cover crockpot until cheese melts. Season with salt and pepper and chili powder. Serve with rice and sour cream.

SERVES 6

Emily Heleniak

CHICKEN ENCHILADAS

2 whole boneless, skinless chicken breasts, cooked and chopped
1 (10¾ ounce) can condensed cream of mushroom soup
1 (4 ounce) can chopped green chiles
¼ cup sour cream
8 ounces Cheddar cheese, shredded
½ cup chopped scallion
1 package soft tortillas
1 (10 ounce) can green enchilada sauce (use another can of red if green is not available)
1 (10 ounce) can red enchilada sauce

Preheat oven to 350 degrees. Combine chicken, soup, chiles, sour cream, cheese and scallion. Spoon a generous amount of chicken mixture onto each tortilla and roll up. Place enchiladas in a 9x13 inch casserole dish. Pour each can of enchilada sauce over top. Bake for 30 minutes.

SERVES 8 TO 10

Jennifer Shirakawa

MY SON'S FAVORITE POST-FOOTBALL PRACTICE DINNER

Olive oil or olive oil spray for sautéing
½ small onion, chopped (optional)
1½ to 1¾ pounds chicken breast, cut into strips
¼ to ¾ teaspoon chili powder, depending on taste
¼ teaspoon paprika
Kosher salt and freshly ground black pepper to taste
4 large tortillas, white or whole wheat
¾ cup shredded Cheddar-Jack cheese
½ head iceberg lettuce, shredded
Salsa

Coat a skillet with olive oil. Add onion and sauté until translucent. Add chicken strips to pan and cook and stir until cooked through. Season with chili powder, paprika and salt and pepper while cooking. Portion chicken mixture onto each tortilla. Sprinkle with cheese. One at a time, microwave 20 to 30 seconds or until cheese melts. Top with lettuce and salsa. Wrap up and serve to your hungry athlete.

SERVES 4

Wendi Brandeis

(continued)

of me in them, and so they take me wherever they go, in much the same way your teachers from Germantown Academy are with you now—guiding your thoughts, guarding your character, and informing your intellect. This is what I love about GA. I'm sure this is one thing you love about GA. This is one thing that will never change."

Paul Savering,
Old Guard Luncheon, 2009

*A*large commodious school-house should be erected in said town, near the centre thereof, two rooms on the lower floor whereof should be for the use of English and High Dutch, or German Schools, and should be continued for that use, and no other, forever; and that there should be convenient dwellings built for the schoolmasters to reside in."

First Minutes December, 1759

LEMON-LIME BROWN SUGAR MARINADE
(FOR CHICKEN)

3 medium cloves garlic, crushed
1½ teaspoons salt
½ cup firmly packed brown sugar
3 tablespoons coarse grain
     mustard
¼ cup cider vinegar

Juice of 1 lime
Juice of ½ large lemon
6 tablespoons canola oil
Salt and pepper to taste
6 small boneless chicken breasts

Combine garlic, salt, sugar, mustard, vinegar, and citrus juices in a bowl and blend by hand. Whisk in oil and season with salt and pepper. Pour mixture over chicken in a zip-top plastic bag. Refrigerate overnight, turning occasionally.

When ready to cook, preheat a grill. Grill chicken about 4 minutes on each side.

SERVES 6   *Lisa Butler*

HAWAIIAN MARINADE
(FOR CHICKEN OR STEAK)

1 cup soy sauce
1 cup sugar
2 tablespoons shredded ginger
1 tablespoon sesame oil

6 cloves garlic, chopped
4 chicken breasts, rinsed
Pineapple rings for garnish

Combine all ingredients except chicken in a zip-top bag. Add chicken and marinate in refrigerator for about 12 hours.

When ready to cook, preheat oven to 350 degrees. Drain chicken and place in a baking dish. Bake for 25 minutes or until chicken is done. Garnish with pineapple rings.

SERVES 4   *Laurel Stack*

Chicken can also be grilled and sliced on top of a salad.

Mom's Marinade
(for Grilled Fish or Chicken)

1½ cups canola oil
¾ cup premium light soy sauce
¼ cup Worcestershire sauce
2 tablespoons powdered mustard
2 teaspoons salt

1 tablespoon ground black pepper
½ cup red wine vinegar
1½ teaspoons dried parsley
2 cloves garlic, crushed
⅓ cup lemon juice

Combine all ingredients in a blender or food processor and blend well. Marinate chicken in mixture overnight or marinate fish for 3 to 5 hours. While grilling, marinade can be reduced in a saucepan by gently boiling for 10 to 15 minutes. Drizzle reduction over meat to serve.

MAKES 4 CUPS MARINADE

Alison Rosenberg

Coriander Sauce (for Chicken)

1 tablespoon Worcestershire
   sauce
1 tablespoon ketchup
1 tablespoon honey

½ teaspoon Tabasco sauce
   (optional)
½ teaspoon ground coriander
6 chicken pieces, bone-in thighs
   work well

Combine all ingredients except chicken in a large zip-top plastic bag and shake well. Add chicken, reseal bag and toss to coat chicken with marinade. Refrigerate at least 2 hours or up to 24 hours, turning bag occasionally.

When ready to cook, preheat broiler. Remove chicken from marinade and arrange skin-side down in a foil-lined pan. Broil chicken about 5 inches from heat source for 4 to 5 minutes. Turn chicken and broil 4 to 5 minutes longer or until done. Remove chicken to a platter and keep warm. Add 2 tablespoons water to pan and stir to dissolve or loosen pan juices. Pour juices over chicken and serve.

SERVES 4

Caren Levin

Avocado, Tomato, Cilantro Salsa
(for Grilled Seafood or Steak)

2 tomatoes, chopped
2 avocados, peeled and
   chopped
1 red onion, chopped
1 mango, peeled and
   chopped (optional)
Juice of 1 lime
1 clove garlic, minced
Small handful chopped fresh
   cilantro
Splash of rum

Combine all ingredients.

MAKES 1½ CUPS

Serve with Orzo Feta Salad (page 85).

Peach Apple Sauce
(for Chicken or Pork)

2 peaches, peeled and chopped

1 Granny Smith apple, peeled and chopped

1 red apple, peeled and chopped

2 tablespoons lime juice

3½ tablespoons honey

½ cup chopped fresh cilantro

¼ teaspoon allspice or nutmeg

¼ teaspoon cinnamon

¼ teaspoon apricot preserves

Combine all ingredients in a small to medium saucepan. Cook until apples are soft and sauce is syrupy. Serve over chicken or pork.

S E R V E S   6   T O   8

Jo Ann Chalal Engleman

Classic Chicken Marinade

Juice of 6 lemons

½ cup virgin olive oil

⅓ cup Worcestershire sauce

2 tablespoons crushed garlic cloves

1 tablespoon salt

1 tablespoon chopped fresh rosemary

Whisk together all ingredients. Use as a marinade for chicken, pork loin and shrimp.

For best results, completely immerse meat in marinade for 24 hours, or freeze meat in marinade for later use.

M A K E S   1 ¼   C U P S

Cathy Black

Absolutely Fabulous Marinade

2 tablespoons Worcestershire sauce

½ cup Dijon mustard

¼ cup plus 2 tablespoons bourbon

¼ cup soy sauce

½ cup firmly packed brown sugar

⅓ cup chopped scallion (optional)

Mix all ingredients. Use as a marinade for beef, chicken, pork or shrimp.

S E R V E S   8   T O   1 0

Meredith Schoff

For pork, use pork tenderloin and marinate at least 2 hours.
Cook 20 minutes per pound at 350 degrees. Delicious!

ALL PURPOSE BASTING RECIPE

½ cup salad oil or olive oil
½ cup lemon juice or frozen
   lemonade concentrate
½ cup wine vinegar

¼ cup soy sauce
Salt and pepper to taste
Herbs of choice to taste

Combine all ingredients. Store in a covered jar in refrigerator. Brush on meat while grilling.

MAKES 1³/₄ CUPS

George Laedlein

MEMORABLE MARINADE

½ cup balsamic vinegar
½ cup soy sauce
1 cup olive oil
1 teaspoon dry mustard

1 teaspoon minced garlic
Black pepper to taste
2 sprigs fresh rosemary

Mix together all ingredients.

MAKES 2 CUPS

Beth Mulford

LONDON BROIL MARINADE

Juice of ½ lime
½ cup balsamic vinegar
2 tablespoons firmly packed
   brown sugar

2 tablespoons Worcestershire
   sauce
¼ cup soy sauce
4 to 5 cloves garlic, crushed
Garlic powder to taste

Combine all ingredients. Add meat to marinade. Marinate in refrigerator for at least 1 hour before grilling or broiling.

MAKES 1 CUP

Carol DeLucca

STEAK MARINADE

3 tablespoons vegetable oil
2 large shallots, finely
   chopped
2 large cloves garlic, minced
⅔ cup soy sauce
⅓ cup Worcestershire sauce
¼ cup chili sauce
¼ cup honey
¼ cup white wine vinegar
1 tablespoon grated ginger
2 teaspoons mustard
Freshly ground black pepper

Heat oil in a saucepan. Add shallot and garlic and simmer over low heat for 5 minutes or until tender. Add soy sauce, Worcestershire sauce, chili sauce, honey, vinegar, ginger, mustard and pepper and stir to mix. Simmer for 15 minutes, stirring occasionally. Marinate meat in mixture for at least 1½ hours, or overnight.

MAKES 2 CUPS

Kris Henry

Seafood Parmesan Sauce (for Fish)

2 pounds flounder, sole or
  cod fillets
1 cup sour cream
¼ cup freshly grated
  Parmesan cheese
1 tablespoon minced onion
1 tablespoon lemon juice
½ teaspoon garlic salt
Cayenne pepper to taste
¼ cup chopped fresh parsley
Paprika

Preheat oven to 375 degrees.
Place fillets in a 9x13 inch
casserole dish. Combine sour
cream, Parmesan cheese,
onion, lemon juice, garlic salt,
cayenne pepper and parsley
and spread over fish. Bake
for 10 to 15 minutes or until
fish flakes easily. Sprinkle with
paprika and serve.

SERVES 8

Will Newbold

Coconut Marinade

1 (13½ ounce) can lite coconut
  milk
¼ cup soy sauce
¼ cup teriyaki sauce
2 tablespoons sesame oil
Juice of 1 lime
1 tablespoon grated fresh ginger
1 tablespoon minced garlic
1 tablespoon cilantro
1½ pounds swordfish or tuna
  steaks, or scallops, rinsed and
  patted dry

Combine all ingredients except fish in a zip-top plastic bag. Add fish to bag
and marinate 20 to 30 minutes.

When ready to cook, preheat a grill to high. Grill fish 5 to 7 minutes on each
side or until done.

SERVES 4

Kris Henry

Mango-Avocado Chutney (for Fish)

1 avocado, chopped
1 mango, chopped
½ green chile pepper, diced
Juice of 1 lime
½ to 1 cup chopped fresh cilantro
Salt and pepper to taste

Toss avocado and mango in a bowl with chile pepper, lime juice and cilantro; mix well. Season with salt and pepper.

SERVES 4

Alice Bast

An easy and colorful crowd-pleaser that goes especially well with salmon.
However, you may find that it is so popular, you have to protect
it from sneaky snackers before dinner is ready.

Vegetables & Sides

*S*ince 1986, when GA's Upper School launched its Community Service Organization, it has been under the direction of Peter McVeigh 1760 . Lower School and Middle School students have enthusiastically joined in the efforts under the leadership of Julia Blumenreich and Emily Rubinfield 1760. GA students begin volunteering their time to the CSO from their first years at GA, with every student and faculty member bringing a wrapped gift for charity to the all-school Holiday Assembly. In 2009, CSO collected over 1,400 gifts! The children quickly learn that helping others has benefits on many levels. As one Middle School CSO student puts it: "I love CSO because it is a fun way to hang out with your friends while helping other people at the same time."

One hundred 4th and 5th graders meet weekly to help plan CSO activities in Lower School, which include the Thanksgiving Food Drive, benefitting 200 needy families in North Philadelphia, and the Martin Luther King Day of Service, where the students help make blankets for residents of local shelters, concoct casseroles for people in need, and raise money for charity via pretzel sales and bake sales. Lower School also raises money for Children's Hospital of Philadelphia, the Humane Society, Hurricane Katrina relief, and Alex's Lemonade Stand. Most importantly, the kids get to brainstorm on how to raise funds.

In Middle School, students love to work on Alex's Lemonade Stand sales, and Dress Down Day is a popular fundraiser. "GA Goes Green" reusable shopping bags raise money and help keep the environment free of plastic bags. Upper School students participate in activities as varied as hosting an appreciation dinner for the school's maintenance and service staff to organizing a canned food and clothing drive.

Off-campus, students donate their time to Habitat for Humanity and to serve meals at organizations such as St. John's Hospice and Neighborhood Rehab at Dignity Housing. Sports teams contribute, too, with teams "adopting" a charity, such as the girls' field hockey hosting a tournament that supports Ronald McDonald House and the boys' wrestling team work at Dignity Housing. In the past, Mr. McVeigh has pioneered weekend conferences on community service. They have included four conferences on hunger and homelessness, and have attracted 33 schools and more than 250 participants.

The habit of volunteering is one that can last a lifetime, and provide untold benefits to the giver as well as the recipient. As one Middle-Schooler puts it: "I love CSO, because by helping other people, you realize how fortunate you are."

GREEN BEAN AND POTATO SALAD

1 medium potato, peeled
½ pound fresh green beans, cut
  into 2 inch pieces
1 medium tomato, cubed
½ small red onion, sliced and
  separated into rings
2 tablespoons red wine vinegar

2 tablespoons olive oil
2 tablespoons minced fresh
  oregano, or 1 teaspoon dried
2 tablespoons minced fresh
  parsley
½ teaspoon salt

Place potato in a saucepan and cover with water. Bring to a boil and cook 15 minutes or until tender; drain, cool and cut into cubes. Meanwhile, place green beans in saucepan and cover with water. Cook beans, uncovered, for 6 to 8 minutes or until tender-crisp; drain and cool.

In a bowl, combine beans, potato, tomato and onion. In a jar with a tight-fitting lid, combine vinegar, oil, oregano, parsley and salt. Shake well to mix and pour over vegetables. Toss to coat.

SERVES 4   *Barbara Buckley*

BALSAMIC SUGAR BEANS

1 pound fresh string beans
3 tablespoons butter
2 tablespoons balsamic vinegar

3 tablespoons firmly packed light
  or dark brown sugar
Salt and pepper to taste

Snap off ends of beans and cut or break beans in half. Rinse beans in cold water. Place beans in a large pot and cover with cold water. Cook in boiling water for 15 minutes or until beans are done to taste. Drain beans and return to pot. Melt butter with vinegar and brown sugar on stovetop. Pour mixture over beans and mix well. Season with salt and pepper and transfer to a bowl to serve.

SERVES 4   *Marie B. Koals*

Adjust amounts of the sugar, butter and vinegar to taste or dietary needs.
The recipe easily doubles. It can be made ahead, refrigerated for a
few days and then heated in the microwave before serving.

Community Partnership School is a coeducational, nonsectarian, independent school located in the heart of Philadelphia. Currently in our fourth year, we are excited about the opportunity to be a part of the revitalization taking place here in inner-city Philadelphia. As we continue to grow, we are committed to serving more families, particularly those from households and neighborhoods that traditionally have not accessed independent schools, and crafting a program that effectively nurtures the hopes that loving parents and guardians naturally have for their children.

FRIED BEAN SPROUT SALAD

½ pound sliced bacon, cut into fourths

2 tablespoons minced garlic

1 pound bean sprouts, washed and drained

4 to 6 scallions including green ends, cut into ½ inch pieces

1 stalk broccoli, excluding florets, thinly sliced

¼ to ½ teaspoon soy sauce

¼ teaspoon salt

¼ teaspoon black pepper

Fry bacon in a large skillet over medium-high heat until crisp; remove with a slotted spoon and drain on paper towel. Add garlic to bacon grease in skillet and stir. Add bean sprouts and stir. Add scallion, broccoli slices and soy sauce. Sauté, stirring, for about 5 minutes. Season with salt and pepper. Add bacon and serve hot.

SERVES 4 TO 6

Susan McCune

CHICKPEA (CHOLE) CURRY

3 tablespoons oil

2 medium onions, finely diced

3 medium tomatoes, finely diced

2 green chiles, sliced

1 tablespoon julienned ginger

2 teaspoons Badshah brand Punjabi Chole masala

2 (15 ounce) cans chickpeas, drained and rinsed

2 cups water

1 tablespoon chopped cilantro leaves for garnish

Heat oil over medium heat in a deep, heavy pan. Add onion and sauté until golden brown. Add tomato and sauté until cooked and mixture resembles gravy. Add chiles, ginger and masala and cook and stir a couple minutes more. Carefully stir in chickpeas and 2 cups water so as to not mash chickpeas. Bring to a boil. Reduce heat to low and simmer, uncovered, until gravy is thick. Stir occasionally to make sure chickpeas do not stick to the bottom of pan. Serve with any rice (plain, jeera or pulao) or nan bread.

SERVES 6

Rajni Patel

UNCLE LAURENT'S FRENCH BEAN SALAD

2 tablespoons Dijon mustard

2 tablespoons red wine vinegar

6 tablespoons extra virgin olive oil

½ medium-size red onion, diced

1 (15 ounce) can chickpeas, drained

1 (15 ounce) can lentils, drained

Salt and pepper to taste

Mix mustard, vinegar and oil in order listed for a dressing; set aside.

Combine onion, chickpeas and lentils with dressing. Season with salt and pepper. Serve at room temperature. Flavors will develop further if not served until next day.

SERVES 4

Laura Blair

Can be served as a side dish or as a meal with crusty bread. This dish is vegan.

Spinach and Cheese Stuffed Tomatoes

6 small tomatoes
⅛ teaspoon salt, plus extra to season inside of tomatoes
⅛ teaspoon black pepper, plus extra to season inside of tomatoes
1 tablespoon olive oil

2 (10 ounce) packages fresh or frozen spinach
1 (6 ounce) package garlic and herb Boursin cheese
¼ cup chopped pecans, toasted
1 tablespoon chopped scallion
2 tablespoons chopped water chestnuts

Preheat oven to 350 degrees. Cut off top of each tomato and scoop out pulp. Invert tomatoes onto paper towels and drain for 10 minutes. Sprinkle inside of tomatoes with salt and pepper and arrange tomatoes in an 8 inch square baking pan.

Heat oil in a large skillet over medium heat. Add spinach and cook for 4 minutes; cool, drain and chop. Mix spinach with cheese, pecans, scallion and water chestnuts. Season with ⅛ teaspoon each salt and pepper. Spoon mixture into tomatoes. Bake for 15 minutes.

SERVES 6

Kris Henry

Roasted Cherry Tomatoes

1 teaspoon kosher salt
1 tablespoon olive oil
1 teaspoon dried herbs, such as basil, oregano or parsley
8 ounces cherry tomatoes, halved

Preheat oven to 350 degrees. Mix salt, oil and herbs in a bowl. Add cherry tomato halves and mix until well coated. Pour mixture onto a baking sheet. Bake for 30 minutes. Remove from oven and cool slightly before serving.

SERVES 4

Alice Biggs-Smith

Italian Green Beans

1 pound fresh green beans
½ teaspoon oregano
Salt and black pepper to taste
¼ cup red wine vinegar

¼ cup olive oil
5 cloves garlic, crushed
⅛ to ¼ cup shredded Locatelli cheese

Snap ends off beans. Cook beans until tender. Drain and immediately add remaining ingredients. Mix lightly. Refrigerate to cool. Serve at room temperature or chilled.

SERVES 6

Carol DeLucca

Do not substitute balsamic vinegar for the red wine vinegar.

TOMATO PIE

1 (9 inch) deep dish pie crust, baked and cooled

4 to 5 large tomatoes, peeled, seeded, drained and thickly sliced

2 to 3 scallions, chopped

Salt and pepper to taste

Several leaves basil, cut into strips with a scissors

Chopped fresh chives

1 cup shredded extra sharp Cheddar cheese

½ to ¾ cup light mayonnaise

Preheat oven to 350 degrees. Fill cooled pie crust with alternating layers of tomato slices, scallion, salt and pepper, basil and chives.

Combine cheese and mayonnaise and spread over top of pie. Bake for 30 minutes.

SERVES 6

Polly O'Brien

TOMATO CORN PIE

Crust

2 cups flour

1 tablespoon baking powder

¾ teaspoon salt

6 tablespoons chilled unsalted butter

¾ cup milk

Filling

⅓ cup mayonnaise

2 tablespoons lemon juice

1¾ pounds tomatoes, peeled and sliced

1½ cups fresh corn

2 tablespoons chopped fresh basil

1 tablespoon chopped fresh chives

1 teaspoon salt

¼ teaspoon black pepper

7 ounces Cheddar cheese, shredded

2 tablespoons melted butter

Preheat oven to 400 degrees. To make crust, whisk together flour, baking powder and salt. Blend in chilled butter with fingertips until mixture resembles coarse meal. Add milk and stir until dough forms a ball. Divide dough in half. Roll out one piece between 2 sheets of plastic wrap, then transfer to a 9 inch glass pie pan.

For filling, whisk together mayonnaise and lemon juice. Arrange half the tomato slices over pie crust. Sprinkle with half each of corn, basil, chives, salt and pepper. Repeat all layers. Top with 1 cup cheese. Pour mayonnaise mixture over all and sprinkle with remaining cheese.

Roll out remaining half of dough and place over pie. Cut vents in top of crust and brush with melted butter. Bake for 35 minutes or until crust is golden.

SERVES 8

Kris Henry

Can be made a day ahead and reheated at 350 degrees when ready to serve.

BROCCOLI SLAW

½ cup slivered almonds
2 to 3 heads broccoli, finely chopped
⅓ cup golden raisins

⅓ cup minced onion, Vidalia or other sweet onion preferred
5 slices bacon, cooked crisp and crumbled
8 to 16 ounces slaw dressing

Preheat oven to 350 degrees. Toast almonds in oven for 5 to 10 minutes; cool. Combine almonds with broccoli, raisins, onion and bacon in a large bowl. Add slaw dressing, starting with about 1 cup to coat and adding more dressing as needed. Serve immediately.

SERVES 6 TO 8

Stacy Palmer

BROCCOLI CHEESE CASSEROLE

2 pounds fresh broccoli, chopped and steamed until just crisp-tender
1 (10¾ ounce) can condensed cream of mushroom soup
1 medium onion, diced

1 pound shredded Cheddar cheese
2 large eggs
Salt and pepper to taste
1 sleeve round butter crackers, crushed

Preheat oven to 350 degrees. Combine all ingredients except crackers in a large bowl and mix well. Transfer mixture to a 9x13 inch glass dish and cover with foil.

Bake for 45 minutes. Remove foil and sprinkle with crushed crackers. Bake, uncovered, for 10 minutes longer. Remove from oven and let stand 10 minutes before serving.

SERVES 8

Rose Mary B. Hoy

For a lower fat, lower calorie version, low fat soup, low fat cheese and Egg Beaters can be used.

After several years of research and conversation, Head of School Jim Connor 1760 is proud to announce the creation of the "House System" in the Upper School. Beginning in 2007-08, this unique House System will incorporate the current advisor system (a group of 9-10 students working closely with one advisor, or homeroom teacher, for two years), into a larger system where a "House Head" oversees those advisories through each students' four-year academic period at GA. The main focus of this system is to increase the amount of individual attention for each student, offer more opportunities for student leadership and to give students a feeling of belonging to something a little smaller, and perhaps more intimate, than their grade or the entire Upper School can give them.

Dressing

¼ cup apple juice
¼ cup canola oil
½ teaspoon ground ginger
¼ teaspoon cinnamon
¼ teaspoon cardamom

Whisk together all dressing ingredients in a bowl.

Butternut Squash
with Wild Rice and Cranberries

3 cups peeled and cubed
   butternut squash
Oil
¼ cup maple syrup
Dash of cinnamon
2 cups cooked wild rice

2 cups cooked white rice
1 cup dried cranberries
½ cup raisins
1 cup chopped scallion
Dressing (recipe in sidebar)
Sliced almonds, toasted (optional)

Preheat oven to 400 degrees. Brush squash lightly with oil and place on a nonstick pan. Bake for 10 minutes. Drizzle syrup over squash and dust with cinnamon. Bake for 5 minutes longer; remove from oven and set aside.

In a medium bowl, combine rice, cranberries, raisins, scallion and dressing; mix well. Add squash and toss gently. Garnish with toasted almonds.

S E R V E S   8

Lisa Butler

Mom's Broccoli Casserole

2 tablespoons butter or margarine
2 tablespoons all-purpose flour
4 ounces cream cheese, softened
¼ cup milk
8 ounces blue cheese salad
   dressing

1 (32 ounce) package frozen
   broccoli cuts or florets,
   cooked and drained
½ cup crushed herb and garlic
   croutons

Preheat oven to 350 degrees. Melt butter in a large saucepan. Blend in flour and cream cheese. Stir in milk and salad dressing. Cook and stir over medium heat until mixture boils, adding more milk if mixture is too thick. Stir in broccoli. Transfer mixture to a lightly greased 1½ quart casserole dish. Top with crushed croutons. Bake for 30 minutes.

S E R V E S   10

Jessica Chadwin

ZUCCHINI ROUNDS

⅓ cup baking mix
¼ cup grated Parmesan cheese
⅛ teaspoon black pepper
2 large eggs, lightly beaten

2 cups peeled and shredded
  zucchini
2 tablespoons butter

Combine baking mix, cheese and pepper in a bowl. Add egg and mix until moistened. Fold in zucchini.

Melt butter in a large skillet. Spoon four 2 tablespoon portions of batter into skillet. Cook 2 to 3 minutes on each side or until brown. Repeat with remaining batter.

MAKES 12 ROUNDS   *Becky Harobin*

SUMMER SQUASH CASSEROLE

5 to 6 small yellow squash, sliced
  into rounds
1 medium onion, thinly sliced
6 to 8 ounces extra sharp Cheddar
  cheese, shredded
4 tablespoons flour

2 tablespoons sugar
3 pinches of salt and pepper
¼ teaspoon nutmeg
1½ cups heavy cream
Bread crumbs

Preheat oven to 325 degrees. In a greased 2 quart casserole dish, layer one-third each of squash, onion and cheese. Sprinkle with 2 tablespoons flour, 1 tablespoon sugar and a pinch each of salt and pepper. Repeat for second layer. For third layer, repeat squash, onion and cheese and top with salt, pepper and nutmeg. Pour cream over all and sprinkle bread crumbs on top. Bake, covered, for 1 hour, then uncover and bake 30 minutes longer or until browned.

SERVES 6 TO 8   *Tabb Champlin*

Do not substitute green squash for the yellow.

"*Volunteering is much more than just running events. It's becoming a true member of the community by attending Parents' Committee Meetings, Divisional Meetings, Meet the Teacher Nights, concerts, shows, athletic events, PC events... it makes your connection with the school so much more personal when you can walk in the hall-way and a teacher recognizes you, or a friend of your child says hello. That's when it really feels like a community.*"

Parent Volunteer

STUFFED SQUASH

2 cups sun-dried tomatoes
4 green squash
3 ounces black olives (oil-cured or kalamata), finely chopped
2 or 3 cloves garlic, finely chopped
1 tablespoon chopped fresh oregano
1 tablespoon chopped fresh basil
1 tablespoon chopped fresh coriander
Salt and pepper to taste
3 shallots, finely chopped
1 tablespoon olive oil
1 large egg, beaten
1 ounce Gruyère cheese, shredded

Preheat oven to 350 degrees. Soak tomatoes in hot water for 30 minutes. Slice squash in half lengthwise and discard seeds. Scoop out some pulp, leaving outer shell intact. Place pulp in a bowl. Drain and finely chop tomatoes and add to pulp along with olives, garlic, oregano, basil, coriander and salt and pepper. Mix well.

Cook shallot in oil until translucent. Add squash mixture and cook 5 to 8 minutes or until just tender; remove from heat and cool. Mix in egg.

Fill each squash shell with vegetable mixture. Arrange shells in a greased ovenproof dish. Top with cheese. Bake for 25 to 30 minutes. Serve on warm plates garnish with fresh herbs.

SERVES 8   *Micki and Bernard Vieille*

GRILLED CORN ON THE COB

½ cup mayonnaise
1 teaspoon ground cumin
1 teaspoon chili powder
1 teaspoon onion powder
1 teaspoon garlic powder
1 teaspoon hickory flavored sea salt
1 teaspoon smoked paprika
6 ears fresh corn, shucked

Preheat a grill over high heat. Combine all ingredients except corn. Brush mixture over corn. Grill 15 to 20 minutes or until browned, turning frequently.

SERVES 6   *Chris Hibbitts*

PORTABELLO MUSHROOMS STUFFED WITH WILD RICE

Mushrooms

8 medium portabello mushrooms caps
Vegetable oil
Salt and pepper to taste

Wild Rice Pilaf (recipe below)
Roasted Pepper Vinaigrette (see side bar)

Wild Rice Pilaf

3 cups plus ½ cup chicken or vegetable broth, divided
2 cups water
1 tablespoon salt
1½ cups dry wild rice
2 tablespoons vegetable oil
1 large onion, finely chopped
3 cloves garlic, finely chopped

1 cup white wine
2 teaspoons chopped fresh thyme, or 1 teaspoon dried
2 teaspoons chopped fresh rosemary, or 1 teaspoon dried
1 teaspoon black pepper
¼ cup chopped fresh parsley

Brush mushrooms with oil and season with salt and pepper. Broil mushrooms on both sides for 10 to 12 minutes or until golden brown; set aside.

Combine 3 cups broth and 2 cups water with salt in a large saucepan and bring to a boil. Add rice and simmer 1 ½ to 2 hours or until tender; drain well. Heat oil in a skillet. Add onion and sauté until softened. Add garlic and cook 1 minute. Add wine and cook until reduced by half. Stir in cooked wild rice, thyme, rosemary, pepper and remaining ½ cup broth. Simmer 15 minutes. Add parsley.

To assemble, spoon rice onto mushroom caps. Drizzle vinaigrette over stuffed mushrooms. Serve extra vinaigrette on the side.

SERVES 8

Cheryl Koons

ROASTED PEPPER VINAIGRETTE

5 roasted peppers, chopped
¼ to ½ red onion, chopped
8 cloves garlic, roasted and peeled
¼ cup sherry vinegar
1 ½ tablespoons honey
1 tablespoon Dijon mustard
Kosher salt and freshly ground black pepper
½ cup canola oil

Combine all ingredients except oil in a blender and process until smooth. With motor running, slowly add oil until emulsified.

Rice and vinaigrette can be made ahead.

EILEEN'S SPINACH SOUFFLÉ

1 (10 ounce) package frozen chopped spinach, cooked and drained
1 large egg
4 tablespoons butter
1¼ cups croutons or seasoned stuffing
1 (10¾ ounce) can condensed cream of mushroom soup
1 cup shredded sharp Cheddar cheese
¼ cup grated onion (optional)

Preheat oven to 350 degrees. Combine all ingredients and place in a 7x11 inch casserole dish. Bake for 30 minutes.

SERVES 12

Karen Gallagher

My sister Eileen's recipe is a must have at all of our family get-togethers. You'll love it!

CREAMED SPINACH

2 to 4 slices bacon
1 (10 ounce) package frozen chopped spinach
1 teaspoon vinegar
1 teaspoon sugar
1 to 2 tablespoons reserved bacon fat or butter
2 tablespoons sour cream
Salt and pepper to taste

Cook bacon until crisp; drain, reserving fat. In a 1½ quart saucepan, cook spinach as directed on package, drain. Crumble bacon into drained spinach in saucepan. Add vinegar, sugar, 1 to 2 tablespoons reserved bacon, and sour cream. Simmer until blended. Season with salt and pepper and serve.

SERVES 2 TO 4

Jennifer Shirakawa

ECUARDORIAN HUMITA (CORN CASSEROLE)

2 sticks butter
1 white onion, diced
4 large eggs
1 (2 pound) package frozen yellow corn, or fresh corn
6 slices Muenster cheese
4 slices American cheese
1 teaspoon salt
1 tablespoon sugar

Preheat oven to 350 degrees. Melt butter in a skillet. Add onion and sauté 3 to 4 minutes or until soft and translucent but not browned; set aside to cool.

Place eggs in a blender or food processor and blend. Gradually add corn and blend. Add sautéed onion with butter to mixture. Add cheeses, salt and sugar and blend until mixed. Transfer mixture to a greased 8 inch casserole dish with high sides. Cover with foil and bake for 35 to 40 minutes. Check for doneness with a toothpick. If toothpick comes out clean, remove foil and bake 5 to 10 minutes longer to allow top to brown. If not done, re-cover with foil and bake 5 to 10 minutes longer, then remove foil and bake 5 to 10 minutes to brown top.

SERVES 8 TO 10

Mabel C. Johnson

Place a sheet pan under the casserole while baking to catch overflow.

BAKED CAULIFLOWER

1 head cauliflower, cut into bite-size pieces
1 red onion, chopped
2 cups mayonnaise
1 cup Parmesan cheese
Salt and pepper to taste
Garlic powder to taste

Preheat oven to 350 degrees. Steam or microwave cauliflower. Spread cauliflower evenly in a round glass casserole dish. Mix onion, mayonnaise and cheese and spread evenly over cauliflower. Season with salt and pepper and garlic powder. Bake for 30 to 40 minutes.

SERVES 6

Stephanie Frost

CAULIFLOWER AND TOMATOES AU GRATIN

2 cups water
1¼ teaspoons salt, divided
1 head cauliflower, cut into pieces
5 tablespoons margarine, melted and cooled
1 cup shredded Swiss cheese
½ cup fine dry bread crumbs
½ teaspoon celery salt
⅛ teaspoon black pepper
3 medium tomatoes, sliced ½ inch thick

Preheat oven to 375 degrees. Bring water and 1 teaspoon salt to a boil in a large saucepan. Add cauliflower. Cover pan and return to a boil. Reduce heat and cook 10 minutes or until tender; drain and set aside.

Combine cooled margarine, cheese, bread crumbs, celery salt, remaining ¼ teaspoon salt and pepper. Sprinkle half of mixture over the bottom of a shallow 1 ½ quart baking dish or 9x13 inch pan. Arrange tomato slices on top. Spread cauliflower on top. Sprinkle remaining bread crumb mixture over vegetables. Bake for 20 minutes or until golden brown.

SERVES 8 TO 10

Laura Martin

CARROT SOUFFLÉ

2 cups puréed cooked carrot
2 teaspoons lemon juice
2 tablespoons minced scallion
1 stick butter, softened
¼ cup sugar
1 tablespoon flour
1 teaspoon salt
¼ teaspoon cinnamon
1 cup milk
3 large eggs, beaten

Preheat oven to 350 degrees. Combine all ingredients in a bowl and beat until smooth. Pour mixture into a greased 2 quart soufflé dish or casserole dish. Bake for 45 to 60 minutes or until the center is set.

SERVES 4 TO 6

Annamarie Geppert Hellebusch

Current Director of Admissions Barbara Serrill reminisces, "They never seemed to know what to do with the girls yet we were by no means left out, we were made to feel very special!" As a member of the Class of 1968, the first class to graduate with girls, Barbara recalls:

• In the fall of '61, only Lower School was located in Fort Washington.

• In the fall of '65, the Middle and Upper Schools moved from Germantown to Fort Washington; there were 17 girls and 40 boys in the Class of 1968.

• In the Lower School, the classes were coed; in the Middle and Upper Schools, all of classes were single sexed.

• `The first Holiday Program was held in the Dining Hall, which was really just a shell. The floor was dirt, and we wore both hats and mittens.

OVEN ROASTED PARMESAN VEGETABLES

1 medium to large zucchini, cut into bite-size pieces
1 medium to large yellow squash, cut into bite-size pieces
1 medium-size red bell pepper, cut into strips or pieces, or color of choice
1 onion, sliced
1 teaspoon salt
½ teaspoon black pepper
1 (14½ ounce) can petite diced tomatoes, slightly drained
⅓ cup Parmesan cheese, or to taste

Preheat oven to 375 degrees. Combine zucchini, squash, bell pepper, onion, salt and pepper in a lightly greased 9x13 inch baking dish. Add diced tomatoes, trying not to get too much juice in the pan. Mix well. Sprinkle cheese on top. Bake, uncovered, for 35 to 40 minutes, stirring occasionally.

SERVES 6 TO 8   *Michelle Wood*

ROASTED ASPARAGUS WITH GOAT CHEESE AND BACON

6 slices bacon
2 pounds asparagus, ends trimmed, peeled if large
3 tablespoons plus 2 teaspoons olive oil, divided
Salt and pepper to taste
1 (3½ to 4 ounce) package goat cheese, crumbled
2 teaspoons freshly squeezed lemon juice
1 teaspoon lemon zest

Preheat oven to 500 degrees. Cook bacon in a heavy skillet over medium heat until brown and crisp; drain on paper towel, then crumble.

Place asparagus on a baking sheet. Drizzle with 3 tablespoons olive oil, turning asparagus to coat. Sprinkle with salt and pepper. Roast 7 minutes or until asparagus is crisp-tender when pierced with a knife.

Arrange asparagus on a platter. Sprinkle with goat cheese and bacon. Drizzle remaining 2 teaspoons olive oil and lemon juice on top. Sprinkle with lemon zest.

SERVES 6   *Becky Harobin*

Sandy's Asparagus

1 pound asparagus
4 tablespoons butter, softened
1 tablespoon Dijon mustard
1 clove garlic, crushed

Frozen phyllo dough, thawed and
  cut into 2½ inch squares
Olive oil or melted butter

Preheat oven to 350 degrees. Blanch, steam or quickly grill asparagus on a grill pan; cool. Meanwhile, combine softened butter, mustard and garlic. Rub butter mixture over cooled asparagus.

Wrap 3 asparagus spears in dough squares, beginning and ending with a corner. Repeat with remaining asparagus. Brush olive oil over phyllo wraps. Bake for 15 minutes or until golden brown.

SERVES 10 TO 12   *Sandy Budinsky*

Sweet Potato Casserole

3 cups mashed cooked sweet
  potato
½ cup sugar
2 large eggs

1 teaspoon vanilla extract
½ cup milk
2 tablespoons butter

Topping

½ cup firmly packed light brown
  sugar
¼ cup flour

1 to 2 tablespoons butter,
  softened
⅓ cup chopped pecans (optional)

Preheat oven to 350 degrees. Combine all casserole ingredients in a blender and process until smooth. Pour mixture into a greased 9 inch square casserole dish.

For topping, mix brown sugar and flour. Cut in butter until mixture crumbles. Add pecans. Crumble topping over casserole. Bake for 45 minutes or until firm.

SERVES 6 TO 8   *Stacy Palmer*

(continued)

• The boys wore the traditional blue blazers we see today; yet, the girls wore red blazers.

• The girls wore uniform skirts and had to kneel on the floor to prove appropriate length.

• The girls and boys had separate class officers.

• Upper School Librarian Carolyn Baldi walked the halls, ringing a hand bell that indicated time for class change, as the Upper School did not have an intercom system.

• The cheerleaders were boys!

• There was an active Philomathean Society (debate club) where the girls actually debated the boys to prove their worthiness to the Society.

• Girls wore dresses for dances; the prom was in the Dining Hall.

• Girls wore white dresses and carried daisies at graduation.

(continued on next page)

(continued)

- The girls performed a variety show at the Father/Daughter dinner held at the Germantown Cricket Club.
- During morning chapel, the students sang the "Doxology" and repeated the "Nicene Creed."
- Students played tennis at the Stroud's residence on their backyard court.
- They never seemed to know what to do with the girls yet we were by no means left out, we were made to feel very special!

GRILLED EGGPLANT

2 eggplants
1 cup olive oil
1 tablespoon garlic powder
1 teaspoon seasoned salt
2 tablespoons Parmesan cheese
Black pepper to taste
Pinch of kosher salt

Preheat a grill. Cut eggplant into ¼ to ½ inch slices. Combine all remaining ingredients. Brush mixture over both sides of eggplant slices. Grill over medium heat for 3 to 4 minutes per side or until crispy.

SERVES 4 TO 6   *Tara Schwartz*

ALOO GOBHI VEGETABLE

½ inch ginger, shredded
1 tablespoon ground coriander
¼ teaspoon ground turmeric
¼ teaspoon cayenne pepper
5 tablespoons water, divided
3 tablespoons oil
Pinch of asafoetida (optional)
½ teaspoon cumin seeds
2 bay leaves
2 green chiles, cut into long slices
2 cups cauliflower small florets
2 medium potatoes, cut into bite-size cubes
1 teaspoon salt, or to taste
1 teaspoon mango powder (optional) or ½ teaspoon lemon juice
2 tablespoons chopped fresh cilantro

Combine ginger, coriander, turmeric, cayenne pepper and 3 tablespoons water to make a paste; set aside. Heat oil in a large pan. When hot, add asafoetida and cumin seeds. When seeds start to crackle, add bay leaves and chiles and stir a few seconds. Add spice paste and stir over heat for a minute or until spices and oil separate. Add cauliflower, potato, remaining 2 tablespoons water and salt and mix well. Cover pan and cook over medium heat for 15 to 20 minutes or until vegetables are tender. Gently stir every 3 to 4 minutes while cooking. Mix in mango powder and cilantro. Cover and cook for a minute. Adjust salt to taste. Serve hot with Roti/Nan bread and rice.

SERVES 4 TO 6   *Rini Shah*

For extra color and nutrients, try adding some green peas and/or sliced red bell pepper; the bell pepper should be added at the end of the recipe as they cook quickly.

SWEET POTATO, WHITE BEAN AND PEPPER TIAN

3 medium to large sweet potatoes, peeled

1 (14 ounce) can small white beans, rinsed and drained

1 red bell pepper, cut into 1 inch chunks

1 green bell pepper, cut into 1 inch chunks

1 medium-size red onion, cut into 2 inch chunks and sections separated

2 plum tomatoes, cut into 1½ inch chunks

3 cloves garlic, thinly sliced

½ teaspoon salt

Generous amount of freshly ground black pepper

⅓ cup olive oil

Topping

3 slices home-style white bread

1 tablespoon olive oil

Preheat oven to 375 degrees. Quarter sweet potatoes lengthwise, then slice into ¼ inch thick pieces. Combine sweet potato, beans, bell peppers, onion, tomato, garlic, salt, pepper and olive oil in a large bowl. Toss well. Pack mixture into a 2½ to 3 quart shallow baking dish and flatten top surface. Bake for 45 minutes.

For topping, tear bread into pieces and place in a food processor. Process into crumbs. Transfer crumbs to a bowl. Drizzle with oil and rub oil into crumbs with fingertips until evenly moistened.

Spread topping over baked tian. Return to oven and bake 15 minutes longer or until topping is golden. Remove from oven and let stand 10 minutes before serving.

SERVES 4   *Trish Reger*

CAN YOU BELIEVE?

At the first coed graduation in June of 1968, a male student was announced as valedictorian and delivered the commencement address. A few days prior to graduation, GA's headmaster informed Barbara Serrill's parents that Barbara was the true valedictorian. No one had thought to consider the grades of the female students in determining the student with the highest academic achievement.

William Kershaw led GA for
36 years as Headmaster and was
recognized for increasing the
school's student body from
11 boys to 300 boys in 1903.

ELEGANT APRICOT SWEET POTATOES

6 medium sweet potatoes, peeled and cooked

½ pound dried apricots, cooked and drained, cooking liquid reserved

1 cup lightly packed brown sugar

3 tablespoons butter or margarine, melted

2 teaspoons orange juice

1 teaspoon orange zest

¼ cup pecan halves

Preheat oven to 350 degrees. Cut potatoes into ½ inch lengthwise slices. Arrange a single layer of potato slices in a lightly greased shallow 9x13 inch glass casserole dish. Scatter half of apricots over potato slices. Sprinkle with half of brown sugar. Repeat layers.

Combine butter, orange juice, orange zest and ¼ cup reserved apricot cooking liquid. Pour mixture over layers. Bake for 40 minutes, basting twice while cooking. Arrange pecan halves on top. Bake 5 minutes longer.

SERVES 6 TO 8   *Jo Ann Chalal Engleman*

"HAVE A PARTY" POTATOES

8 to 10 potatoes, peeled and cooked

8 ounces cream cheese, softened

8 ounces sour cream

3 tablespoons chopped chives, fresh preferred

Salt and pepper to taste

Butter

1 cup shredded Cheddar cheese

Preheat oven to 325 degrees. Mash potatoes until smooth. Blend cream cheese and sour cream by hand in a small bowl. Add mixture to potatoes and beat by hand until thoroughly blended. Stir in chives and season with salt and pepper.

Transfer mixture to a casserole dish. Dot with butter and sprinkle with cheese. Bake for 1 hour.

SERVES 8 TO 10   *David Oberkircher*

*Potatoes can be prepared a day ahead. Once transferred
to casserole dish, cover potatoes and refrigerate until ready to cook.
Remove from refrigerator 1 hour before baking.*

PATIO POTATOES

1 stick butter, divided

1 (10¾ ounce) can condensed
    cream of chicken soup

16 ounces sour cream

⅓ cup chopped scallion

1½ cups shredded Cheddar
    cheese

2 pounds frozen shredded hash
    brown potatoes, thawed

1½ cups crushed corn flakes

Preheat oven to 350 degrees. Heat 4 tablespoons butter with soup until blended. Mix in sour cream, scallion and cheese. Add potatoes and mix lightly. Spoon mixture into a 9x13 inch casserole dish.

Melt remaining 4 tablespoons butter and mix with crushed corn flakes. Spread mixture over top of potatoes. Bake for 40 minutes or until bubbling.

SERVES 10

Eileen Guers

POTATO, TOMATO, ZUCCHINI GALETTE

1 large onion, sliced

1 tablespoon olive oil, plus extra
    for drizzling

1 to 2 cloves garlic, chopped

2 to 3 large Yukon Gold potatoes,
    peeled and sliced ⅛ inch thick

2 large tomatoes, thinly sliced

2 zucchini, thinly sliced

Salt and pepper to taste

1 tablespoon rosemary

4 ounces Gruyère cheese,
    shredded

Preheat oven to 350 degrees. Sauté onion in 1 tablespoon oil for 7 minutes or until soft. Add garlic and sauté 2 minutes. Spread sautéed mixture on a greased 12 to 14 inch ovenproof platter. Starting on edge of platter, arrange potato, tomato and zucchini slices in an alternating pattern, spiraling to the center. Drizzle with olive oil and season with salt and pepper and rosemary. Sprinkle cheese on top. Bake for 30 to 40 minutes or until potatoes are fork-tender.

SERVES 8

Katelyn Koons

GREEK POTATO

4 large russet potatoes

2 (10 ounce) packages
    frozen chopped spinach,
    thawed and squeezed
    dry

4 ounces crumbled feta
    cheese

Salt and pepper to taste

Preheat oven to 425 degrees. Bake potatoes for 50 to 60 minutes or until tender. Cut potatoes in half lengthwise. Scoop potato pulp into a bowl, leaving shells intact. Add spinach and cheese to pulp. Season with salt and pepper and mix. Spoon filling mixture into potato shells. Bake for 10 minutes.

SERVES 4

Kirsten Karr

*Use a mandoline for slicing potatoes, tomatoes and zucchini.
Thyme can be substituted for the rosemary. Instead of Gruyère,
substitute cheese of your choice.*

Armenian Rice Pilaf

3 tablespoons butter, plus
    extra for coating skillet
1½ cups fine egg noodles
1 cup Carolina rice
2½ cups water
1½ teaspoons salt

Coat bottom of a skillet with
butter over medium heat.
Add noodles to skillet and
sauté until golden brown.
Add rice, water, salt and 3
tablespoons butter. Bring to
a boil. Stir well, reduce heat
to low and cover. Simmer 20
minutes.

S E R V E S 4

*Carol Momjian and
Michael Hanamarian*

Refrigerator Mashed Potatoes

5 pounds red bliss potatoes,
    peeled and quartered
6 ounces cream cheese
8 ounces sour cream

1 to 2 teaspoons salt, or to taste
¼ teaspoon black pepper
2 tablespoons butter, plus extra
    for dotting

Cook potatoes in boiling salted water until tender; drain well. Mash potatoes until smooth with a mixer. Add cream cheese, sour cream, salt, pepper
and butter and beat until smooth and fluffy. Spoon potato mixture into a
greased 2½ quart casserole dish. If preparing ahead, cover and refrigerate
up to 2 weeks, or freeze.

When ready to bake, preheat oven to 350 degrees. Dot top of potatoes
with butter. Bake, covered, for 30 minutes.

S E R V E S 1 0 T O 1 2   *Jill Hotte*

Scalloped Potatoes with Fennel

3 to 4 tablespoons butter, melted,
    divided
3 pounds gold potatoes, peeled
    and thinly sliced
2 large bulbs fennel, sliced
2½ cups chicken broth

2½ cups cream
2 tablespoons flour
2 cloves garlic, minced
2 teaspoons salt
Black pepper to taste
½ teaspoon nutmeg

Preheat oven to 400 degrees. Use 1 tablespoon melted butter to coat a
9x13 inch baking dish. Arrange half each of potato and fennel slices in dish.
Combine broth, cream, flour, garlic, salt and pepper in a bowl. Pour half of
broth mixture over slices. Add remaining potato and fennel slices and top
with remaining broth mixture. Drizzle remaining melted butter over all and
sprinkle with nutmeg. Bake for 1 hour or until potato and fennel are fork-
tender.

S E R V E S 6 T O 8   *Donna Dreier*

*The fennel is not necessarily discerned but
gives this comfort food dish a bright, fresh taste!*

PULAO RICE

1 cup basmati rice
1 tablespoon ghee (clarified
    butter)
2 cloves
1 cinnamon stick
½ teaspoon cumin seeds

8 cashews or almonds
2 to 3 curry leaves (optional)
1 cup frozen mixed vegetables
1 teaspoon salt
1 teaspoon Rajah tandoori marsala
2 cups water

Rinse rice with cold water and allow to soak in cold water for 15 minutes. Place a heavy saucepan over medium heat. Add ghee. Once ghee is hot but not smoking (to tell if temperature is right, add a couple cumin seeds and if they sizzle, the ghee is ready), add cloves, cinnamon stick and cumin seeds. Wait about 10 seconds and then add cashews and curry leaves. Stir and wait a few seconds before adding mixed vegetables. Stir and add salt. Cook and stir 1 minute or until there is no moisture. Stir in Marsala. Drain rice and add to saucepan. Cook and stir for 1 minute. Add 2 cups water and adjust seasoning as needed. Bring to a boil. Reduce heat to low, cover with a tight fitting lid and cook for 15 minutes. Stir gently and check for doneness and if all water is absorbed. If rice is not tender and there is no water, add a little hot or boiling water; do not use cold water. If rice is cooked and there is still a lot of moisture, cook uncovered until all water is absorbed. Serve with chole, bharatha or raita.

SERVES 4

Raju Patel

RICE PILAF

9 tablespoons butter, divided
1 cup dry long grain and wild
    rice mix
2½ cups chicken broth
Salt to taste
¾ cup pine nuts

Melt 5 tablespoons butter in a medium saucepan. Add rice and cook until slightly browned. Add broth and salt and bring to a boil. Reduce heat, cover and simmer for 20 minutes.

When ready to serve, melt 4 tablespoons butter in a skillet. Add pine nuts and sauté until light brown. Add pine nuts to top of rice.

SERVES 4

Pauline Papadakes

The amount of water the rice needs depends on the variety and age of the rice grain. Usual measurements are 2 cups water to 1 cup rice. If you know that the rice you are using uses more or less water, adjust water amount accordingly.

A Look At 7th Grade, 2009

Williamsburg Trip

Picture Books for History

To the Edge of the World, Fahrenheit 451, Miracle Worker, 12 Angry Men

CPS Trip

Independent Research Project

TAPAS Tuesday

Salsa Contest

French Café

Dia Delos Muertos

Drug Education

Miam Miam Monday

Speech Poems

LS Buddies

JEERA RICE

8 cups water
1 cup basmati rice
1 teaspoon salt
2 teaspoons oil
2 teaspoons ghee (clarified butter)

1 teaspoon cumin seeds
1 teaspoon garam masala
1 small onion, thinly sliced lengthwise

Bring 8 cups water to a boil in a saucepan. Rinse rice in cold water; drain. Add rice, salt, and oil to boiling water. Stir and return to a boil. Cook until rice is tender and so each grain is separate; do not overcook. Drain rice well in a colander. Remove rice to a serving dish.

In a small pan, heat ghee. Add cumin seeds and remove from heat. Stir in garam masala. Pour mixture over rice. Using a flat wooden spatula, stir until spices are evenly mixed through the rice. Serve with chole, bharatha or raita.

SERVES 4

Rajni Patel

NEVER FAIL RICE

This is not really a recipe but a navigation chart. You will need a heavy pot with a tight-fitting cover such as a Le Creuset small Dutch oven. Melt enough butter in the Dutch oven to well coat the amount of raw natural rice being used.

The ratio of rice to liquid is one part rice to a scant two parts liquid. So if cooking for two, a half cup rice to about a cup of liquid (water, chicken broth or white wine, or a combination of all three!) When the rice is coated with butter, add salt and pepper to taste (an option some finely chopped shallot would go amiss.)

Bring the above concoction and the appropriate amount of liquid to a boil; put on the lid and lower temperature to near or at simmer. Check in about 15 minutes to see if liquid has been absorbed; sometimes it takes 17 minutes.

Transfer rice to a double-boiler to keep hot, or put rice in a microwave-safe casserole dish with a cover. The latter is good for advanced preparation and can be heated in the microwave with a sufficient amount of water to serve the rice piping hot.

Here, I might add that this mixture can easily support leftover vegetables and some meats like chicken or shrimp.

Edwin Probert

PEARLS AND RUBIES

1 teaspoon butter
1½ cups fresh or frozen pearl
   onions
¼ cup sugar

¼ teaspoon salt
½ teaspoon black pepper
1 cup cranberries
¼ cup chicken broth

Preheat oven to 400 degrees. Melt butter in a large skillet. Add onions and sauté until brown. Remove from heat. Sprinkle with sugar, salt and pepper. Add cranberries and toss to mix. Spoon mixture into an ovenproof dish. Bake for 30 minutes.

SERVES 4

Jennifer Gobora

SAFFRON STEAMED BASMATI RICE

9 cups cold water, divided
2 tablespoons salt
3 cups long-grain white basmati
   rice
⅛ teaspoon ground saffron

1 tablespoon hot water
¾ cup vegetable oil or butter,
   divided
2 tablespoons plain yogurt
½ cup lukewarm water

Bring 8 cups cold water and salt to a boil in a large nonstick pot. Add rice and boil for 10 minutes. Once the rice rises to the top, it is done. Drain rice into a large fine mesh strainer and rinse with warm water.

Dissolve saffron in 1 tablespoon hot water. Whisk together ½ cup oil, 2 spatulas full of rice, yogurt, ½ cup lukewarm water and 1 tablespoon saffron water. Spread mixture over the bottom of the pot used for cooking rice. One spatula full at a time, gently mound the remaining rice into the pot, shaping it like a pyramid to leave room for expansion of the rice. Cover pot and cook for 10 minutes over medium heat.

Mix 1 cup cold water with remaining ¼ cup oil and pour over rice. Place a clean towel over pot to absorb condensation and cover with a lid. Reduce heat to low and cook 50 minutes longer. Remove pot from heat and serve.

SERVES 6

Roya Azizi

*While the rice is boiling, stir with a wooden spoon to loosen any
grains that stick to the bottom of the pot. The yogurt and saffron
mixture will form a golden crust at the bottom of the pot.*

The library in the old building on Schoolhouse Lane in Germantown was the gift of Judge and Mrs. Francis Shunk Brown, Jr., in memory of their son Lt. Maxwell McKeen Brown '40, who leading his platoon in the Battle of the Bulge, was killed by machine gun fire. There were plans to have a new memorial to this hero, whose ancestors were three governors of Pennsylvania, when the campus relocated to Fort Washington. Unfortunately, these plans were abandoned. When Edwin Lavino heard about the plans to abandon the memorial he arranged, at his own expense, for the design and construction of a beautiful alcove in the present Upper School Library. This is now the Maxwell McKeen Brown Memorial. This is known to the students as the Brown Alcove.

CRANBERRY RELISH

1 pound whole cranberries
4 apples, unpeeled and sliced
½ orange, quartered with
    peel intact
1 pound sugar (2½ cups)
1 (20 ounce) can crushed
    pineapple
Juice of 1½ oranges

Combine cranberries, apple and orange quarters in a food chopper and process. Add sugar, pineapple and orange juice and blend. Refrigerate 3 to 5 days before serving.

SERVES 24

Christine McDade

Use an old-fashioned hand crank food chopper or the Kitchen Aid food chopper attachment; use a coarse grind. Most electric food processors create too fine a grind to get the right flavor development.

BARLEY CASSEROLE

4 tablespoons butter
2 medium onions, coarsely
    chopped
12 ounces fresh mushrooms,
    chopped
¾ cup dry pearl barley
3 pimentos, chopped (optional)
2 to 3 cups chicken broth

Preheat oven to 350 degrees. Melt butter in a saucepan. Stir in onion and cook until golden brown. Add mushrooms and cook until tender. Add barley and cook until lightly browned; do not burn. Transfer mixture to a greased 2 quart casserole dish. Add pimentos and 2 cups broth.

Bake, covered, for 50 to 60 minutes or until liquid is absorbed and barley is tender. If mixture seems too dry while cooking, add more broth.

SERVES 6

Mary Anne Burton
Rick Weber

SPANISH GREEN PLANTAINS

3 to 4 green plantains
½ cup corn oil
Salt to taste

Peel off skin of plantains by cutting off both ends. Slide a dull knife down along the back lengthwise, then peel off entire skin. Cut plantains into ½ inch thick slices on an angle. Soak slices in salt water for about 1 hour, then pat dry.

Heat oil to 350 degrees in a medium skillet. Fry plantain slices in oil until golden brown on each side; drain and cool on paper towel. Flatten plantains to about ⅛ inch thick with a paper bag. Return to oil and fry until brown. Pat dry with paper towel. Serve with dipping sauce.

Dipping Sauce

4 to 6 cloves garlic, mashed
Olive oil to taste
2 teaspoons salt, or to taste

Combine all sauce ingredients. Serve sauce with plantains.

SERVES 4 TO 6

Alma Torres

Plantains can usually be found in the produce area of most grocery stores.

APPLE NOODLE KUGEL

1 pound egg noodles
10 tablespoons margarine or
     butter, plus extra for dotting
     on top
4 large eggs, lightly beaten
½ cup sugar

1 scant teaspoon cinnamon, plus
     extra for topping
1 teaspoon vanilla extract
½ cup orange juice
2 large apples, peeled and sliced
Frosted corn flakes, crushed, or
     other sugared cereal

Preheat oven to 350 degrees. Cook noodles in boiling water about 8 min-utes; drain and return to pan on stovetop. Stir margarine into hot noodles until melted. Add egg, sugar, cinnamon, vanilla and orange juice. Stir well. Add apple slices.

Pour mixture into a greased 9x13 inch pan. Cover with crushed cereal. Sprinkle with cinnamon and dot with margarine. Bake in center of oven for 1 hour or until brown.

SERVES 10 TO 12   *Cari Lasdon*

SYLVIA'S GARLIC KUGEL

1 pound medium egg noodles
6 large eggs
2 sticks butter, melted and cool to
     room temperature

1 large onion, grated
2 cloves garlic, pressed
Salt and pepper to taste

Preheat oven to 350 degrees. Cook noodles in boiling water until tender; drain and rinse with cool water. Meanwhile, beat eggs in a bowl. Beat in cooled butter, onion and garlic. Mix in cooled noodles. Season with salt and pepper. Transfer mixture to a 9x13 inch baking pan. Bake for 45 min-utes. Cut into pieces to serve.

SERVES 12 TO 16 SERVINGS   *Jamie Aronow*

Kugel can also be baked in large muffin tins.

I believe that the presence of all grades in a House will allow younger and older students to mix naturally on a regular basis as they do now in the arts and athletics. Students will stay in one House for their four years, which will ensure greater "continuity of care" and simplify who oversees each student's progress. The House Head will provide one-stop shopping for most concerns. We are very excited about the inaugural start of this system.

PINEAPPLE STUFFING

2 sticks butter, softened
1¼ cups sugar
2 large eggs
1 (20 ounce) can pineapple chunks, undrained
½ cup half & half
1 large loaf white bread, cut into cubes

Preheat oven to 350 degrees. Cream butter and sugar together. Add eggs. Fold in pineapple with juice and half & half. Mix in bread cubes. Place mixture in a greased 9x13 inch casserole dish. Bake, uncovered, for 1 hour.

SERVES 10

Linda Logan

APPLES STUFFED WITH DRIED FRUITS

2 ounces dried figs, chopped
2 ounces dried apricots, chopped
2 ounces dried prunes, chopped
2 ounces raisins, chopped
2 ounces walnuts or pecans, chopped
2 ounces almonds, chopped
2 ounces pine nuts, chopped
Juice of 1 lime
Juice of 1 orange
1 tablespoon Kirsch
6 apples (Golden Delicious work well)
Melted butter

Combine all chopped fruit in a bowl with lime juice, orange juice and Kirsch. If fruit is too dry, extra lime or orange juice can be added. Let mixture stand for 24 hours.

When ready to bake, preheat oven to 375 degrees. Core apples. Fill apples with macerated fruit mixture and arrange in a baking dish that can tightly hold the apples. Brush melted butter over top of apples. Bake for 1 hour.

SERVES 6

Micki and Bernard Vieille

Desserts

With names ranging from Alcott to Washington, Germantown Academy's Upper School "House System" honors distinguished trustees, parents, alumni, headmasters and teachers, and United States leaders who have impacted GA history. The Seven Houses, established in 2007 by Head of School James W. Connor 1760, are comprised of eight advisories with approximately 70 students, including two student prefects who help run each House. The Houses meet once a week and participate in various activities/competitions throughout the year, including the popular House Olympics and the Knowledge Bowl.

A. Bronson Alcott was hired in 1831 as part of a push to create a co-ed grade school at the then all-male GA; his daughter, *Little Women* novelist Louisa May Alcott, was born the following year. Unfortunately, the co-ed experiment didn't work out, but Alcott is credited for being a pioneer in its conception. **Joseph Galloway**, a founding trustee, was Benjamin Franklin's lawyer, and speaker of the Pennsylvania Assembly. **William W. Kershaw** served as GA head of school for 38 years, from 1877 to 1915, helped start the Inter-Ac, and founded GA's Alumni Society.

Headmaster **Samuel Osbourn** succeeded Kershaw, and his 30-plus-year tenure was nearly as long as his predecessor's. Osbourn was progressive and forward-looking, and is credited with renovating the campus, including its main building, the gym, and the elementary school, and with overseeing the establishment of GA's endowment, thereby opening up enrollment to a more diverse student body. GA's planned giving society is named for Osbourn.

Supreme Court Justice **Owen J. Roberts**, who graduated from GA in 1891, was known as The Fighting Welshman for his insistence on justice and exposing scandal. He was the youngest of the justices when President Herbert Hoover nominated him to the bench in 1930, and in 1941, helped President Roosevelt investigate the attack on Pearl Harbor; he's credited with helping unify efforts by the U.S. Armed Forces in World War II. Roberts also headed Philadelphia's chapter of the United Negro College Fund in the 1940s.

Wallace S. Truesdell was a beloved teacher of classics at GA from 1891 to 1925. And the seventh GA house is named for **George Washington**, whose stepson attended GA and was among its first graduates. As President, Washington was based in Philadelphia, and in 1793 fled a yellow fever epidemic in the city for the healthier climate of Germantown, where he rented a house built by GA's headmaster James Dove. Later, the school acquired the building, and named it Washington-Kershaw Hall.

PECAN PIE BARS

Crust

1⅓ cups all-purpose flour
⅓ cup firmly packed brown sugar

1½ sticks butter

Filling

1 cup firmly packed brown sugar
4 large eggs
1 cup dark corn syrup
4 tablespoons butter, melted

1 teaspoon vanilla extract
⅛ teaspoon salt
2 cups chopped pecans

Preheat oven to 350 degrees. Combine flour and brown sugar. Cut in butter with a pastry blender until crumbly. Press mixture into a greased 9x13 inch baking pan. Bake for 15 to 17 minutes.

Combine all filling ingredients except pecans and stir well. Mix in pecans. Pour filling into crust. Bake for 35 minutes or until set. Cool in pan on a rack before cutting into bars.

MAKES 2½ DOZEN   *Stacy Palmer*

SEVEN LAYER BARS

1½ cups graham cracker crumbs
1 stick butter, melted
1 (12 ounce) package semisweet
    chocolate chips
1 cup golden raisins
1 cup flaked sweetened coconut

1½ cups chopped walnuts
1 (11 ounce) package butterscotch
    chips
1 (14 ounce) can sweetened
    condensed milk

Preheat oven to 350 degrees. Mix cracker crumbs and melted butter. Press mixture into the bottom only of a well greased 7x11x2 inch baking pan. Layer half the chocolate chips, raisins, coconut, walnuts, butterscotch chips and remaining chocolate chips in order listed. Pour condensed milk over the top. Use a knife to make a few wells in the layers to allow the milk to penetrate.

Bake for 30 minutes or until the top is brown and it appears firm. It is almost impossible to overbake these and it is always better to overbake than underbake these bars. Cool, then refrigerate, preferably overnight. Remove from pan and cut into small bars.

MAKES 20 TO 24 BARS   *Jocelyn Hillman*

Dr. William "Pop" Kershaw reigned as Headmaster from 1877 until 1915. Under his leadership enrollment climbed from 11 students in 1876 to 300 in 1903. Activities were born that are still vital today—The Academy Monthly began in 1884; Alumni Society organized in 1886; Inter-Ac League started in 1887; Belfry Club, the oldest continuous existing dramatic club in the country, began 1894; Ye Primer, the senior yearbook, first was issued in 1895.

The Student Senate is comprised of sixteen hard working, dedicated, and responsible students—two from each of the fourth and fifth grade classes—who are elected by their classmates each autumn. They meet once a week during lunch to take a leadership role on issues and initiatives relevant to the life of Lower School students. A few of the annual highlights are: running the UNICEF campaign (especially counting the money), periodically sorting and displaying the Lost and Found items (a daunting task), promoting a Relax and Read Week in April (there's a new commemorative bookmark every year), organizing and hosting the annual Variety

CRUMBLE BARS

2 sticks butter, softened
2 cups flour
½ cup sugar
¼ teaspoon salt

1 (12 ounce) package chocolate chips, divided
1 (14 ounce) can sweetened condensed milk
1 teaspoon vanilla extract

Preheat oven to 350 degrees. Combine butter, flour, sugar and salt and mix by hand until crumbly. Press all but ½ cup of mixture into the bottom of a greased 9x12 inch baking dish. Bake for 10 minutes.

In a glass bowl, combine three-fourths of chocolate chips and condensed milk. Microwave on high for 1 minute. Add vanilla and stir until smooth. Pour mixture over baked crust. Crumble reserved dough mixture over chocolate layer and sprinkle with remaining chocolate chips. Bake for 20 minutes longer.

MAKES 20 TO 24 BARS   *Shawn Towne*

RASPBERRY BARS

2½ cups flour
1 cup sugar
1 cup chopped pecans
2 sticks butter, softened

1 large egg
10 ounces seedless raspberry preserves (¾ cup)

Preheat oven to 350 degrees. In a large mixing bowl, combine all ingredients except raspberry preserves. Beat with an electric mixer on low speed until well mixed. Reserve 1½ cups of mixture. With floured fingertips, press remaining mixture into the bottom of a 10 inch square pan.

Spread preserves to within ½ inch of sides. Crumble reserved mixture over preserves. Bake for 40 to 50 minutes or until lightly browned; do not overcook. Cool completely before cutting into 1 inch bars.

MAKES 25 BARS   *Maria Kiley*

These bars are delicious! Cut into small bars as they are rich.
Bars freeze well and can be quickly thawed.

S'MORES BARS

1 stick butter, softened
¾ cup sugar
1 large egg
1 teaspoon vanilla extract
1⅓ cups all-purpose flour
¾ cup graham cracker crumbs

1 teaspoon baking powder
¼ teaspoon salt
4 to 5 (1½ ounce) milk chocolate candy bars
1 cup marshmallow creme

Preheat oven to 350 degrees. In a large bowl, beat butter and sugar with an electric mixer on medium speed until creamy. Add egg and vanilla and beat until combined.

In a small bowl, combine flour, cracker crumbs, baking powder and salt. Add dry ingredients to creamed mixture and beat until combined. Press half of dough evenly into a greased 8 inch baking pan.

Arrange chocolate bars on top of dough, breaking bars apart as needed to create an even layer of chocolate. Spread marshmallow creme over chocolate. Spread remaining dough over marshmallow creme.

Bake for 30 to 35 minutes. Cut into squares.

MAKES 24 BARS

Kelli Stack

LINDA'S PEANUT BUTTER SQUARES

1 cup milk
2 tablespoons butter or margarine
4 large eggs
1 teaspoon vanilla extract
Pinch of salt
2 cups sugar

2 cups all-purpose flour
2 teaspoons baking powder
1½ cups peanut butter
1 (8 ounce) milk chocolate candy bar

Preheat oven to 350 degrees. Scald milk and butter; set aside. Mix together eggs, vanilla, salt, sugar, flour and baking powder. Pour in scalded milk and mix until blended. Spread mixture in a greased jelly roll pan. Bake for 20 to 25 minutes.

Spread peanut butter over hot cake. Cool in refrigerator. Melt chocolate in a double boiler. Spread chocolate over top. Refrigerate 30 minutes before serving.

Sally Beil

LOWER SCHOOL
STUDENT SENATE
(continued)

Show, where up to 24 acts of every variety entertain the students on the last day before Spring Break. And finally, the Senate helps to organize the Lower School Fair in June, overseeing 18 class booths, lemon sucker and snow-cone stands, and the Western Union music station, where requests for favorite songs are played and dedications are announced. Through these many activities, the representatives develop leadership skills while concurrently providing a service to the school.

In 1831 A. Bronson Alcott, educator and father of Louisa May Alcott, was Master and 19 girls were registered at the Academy. This venture was soon terminated, and for the next 125 years only young men were graduated. Today one of Upper School Houses is named in his honor.

Pumpkin Streusel Squares

Crust

1 cup all-purpose flour
¾ cup firmly packed dark brown sugar
½ teaspoon salt
1 stick butter, chilled
1 cup pecans halves
¾ cup old-fashioned oats

Filling

6 ounces cream cheese
1 cup canned solid pumpkin pack
½ cup sugar
1 egg
1½ tablespoons cinnamon
1 teaspoon ginger

Topping

1 cup sour cream
2 tablespoons sugar
¼ teaspoon vanilla

Preheat oven to 350 degrees. Blend flour, brown sugar, salt and butter in a food processor and pulse until mixture forms coarse meal. Add pecans and process until nuts are chopped. Add oats and process until mixture is moistened. Press 3½ cups of mixture into a greased 9 inch square baking pan. Spread remaining crumb mixture on a parchment paper-lined rimmed baking sheet. Bake crumb mixture for 12 minutes or until browned, stirring once. Bake crust for 30 minutes or until browned.

Blend all filling ingredients until smooth. Spread filling over baked crust. Bake for 20 minutes or until set. Remove from oven.

Mix all topping ingredients in a small bowl. Spread topping over hot filling. Bake for 5 minutes or until set and bubbly at the edges. Cool completely on a rack. Sprinkle baked crumbs on top and gently press into topping. Chill for 2 hours or until cold before cutting into squares.

MAKES 16 SQUARES   *Cheryl Koons*

Supreme Lemon Squares

Crust

2 sticks butter, melted
½ cup confectioners' sugar

2 cups flour

Filling

4 large eggs
2 cups granulated sugar
6 tablespoons freshly squeezed
    lemon juice

1 tablespoon flour
½ teaspoon baking powder
Confectioners' sugar for topping

Preheat oven to 325 degrees. Combine all crust ingredients. Press mixture into a greased 11x14 inch baking pan. Bake for 20 minutes or until edges just begin to brown.

In a separate bowl, mix together all filling ingredients, except confectioners' sugar. Pour filling over crust. Bake for 30 to 35 minutes or until top is brown and center begins to set. Cool. Sift confectioners' sugar over top of bars.

YIELD 20 TO 25 BARS

Kim Sloane

DID YOU KNOW...

The last commencement in Germantown was held in June 1965?

A LOOK AT 8TH
GRADE, 2009

Washington, DC

Day Off Campus

ERB's

Memoir

To Kill a Mocking Bird

Romeo and Juliet Monologues

1968

Science Fair

French Faculty Luncheon

Oui, Oui Wednesday

Sex Ed

Course Selection

Shear Madness

DECADENT CHOCOLATE BROWNIES

4 (1 ounce) squares unsweetened
    chocolate
2 sticks butter
2 cups sugar
4 large eggs

1 cup flour
1 teaspoon vanilla extract
1 (12 ounce) package semisweet
    chocolate chips
Confectioners' sugar for topping

Preheat oven to 350 degrees. Melt unsweetened chocolate with butter in a double boiler or microwave; do not overheat. Stir until smooth.

In a separate bowl, beat together sugar and eggs. Add melted chocolate mixture. Stir in flour and vanilla and beat well. Stir in chocolate chips. Pour batter into a greased 9x13 inch baking pan. Bake for about 25 minutes. Cool for at least 40 minutes. Sprinkle with confectioners' sugar.

MAKES 20 TO 24 BARS   *Laurel Stack*

ROBERT'S ROCKY ROAD BROWNIES

4 (1 ounce) squares unsweetened
    chocolate
1½ sticks margarine
2 cups sugar
4 large eggs

1 teaspoon vanilla extract
1 cup flour
2 cups mini marshmallows
1 cup chocolate chips
1 cup coarsely chopped nuts

Preheat oven to 350 degrees. Heat chocolate with margarine in a glass bowl on high for 2 minutes or until completely melted. Blend in sugar. Beat in eggs and vanilla. Mix in flour until well blended. Spread mixture into a greased 9x13 inch baking pan.

Bake for 35 minutes. Remove from oven and immediately sprinkle with marshmallows, chocolate chips and nuts. Bake for 3 to 5 minutes longer or until topping begins to melt together. Cool in pan before cutting into small squares.

MAKES 24 BARS   *Robert and Pamela Di Donato*

In a hurry? Substitute an 18 ounce package dark chocolate brownie mix for the base. Use coarsely chopped pecans, almonds or walnuts for a traditional recipe; or salted peanuts for a twist.

CHOCOLATE ICED CHECKERBOARD BROWNIES

(GRANDMA ZICK'S MARBLE BROWNIES)

2 sticks butter, softened
2 cups sugar
4 large eggs
1½ teaspoons vanilla extract
2 cups cake flour, sifted

Dash of salt
2 cups English walnuts, chopped (optional)
1 (1 ounce) square unsweetened chocolate, melted
Frosting (recipe below)

Preheat oven to 350 degrees. Cream together butter and sugar. Add eggs, one at a time, beating after each addition. Stir in vanilla. Add sifted cake flour and salt. Stir in walnuts.

Divide batter equally between 2 bowls. Mix melted chocolate into batter in one bowl. Arrange small scoops of each batter in a greased and floured 9x13 inch pan, making a checkerboard pattern. Bake for 40 minutes. Cool brownies before spreading with frosting.

Frosting

½ cup milk
2 tablespoons butter
½ teaspoon vanilla extract

1 (1 ounce) square unsweetened chocolate, melted
2 cups sifted confectioners' sugar

Heat milk and butter until butter is melted. Add vanilla and melted chocolate and mix well. Remove from heat and mix in confectioners' sugar. Cool slightly before spreading over brownies.

Ronalyn Sisson and Coralyn Zick

ONE-BOWL BROWNIES

1 stick butter
2 (1 ounce) squares unsweetened chocolate
1 cup sugar
½ cup flour
2 large eggs, beaten
1 teaspoon vanilla extract

Preheat oven to 350 degrees. Melt butter with chocolate in a medium saucepan over low heat. Remove from heat and stir in sugar, flour, egg and vanilla. Mix well. Pour batter into a greased and floured 8 or 9 inch square pan.

Bake for 20 to 25 minutes or until a toothpick inserted into brownies comes out almost clean. Cool slightly in pan before removing.

MAKES 16 BARS

Janet Maurer

Brownies should be a bit under-cooked for maximum fudginess.

This was an absolute favorite recipe for us as kids. God bless Grandmother, Coralyn Hull Zick, for this family recipe. I am happy to share it with Germantown Academy on such an important celebration year.

Each year, The Lower School Community Service Organization attracts about a 100 4th and 5th graders to meet weekly on Tuesdays during lunch and recess. The Fall is spent planning and implementing the Thanksgiving Food Drive benefitting 200 needy families in Northeast Philadelphia. Each January the children break into groups in order to spread their charitable energies and interests over such diverse areas as knitting scarves and making fleece blankets for people in shelters; stitching blankets for premature babies; making large quantities of casseroles for organizations feeding those in need; selling pretzels, and bake goods for fundraisers for organizations such as CHOP, The Humane

Soft Batch Chocolate Chip Cookies

5 cups all-purpose flour
2 teaspoons baking powder
3 sticks margarine, melted and slightly cooled
3 cups firmly packed light brown sugar

2 large eggs
2 teaspoons vanilla extract
1 teaspoon butter-flavored extract
2 cups semisweet or milk chocolate chunks (16 ounces)

Preheat oven to 350 degrees. Combine flour and baking powder; set aside. In a large bowl, combine melted margarine and brown sugar and mix well. Stir in eggs, vanilla and butter extract until well blended. Add dry ingredients and stir until just combined. Stir in chocolate chunks.

Drop by heaping tablespoons, 2½ inches apart, onto a parchment paper-lined baking sheet. Bake for 9 to 11 minutes or until edges harden and centers are still soft.

MAKES 3 DOZEN COOKIES   *Violet Sible*

Everyone's Favorite Sugar Cookie

2 sticks butter, softened
1 cup granulated sugar, plus extra for rolling
1 cup confectioners' sugar
1 cup vegetable oil

4 cups flour
1 teaspoon salt
1 teaspoon baking soda
1 teaspoon cream of tartar
1 teaspoon vanilla extract

Preheat oven to 350 degrees. Cream together butter, both sugars and oil. Mix in flour, salt, baking soda, cream of tartar and vanilla. Roll dough into walnut-size balls. Roll dough balls in granulated sugar and place on an ungreased baking sheet. Flatten dough slightly with the bottom of a glass. Bake for 15 minutes or until lightly golden brown.

Dovey, Stack, Culligan and Galloway

NANA'S GINGERBREAD CHRISTMAS COOKIES

½ cup firmly packed brown sugar
5 tablespoons butter or margarine
1½ cups dark molasses
½ cup water
¼ teaspoon salt

2 teaspoons ground ginger
2 teaspoons baking soda
1 teaspoon ground allspice
1 teaspoon cinnamon
7 cups all-purpose flour

Toppings

Colored frosting
Colored sugar

Candy
Raisins (optional)

Mix brown sugar, butter, molasses and water in a large mixing bowl. Stir in salt, ginger, baking soda, allspice, cinnamon and flour. Cover and refrigerate at least 2 hours.

When ready to cook, preheat oven to 350 degrees. Roll one-fourth of dough to ¼ inch thickness on a floured surface. Cut out shapes with floured gingerbread cutters. Place cookies about 2 inches apart on a lightly greased baking sheet. Bake for 10 to 12 minutes or until no indentation remains when touched. Cool. Repeat until all dough is used.

Decorate cookies with toppings of choice. Raisins, if using, need to be added to cookies before baking.

Ashley Piszek

(continued)

Society, The Hurricane Katrina relief fund and Alex's Lemonade Stand; making craft items for senior citizens and collecting sports and books for recreation centers and schools in Philadelphia. The philosophy of the group, facilitated by both Lower School teachers and parent volunteers, is that the children brainstorm the ways they can help and then choose the groups they want to join. Visit us in the Common Room on a Tuesday; it's a lively, energizing group!

Use a mixture of flour and confectioners' sugar for rolling out cookies.

FROM THE CLASS OF 1921:

"I extend you a hearty welcome to this yearly ceremony, the planting of the ivy. To us, who are about to step over the threshold of our beloved school into the envied company called "Alumni," this event means much. "Alumni" what a magical word!…The established custom of planting an ivy, to grow at its own will over the walls of our Alma Mater, seems a fitting symbol for our future. We shall branch out in many directions, seemingly quite independent of support, yet in memory always clinging to old G.A. and its associations. Each ivy, added to those already planted, means that the school is expanding— that the vision of years past is

OPULENT OATMEAL COOKIES

1¼ cups all-purpose flour
¾ teaspoon baking powder
½ teaspoon baking soda
½ teaspoon salt
1¼ cups old-fashioned oats
1 cup pecans, toasted
1 cup dried Bing cherries, chopped

4 ounces good-quality bittersweet chocolate, chopped (about ¾ cup)
1½ sticks butter, slightly softened
1½ cups firmly packed dark brown sugar
1½ teaspoons orange zest
1 large egg
1 teaspoon vanilla extract

Preheat oven to 350 degrees. Combine flour, baking powder, baking soda and salt in a medium bowl; set aside. In a separate bowl, combine oats, pecans, cherries and chopped chocolate; set aside.

In another bowl, beat butter and brown sugar with an electric mixer until smooth. Add zest, egg and vanilla and mix until blended. On low speed, add dry ingredients until just combined. Gradually stir in oats mixture using a spatula until incorporated. Scoop dough into ¼ cup portions and roll into balls. Gently press cookies to about 1 inch thickness onto parchment paper or silicone-lined baking sheets, placing them at least 2 inches apart. Bake for 12 minutes. Rotate baking sheets front to back and top to bottom. Bake 8 minutes longer or until edges are brown but centers are still soft. Cool on wire racks.

MAKES 16 BIG COOKIES   *Betty Grant*

Walnuts or any mixed nuts can be substituted for pecans.
Cranberries can be used instead of cherries. Use bittersweet chocolate;
chocolate chips make these cookies too sweet.

ROCKY MOUNTAIN CHIP COOKIES

1 stick margarine, softened
1 stick unsalted butter, softened
1 cup firmly packed brown sugar
1 cup granulated sugar
2 large eggs, lightly beaten
2 tablespoons milk
2 teaspoons vanilla extract
2 cups sifted all-purpose flour

1 teaspoon baking powder
1 teaspoon baking soda
1 teaspoon salt
2 cups quick-cooking oats
1 (12 ounce) package semisweet
    chocolate chips
1 cup coarsely chopped walnuts

Cream together margarine, butter and both sugars in a large mixing bowl until light and fluffy. Add eggs, milk and vanilla and beat until blended.

In a separate bowl, sift together flour, baking powder, baking soda and salt. Add dry ingredients to creamed mixture and stir until blended. Stir in oats. Fold in chocolate chips and walnuts. Cover and refrigerate for at least 1 hour.

When ready to cook, preheat oven to 350 degrees. Shape dough into balls using a rounded teaspoon for small cookies or a tablespoon for large cookies. Flatten balls slightly into round disks and place 2 inches apart on greased baking sheets. Bake for 8 to 10 minutes or until the edges are slightly browned but the cookies are still white. Cool on baking sheets for 5 minutes. Remove to wire racks to cool completely.

MAKES 100 SMALL
OR 50 LARGE COOKIES

Liz Kaufman

FROM THE CLASS OF 1921: *(continued)*

taking form in better facilities; in better equipment. For the dream of the athletic field has now become a reality. If we can be sturdy in growth, as beautiful in character, as this plant, G.A. will have fulfilled its mission. Each ivy recalls a group of our predecessors that have gone forth from the "Old School." Each symbolizes the loyalty and devotion of a graduating class, and these various plants, mingling in loving communion in these walls, exemplify the spirit of unity and comradeship that bands together the many sons of old G.A....".

From "Silver Palate Good Times" cookbook by Julee Rosso and Sheila Lukins.

Icing

2 tablespoons butter,
    softened
2 cups confectioners' sugar
1 teaspoon vanilla extract
1 to 2 teaspoons light cream

Combine butter and confectioners' sugar. Add vanilla. Mix in cream to a creamy consistency.

Ricotta Cookies

1 stick unsalted butter, softened
2 cups sugar
1 teaspoon vanilla extract
2 large eggs, beaten

1 pound ricotta cheese
4 cups all-purpose flour
1 teaspoon salt
1 teaspoon baking soda

Cream butter and sugar together in a medium bowl. Mix in vanilla and egg. Blend in ricotta cheese until well mixed; set aside.

In a large bowl, combine flour, salt and baking soda and mix well. Add ricotta mixture to dry ingredients and mix well with a sturdy spoon; dough will be sticky and you might need to use your hands to fully mix.

Roll dough, using wet fingers so dough does not stick, into tablespoon-size balls. Arrange balls, three across, on ungreased, nonstick baking sheets. Bake 12 to 14 minutes or until bottoms are browned and tops are still white and firm to the touch. Cool completely before frosting with icing (see sidebar).

MAKES 3 DOZEN COOKIES   *Marisa Graziano*

Bibbie's Lace Cookies

2 cups rolled oats
1 tablespoon flour
2 cups sugar
1 teaspoon salt

2 sticks butter (no substitutions)
1 teaspoon vanilla extract
2 large eggs, beaten

Preheat oven to 325 degrees. Mix oats, flour, sugar and salt in a large bowl. Melt butter until very hot. Pour hot butter over dry ingredients and stir by hand until sugar is dissolved. Add vanilla and egg and stir well. The mixture should be a little thicker than pancake batter.

Scoop ½ teaspoon portions, at least 2 inches apart, onto foil-lined baking sheets. Bake for 10 to 12 minutes or until cookie centers are dark golden brown or caramel in color. Cool slightly on foil. Peel cookies from foil before completely cooled; peel gently as cookies are delicate.

MAKES ABOUT 8 DOZEN COOKIES   *Tyler Wellington*

*The use of foil is imperative in the success of
this recipe as cookies would stick to any cookie sheet.*

Dr. J's Famous Vanilla Cookies

2½ cups sifted cake flour
2 sticks butter, well chilled
1 cup sugar

½ teaspoon baking powder
2 large egg yolks
1½ teaspoons vanilla extract

Preheat oven to 375 degrees. Sift and measure cake flour into a bowl. Cut in butter using a pastry blender or fork until thoroughly blended. Add sugar and baking powder. Mix in egg yolks and vanilla. Work dough until smooth.

Roll out dough. Cut dough as desired using cookie cutters. Place cookies on a baking sheet. Bake about 8 to 10 minutes. Decorate cookies as desired.

MAKES ABOUT 5 DOZEN COOKIES   *Heather Foley*

Florentine Crispy Cookies

2 cups old-fashioned oats
½ cup sugar
2 tablespoons flour
2 to 4 tablespoons butter, melted

4 to 5 teaspoons almond extract
1 teaspoon vanilla extract
   (optional)
½ cup light corn syrup

Preheat oven to 325 degrees. Line 2 baking sheets with foil and spray with cooking spray. Combine oats, sugar and flour in a bowl until completely mixed. Add melted butter and mix well. Stir in almond and vanilla extracts. Pour corn syrup evenly over mixture and stir until completely blended.

Drop by spoonfuls into about 1 inch size mounds onto prepared baking sheets, about 12 cookies per sheet. Wet fingers and press dough into flat rounds, the thinner the better. Bake 15 to 20 minutes or until cookies start to turn golden brown. Cool cookies on baking sheets. Gently peel cooled cookies off foil.

MAKES ABOUT 2 DOZEN COOKIES   *Sussi Seybert*

The choice of how much butter to use is yours; how healthy do you want your cookies? I have used 2, 3 and 4 tablespoons on different occasions.

Though each side plays fiercely for every minute of every game, sportsmanship is valued. At the time of the centennial game in 1986, heads of school Earl J. Ball (PC) and James C. Ledyard (GA) wrote, "Many athletic rivalries formed on the fields of the two schools have matured into lasting friendships. The lessons learned from extending oneself individually in pursuit of a goal, from the spirit of teamwork, and from healthy competition are important aspects of education."

MARVELOUS MOLASSES COOKIES

2¼ cups flour
2 teaspoons baking soda
¼ teaspoon salt
1 teaspoon cinnamon
1 teaspoon ground ginger
1½ sticks unsalted butter, softened

1 cup firmly packed brown sugar
1 extra-large egg
¼ cup regular molasses (blackstrap is too strong for this recipe)
Granulated sugar

Preheat oven to 375 degrees. Line 2 baking sheets with parchment paper, silicone liners or foil; if using foil, grease foil with 1 tablespoon butter or vegetable shortening. Sift together flour, baking soda, salt, cinnamon and ginger in a medium bowl; set aside.

Cream butter and brown sugar together in a large mixing bowl with an electric mixer on high speed for 1 minute or until light and fluffy. Reduce speed to medium and beat in egg and molasses. Increase to high speed and beat 1 minute longer or until mixture no longer looks curdled. Scrape sides of bowl with a rubber spatula several times while mixing. Mix in dry ingredients on low speed. The batter will be rather stiff.

Place some granulated sugar in a small plate or saucer. Scoop dough into ¼ cup portions using a scoop or measuring cup. If needed, spray scoop or measuring cup with cooking spray to make it easier to release dough. Roll dough into rough balls with your hands, then roll each ball in sugar. Place 6 balls on each baking sheet, spacing them evenly apart as cookies will spread while baking. Press down lightly on each cookie with damp fingers to flatten them a little and to dampen the top. Refrigerate one filled baking sheet while other bakes.

Bake one tray at a time on center rack for 12 minutes or until cookies have spread and are firm to the touch. Rotate sheet 180 degrees halfway through the baking time. Cool cookies on baking sheet.

Kim Culligan and
Christy Galloway

MAKES 1 DOZEN LARGE COOKIES

This dough can be frozen for slice-and-bake cookies. Just roll into a 2½ inch thick log. Wrap in plastic and then in foil. Can be frozen up to 6 months.

VISCOTI ITALIAN COOKIES

3½ cups all-purpose or cake flour
3½ teaspoons baking powder
Pinch of salt
6 large eggs
¾ cup canola oil
¾ cup sugar

2 teaspoons vanilla or anisette
  flavoring
Frosting (recipe below)
Optional toppings, such as
  coconut, sprinkles or
  chocolate chips

Preheat oven to 350 degrees. Mix flour, baking powder and salt in a bowl; set aside. In a separate bowl, beat eggs with an electric mixer until frothy. Add oil, sugar and flavoring. Turn mixer to low and gradually add dry ingredients. Drop cookies in 1 teaspoon portions onto greased baking sheets. Bake for 4 minutes in center of oven. Transfer baking sheet to bottom rack and bake until cookies are barely brown on the bottom. Cool cookies for 1 minute on baking sheet, then transfer to a rack to cool.

Spread frosting quickly over warm cookies before frosting hardens; frosting will spread easier over warm cookies. Sprinkle with toppings, if desired. Allow cookies to dry for 2 hours on a clean baking sheet. Store in a plastic container with wax paper between each layer to prevent cookies from drying out and sticking to each other.

Frosting

4 tablespoons butter, softened
1 (16 ounce) package
  confectioners' sugar

2 tablespoons hot water, or as
  needed
Food coloring (optional)

Mix butter and sugar. Add hot water until frosting is a thin spreading consistency. Add food coloring, if desired.

MAKES 5 TO 6 DOZEN COOKIES

Frances, Nicos and Camille Scordis

Add candied ginger to make a scone-like cookie. Try different types of flour, such as semolina, to change the consistency from a cake-type cookie to a biscuit-type cookie. Try your favorite flavorings and toppings. These are popular with kids and adults.

COOKING UP WORDS IN ALPHABETIA

Remember our first recipe, CVC, is a delicious blend of consonants and vowels?

Will you ever forget our puppet friends who help us remember their vowel sounds in CVC words?

Madame Adam Apple's wedding was a glorious event complete with a reception and delicious apple treats.

Do you remember Ollie's birthday and his silver pot?
Oh yes, Ollie liked things hot, hot, hot, yes he liked them h-o-t!

Ollie's Rock Out party helped bring out the Rock Star in all Kindergarten students!

Playing games and singing songs helped us to learn and Cherrios helped us to concentrate!

By second grade you were star performers in the Alphabetia Theater, showing us all how talented you were!

DELICIOUS!!!

Baklava

Syrup

2½ cups sugar
2 cups water
Peel of ½ lemon
1 stick cinnamon

2 drops fresh-squeezed lemon juice
½ cup honey

Pastry

1½ pounds crushed walnuts (about 5 cups)
1 teaspoon cinnamon
¼ teaspoon ground cloves

½ cup sugar
¾ pound clarified butter
1 pound frozen phyllo dough, thawed

Combine sugar, water, lemon peel, and cinnamon in a saucepan and bring to a boil. Cook 10 to 15 minutes. Add a couple drops lemon juice. Stir in honey and boil a few minutes longer. Remove from heat and put aside to cool. Syrup yields about 2½ cups.

Mix walnuts, cinnamon, cloves, and sugar in a bowl. Brush all inside surfaces of a 9x13 inch aluminum baking pan with some of clarified butter. Gently unfold phyllo dough on a work surface so it lays flat. Cover with wax paper and a damp tea towel. Working with one sheet of phyllo at a time, lay phyllo sheet in baking pan. Brush lightly with clarified butter and sprinkle lightly with water. Repeat layering process with 10 sheet of phyllo. Sprinkle walnut mixture over layers, using just enough to cover entire surface. Sprinkle lightly with butter. Repeat layering of phyllo, each buttered and sprinkled lightly with water, using 4 sheets of dough. Add a second layer of walnut mixture. Repeat procedure, using 4 sheets of dough and walnut mixture, until all of nut mixture is used. Top final nut layer with 10 sheets of phyllo, each buttered and sprinkled with water as dough sheets are stacked on top of the other.

Preheat oven to 350 degrees. Use a pointed knife to cut slightly into pastry layers, cutting 5 rows lengthwise and 4 rows widthwise. Then cut diagonally to make two triangles out of each square, about 40 triangles total. Bake 30 minutes or until pastry is golden brown. Remove from oven and immediately pour cooled syrup on top. Cool completely.

SERVES ABOUT 40

*Pauline Papadakes and
Sophia Papadakes Frangakis*

IRISH POTATOES

⅓ cup light corn syrup
5 tablespoons butter, softened
½ teaspoon salt
1 teaspoon vanilla extract

1 (16 ounce) package
   confectioners' sugar
1 (10 ounce) container coconut,
   or as desired
Cinnamon

Mix corn syrup, butter, salt and vanilla until smooth. Add sugar and stir until well blended. Turn dough out onto a wooden board and knead until smooth. Add desired amount of coconut while kneading. Form mixture into ¾ inch balls. Place some cinnamon in a bowl. Roll dough balls in cinnamon.

MAKES 2½ DOZEN *Virginia Menno*

FANNIE'S POPPYSEED COOKIES

2 sticks butter, softened
1 cup sugar, plus extra for topping
4 large eggs
1 teaspoon vanilla extract

7 to 8 tablespoons poppy seeds
4 cups flour
4 teaspoons baking powder

Beat together butter and sugar until creamy. Add eggs, one at a time, beating well after each addition. Mix in vanilla. Add poppy seeds and mix well.

In a large bowl, combine flour and baking powder. Gradually add dry ingredients to creamed mixture and blend well. Gather dough into a ball and wrap in wax paper. Refrigerate 3 to 4 hours or until chilled, or overnight.

When ready to cook, preheat oven to 350 degrees. Roll out dough to ⅛ inch thickness on a well-floured surface. Cut dough into circles using a 3 inch cookie cutter or a glass. Place cookies 1 inch apart on a baking sheet. Sprinkle sugar on top. Bake for 12 to 15 minutes or until golden brown around the edges.

MAKES ABOUT 4 DOZEN COOKIES *Bonnie Levinthal*

Sprinkle cinnamon sugar on top instead of sugar.

> "My own remedy is always to eat, just before I step into bed, a hot roasted onion, if I have a cold."
>
> *George Washington*

> "Boil a pan of water containing cloves and cinnamon sticks just before guest arrive. The house will smell Heavenly!"
>
> *George Washington*

Did you know that every child in the Lower School at GA has reading homework every night? It's one of the ingredients that make our language arts program successful. After a busy day, reading homework is a wonderful opportunity for family members to grab a great book or article and relax together. While they enjoy the marvelous words and illustrations in picture books, very young children cuddle up and listen to someone read to them. Children who have acquired a beginning vocabulary read to or with a family member. Older, independent readers get lost in a book of their own choosing; but please, never stop reading aloud to your children. An adult reading interesting parts of books or significant news

SALTINE CHOCOLATE TOFFEE TREAT

40 saltine crackers
2 sticks butter
1 cup firmly packed light brown sugar

1 (12 ounce) package chocolate chips
1 cup chopped pecans or nuts of choice

Preheat oven to 400 degrees. Arrange crackers side by side in a single layer, flat side down, on a foil-lined jelly roll pan. Melt butter and brown sugar in a saucepan. Bring to a rolling boil, stirring constantly for 3 minutes. Pour mixture over crackers. Bake for 5 minutes.

Sprinkle with chocolate chips and return to oven for 1 minute or until chips are softened. Spread melted chocolate chips over toffee layer. Sprinkle nuts on top. Refrigerate for at least 2 hours.

Peel foil from back of crackers and break into pieces.

Bonnie Austin
Lauren Kelly

ICEBOX COOKIES

2 sticks butter
1 cup vegetable shortening
1 cup granulated sugar
1 cup firmly packed brown sugar
4 large eggs

6 cups flour
1 teaspoon baking soda
1 teaspoon cinnamon
1½ cups slivered almonds, lightly toasted and cooled

Preheat oven to 375 degrees. In a large mixing bowl, cream together butter and shortening. Gradually beat in both sugars. Add eggs, one at a time, beating after each addition. Add flour, baking soda and cinnamon and mix well. Stir in almonds.

Roll dough into 2 inch diameter loaves. Wrap loaves in wax paper, then in foil. Place loaves in freezer for 2 hours or up to 1 month. Cut loaves into ¼ inch thick slices and place on baking sheets. Bake for 10 to 12 minutes or until light brown.

Laura Korman

MAKES ABOUT 6 DOZEN

To toast almonds, spread on a baking sheet. Bake at 375 degrees for 15 minutes or until lightly browned. Cool before adding to dough.

BISCOTTI WITH CANDIED ORANGE AND PECANS

1 stick butter, softened
¼ cup sugar
2 large eggs
2 tablespoons orange liqueur
Zest of 1 orange
2 cups plus 2 tablespoons all-
    purpose or unbleached flour

1½ teaspoons baking powder
¼ teaspoon salt
1 cup candied orange peel
    (recipe below)
¼ cup pecans, toasted and
    coarsely chopped

Preheat oven to 325 degrees. Cream butter and sugar together in a mixing bowl until light and fluffy. Beat in eggs, orange liqueur and orange zest. In a separate bowl, combine flour, baking powder and salt and mix until just blended. Fold creamed mixture into dry ingredients. Stir in candied orange peel and pecans.

Divide dough in half. Form each half into a log on a greased and floured or parchment paper-lined baking sheet; spacing logs several inches apart. Press down on logs to flatten. Bake in center of oven for 25 to 30 minutes or until set and lightly browned. Reduce oven to 300 degrees. Transfer logs to a rack to cool for 15 minutes.

Place logs on a cutting board and slice with a serrated knife diagonally at a 45 degree angle about ½ inch thick. Place slices, cut side down, on baking sheet. Bake 8 minutes on each side to dry slightly. Cool thoroughly before storing in an airtight container.

Candied Orange Peel

3 oranges
½ cup sugar

½ cup water, plus extra for
    simmering

Score oranges into 6 to 8 sections and remove peel. Place sections of peel in a saucepan and add enough water to cover. Simmer for 10 minutes. Drain and cool. With a grapefruit knife or melon ball scoop, carefully remove all white pith from orange peel; set side. Combine sugar and ½ cup water in saucepan. Bring to a boil until sugar is dissolved. Reduce heat and add orange peel. Simmer about 1 hour or until liquid is absorbed. Transfer orange peel sections to wax paper to cool. When cool, slice candied peel into very thin slivers, about ¼ inch long. Yields about 1 cup.

MAKES 3 DOZEN COOKIES   *Cathy Black*

This is a beautiful and delicious cookie and well worth the effort. Use Blue Curaçao Liqueur for a pale green cookie, which highlights the vivid orange peel and nuts.

(sidebar continued)

articles models not only what is important in print, but also how reading should sound (fluency). From years of experience, we know that the more children read, the better readers they become; and the better readers they become, the more they want to read. We urge all families to join in this wonderful cycle. Read the cookbook together tonight, and make something tasty while enhancing your child's ability to read and follow directions. Now there's a delicious way to do homework!

Betty Grant,
Lower School Language
Arts Coordinator

Prune-Plum Filling

1 (10 ounce) jar prune-plum
   filling
3 tablespoons chopped
   walnuts (optional)
1 teaspoon lemon juice

Combine all ingredients in
a saucepan. Cook for a few
minutes. Cool before using.

Betty Silow's Hamentashen (Filled Pastry)

Dough

4 large eggs
1 cup vegetable or canola oil
1 teaspoon vanilla extract
1 cup sugar

2 teaspoons baking powder
4 cups flour, plus extra for rolling
   dough

Filling

2 (10 to 12 ounce) jars or cans fruit
   filling, such as strawberry,
   apricot or cherry, or chocolate
   chips or Prune-Plum filling
   (recipe in sidebar)

1 to 2 large eggs, beaten

Preheat oven to 375 degrees. In the large bowl of an electric mixer, beat
together eggs, oil and vanilla until blended. Add sugar and mix until fully
blended. In a separate bowl, sift baking powder with flour. Gradually add
dry ingredients to creamed mixture. Knead dough, being careful to not
over-process if using an electric mixer. If the dough is not cleaning the bowl
and forming a ball, add a bit more flour.

Dust a flat surface and a rolling pin with flour. Divide dough into 4 sections.
Roll out sections one at a time. Cut dough with a 2½ inch round cookie
cutter or a glass and transfer to baking sheets. Combine extra pieces of
dough, roll again and cut into circles until all dough is used.

Spoon a heaping teaspoonful of filling into center of each pastry circle. The
object is to have a triangular-shaped pastry, so gently lift and fold 3 sides
of dough, one at a time, to the center of the pastry; a tiny bit of filling will
show. Shape pastry into a triangle. Brush pastries with egg; this produces a
shiny, golden pastry.

Bake for 10 to 12 minutes. Remove from pan and cool on a rack. Cover
lightly with foil to store; storing in an airtight container will produce soggy
pastries.

MAKES ABOUT 60 PASTRIES   *Deenie Silow*

RICE PUDDING

1 cup dry white rice
2 cups water
1 stick butter
½ gallon whole or 2% milk
5 large eggs, beaten

1 cup sugar
2 teaspoons vanilla extract
1 cup golden raisins
Nutmeg and cinnamon to taste

Combine rice and water in a saucepan and cook for 7 minutes over low heat. Add butter and milk and cook over medium-low heat for 60 to 75 minutes, stirring often. Remove from heat and slowly mix in egg; be sure to add slowly so as to not scramble the egg. Mix in sugar, vanilla and raisins and stir thoroughly. Do not return mixture to hot stove. Pour mixture into a 2 quart casserole dish. Sprinkle with cinnamon and nutmeg. Cool.

SERVES 10 TO 12   *Donna Obrecht*

CRANBERRY PUDDING

Pudding

½ cup sugar
½ cup milk
2 tablespoons butter, melted

1 cup flour, sifted
2 teaspoons baking powder
1 cup raw cranberries

Preheat oven to 400 degrees. Mix together pudding ingredients in order listed. Pour pudding into a pie or cake pan. Bake for 30 minutes. Serve warm with warm sauce (recipe below).

Sauce

½ cup butter
2 cups sugar

¾ cup heavy cream

Melt butter in a saucepan. Add sugar and cook over low heat. Stir in cream. Serve warm over pudding. May be made ahead and reheated.

SERVES 4 TO 6   *Linda Test*

Pudding can be baked ahead and covered loosely with foil.
Reheat briefly in a hot oven before serving.

Field Day is an annual event which began with the opening of the new campus in the early 1960's. Director of Admission Barbara Serrill '68, one of the original girls admitted to GA, remembers it as a family affair with people bringing their barbecues to the festivities. Edwin Probert, GA Archivist, confirms that Field Day premiered as a Lower School tradition in Fort Washington, but is a direct descendant of the Upper School Tug of War that began in Germantown in 1875.

DECADENT BUTTERSCOTCH PUDDING

1¼ cups heavy cream
6 tablespoons unsalted butter
1¼ cups firmly packed brown
    sugar
1½ cups whole milk

4 large egg yolks
¼ cup cornstarch
¾ teaspoon salt
Whipped cream and chocolate
    shavings for topping

Heat cream in a saucepan over low heat until warm. In a separate saucepan, melt butter over medium heat. Stir in brown sugar. Cook, stirring occasionally, for 5 minutes or until mixture is bubbling and smooth. Carefully add warm cream and stir over low heat for 1 minute or until sugar is dissolved. Remove from heat.

In a large double boiler, whisk together milk, egg yolks, cornstarch and salt. Add warm cream mixture in a slow stream, whisking constantly over simmering water. Cook, whisking, for 10 minutes or until pudding starts to thicken. Remove from top of double boiler and cool, whisking, for 5 minutes.

Divide pudding into individual serving bowls. Cover to prevent a skin from forming on the top. Chill for at least 3 hours. Serve with whipped cream and chocolate shavings on top.

SERVES 6

Kris Henry

QUICK BAKED APPLE CRUNCH

6 to 8 Granny Smith apples
1 large egg
1 cup sugar
1 cup flour

1 teaspoon baking powder
3 tablespoons butter, softened
Cinnamon

Preheat oven to 350 degrees. Peel and slice apples. Arrange slices in a greased shallow baking dish, making 1 to 2 layers, depending on size of dish.

Combine egg, sugar, flour, baking powder and butter. Spread mixture over top of apple slices. Sprinkle with cinnamon. Bake for 30 minutes.

SERVES 6

Maggie, Grace and Caroline Sloane

Peaches or 2 pints of blueberries can be substituted for the apples.
My girls' favorite is blueberry!

Jackson Peak Spiked Apple Crisp

Crumb Topping

¾ cup granulated sugar
¼ cup firmly packed light
    brown sugar

¾ cup flour, sifted
¼ teaspoon salt
1 stick butter, softened

Filling

5 cups peeled and sliced apple
½ teaspoon cinnamon sugar
1 jigger Grand Marnier® liqueur

1 jigger Amaretto di Saronno
    liqueur

Preheat oven to 350 degrees. Combine all topping ingredients in a bowl until crumbly.

To make filling, place apple slices in a greased 1 quart casserole dish. Sprinkle with cinnamon sugar and drizzle with both liqueurs. Spread topping over apple slices.

Bake for 1 hour or until top is lightly browned. Serve with vanilla ice cream.

SERVES 6 TO 8   *Samantha Jordan*

Dirt

4 tablespoons butter
8 ounces cream cheese
1 cup confectioners' sugar
2 (3 ounce) boxes instant French
    vanilla pudding mix
3½ cups milk

1 (12 ounce) container frozen
    whipped topping, thawed
1 (18 ounce) package chocolate
    sandwich cookies, crushed
    into small pieces
Gummy worms (optional)

Heat butter and cream cheese in microwave for 1 minute; beat until smooth. Whip in confectioners' sugar.

In a separate bowl, beat pudding mix and milk. Let pudding stand for 5 minutes. Add pudding to cream cheese mixture and mix until blended. Fold in whipped topping until incorporated.

In a trifle bowl or 9x13 inch glass pan, layer pudding and cookie crumbs, starting and ending with cookies (3 layers cookies, 2 layers pudding). Decorate with gummy worms. Chill for 3 to 4 hours before serving.

SERVES 12 TO 15   *Judy Cody*

250th Year Celebration Events

All-School Flag Raising

All-School Parent Social

Historical Photo Essay

Alumni Juried Art Show

Middle School Cricket Exhibition

Tailgate 250 and Reunion Weekend at GA-PC Day

All-School Birthday Party

Coast-to-Coast Toast for Alumni

Class of 1760 Celebration

GA Celebrates!

CSO Showcase

Belfry Club's performance of *An Ideal Husband*, written by Oscar Wilder the same year when the Club was founded, 1895

Patriots' Gala

Patriots' Bounty—GA's Community Cookbook

Candle flames, inclined planes, determining the strength of an egg;

Animal tracks in plaster casts and counting insect legs.

Homemade ice cream, the Wissahickon Creek, experiments galore.

Tall towers, dry ice, chrysalises, butterflies, and more.

Pictures in the darkroom, rivers in diatomaceous earth,

Rock collections, growing seeds, and dinosaurs from moss and dirt.

Nature walks, informative talks through rhyme, projects, and song.

Investigation and celebration, Lower School science all day long!

BLUEBERRY BUCKLE

Topping

½ cup sugar
⅓ cup flour

½ teaspoon cinnamon
4 tablespoons butter, softened

Batter

¾ cup sugar
¼ cup shortening
1 large egg
½ cup milk

2 cups flour
2 teaspoons baking powder
½ teaspoon salt
2 cups blueberries, well drained

Preheat oven to 375 degrees. For topping, combine sugar, flour and cinnamon. Cut in butter until mixture resembles coarse meal using a pastry blender or fork; set aside.

To make batter, mix sugar, shortening, egg and milk. In a separate bowl, sift together flour, baking powder and salt. Add dry ingredients to batter mixture. Carefully fold in blueberries. Batter will be thick. Spread batter in a greased and floured 9 inch square baking pan.

Sprinkle topping over batter. Bake for 45 to 50 minutes.

SERVES 12

Charlotte Dean

As a dessert, serve warm with ice cream. For breakfast, serve as a coffee cake.

Uncle Jake's Apple Brown Betty

6 tablespoons unsalted butter, divided
4 medium Granny Smith apples, peeled and sliced ¼ inch thick
¼ cup granulated sugar
1 teaspoon cinnamon
¼ teaspoon nutmeg
Salt to taste
½ cup apple juice
1½ cups butter cookie crumbs
½ cup firmly packed light brown sugar

Preheat oven to 350 degrees. Use 1 tablespoon butter to grease a 1½ quart baking dish; set aside.

Place apple slices in a large mixing bowl. Add granulated sugar, cinnamon, nutmeg, salt and apple juice. Toss to mix thoroughly and coat apple slices evenly with spices.

Combine cookie crumbs and brown sugar in a small mixing bowl and stir until evenly mixed. Cut the remaining 5 tablespoons butter into ¼ inch slices and set aside until needed.

Sprinkle ¼ cup of crumb mixture over the bottom of prepared dish. Top with half the apple slices, then drizzle with half the juice from the bottom of the mixing bowl. Sprinkle half the remaining crumb mixture over the apple slices. Dot with half the butter.

Add the remaining apple slices and drizzle with remaining apple juice. Top with remaining crumbs. Dot with remaining butter.

Bake for 50 minutes or until apple is tender and crumbs turn a dark golden brown. Cool 10 minutes. Serve warm topped with vanilla ice cream or butter pecan ice cream.

Michael Jacobs

(And you thought my wife was the baker of the family — well, think again!)

Perhaps the greatest challenge any new enterprise faces is the development of a genuine identity. Moving a school from urban to suburban, from all male to coeducation, from a historic setting to unmarked open ground certainly means that a re-birth is underway. What will the new issue look like? What will it grow to become? What will its defining quality be?

Fifty years later, those questions have answers. Initially, precocious but awkward; ambitious but deferential; becoming confident without pretension, gracious without condescension, inclusive without mediocrity. All nourished upon an optimistic, sleeve rolled spirit that is entrepreneurial in nature, extraordinary in execution.

Smells so good...tastes even better!

GAPN is a group of parent volunteers whose purpose is to strengthen the GA community through networking and by providing information and healthy parenting education.

Our dedication to parenting education plays a major role in all of our programming. We are committed to assisting our community with developing skills for one of our most important jobs: meeting the emotional needs of our children.

We offer varied and diverse opportunities for all members of the GA community to develop and enrich skills for effective interaction with children.

PEACH CHEESE COBBLER

Batter

¾ cup flour
1 teaspoon baking powder
½ teaspoon salt
1 (3 ounce) box cook and serve vanilla pudding (not instant)

3 tablespoons butter or margarine
1 large egg
½ cup milk

Topping

1 (20 or 29 ounce) can sliced peaches, drained, 3 to 4 tablespoons juice reserved
8 ounces cream cheese

½ cup sugar
Dash of vanilla extract
1 teaspoon cinnamon sugar

Preheat oven to 350 degrees. Combine all batter ingredients in a mixing bowl. Beat with an electric mixer on medium speed for 2 minutes. Pour batter into a 10 inch pie pan.

Arrange peaches over batter. Mix 3 to 4 tablespoons reserved peach juice, cream cheese, sugar and vanilla until smooth. Spread cream cheese mixture over peaches. Sprinkle with cinnamon sugar.

Bake for 30 to 35 minutes. Serve warm or cold.

SERVES 8 TO 10

Lois Herbine

DELICIOUS GRAPES

3 pounds red and green seedless grapes for color, at room temperature
1¼ quarts sour cream, or enough to cover grapes

3 tablespoons vanilla extract
1 pound firmly packed brown sugar

Preheat a broiler. Combine grapes, sour cream and vanilla. Transfer to a large casserole dish. Sprinkle brown sugar over grapes.

Place casserole dish on top of a large pot filled with ice. Broil until brown sugar melts. Refrigerate until serving.

SERVES 12 OR MORE

Dorothy Harkrader

FABULOUS HOT FUDGE SAUCE

4 ounces bittersweet chocolate
2 ounces unsweetened chocolate
3 tablespoons unsalted butter
⅓ cup heavy cream

⅓ cup sugar
⅓ cup light corn syrup
1 teaspoon vanilla extract

Melt all chocolate and butter in the top of a double boiler over boiling water.

In a separate saucepan, warm cream over low heat. Add sugar and corn syrup and stir until dissolved. Add warm cream mixture to melted chocolate. Continue to heat over simmering water for 10 minutes, stirring constantly. Stir in vanilla.

MAKES ABOUT 2 CUPS   *Jennifer Stack*

GEORGIA PEACH COBBLER

6 tablespoons butter
1¼ cups sugar, divided
3¾ cups flour
2 teaspoons baking powder

½ teaspoon salt
¾ cup milk
3 cups peeled and sliced fresh
   peaches

Preheat oven to 350 degrees. Melt butter in a dry 2 quart deep baking dish in heated oven, remove from oven when melted. In a mixing bowl, combine 1 cup sugar, flour, baking powder, salt and milk. Beat batter until mixed; do not overmix. Mix peaches with remaining ¼ cup sugar.

Pour batter into hot baking dish. Pour peach slices into the center of the batter. Do not stir. Bake for 1 hour. Serve with ice cream or whipped cream.

SERVES 8   *Ken Patrick*

This is my mother's recipe; origin unknown. Other fruits can be substituted, such as blueberries, apples or nectarines.

In 1784, the Trustees were determined to place GA on a firm legal foundation by applying to the state legislature for charter. The school officially became known as the Public School of Germantown, and for legal and financial purposes, continues to use that term.

GRAMMIE'S MARSHMALLOW FUDGE

1 stick butter
5 cups sugar
⅛ teaspoon salt
1 (13 ounce) can evaporated milk

18 ounces semisweet chocolate chips
1 (8 ounce) jar marshmallow creme
2 cups walnuts (optional)
1 teaspoon vanilla extract

Combine butter, sugar, salt and evaporated milk in a saucepan. Cook over medium heat for 8 to 10 minutes or until mixture boils. Stir constantly and boil until mixture reaches soft ball stage (236 degrees). Remove from heat. Quickly add chocolate chips, marshmallow creme, walnuts and vanilla. Stir constantly until blended; fudge will start to stiffen a bit. Pour fudge into a greased 9x13 inch pan. Fudge will set as it cools.

MAKES 6 POUNDS   *Carol Buckley and Laura Martin*

PEACH CLAFOUTI

Butter to grease pan
⅓ cup plus 2 tablespoons
    granulated sugar, divided
3 cups ripe peaches, peeled and
    sliced
¾ cup milk
¾ cup light cream

3 large eggs
¼ cup flour
Pinch of salt
1 teaspoon vanilla extract
½ teaspoon cinnamon
Confectioners' sugar

Preheat oven to 375 degrees. Use butter to generously grease a 1½ quart shallow baking dish. Sprinkle dish with 2 tablespoons sugar. Spread peach slices evenly over the bottom of the pan.

In a blender, combine milk, cream, eggs, flour and salt. Process mixture for 2 minutes. Add remaining ⅓ cup sugar, vanilla and cinnamon. Blend for a few seconds and pour mixture over fruit.

Bake for 45 minutes or until puffed and golden. Cool slightly and dust top with confectioners' sugar. Serve warm with vanilla ice cream, if desired.

SERVES 6 TO 8   *Susan McCune*

If peaches are juicy, only use 2 cups to prevent mixture from being too liquidy.

LEMON WALNUT DESSERT

Crust

1 stick margarine
1 cup flour

½ cup small walnut pieces, plus
extra to sprinkle on top

Filling

1 (16 ounce) container frozen
whipped topping, thawed,
divided
16 ounces cream cheese, softened

2 cups confectioners' sugar
2 (3½ ounce) boxes instant lemon
pudding mix
1¾ cups milk

Preheat oven to 350 degrees. To make a crust, combine margarine, flour and walnuts with a fork and pat mixture into the bottom of a 9x13 inch pan. Bake crust for 15 to 20 minutes or until crust is just turning brown. Cool for a few minutes.

For filling, in a mixing bowl, cream together one-third of whipped topping, cream cheese and confectioners' sugar until smooth. Spread mixture over crust.

Prepare pudding mix according to directions on package using 1¾ cups milk. Spread pudding over cream cheese layer. Cover pudding with remaining whipped topping. Sprinkle with extra walnut pieces. Refrigerate at least 2 hours before serving.

Genie Ferguson

CHOCOLATE POTS DE CRÈME

1 pint light cream
3⅓ cups semisweet chocolate
chips

5 ounces brewed extra strong
coffee
¼ cup Kahlúa liqueur
6 large eggs

Heat cream to just boiling. Combine hot cream with all other ingredients in a blender. Blend on high speed for 3 minutes. Pour mixture into individual serving cups. Chill at least 4 hours or preferably overnight. Top with whipped cream and shaved chocolate.

SERVES 8

Godsey Meriwether Co.

*Other liqueurs may be substituted for the Kahlúa,
such as Grand Marnier, Bailey's or Chambord.*

The Germantown Academy chapter of the Cum Laude Society, founded in 1921, is the second oldest chapter in Pennsylvania. The Cum Laude Society was founded in 1906. Only seven school chapters in the nation predate Germantown Academy's chapter. The Society's Constitution states: "Its object is to promote learning and sound scholarship in secondary schools." Twenty percent of the senior class may be inducted, of whom no more than half may enter as juniors, based on criteria including honors courses, grades, "excellence in the moral sense and… the ideal of superiority in scholarship."

"Today the workmen affix a flag to the first iron beams that is put in place on the top, marking the attainment of the final height of the building. In the 18th century they observed a different and rather more convivial custom. Those in charge set out the "cake and ale" for the workman when this point in the construction of a public building was reached. It may be recalled that there was such an entertainment when the old State House in Philadelphia, now called Independence Hall, was near completion, and the founders of Germantown Union School were adherents to the same old custom…each Trustee and Treasurer do contribute ten shillings to this purpose."

From Trustee Minutes 1760

TRIFLE

- 1 (3 ounce) package instant chocolate pudding
- 1 (3 ounce) package instant vanilla pudding
- 4 cups milk
- 2 (12 ounce) container frozen whipped topping, thawed, regular or light, divided
- 1 (12 ounce) package pound cake, regular or light
- 1 jar jam or jelly, flavor of choice
- 2 packages fresh strawberries, sliced
- 2 packages fresh blueberries
- 2 packages fresh raspberries
- 4 kiwi fruit, sliced

Prepare each pudding in separate bowls according to directions on packages, using 4 cups milk total. Fold half a container of whipped topping into each pudding until blended.

Cut cake into 12 slices. Spread jelly on 6 slices. Place remaining slices on top, like a sandwich. Cut cake sandwiches into small cubes.

In a trifle bowl, spread a layer of half of the cake cubes. Top with a layer of all the chocolate pudding. Add half the fruit. Add another layer of remaining cake cubes. Top with all the vanilla pudding. Add remaining fruit. Spread remaining container of whipped topping over all and smooth top. Garnish, if desired, with extra fruit.

SERVES ABOUT 10   *Kirsten Gambone*

MEADOW GLEN LEMON TRIFLE

5 tablespoons butter
2 teaspoons lemon zest
½ cup freshly squeezed lemon juice
¼ teaspoon salt
1 cup sugar

3 large eggs
1 (16 ounce) package frozen pound cake, cut into ½ inch thick slices
3 pints vanilla ice cream, softened
6 to 8 fresh lemon slices for garnish

Melt butter in the top of a double boiler. Stir in lemon zest, lemon juice, salt and sugar. Blend in eggs, one at a time. Cook over boiling water, stirring constantly, until mixture begins to thicken. Remove from heat and cool for 10 to 15 minutes.

Line the bottom of a glass bowl or trifle dish with a single layer of cake slices. Spoon 1 pint of softened ice cream over cake. Pour one-third of lemon sauce over ice cream. Repeat layers twice. Garnish with lemon slices. Freeze 1 to 2 hours or until firm.

SERVES 8   *Sherrea Chadwin*

NORMA'S TREATS

2 sticks butter, softened
1 cup firmly packed brown sugar
1 large egg yolk

1 cup flour
6 (1½ ounce) chocolate candy bars
⅔ cup crushed nuts

Preheat oven to 350 degrees. Cream butter, brown sugar and egg yolk together. Mix in flour. Spread mixture into a lightly greased jelly roll pan. Bake for 15 to 20 minutes.

Remove from oven and turn off heat. Arrange candy bars on crust. Return to turned-off oven for a minute or two to allow chocolate to melt. Spread melted chocolate and sprinkle with nuts. Cut into bars or break into pieces.

SERVES 8 TO 10   *Carol R. Buckley*

Norma Tornetta (Mothers' Committee Chairman 1976-1977) gave me this recipe when I told her how much I loved Heath bars. Since she didn't tell me what they were called, I named these wonderful little bars after her!

One day we thought we would plant a tree. Our class asked a boy to get the tree for us. He sent us a letter and told us he saw one that he thought was good. So each boy brought twenty-six cents to help pay for it. When the day came for planting it, we went out on the campus. We each put a trowel full of dirt on it. Then we cheered the teachers, and also the janitor because he dug the hole for the tree. Doctor Kershaw said he hoped he lived long enough to climb the tree when it was big.

Charles Brigham,
Fourth Form
Primary News 1927

Patriots' Dinner Party Mocha Roll

Batter
6 large egg whites, room temperature
1 cup confectioners' sugar, divided
1 tablespoon all-purpose flour, plus extra for dusting pan

6 large egg yolks
1 tablespoon vanilla extract
6 ounces semisweet chocolate chips
3 tablespoons water

Filling
1½ cups heavy cream
½ cup confectioners' sugar
¼ cup unsweetened cocoa powder

1½ teaspoons instant coffee granules
1 teaspoon vanilla extract

Preheat oven to 350 degrees. Grease a 10x15 inch jelly roll pan. Line bottom of pan with wax paper and grease wax paper and dust with flour.

To make crust, in a small bowl, beat egg whites until soft peaks form. Gradually beat in ½ cup confectioners' sugar and flour until stiff peaks form. Cover and set aside.

In a large mixing bowl, beat egg yolks with vanilla and remaining ½ cup confectioners' sugar for 10 minutes or until thick. In a small saucepan, melt chocolate chips with water until smooth. Cool slightly. Stir chocolate into yolk mixture. Fold in egg whites. Spread batter into prepared pan. Bake for 15 to 20 minutes. Cool for 15 minutes.

Meanwhile, prepare filling. Beat together all filling ingredients until cream is whipped.

Turn cooled cake onto a damp tea towel. Carefully remove wax paper and let cake stand about 10 minutes. Spread filling over cake. Roll up cake in jelly roll fashion, lifting towel to roll the cake. Dust with confectioners' sugar. Wrap tightly and refrigerate.

Before serving, sprinkle with confectioners' sugar again and garnish around the edge with piped whipped cream rosettes.

SERVES 12

Kris Henry

A dessert fit for a king.

MAMA JACOBS' CHOCOLATE CHIP (CARAMEL SURPRISE) CUPS

1 (16½ ounce) package mini chocolate chip refrigerated cookie dough

24 Rolo candies, unwrapped (3 rolls)

Preheat oven to 350 degrees. Cookie dough is already divided into 40 squares. Roll dough into balls, using 1½ squares for each ball. Place balls in paper-lined mini muffin cups.

Bake for 8 minutes or until light golden brown. Remove from oven; the centers will be soft. Press a candy, narrow side down, into each cup. Leave top of candy showing and flush with top of batter. Return to oven and bake 3 minutes longer or until cups are golden brown; do not overbake. Cool completely before removing cups from muffin pan.

MAKES 24 CUPS   *Carolyn K. Jacobs*

DID YOU KNOW…

The GA swimming pool was built in 1965?

These can be made with your own chocolate chip cookie recipe, but make sure to use mini chocolate chips. Fill each liner three-fourths full. Your own recipe will probably yield more cups, so be sure to have more paper liners and Rolo candies on hand. There will be 4 squares left over after filling muffin cups; perfect for nibbling while cups are baking. Suggesting eating raw cookie dough may not be politically correct, but that's what we do.

Apple Walnut Pie

1 prepared pie crust, unbaked

Filling

1 large egg, lightly beaten
1¼ cups sour cream
¾ cup sugar
½ teaspoon salt

2 teaspoons vanilla extract
¼ cup flour
6-8 tart apples, sliced
(enough to fill pie shell)

Topping

⅓ cup firmly packed brown sugar
⅓ cup granulated sugar
1 teaspoon cinnamon
½ cup flour

Pinch of salt
1 cup walnut pieces
6 tablespoons butter, melted

Preheat oven 450 degrees. Mix all filling ingredients except apples. Add apples and mix until lightly coated. Spoon filling into pie crust. Bake 10 minutes. Reduce heat to 350 degrees and bake 40 minutes longer.

In the meantime, mix all topping ingredients. When pie is done baking, spoon topping over pie and bake another 10 minutes.

SERVES 8   *Virginia Menno*

Fresh Blueberry Pie

1 cup sugar
3 tablespoons cornstarch
⅛ teaspoon salt
1 cup water

1 quart fresh blueberries, divided
1 teaspoon butter (optional)
1 (10 inch) pie crust, baked

Combine sugar, cornstarch and salt in a large saucepan. Add water and 1 cup blueberries. Cook over medium-high heat, stirring constantly, for 20 minutes or until all the berries have burst and liquid is bubbly and thick. Remove from heat and stir in butter for added shine.

Fold in remaining blueberries until just coated. Pour filling into baked pie crust. Cool to allow filling to set. Serve with vanilla ice cream or lemon sherbet.

SERVES 8   *Kristine Thum*

Cooking time and amount of sugar may need to be adjusted depending on the size, sweetness and firmness of the berries.

Favorite Apple Pie

1 double-crust pie pastry

Filling

6 cups peeled and sliced cooking
    apples
1 tablespoon lemon juice
½ cup granulated sugar
½ cup packed light brown sugar

2 tablespoons quick-cooking
    tapioca
½ teaspoon cinnamon
¼ teaspoon nutmeg
Butter

Glaze

1 large egg white
1 teaspoon lemon juice

1 cup confectioners' sugar

Preheat oven to 450 degrees. Fit 1 pastry crust into a 9-inch pie pan. Combine all filling ingredients except butter and spoon into crust in pan. Dot filling with butter. Cut remaining pastry crust into strips and arrange in a basket-weave design over filling. Seal edges of crust.

Combine all glaze ingredients and mix until creamy. Slowly drizzle glaze over pie in a small stream until pie is covered. Cover crust edges with foil. Bake for 15 minutes. Reduce heat to 350 degrees and bake 50 minutes longer.

SERVES 8

Horace "Pete" Deacon III

Each of the seven "Houses" has approximately 70 students, eight advisors and a House Head.

- Each House will have two advisories from each class — that is, two 9th grade, two 10th grade, two 11th grade, and two 12th grade advisories, for a total of eight advisories.

- Rising eighth graders and all other entering 9th graders will be placed randomly in Houses as they enter the Upper School.

- Students will continue to have one advisor for both their 9th and 10th grade years and a second, different advisor, for their 11th and 12th grade years.

George Hastings

The ivy has been planted

By the side of old GA

And may it grow and flourish,

By the walls so old and gray,

Comrades we are leaving now,

Our hearts are bea'ing high,

And friendship warms each

heart I trow

Dear Germantown, Goodbye.

Oft to our student days

Fond memories will revert,

Tender the influence

They'll on our lives exert.

Down through the coming years,

True to thee we'll be,

Germantown, dear Germantown,

Would we were still with thee.

Chorus

O Germantown, dear Germantown

We're leaving you to-day,

But the days of cheer

And friendship dear

Will remain with us always.

APPLE PIE WITH CRUMB TOPPING

1 refrigerated single-crust pastry

Filling

7 cups peeled and thinly sliced apples

⅓ cup plus 1 tablespoon granulated sugar, divided

Juice and zest of 1 lemon

¼ teaspoon nutmeg

1½ tablespoons cornstarch

Crumb Topping

1 cup all-purpose flour

½ cup rolled oats

⅔ cup firmly packed brown sugar

½ teaspoon cinnamon

½ cup unsalted butter, chilled and cut into pieces

While preparing apples, prepare pastry if not already made, and refrigerate 30 to 60 minutes or until firm enough to roll. Roll out pastry and place into a 9-inch pie pan, trimming the edges. Place in freezer 15 minutes.

For filling, combine apples, ⅓ cup granulated sugar, lemon juice, and lemon zest in a large bowl. Mix well, then let rest 10 minutes.

Preheat oven to 400 degrees. In a small bowl, combine remaining 1 table-spoon sugar, nutmeg, and cornstarch. Sprinkle mixture over apples and stir well. Spoon filling into chilled pie crust and smooth into place. Place pie on center oven rack and bake 30 minutes.

While pie is baking, prepare topping. Mix flour, oats, brown sugar, and cinnamon in a food processor. Pulse several times to mix. Scatter butter over top of mixture and pulse until mixture resembles fine crumbs. Refrigerate until ready to use.

Remove pie from oven and reduce temperature to 375 degrees. Spoon crumbs onto center of pie, then spread them over the surface of the pie. Tamp the crumbs down lightly. Return pie to oven and bake 30 to 35 minutes or until topping is golden brown and the juices bubble at the edge. Cover pie loosely with aluminum foil if browning too much. Remove from oven and cool on a wire rack for about 1 hour before serving.

SERVES 6 TO 8

Abigail Korth

CRANBERRY-APPLE PIE

Crust

1¼ cups all-purpose flour

1 teaspoon sugar

½ teaspoon salt

¼ cup shortening, chilled and cut into pieces

¼ cup unsalted butter, chilled and cut into pieces

3 tablespoons ice water

Filling

1½ pounds tart green apples, peeled and cut into 1½-inch chunks

2 cups fresh or frozen cranberries

1¼ cups sugar, divided

¼ cup plus 2 tablespoons flour, divided

1 tablespoon cinnamon

3 tablespoons unsalted butter, melted and slightly cooled

1 large egg

Mix flour, sugar, and salt in a food processor. Add shortening and butter and process until mixture resembles coarse meal. Add ice water and process until moist clumps form. If too dry, add more water, 1 teaspoon at a time. Gather dough into a ball, then flatten into a disk. Wrap dough in plastic wrap and chill 1 hour, or up to 3 days. Roll out dough on a lightly floured surface into a 12-inch circle. Transfer to a 9-inch pie pan and trim overhanging dough to ½ inch. Fold crust under and crimp edge. Freeze crust 15 minutes.

Preheat oven to 400 degrees. Line crust with foil and fill with dried beans or pie weights. Bake 15 minutes. Remove foil and beans or weights. Bake 10 minutes longer or until golden, piercing bubbles as needed. Cool completely. Reduce oven temperature to 325 degrees.

To prepare filling, mix apples, cranberries, 1 cup sugar, ¼ cup flour, and cinnamon in a large bowl. Spoon fruit filling into baked pie crust. Bake 30 minutes. Meanwhile, whisk together butter, egg, remaining ¼ cup sugar, and remaining 2 tablespoons flour in a small bowl until blended. Pour mixture evenly over filling and spread to cover. Bake 1 hour longer or until apples are tender and filling begins to brown. Transfer to a rack and cool completely.

SERVES 8

Liz Kaufman

To save time, use a store-bought refrigerated pie crust.

very year 5th graders create large, 3-dimensional clay busts based on fictional characters. You can find these amazing sculptures displayed in the entrance of the Lower School in the Spring.

THE BEST KEY LIME PIE

Crust

1 cup graham cracker crumbs
½ cup firmly packed brown sugar

½ cup crushed walnuts
1 stick butter, melted

Filling

8 ounces cream cheese, softened
1 (14 ounce) can sweetened condensed milk

1 large egg
½ cup Key lime juice

Preheat oven to 350 degrees. Combine all crust ingredients and mix well. Press mixture into a 9 inch pie pan. Refrigerate while preparing filling.

Blend all filling ingredients until smooth. Pour filling into chilled crust. Bake for 8 to 10 minutes. Cool to room temperature, then refrigerate until ready to serve.

SERVES 8   *Linda Weber*

LEMON CUPCAKES WITH ORANGE GLAZE

Batter

1 (18 ounce) package moist yellow cake mix
1 (3.4 ounce) box instant lemon pudding mix

4 large eggs
½ cup vegetable oil
1 cup orange juice, freshly squeezed preferred

Glaze

1½ cups confectioners' sugar

4 to 6 tablespoons orange juice

Preheat oven to 350 degrees. Mix all batter ingredients with an electric mixer until smooth. Pour batter into greased or paper-lined muffin cups, filling three-fourths full. Bake for about 15 to 20 minutes. Drizzle baked cupcakes with glaze.

To make glaze, combine confectioners' sugar and orange juice.

SERVES 18 TO 24   *Elizabeth Dovey*

Also makes a wonderful breakfast muffin or Bundt cake.
For Bundt cake, bake 42 to 45 minutes.

BLUEBERRY/LEMON POUND CAKE

4 sticks unsalted butter, softened
3 cups sugar
2 teaspoons lemon zest
6 large eggs
4 cups unbleached all-purpose flour
1 tablespoon baking powder
¼ teaspoon baking soda

½ teaspoon salt
¾ cup milk
¼ cup freshly squeezed lemon juice
2 teaspoons vanilla extract
1½ teaspoons lemon extract
2 cups fresh blueberries, not canned or frozen (optional)
Confectioners' sugar (optional)

Preheat oven to 350 degrees. Combine butter and sugar in a mixing bowl. Beat with an electric mixer on high speed until light and fluffy. Beat in lemon zest. Add eggs, one at a time, beating well after each addition.

Sift together flour, baking powder, baking soda and salt in a separate bowl. In another bowl, mix milk, lemon juice and extracts. Add dry ingredients and liquid ingredients alternately to creamed mixture, beginning and ending with dry ingredients. Stir gently from the bottom of the bowl after each addition, stirring just enough to blend. Try not to overmix. Gently fold in blueberries. Spread batter into a generously greased and floured Bundt pan.

Bake for 50 to 60 minutes or until a sharp knife inserted all the way into the center comes out clean. Cool in pan for at least 20 minutes. Rap pan sharply on counter and invert cake onto a serving plate. Cool completely before sprinkling with confectioners' sugar and slicing.

SERVES 15 TO 25

Peter Waxler

During a periodic down cycle in Germantown Academy history, Haddington College proposed a merger of the two schools. The Board voted to proceed, and then the storm broke. The whole Germantown community protested and the agreement was cancelled. Haddington College did quite well for itself. It is now Bucknell University.

Lemon Sponge Pie

1 (9 inch) homemade or store bought pie crust, unbaked
4 tablespoons butter, softened
1 cup sugar
3 tablespoons flour

3 large eggs, separated
6 tablespoons freshly squeezed lemon juice
1 teaspoon lemon zest
1½ cups milk

Preheat oven to 425 degrees. Refrigerate pie crust in pan while preparing filling. Cream butter with an electric mixer. Gradually beat in sugar and flour and mix thoroughly. Add egg yolks, lemon juice, lemon zest and milk and beat well.

In a separate bowl, beat egg whites until stiff peaks form. Gently fold egg whites into filling. Pour filling into pie crust. Bake for 15 minutes. Reduce heat to 325 degrees and bake 30 minutes longer or until a toothpick inserted into the center comes out clean.

Serve with a dollop of whipped cream or drizzle with fresh raspberry or blueberry sauce.

SERVES 8

Sara Gowing

For lemon sponge "pudding", omit pie crust and bake in a greased 9 inch square glass baking pan.

Lemon Mousse Fruit Tart

Tart Shell

1¼ cups graham cracker crumbs
¼ cup sugar

5 tablespoons butter, melted

Lemon Mousse

Juice and zest of 2 lemons
2 large eggs
½ cup sugar
6 tablespoons butter, softened

1 cup heavy cream
1 pint fresh blueberries
1 pint raspberries

Preheat oven to 375 degrees. Combine all tart shell ingredients in a bowl. Press mixture into a 10 inch pie or tart pan. Bake for 6 to 8 minutes; cool.

For mousse, combine lemon juice and zest, eggs and sugar in a saucepan. Cook over low heat, stirring constantly with a wooden spoon, until mixture heavily coats the spoon; do not bring to a boil. Turn off heat and immediately stir in butter. Cool to room temperature or refrigerate.

In a separate bowl, beat cream to soft peaks. Gently fold whipped cream into lemon mixture. Spoon mousse into cooled shell. Refrigerate at least 6 hours. Cover tart completely with berries.

SERVES 6

Nicole Riter

Come spend a wonderful year in Leas Hall,

New friends, learning adventures, and Monarch butterflies in the fall.

Winter brings a chill to the air,

As you'll learn about the polar bear.

The colorful Eric Carle brightens the rainy days of spring,

A year in kindergarten is a magical thing!

Kindergarten, 2009

Tart shell and lemon mousse can be made a day ahead. When adding eggs to saucepan, it is very important to whisk fast over very low heat so eggs do not scramble.

In November of 1884, the class of 1885 profiled itself: "We number 29, averaging in age seventeen years, five months and eight days…Politically the Democrats have a hard time of it, as they number but 5 against 21 Republicans, 2 Prohibitionists and an Independent. In religious denominations we stand 18 Episcopalians' to seven Presbyterians and four Methodists.

APPLE PIE CAKE

1 stick butter
¾ cup sugar
1 large egg, lightly beaten
1 cup flour
1 teaspoon baking powder
1 teaspoon cinnamon
½ teaspoon salt
½ teaspoon nutmeg
½ teaspoon ground cloves
¼ teaspoon vanilla extract
2 cups peeled and chopped apple
½ cup pecans or walnuts, chopped

Preheat oven to 350 degrees. Melt butter in a saucepan. Remove from heat and blend in sugar and egg. In a medium bowl, combine flour, baking powder, cinnamon, salt, nutmeg and cloves. Mix in butter mixture. Fold in apple and nuts. Spread batter in a greased 9 inch pie pan.

Bake for 40 to 45 minutes. Serve warm with a scoop of vanilla ice cream.

SERVES 6 TO 8   *Gretchen Murray*

PRIBITKIN FRESH PEAR CAKE

4 cups peeled and chopped pear, cut into ½ inch chunks
1½ cups turbinado sugar (sugar in the raw)
4 large egg whites, lightly beaten
⅔ cup canola oil
2 cups unbleached all-purpose flour
1 cup whole wheat pastry flour
1 teaspoon salt
1 teaspoon pumpkin pie spice
1½ teaspoons baking soda

Combine pear and sugar and let stand for at least 1 hour in a covered dish.

Preheat oven to 325 degrees. Add lightly beaten egg whites and oil to pear mixture. In a separate bowl, combine both flours, salt, pumpkin pie spice and baking soda. Stir dry ingredients into pear mixture. Pour batter into a greased nonstick 10 inch Bundt pan.

Bake for 70 minutes. Cool on a rack for 10 minutes before inverting onto a serving plate and removing pan.

SERVES 12   *Edmund Pribitkin*

This is a recipe we use with the fresh pears we get from our pear tree in September. If using store bought pears, look for firm, crisp pears like Bosc pears rather than ripe Anjou or Bartlett pears.

COACH SHOULBERG'S FAVORITE CHEESECAKE

Crust
1½ cups graham cracker crumbs
¼ cup sugar

4 tablespoons butter, melted

Filling
24 ounces regular cream cheese, softened
1½ cups sugar
⅛ teaspoon salt

4 large eggs
1 to 2 teaspoons vanilla extract
1 teaspoon lemon zest or juice (optional)

Topping
2 cups regular sour cream
¼ cup sugar

2 teaspoons vanilla extract
Fresh fruit for garnish (optional)

Preheat oven to 350 degrees. Combine all crust ingredients. Press mixture into a 10 inch springform pan. Chill while preparing remainder of recipe.

To make filling, beat cream cheese. Slowly blend in sugar and salt and beat until smooth. Beat in eggs, one at a time. Mix in extract to taste and lemon zest. Pour filling into crust. Bake for 50 minutes or until firm. Remove from oven and allow to stand for 15 minutes; cake will fall as it stands.

Mix all topping ingredients except garnish and spread over baked cake. Increase oven to 450 degrees. Bake for 10 minutes; watch carefully so as to not overbake. Garnish with fresh fruit, if desired.

Dick Shoulberg

IT IS A FACT... GA SWIMMING

To date, the girl's team NEVER lost an Inter-Ac swim meet since 1969 . . . The boy's team won 26 Inter-Ac championships . . . Many days there are 5 PE classes in the pool, without a break . . . There is a parent/alumni swim in the pool every day from 7:40 to 9:00 am, and a faculty swim time at 2:00 pm.

In 2003, Robert L. Mc-Neil Jr., class of 1932, and long time Trustee and Benefactor of the Academy, established The McNeil Patriot Awards Scholarship Program. The purpose of this program is to award annually full tuition scholarships to four rising seniors', two boys and two girls, for their final year at the Academy. The students are chosen in recognition of the roles they have played as models for the younger Germantown Academy community.

Chocolate Chip Cheesecake

Crust
2½ cups graham cracker crumbs
¼ cup sugar

1 stick butter, melted

Filling
24 ounces cream cheese, softened
½ cup sugar
4 large eggs

1 cup sour cream
1 to 2 cups semisweet chocolate chips, or to taste

Topping
¼ cup sugar
1 cup sour cream

Semisweet chocolate chips

Preheat oven to 350 degrees. Mix cracker crumbs with sugar and place in a greased 9 inch springform pan. Drizzle butter over crumbs and mix until evenly moistened. Press mixture against the bottom and up the sides of the pan to form a crust. Refrigerate crust while preparing filling.

Combine cream cheese and sugar in a bowl and mix with a large spoon. Transfer mixture to a blender. Add eggs, one at a time, blending after each addition. Blend until very smooth. Return to bowl and stir in sour cream until smooth and completely mixed. Stir in chocolate chips. Pour filling into chilled crust. Bake for 45 minutes or until the top starts to crack and turn golden brown.

For topping, mix sugar into sour cream. Spread topping over baked cake to completely cover top. Sprinkle with chocolate chips. Bake about 5 minutes longer.

Cool cake on counter until cake separates from the side of the pan. Refrigerate cake in pan to cool overnight. The next day, remove cake from pan and return to refrigerator until ready to serve.

Jessica S. MacNair

This is my tried and true Chocolate Chip Cheesecake recipe.

APPLE BRANDY CHEESECAKE

Cinnamon Crust

1¼ cups graham cracker crumbs
⅓ cup ground walnuts

5 tablespoons butter, melted
½ teaspoon cinnamon

Filling

32 ounces cream cheese, softened
1 cup sugar
3 tablespoons apple brandy or
    Applejack liqueur
1 teaspoon cinnamon

½ teaspoon vanilla extract
⅛ teaspoon nutmeg
4 large eggs
1 cup chunky applesauce
¼ cup heavy cream

Crumb Topping

¾ cup firmly packed brown sugar
¾ cup flour
5 tablespoons butter, melted

½ teaspoon cinnamon
¼ teaspoon nutmeg

Preheat oven to 350 degrees. Combine all crust ingredients and press onto the bottom and 1½ inches up the sides of a 10 inch springform pan. Bake for 10 minutes; cool.

For filling, beat cream cheese until smooth. Gradually beat in sugar. Add brandy, cinnamon, vanilla and nutmeg and blend well. Add eggs, one at a time, beating well after each addition. Stir in applesauce and cream. Pour filling into cooled crust. Bake for 50 minutes or until center appears set.

Meanwhile, prepare topping. Combine all topping ingredients until crumbly. Sprinkle topping over baked cake. Return to oven and bake 10 minutes longer. Cool 5 minutes on a wire rack. Carefully loosen sides of pan and remove. Cover and chill thoroughly.

SERVES 8

Michelle Gill

The first class stone and ivy were dedicated in 1885. Dr. William Kershaw, who was the Headmaster at the time, was instrumental in fostering this new tradition. An Ivy Oration, much like valedictory speech, was read at graduation and was included in the *Ye Primer*. The oration stated the sentiments of the class as they prepared to leave GA. If the ivy was considered a living memorial, the class stone was a permanent testament to the class.

LOWER SCHOOL MATH RECIPE FOR PROBLEM SOLVING

R – Read the problem

E – Estimate the answer

C – Circle important numbers

I – Investigate information for too much or too little to solve

P – Plan a strategy like drawing a picture or making a chart

E – Evaluate the answer — does it make sense?

ROUGH APPLE CAKE

8 ounces self-rising flour
4 ounces sugar
1 stick butter

4 or 5 tart apples, peeled and roughly chopped
1 large egg, beaten
Milk

Preheat oven to 375 degrees. Gently mix flour, sugar and butter. Add apples and stir to mix well. Add egg and enough milk to make a thick, sticky batter. Spoon batter into a loaf pan.

Bake in center of oven for 35 to 45 minutes or until top turns golden brown. Reduce heat to 340 degrees and bake 30 minutes longer or until top is browned. Cool in pan 10 minutes. Remove pan and cool further on a rack. Serve warm with custard or cream.

SERVES 6 TO 8   *Gill Newbery*

DR. SAMUEL OSBOURN'S (BELOVED!) CAMP SUSQUEHANNOCK POUND CAKE

2 sticks unsalted butter
1 cup sugar
3 large eggs
2½ cups all-purpose flour
2 teaspoons baking powder

2 teaspoons baking soda
1 teaspoon salt
1 cup sour cream
5 teaspoons vanilla extract

Preheat oven to 350 degrees. Cream butter. Blend in sugar. Add eggs, one at a time, beating after each addition.

In a separate bowl, mix flour, baking powder, baking soda and salt. Add dry ingredients to creamed mixture. Stir in sour cream. Mix in vanilla. Pour batter into a greased or nonstick 10 inch Bundt pan. Bake for 45 minutes.

SERVES 12 OR MORE   *Cannie Shafer*

Serve cake alone (we know Dr. Osbourn liked this with coffee) or serve with fresh fruit or ice cream! Dr. Osbourn was a close friend of George Carlton "King" Shafer. They founded Camp Susquehannock together in 1905 in Brackney, PA. He came to Camp Susquehannock until he was 92 years old!

Jewish Apple Cake

2 teaspoons cinnamon
5 tablespoons plus 2 cups sugar, divided
3 cups flour
1 tablespoon baking powder

4 large eggs, room temperature
1 cup canola oil
1 tablespoon vanilla extract
½ cup orange juice
4 to 5 Granny Smith apples

Preheat oven to 350 degrees. Combine cinnamon and 5 tablespoons sugar; set aside. In the bowl of an electric mixer, combine remaining 2 cups sugar, flour, baking powder, eggs, oil, vanilla and orange juice. Beat until smooth.

Peel and quarter apples. Cut each quarter into 3 slices. Pour about half of batter into a greased and floured 10 inch tube pan with a removable bottom. Add a layer of apple slices. Sprinkle with about half of cinnamon mixture. Repeat layers, using remaining ingredients and arranging apple layer in a decorative fashion with all slices pointing in the same direction and nesting the slice before it. Bake for 1 hour, 40 minutes.

Cool cake for at least 30 minutes (more is better) before removing from pan. To remove, cut around edges with a knife. Keeping cake on its base, pull up center to remove cake from sides of pan. Use a knife to loosen cake bottom from base. Invert cake onto a plate, then invert again onto a serving plate.

Cake keeps for several days and freezes well.

SERVES 10 TO 14

Lynne Garbose
Phy Chauveau
Ethel Massey

*W*hitechapel Foundry in London, the same foundry that cast the Liberty Bell, cast the original bell for the belfry. When the bell was installed after the American Revolution, it did not have any resonance because the foundry had used too much iron and lead but not enough brass. The bell thus rang on E flat, a thud more than a brilliant peel. The bell was recast delivering the sound we hear today!

We provide carefully selected, fully trained student Writing Advisors to work on writing assignments in all subjects, in all grades in the Upper School. Students can bring assignments at any stage of development; brainstorming, outlining, rough or polished drafts. We'll help them wherever they are to make their writing clearer and more effective.

We are also the "home base" for creative writing here at GA. We will sponsor several programs each year that bring professional, working writers to campus to meet and work with our students. We hope to bring writers of all type and description: poets, fiction writers, journalists, editors, playwrights among others.

Easterns Carrot and Pineapple Cake

1½ cups oil
2 cups sugar
3 large eggs
2 teaspoons vanilla extract
2 cups flour
2 teaspoons cinnamon
2 teaspoons baking soda
1 teaspoon salt
2 cups shredded carrot
1 cup chopped nuts
½ cup crushed pineapple, drained (about 8 ounces)
1 cup raisins

Preheat oven to 350 degrees. Beat together oil, sugar and eggs. Add vanilla. In a separate bowl, sift together flour, cinnamon, baking soda and salt. Add dry ingredients to batter. Stir in carrot, nuts, pineapple and raisins until thoroughly blended. Pour batter into a greased and floured 9x13 inch baking pan.

Bake for 1 hour. Cool completely. Spread icing over cake.

Cream Cheese Icing

3 ounces cream cheese, softened
1¼ cups confectioners' sugar
1 stick butter, softened

Beat all icing ingredients together until smooth. Spread over cooled cake.

SERVES 12 TO 14

Tink McDevitt

When eaten immediately, this cake is light. It is an excellent dessert to make ahead and freeze. When the cake is frozen, it becomes more dense and moist.

AUNT MARTHA'S CARROT CAKE

1½ cups oil
2½ cups sugar
4 large egg yolks
5 tablespoons hot water
2½ cups flour
1½ teaspoons baking powder
½ teaspoon baking soda

1 teaspoon nutmeg
¼ teaspoon salt
1 teaspoon cinnamon
1 teaspoon ground cloves
1½ cups shredded carrot
4 large egg whites

Preheat oven to 350 degrees. Cream oil and sugar until well mixed. Add egg yolks, one at a time, beating well after each addition. Beat in hot water.

In a separate bowl, sift together flour, baking powder, baking soda, nutmeg, salt, cinnamon and cloves. Mix dry ingredients into batter. Stir in carrot; batter will be thick.

Using a chilled bowl and beaters, beat egg whites with an electric mixer. Fold egg whites into batter; do not overmix. Pour batter into a greased and lightly floured 9 inch tube pan. Bake for 60 to 70 minutes or until a toothpick inserted in the center comes out clean. Cool before spreading frosting on top.

Frosting

6 tablespoons butter, softened
8 ounces cream cheese, softened
2 teaspoons vanilla extract

1 (16 ounce) package
   confectioners' sugar

Cream together butter and cream cheese. Mix in vanilla and confectioners' sugar until smooth.

SERVES 10 TO 12   *Patti Cannon*

Use a separate cold bowl to beat egg whites;
place bowl and beaters in refrigerator ahead of time.

The Writing Center will also promote opportunities for students to participate in writing competitions and to send their work out for publication. We plan to institute a program of coffeehouses, where students can share their work with each other and with the community. Through connections with off-campus programs, such as the Kelly Writers House at the University of Pennsylvania, we will seek out opportunities to connect with the larger writing community, and to expand and promote creative writing here at GA. We also plan to support our on-campus publications, and to offer an ongoing writing workshop for students interested in sharing and critiquing their original creative writing.

The 250th anniversary happens to coincide with our welcoming Mr. Schellhas as our new Head of Upper School. What are his plans for the anniversary? For one, he hopes to create a 21st Century GA committee comprised of Upper School faculty. The committee will work on shifting the school from a subject-oriented to an interdisciplinary curriculum and increasing the use of technology in classes. The goal is to prepare students for the future in an interdisciplinary and computer-based world. On a social front, Mr. Schellhas looks forward to celebrating some of GA's traditions, the biggest one being GA/PC day. "I'm excited about the school unity," Mr Schellhas says, "especially the unity between the Upper, Middle, and Lower Schools."

Peanut Butter Dream Pie

8 ounces cream cheese, softened
¾ cup peanut butter
1 cup confectioners' sugar
½ cup milk

1 (9 ounce) container frozen whipped topping, thawed
1 graham cracker crust or chocolate cookie crust
Chocolate syrup or nuts for garnish

Beat cream cheese with an electric mixer until fluffy. Add peanut butter and sugar and beat until smooth. Mix in milk. Fold in whipped topping. Pour filling into crust. Freeze overnight. Garnish with chocolate syrup or nuts.

SERVES 8

Mitzi Singmaster

Oreo Ice Cream Explosion

1 (18 ounce) package Oreo cookies
1 stick butter or margarine, melted
1 (10 ounce) jar hot fudge

2 (½ gallon) containers ice cream, flavor of choice, softened
1 (10 ounce) jar caramel sauce
Chopped nuts or sliced banana (optional)

Crush cookies in a plastic bag. Add melted margarine to bag and mix well. Pat mixture into the bottom and up the sides of a deep dish pie pan.

Pour three-fourths of hot fudge over the crust. Pack 1 container of ice cream into pie. Pour caramel sauce over ice cream. Pack second container of ice cream on top. Drizzle with remaining hot fudge. Top with nuts or banana slices. Freeze for several hours before serving.

SERVES 8

Amy Abrams

Mama Jacobs' Best Ever Butter Cake

Batter

1 (18½ ounce) package yellow
  cake mix

1 large egg

1 stick butter, melted

Filling

8 ounces cream cheese, softened

2 large eggs

½ tablespoon vanilla extract

1 (16 ounce) package
  confectioners' sugar

1 stick butter, melted

Preheat oven to 350 degrees. In the bowl of an electric mixer, combine all batter ingredients. Pour batter into a lightly greased 9x13 inch baking pan; set aside.

To prepare filling, beat cream cheese with an electric mixer until smooth. Beat in eggs and vanilla. Add confectioners' sugar and beat well. Reduce speed of mixer and slowly pour in butter. Mix well. Pour filling over batter and spread evenly.

Bake for 40 to 45 minutes or until cake is light golden brown. Do not over-bake; better moist than dry. Cool completely before cutting into squares.

MAKES 20 TO 24 SQUARES   *Carolyn K. Jacobs*

Kahlúa Cake

Batter

1 (18 ounce) package devil's
  food cake mix

1 (4½ ounce) package instant
  chocolate pudding mix

½ cup Kahlúa liqueur

½ cup crème de cacao
  liqueur

¾ cup strong brewed coffee

½ cup oil

4 large eggs, room
  temperature

Glaze

2 tablespoons Kahlúa liqueur

2 tablespoons brewed coffee

2 tablespoons crème de
  cacao

1 cup confectioners' sugar

Preheat oven to 350 degrees. Beat all batter ingredients together with an electric mixer. Pour batter into a greased Bundt pan. Bake for 40 to 45 minutes; do not overbake.

Meanwhile, combine all glaze ingredients. When done baking, pierce top of cake all over with a fork. Pour glaze over cake. Cool before removing pan.

Jane Schmidt

Cake should be very moist; cutting will be a little messy. It helps to wipe your knife clean with a warm moist cloth between slices. It is so good I don't think your guests will mind it not being perfect!

The Glee Club from the Old Campus performed with girls' schools such as the Stevens School, The Lankenau School and Abington Friends School. After their performance, there was dancing and refreshments served by the schools' Mothers' Committee.

RED VELVET CAKE

3 tablespoons unsweetened cocoa
2 ounces red food coloring
½ cup shortening
1½ cups sugar
2 large eggs
2¼ cups sifted flour

¾ teaspoon salt
1 cup buttermilk
1 teaspoon vanilla extract
1 teaspoon vinegar
1 teaspoon baking soda

Preheat oven to 350 degrees. Mix cocoa and food coloring into a paste. Cream together shortening and sugar. Add eggs and mix well. Mix in cocoa paste. Combine flour and salt and add to mixture alternately with buttermilk and vanilla. Fold in vinegar and baking soda.

Pour batter evenly into two greased and lightly floured 8 or 9 inch round cake pans. Bake for 25 to 30 minutes. Cool slightly before removing from pans. Cool completely before spreading icing between layers and over outside of cake.

Icing

3 tablespoons flour
1 cup milk
2 sticks butter, softened

1 cup sugar
1 teaspoon vanilla extract

Blend flour and milk in a saucepan. Heat and stir until thickened and smooth. Refrigerate until very cold. Icing will fall apart at room temperature. In a separate bowl, cream butter and sugar together with an electric mixer for 15 minutes or until fluffy. Add vanilla. Blend in refrigerated mixture until combined.

SERVES 12

Lauren Hellman

RAKOWSKY ZUCCHINI CAKES

3 large eggs
1¼ cups olive oil
1½ cups sugar
1 teaspoon vanilla extract
2½ cups shredded unpeeled
    zucchini
2 cups all-purpose flour

2 teaspoons baking soda
1 teaspoon baking powder
1 teaspoon salt
1 teaspoon cinnamon
1 teaspoon ground cloves
1 cup chopped walnuts
Icing (recipe below)

Preheat oven to 350 degrees. Beat eggs, olive oil, sugar and vanilla in a large mixing bowl until light and fluffy. Fold in zucchini.

In a medium mixing bowl, sift together flour, baking soda, baking powder, salt, cinnamon and cloves. Add dry ingredients to batter and mix until just blended. Fold in walnuts. Pour batter into paper-lined muffin cups, filling three-fourths full.

Bake 20 to 25 minutes or until a toothpick inserted in the center comes out clean. Cool completely before spreading icing over cupcakes.

Icing

2 sticks butter, softened
12 ounces cream cheese, softened

4 cups sifted confectioners' sugar
¾ teaspoon vanilla extract

Beat butter and cream cheese together in a medium mixing bowl until fluffy. Add sugar, ½ cup at a time, beating after each addition. Add vanilla and beat until smooth. If not using immediately, refrigerate for up to 3 days; bring to room temperature and beat until smooth before spreading on cupcakes.

SERVES 22 TO 24

Evelyn Rakowsky

MRS. McCLURE'S GREAT MOIST CAKE

6 large eggs
1 cup vegetable oil
2 cups flour
2 cups sugar
1 teaspoon vanilla extract
2 teaspoons baking powder

Preheat oven to 350 degrees. Beat together all ingredients until well blended. Pour batter into a greased and floured Bundt pan. Bake for 1 hour. Cool in pan 10 minutes. Invert onto a rack and remove pan to cool completely.

SERVES 12

*Rosemarie Beltz
Diane Doyle*

Warm cake can be glazed or sprinkle with confectioners' sugar. Yum!

Great way to use up zucchini!

SNICKERS BAR PIE

1 (½ gallon) vanilla ice cream, softened
1 large Snickers bar, chopped
1 ready-made chocolate cookie pie crust

Place softened ice cream in a bowl. Mix chopped Snickers into ice cream and spoon into pie crust. Cover and freeze for 2 hours.

SERVES 8

Elise Shirakawa

Any combination of candy, cookies and pie crust can be used.

AUNT CLARE'S HOMEMADE CHOCOLATE CAKE

2 cups flour
2 cups sugar
¾ cup cocoa powder
1 teaspoon salt
½ cup oil
1 cup milk

2 large eggs
1 teaspoon vanilla extract
1 teaspoon baking powder
2 teaspoons baking soda
1 cup boiling water

Preheat oven to 350 degrees. Combine all ingredients in order listed and mix well. Pour batter into a lightly greased 10 inch tube pan. Bake for 40 to 45 minutes. Cool in pan. Remove from pan to frost.

Frosting

1 stick butter, softened
1 (16 ounce) package confectioners' sugar

1 teaspoon vanilla extract
3 to 5 tablespoons milk, or as needed

Mix all ingredients, adding enough milk to reach a spreading consistency. Spread over cooled cake.

SERVES 12 TO 16

Clare M. Toland

EASY CHOCOLATE CHIP CAKE

4 large eggs
½ cup oil
1 cup water
1 (18¼ ounce) package yellow cake mix
1 (3 ounce) package instant vanilla pudding mix

1 (6 ounce) package semisweet chocolate chips
1 (1 ounce) square unsweetened chocolate, shaved
1 (16 ounce) container chocolate frosting

Preheat oven to 350 degrees. Combine eggs, oil, water, cake mix and pudding mix in a bowl. Beat until batter is smooth. Stir in chocolate chips. Fold in shaved chocolate. Pour batter into a greased and floured tube pan.

Bake for 40 minutes or until a toothpick inserted in the center comes out clean. Cool before removing from pan. Ice cooled cake with frosting.

SERVES 12 TO 16

Susan R. Miller

SOUR CREAM DOUBLE CHOCOLATE CAKE

1 (18¼ ounce) package chocolate
   cake mix
1 (3 ounce) package instant
   chocolate pudding mix
4 large eggs
½ cup oil

¾ cup water
1 cup sour cream
1 (6 ounce) package chocolate
   chips
Confectioners' sugar (optional)

Preheat oven to 350 degrees. Combine all ingredients except chocolate chips and confectioners' sugar in a bowl. Beat for 3 minutes with an electric mixer. Stir in chocolate chips. Pour batter into a greased Bundt pan.

Bake for 50 to 55 minutes. Cool in pan 20 minutes. Remove from pan and dust with confectioners' sugar.

SERVES 12 TO 16

Betsy Palmer

DERBY PIE

2 large eggs
1 cup sugar
1 stick butter or margarine,
   melted
1 to 4 tablespoons bourbon
   (optional)

¼ cup cornstarch
1 cup chopped pecans
1 cup semisweet chocolate chips
1 pie crust, unbaked
Frozen whipped topping, thawed
   (optional)

Preheat oven to 350 degrees. Lightly beat eggs in a medium mixing bowl. Stir in sugar, melted butter and bourbon.

In a smaller bowl, mix cornstarch with chopped pecans and chocolate chips. Add to filling and mix. Pour filling into pie crust. Bake 45 to 50 minutes. Cool completely. Top with whipped topping.

SERVES 8

Janie Stack

CANDY CANE PIE

1 (½ gallon) vanilla ice cream,
   softened
4 candy canes, crushed
1 ready-made vanilla cookie
   pie crust

Place softened ice cream in a bowl. Mix crushed candy cane into ice cream and spoon into pie crust. Cover and freeze for 2 hours.

SERVES 8

Elise Shirakawa

Any combination of candy, cookies and pie crust can be used.

*G*ermantown Academy continued its celebration of 250 years on Saturday, January 2, 2010 with a special event to kick off the New Year — GA Celebrates! The audience was in awe during this unique day where the GA's Upper School choral group, the Singing Patriots, and the first-ever Singing Patriots alumni, gathered on the same stage to help take us on a walk through GA history and American history in song and speech. The production was the brainchild of Upper School choral director Michael Kemp, and was written by faculty emeriti and archivist Edwin Probert 1760.

FOOD PROCESSOR PIE CRUST

3 cups all-purpose flour
1 tablespoon sugar
1 teaspoon salt
1 stick unsalted butter, chilled and cut into small pieces
½ cup shortening, chilled and cut into small pieces
½ cup cold water

Combine flour, sugar and salt in a food processor. Pulse twice to mix. Add butter and pulse 5 to 6 times to cut in. Fluff mixture with a fork, lifting it from the sides and bottom of the processor bowl. Add shortening and pulse 5 to 6 times to cut in. Fluff mixture as before. Drizzle half of water over mixture and pulse 5 or 6 times. Fluff as before. Test pastry by squeezing a small portion between fingers. If it does not pack, add remaining water and pulse 5 or 6 times. The dough will form clumps. Transfer contents of processor into a large bowl. Test pastry again by squeezing a small portion between fingers. If is does not pack, drizzle a teaspoon of cold water over pastry and work it in with fingertips.

MAKES 2 (9 INCH) SINGLE CRUSTS   *Joan Korth*

A couple of years ago, the GA girls crew team took turns making pies and bringing them as a snack after the Saturday morning practices. Although store bought pies were welcome, the girls and their coach took pride in making them from scratch.

DULCE DE LECHE CAKE
(PASTEL DE CUATRO LECHES)

2 teaspoons butter
1 tablespoon plus 2 cups flour, divided
2 teaspoons baking powder
1½ teaspoons fine salt
6 large eggs, room temperature, separated
1¼ cups sugar
½ cup whole milk
1½ tablespoons dark rum

1 tablespoon vanilla extract
1 (14 ounce) can sweetened condensed milk
1 (12 ounce) can evaporated milk
1 cup heavy cream
1 (16 ounce) jar dulce de leche (milk caramel) (Available online at igourmet.com, or check at the Chestnut Hill Cheese Shop.)

Preheat oven to 350 degrees. Use butter to grease a 9x13 inch baking pan. Dust pan with 1 tablespoon flour; invert and tap out excess flour and set aside. Sift together remaining 2 cups flour, baking powder and salt in a bowl; set aside.

Beat egg whites in a large bowl with an electric mixer on medium speed for 2 minutes or until soft peaks form. While mixer is still running, add sugar in a gradual stream and continue beating again to soft peaks. Add egg yolks, one at a time, beating well after each addition. Add dry ingredients alternately with whole milk in 3 parts, beating until smooth after each addition. Add rum and vanilla and beat until mixed.

Pour batter into reserved pan. Bake for 30 minutes or until golden brown. Cool for 30 minutes.

Whisk together condensed milk, evaporated milk and cream in a bowl. While cake is still warm, use a knife to poke holes all over cake, penetrating to the bottom of the pan. Pour milk mixture over warm cake and set aside to cool completely. Cover with plastic wrap and refrigerate at least 4 hours or until cake is well chilled and liquid is absorbed.

Spread dulce de leche over cake and serve.

Emily Wagner

Instead of topping with dulce de leche, cake can be topped with whipped cream or a dusting of confectioners' sugar and served with fresh fruit. Luxuriant moistness is this dessert's calling card.

More than 80 performers gathered on stage, including the Select Strings orchestral group, featuring senior Sophia Wu '10 and alumna Joanna Frankel '01, performing a special Bach Double Violin Concerto. Narrators who helped tell the stories included Bobbie Crane Devlin 1760, Keith Williams, Francis Ballard 1760, Richard House, Shelby Hightower '10, Maggie McVeigh 1760, Kathryn Kleppinger '00, Michael Meloro '08, Ryan LaMont '04, Aaron Sprecher '07 and Jim Connor 1760. After each of the eight narrations, Mr. Kemp conducted music to match each era while a slideshow was going on either side of the stage.

To end the evening, Mr. Kemp introduced his premier of "A Tribute to our Forefathers," which combined God Bless America, America the Beautiful, and the Germantown Academy alma mater. It was the perfect ending to a special celebration of GA's rich history.

President Washington, in gratitude for both the professional and the personal services rendered to him and to his family by the Academy, planted a chestnut tree on the campus in Germantown. The planting of the tree symbolized the eternal quality of his connection to our school, a connection that we are re-vitalizing and re-planting, permanently, here in Fort Washington with the presence of the Fairbanks' bust, a sculpture that can only be displayed by institutions which can authenticate a true relationship with our Founding Father. Permission to have and display the bust has been granted by the Fairbanks family.

SWEET POTATO PIE

1 stick butter, softened
2 cups cooked and mashed sweet potatoes
2 cups sugar
1 (5 ounce) can evaporated milk
1 teaspoon vanilla extract
3 large eggs, beaten
1½ teaspoons cinnamon
2 pie crusts, unbaked

Preheat oven to 350 degrees. Combine butter, sweet potatoes, sugar and milk in a bowl and mix until well blended. Add vanilla, egg and cinnamon and mix well. Pour filling into unbaked pie crusts.

Bake for 1 hour or until pie is firm but not hardened.

SERVES 12 TO 16

Leslie Feggans-Haynes

AUTUMN BUTTERSCOTCH PUMPKIN CAKE

1 cup butterscotch chips
2 cups all-purpose flour
1¾ cups sugar
1 tablespoon baking powder
1½ teaspoons cinnamon
½ teaspoon nutmeg
1 teaspoon salt
1 cup canned solid pumpkin pack
½ cup vegetable or canola oil
3 large eggs, beaten
1 tablespoon vanilla extract

Preheat oven to 350 degrees. Microwave butterscotch chips for 1 minute on 70% power; chips should retain some of their original shape. Stir and microwave in 10 to 15 second intervals, as needed, until melted and smooth; set aside.

Combine flour, sugar, baking powder, cinnamon, nutmeg and salt in a medium bowl. In a separate large bowl, stir together melted butterscotch, pumpkin, oil, egg and vanilla with a wire whisk. Blend in dry ingredients. Spoon batter into a greased and floured 12 cup Bundt pan.

Bake for 40 to 50 minutes or until a toothpick inserted comes out clean. Cool in pan on a rack for 30 minutes. Remove from pan and cool completely on rack.

SERVES 12 TO 16

Kathie Vit

GH's Neighborhood

We are truly at an extraordinary time in Germantown Academy history. In addition to celebrating 250 years of independent school education - the oldest school of its kind in America - the school announced plans to move forward in spring 2010 with Phase 1 of a $120 million Campus Master Plan. Phase I includes the construction of a new Middle/Upper School buildings for grades 6 through 12. Construction of a Wet Meadow project and new athletic fields, on the premise that funding is available, has also been approved. Phase ll includes the renovation of the Lower School and construction of an indoor athletic complex, complete with a competition gym, swimming pool, wrestling complex, squash courts and community fitness facility. Phase lll will address the arts with a 700+ Seat Theater, digital media lab and performance rooms.

The new Middle/Upper School building will give GA approximately 40% more space than it currently has to serve those students and faculty, and will be a testament to the plan's integration of the environment and academics. It will offer state of the art facilities, accessibility enhancements, environmental sustainability and increased technology.

It is imperative that we continue to serve the ambitious and sophisticated programs our Middle and Upper School students and faculty have developed, and rely upon, on a daily basis," said Head of School Jim Connor 1760. "We are on the cutting edge of some exciting things for a history as long as ours, and I am pleased that we will be able to deliver this plan for the current and future GA community."

The Wet Meadow/Outdoor Athletic Complex will be a highlight all on its own, as the project has the makings of being the first of its kind to become LEED (Leaders in Energy and Environment Design) certified. By returning 12 acres of floodplain to its intended natural state and building an environmentally friendly outdoor educational space, Germantown Academy will become a leader in 21st century learning.

Roasted Brussels Sprouts with Balsamic Bacon and Parmesan

1¼ pounds Brussels sprouts
(about 25)
Dash of salt

1 cup oil, such as peanut, blended
or corn, divided
Salt and pepper to taste
4 tablespoons butter, divided

Vinaigrette

¼ cup balsamic vinegar
¾ cup olive oil
2 to 3 tablespoons Dijon mustard

2 tablespoons honey
Kosher or sea salt and freshly
ground black pepper to taste

Garnish

6 slices bacon, thickly sliced,
cooked and chopped or
crumbled

½ cup shaved Parmigiano-
Reggiano cheese

Preheat oven to 350 degrees. Cut Brussels sprouts in half lengthwise. Blanch Brussels sprouts in boiling salted water for about 10 seconds or until just cooked and still firm. Drain and immediately submerge in ice water. Drain again and dry sprouts.

Heat a sauté pan with a thin film of about ½ cup oil until hot but not smoking. (Note: only cover the bottom of the pan – the Brussels sprouts should not soak in the oil.) Add half the sprouts to the pan, cut side down. Cook over high heat for 5 minutes or until brown; do not shake pan. Sprinkle with salt and pepper. Finish by adding 2 tablespoons butter to pan and cook, shaking pan, to brown. Transfer to oven and bake 2 to 3 minutes. Repeat process with remaining Brussels sprouts, oil and butter.

Whisk together all vinaigrette ingredients.

To serve, mound Brussels sprouts on a plate. Drizzle with vinaigrette. Sprinkle with bacon and top with shaved Parmesan cheese.

SERVES 4

*A*lison two is a 120-seat restaurant with two private dining rooms, a full bar with its own menu and a cozy "living room "with a fireplace and flat screen television. The 150-year-old stone building is a warm and lush dining space with unusual architectural accents and a glowing atmosphere.

ALISON
two

Chef Alison Barshak serves contemporary American cuisine with ethnic twists and an emphasis on seafood. The cuisine reflects her interest in travel and each dish presents a complete experience from the country of its origin.

Alison two
424 S. Bethlehem Pike, Fort Washington, PA 19034 215 591-0200
www.alisontwo.com

*Y*our appetizer and dessert party is covered! Beginnings offers a variety of frozen hors d'oeuvres, homemade by Kris Henry, ready to heat and serve to your guests.

BEGINNINGS

*F*or a sweet ending to your party try some specialty cookies or cakes by *Sara's Sweets.*

SARA'S SWEETS

BAKED GOAT CHEESE WITH CARAMELIZED ONION, GARLIC AND FIGS

1 pound goat cheese
½ cup sliced dried Mission figs
¼ cup dry sherry
3 tablespoons olive oil
1 large Spanish onion, sliced
5 cloves garlic, crushed
2 sprigs rosemary
1 teaspoon salt
Freshly ground black pepper to taste
1 baguette, sliced, for dipping

Preheat oven to 350 degrees. Crumble goat cheese into a baking dish. In a saucepan, combine figs and sherry with enough water to just cover figs. Bring to a boil. Cover and remove from heat; let figs stand to plump.

Heat olive oil in a skillet over medium heat. Add onion, garlic, rosemary, salt and pepper. Cook, stirring often, for 10 minutes. Using a slotted spoon, remove figs from liquid. Add figs to onion mixture. Spoon onion/fig mixture over goat cheese. Bake for 20 minutes or until edges bubble.

SERVES 12 TO 14

SPICE COOKIES

⅔ cup dark corn syrup
1½ cups sugar, plus extra for sprinkling
1½ sticks butter, softened
1 tablespoon cinnamon
1 tablespoon ginger
1 tablespoon ground cloves
½ teaspoon salt
1½ teaspoons baking soda
4 cups flour, divided
⅔ cup heavy cream

Preheat oven to 350 degrees. Heat corn syrup in a saucepan; do not boil. Place sugar in a mixing bowl. Pour hot syrup over sugar and beat with an electric mixer for 10 minutes or until dissolved. Beat in butter, cinnamon, ginger, cloves and salt.

In a separate bowl, mix baking soda and 2 cups flour. Add to syrup mixture. Mix in cream and remaining 2 cups flour.

Drop dough by teaspoonfuls onto baking sheets. Sprinkle with sugar, if desired. Bake for 6 to 7 minutes.

MAKES 2 DOZEN

Beginnings
215.540.0258, 208khenry@verizon.com
Sara's Sweets
215 872-8431, saragara@comcast.net

BLUE BELL INN LENTIL SALAD

2 cups French green lentils
5 cups chicken broth
1 small onion, chopped
1 stalk celery, chopped

¼ bunch flat leaf parsley
¼ cup tarragon vinegar
1 cup light olive oil
Salt and pepper to taste

Wash lentils and pick out any particles; drain and transfer to a pot. Add chicken broth and let soak for 1 hour.

Place onion, celery and parsley in a cheesecloth bag and add to lentils and broth. Bring to a boil. Reduce heat to a simmer and cook for 10 minutes or until tender. Drain lentils and cool; discard vegetables.

Whisk together vinegar, oil and salt and pepper until thoroughly blended. Add vinaigrette to drained lentils and toss to mix. Serve with finely chopped onion and hot pepper infusion or Louisiana hot sauce.

SERVES 4

Since 1743, the Blue Bell Inn has been serving guests food and beverage, and, in its earliest days, offered lodging. The historic building was known as the White House until 1796 and was marked on George Washington's military maps of 1777 in which he led his troops to the battle of Germantown. Washington stayed at the inn during these times. In 1796 when the name was changed to the Blue Bell Inn, a Blue Bell was hung on the building so the people who did not know how to read could know the name of the inn. Today, it is still prominently displayed! In 1840, the name of the town changed from Pigeontown to Blue Bell because the Inn was so prominent in the town's history.

Blue Bell Inn
601 West Skippack Pike, Blue Bell, PA 19422
215 646-2010, www.bluebellinn.com

*T*oday, the award winning Blue Bell Inn is famous throughout the Delaware Valley for its fine food. John Lamprecht has followed a family tradition started by his father, who was once the garde-manager at the Warwick Hotel, and is known to be the creator of Lamaze Sauce.

BLUE BELL INN

The building has been extensively remodeled, adding the upscale casual Blue Bell Bistro, complete with fireplace, cathedral ceiling, and French doors that lead outside to the popular Blue Bell Café-all the while the exterior still remains an imposing 18th century building.

*S*erving Ambler's finest food. Head Chefs Peter Sherba and Floyd Powell offer a delectable "New World" menu, featuring prime meats, fresh pastas and ocean-fresh fish.

BRIDGET'S MODERN STEAKHOUSE

The menu now also features "small plates", for a quick bite, and savory choice cuts from the Butcher Block menu. Bridget's is a great place to gather with friends and family for a relaxed meal in the beautiful dining room or a few cocktails in the expanded bar!

BRIDGET'S PORK TENDERLOIN

2 pounds pork tenderloin
Lemon pepper seasoning
¼ cup olive oil
¼ cup soy sauce

2 cloves garlic, crushed
½ teaspoon dried thyme
3 shakes of Tabasco sauce

Remove silver skin from pork and cut meat into 2 inch thick medallions. Lightly coat pork with lemon pepper seasoning; set aside.

In a medium mixing bowl, whisk together olive oil, soy sauce, garlic, thyme and Tabasco until well mixed. Add pork to marinade mixture and let stand 30 to 60 minutes.

When ready to cook, preheat a grill. Grill pork over medium-high heat until done.

SERVES 4 TO 5

Bridget's Modern Steakhouse
8 West Butler Pike, Ambler, PA 19002
267 465-2000, www.bridgetssteak.com

CRÈME BRÛLÉE

1 vanilla bean
1 quart heavy cream
1¼ cups sugar, divided

12 egg yolks
Fresh fruit or mint for garnish

Preheat oven to 325 degrees. Split vanilla bean in half lengthwise and scrape out seeds. Place seeds and pod into a saucepan with cream and ½ cup sugar. Bring to a simmer, then remove from heat.

In a mixing bowl, whisk together ½ cup sugar and egg yolks until well mixed. Slowly whisk warm cream mixture into egg yolk mixture. Strain mixture and chill.

When mixture is cool, ladle into individual shallow baking dishes. Place dishes in a large baking pan. Fill large pan halfway up sides of dishes with hot water. Bake until custard is set; cool.

Spread a thin layer of remaining ¼ cup sugar over each custard. Caramelize sugar topping with a blow torch or broiler. Garnish with fresh fruit or mint.

SERVES 6

The historic Broad Axe Tavern was built in 1681, making it the oldest Tavern in Pennsylvania.

BROAD AXE TAVERN

The recently renovated Broad Axe Tavern promises a unique experience for everyone, including a large selection of beers on tap, a comprehensive wine list and a broad array of tavern food that focuses on small plates.

Broad Axe Tavern
901 West Butler Pike, Ambler, PA 19002
215 643-6300, www.broadaxetavern.com

*J*anet Binswanger '79 first started cooking while at GA. She made the food for the 5th grade Greek feast, she baked for every bake sale, she even made the brown bag lunches daily for her three siblings.

CULINARY CONCEPTS INC.

In 1987, she fulfilled her dream, when she started Culinary Concepts Catering with her husband Jim Israel. Now 22 years later, they are still catering for all sorts and sizes of events, including the GA 250th!

Enjoy this dish for any celebration! You can make it as an entrée, make it in miniature for an appetizer or even on a bun as an alternative burger.

CHICKEN AND SPINACH CAKES

2½ pounds boneless, skinless chicken breast
5 slices bacon, chopped
2 teaspoons crushed garlic
½ cup minced shallot
3 cups frozen chopped spinach, thawed and well drained
1 cup bread crumbs
1½ cups heavy cream
1 teaspoon salt
1 teaspoon black pepper
Pinch of cayenne pepper
Olive oil for sautéing

Cube chicken and process in a food processor until minced. Cook bacon in a hot pan until crisp and brown. Add garlic and shallot and sauté until softened; cool slightly. Add chicken and spinach to bacon mixture. Stir in bread crumbs, cream, salt, pepper and cayenne and mix well. Mold mixture into palm-size cakes.

Heat olive oil in a sauté pan. Sauté a thumb-size cake to test for seasoning. Sauté cakes on both sides until golden brown. Serve with lemon basil mayonnaise or sautéed mushrooms.

YIELDS 25 (2 1/2 OUNCE) CAKES, 2 CAKES PER ENTRÉE OR 60 MINI HORS D'OEUVRE-SIZE CAKES

Cakes can be frozen, or heated in oven when ready to serve.

Culinary Concepts Inc.
1406 South Front Street, Philadelphia, PA 19147
215 755-7747, www.culinary-concepts.com

VEAL SALTIMBOCCA

5 tablespoons canola oil
8 (3 ounce) slices veal
1 cup flour
1 stick butter
1 cup Madeira wine
1 cup chicken, veal or beef broth

1 (16 ounce) package fresh leaf
  spinach
8 thin slices prosciutto
8 slices mozzarella cheese
Salt and pepper to taste

Heat oil in a sauté pan until hot. Dust veal with flour and sear in hot oil on both sides until lightly browned. Drain oil from pan. Add butter to pan. Turn heat to medium-high and cook for 1 minute. Remove pan from heat and add wine. Return to heat and simmer for 5 minutes. Add broth, spinach and salt and pepper. Cover pan and cook until spinach cooks down.

Move spinach to one side of the pan. Place prosciutto on top of veal slices. Stack spinach on top. Place mozzarella on spinach. Cover pan until cheese melts. Remove veal from pan and plate, return to high heat. Season with salt and pepper. Cook until sauce reduces to coat the back of the spoon. Slowly pour sauce over each stack. Plate and serve.

SERVES 4

From the Boot opened in Lafayette Hill 1999 as a carry-out restaurant and evolved into an full service sit-down restaurant. A second location opened in Ambler in 2009 with a full bar and restaurant.

FROM THE BOOT

From the Boot offers family recipes made from the freshest ingredients in the company of friends and family. It's place where you are truly welcomed.

From the Boot.
110 East Butler Pike, Ambler, PA 19002
215 646-0123, www.fromtheboot.com

*D*esigned and built by owner Frank Lutter, Dettera is located in the heart of Ambler. Dettera brings sophisticated dining to the suburbs. Centrally located on Butler Pike, the main street of the newly revitalized downtown Ambler, Dettera merges executive chef Thomas Groff's progressive American cuisine with wine bar chic in a beautifully restored, historic building.

DETTERA RESTAURANT & BAR

From casual dining on the outside deck with an intimate brick fireplace, to the first floor dining level, which opens to a dramatic curving black granite bar and oversized round banquettes, Dettera creates the perfect atmosphere for your dining experience. There is a second floor that is used for private parties during the week and ala carte dining on the weekends.

Roast Rock Cod or Striped Bass with Fennel and Beurre Blanc

6 (6 to 8 ounces) fillets Rock Cod or Wild Striped Bass
Salt and freshly ground black pepper to taste
2 fennel bulbs, sliced lengthwise ½ inch thick, stalks discarded, some fronds reserved

1 pound fingerling potatoes, halved lengthwise—blanched for 10 minutes
2 medium onions, sliced ½ inch thick
6 plum tomatoes, cut into wedges
Pinch of dried red pepper flakes
Extra virgin olive oil
¾ cup dry white wine

Sauce

3 tablespoons olive oil, plus extra for drizzling
3 shallots, finely chopped
½ fennel bulb, finely chopped
2 tablespoons Pernod or Anesette
¾ cup dry white wine

1 stick unsalted butter, softened, cut into pieces
Juice of ½ lemon
2 lemons, halved or cut into wedges
Fresh parsley sprigs

Preheat oven to 400 degrees. With a sharp knife make incisions in skin side of filets at 1 inch intervals. Season fish all over, including incisions with salt and pepper.

Spread fennel slices, potatoes, onion slices and tomato wedges on a rimmed baking pan. Sprinkle vegetables with salt, pepper and dried chili flakes. Drizzle generously with olive oil. Place fish on vegetables, skin side up. Drizzle fish with olive oil. Pour wine in pan with vegetables.

Place pan over two burners on stovetop over medium-high heat. As soon as liquid starts to steam, transfer to oven. Roast for 15 minutes, basting occasionally with pan juices. Remove fish when firm to touch.

Dettera Restaurant & Bar
129 East Butler Avenue, Ambler, PA 19002
215 643-0111, www.dettera.com

Meanwhile, prepare sauce. Heat olive oil over medium-high heat in a saucepan. Add shallot and chopped fennel and sauté for 3 to 5 minutes until translucent but not browned. Add Pernod, which may flare up as the alcohol burns off. Add white wine and stir and scrape to deglaze bottom of pan. Simmer briskly for about 10 minutes or until liquid reduces to about ¼ cup.

Whisking continuously, add butter to sauce, 2 pieces at a time, until sauce is smooth, thick and creamy. Season to taste with salt and pepper. Stir in lemon juice. Pour sauce through a fine strainer held over another saucepan. Press down solids with the back of a wooden spoon to press out all the liquid. Finely chop reserved fennel fronds. Stir all but about 1 tablespoon of fronds into sauce and adjust seasonings to taste. Keep sauce warm over low heat.

Use a pair of large spatulas to transfer fish to a serving platter. Arrange roasted vegetables around fish. Drizzle a spoonful or two of sauce over the top. Garnish platter with lemon, parsley and remaining fennel fronds. Drizzle fish with a little more olive oil. Serve, passing remaining sauce separately.

SERVES 6

The Jarrettown Hotel offers a unique combination of extraordinary Italian cuisine, exquisite décor, and affordable prices. Owner Giovanni Agresti delivers a true taste of Italy with passion and gusto!

Since we opened The Jarrettown Hotel, our food has been known for its freshness and flavor. We believe that food, and process of crafting food deserves the utmost care and respect. We bring together sensational imported ingredients, the freshest seasonal produce, local meats, and seafood (delivered daily) with authentic family recipes.

JARRETTOWN HOTEL ITALIAN RESTAURANT & BAR

"Our goal is to carry on the established traditions of Italian cooking from previous generations and deliver them to our customers. The result is deliciously simple, rustic and uncompromised cuisine."

Giovanni Agresti

POLLO JARRETTOWN AND SPINACH FETTUCCINE

12 ounces chicken breast
2 tablespoons chopped shallot
4 ounces fresh mushrooms, chopped
4 tablespoons butter
4 asparagus spears, cut into pieces

3 tablespoons brandy
6 ounces cream
Salt and pepper to taste
4 slices mozzarella cheese
8 ounces dry spinach fettuccine, cooked al dente
2 ounces Parmesan cheese

Preheat oven to 350 degrees. Sauté chicken breast with shallot and mushrooms in olive oil in a hot pan for 6 to 8 minutes. Add asparagus. Deglaze pan with brandy and cook 1 to 2 minutes. Add cream and season with salt and pepper. Cook until sauce reduces. Spoon asparagus and mushrooms on top of chicken breasts. Place mozzarella on top.

Bake for 2 to 3 minutes. Serve over fettuccine. Sprinkle Parmesan on top.

SERVES 2

Jarrettown Hotel Italian Restaurant & Bar
1425 Limekiln Pike, Dresher, PA 19025
215 654-6880, www.jarrettownrestaurant.com

KC's ROCKHILL SALAD

3 heads romaine hearts, cut to desired size pieces
6 ounces balsamic vinaigrette
¼ cup sun-dried cranberries

¼ cup crumbled bleu cheese
¼ cup chopped walnuts
1 Granny Smith apple, cored and sliced

Place romaine in a large mixing bowl. Add vinaigrette and toss well. Add cranberries, cheese and walnuts. Toss again. Garnish with apple slices on top. Enjoy!

SERVES 5

K C's Alley is Ambler's FIRST family tavern, serving great food and spirits since 1999. Head Chefs Peter Sherba & Floyd Powell offer a fantastic menu including salads, sandwiches, wraps, ribs, wings and the area's best burgers.

KC'S ALLEY

KC's Alley offers varied culinary offerings throughout the week, daily drink specials and serves as a great place to host your own special event.

KC's Alley
10 West Butler Pike, Ambler, PA 19002
215 628-3300, www.kc-alley.com

A local neighborhood bar and grill not to be missed is MaGerk's Pub and Grill, formerly known as the *Bent Elbow Tavern*.

MaGERK'S PUB AND GRILL

This restaurant is the third venture stemming from two other successful locations in Maryland and is a homecoming for the owners who are from the greater Philadelphia area. MaGerk's is designed to be a "sports pub with good grub". Signature cheese steaks along with several menu items with a Baltimore flair keep customers coming back. The lively atmosphere boasts musical entertainment several times throughout the week and over 30 flat screen TV's to watch your favorite Philly teams.

HOT CRAB DIP

16 ounces cream cheese
1 cup mayonnaise
1 tablespoon Dijon mustard
1 tablespoon sherry
1 tablespoon Old Bay seasoning, or more to taste
1 tablespoon Worcestershire sauce
3 tablespoons onion powder
1 can lump crabmeat
2 cans backfin crabmeat
Hot pepper sauce to taste (optional)

Preheat oven to 350 degrees. Blend cream cheese and mayonnaise until smooth. Mix in mustard, sherry, Old Bay, Worcestershire sauce and onion powder. Fold in all crabmeat. Transfer mixture to a baking dish.

Bake for 20 to 30 minutes or until hot and bubbly. Serve with warm bread, and celery and carrot sticks.

SERVES 10

MaGerk's Pub and Grill
582 South Bethlehem Pike, Fort Washington, PA
19034 215 948-3329, www.magerks.com

CHESAPEAKE BAY CRAB SOUP

1 stick margarine
½ cup chopped onion
½ cup all-purpose flour
1 quart half & half
1 quart milk
1 pound backfin crabmeat

¼ cup sherry wine
½ teaspoon salt
¼ teaspoon cayenne pepper
1 tablespoon chopped fresh parsley

Melt margarine in a saucepan. Add onion and sauté until translucent. Blend in flour. Stir in half & half and milk. Simmer for 5 minutes over medium heat. Add crabmeat, sherry, salt and cayenne pepper. Cook until heated through; do not boil. Sprinkle with parsley and serve immediately.

SERVES 12

*M*eriwether Godsey has proudly served Germantown Academy since 2005.

MERIWETHER GODSEY AT GERMANTOWN ACADEMY

An employee-owned Dining Management Company, MG was started by Marie "Rie" Meriwether Godsey and her husband Eddie with this simple belief: real service and wonderful food is possible in schools just as it is in restaurants. MG serves communities from Pennsylvania to North Carolina, and is a team of nearly 500 managers, chefs and dedicated staff.

Meriwether Godsey at Germantown Academy
4944 Old Boonsboro Road, Lynchburg, VA 24503
434 384-3663, www.merig.com

*R*ich Rosenau and Rich's Delicatessen have been fixtures in Fort Washington since Memorial Day of 1978. Having purchased the business from Bea's Cold Cuts, Rich's Deli has become an annex of German-town Academy, having watched 32 years of graduating classes and befriending thousands of students and their families.

RICH'S DELI

Rich's son Philip was a GA Lifer graduating in 2002. Rich has cemented a bond between him-self and the GA Community. He knows everyone, from the head-master, teachers, administrators, coaches, to the maintenance staff and is deeply involved in the GA community.

Rich's has been providing customers with Philly staples such as hoagies, cheese steaks, sandwiches and a full line of breakfast sandwiches and plat-ters. He takes special pride in the superb catering that comes out of his deli.

MELANIE OMELETTE

(Named after Melanie Rosenau, Rich's wife, and Philips' Mom a volunteer at GA)
(Low Cholesterol Omelette)

4 egg whites
3 teaspoons finely chopped onion
3 teaspoons finely chopped tomatoes

3 teaspoons finely chopped green peppers
Oil to coat frying pan

In a small bowl, whip together all ingredients. Coat a frying pan with oil and preheat to medium heat. Pour ingredients into a frying pan. Let cook thoroughly on one side, then flip and cook other side. After omelette is firm, fold sides in to form a rectangle and flip onto platter. Serve with home fries, fruit or toast.

Rich's Deli
430 South Bethlehem Pike, Fort Washington, PA 19034, 215-646-9860
www.richsdeli.com

POLLO SAN MARCO

4 (4 ounce) chicken breasts
All-purpose flour for dusting
3 tablespoons cooking oil
4 tablespoons butter
1 ounce shallot, chopped

2 ounces sun-dried tomatoes
1½ cups chicken broth
Salt and pepper to taste
4 paper thin slices prosciutto
4 (1 ounce) slices fontina cheese

Pat dry chicken and dust with flour to prevent sticking. Sear chicken in hot oil over medium-low heat in a 12 inch skillet until golden brown on both sides.

Add butter, shallot, sun-dried tomato and broth. Reduce heat to medium and cook until chicken is done throughout. Season with salt and pepper. Top with prosciutto and cheese. Cover skillet with a lid to melt cheese prior to serving.

SERVES 4

Ristorante San Marco has been in business for the past 11 years. This well-established restaurant is immeasurable, with impeccable service, attention to detail and beautiful grounds, all of which make San Marco a great place to visit. The menu selection is always innovative, with great daily specials.

RISTORANTE SAN MARCO

When you visit San Marco you will be in for a treat, and you'll be able to catch a piece of the Old Country, right here in Ambler.

Ristorante San Marco
504 North Bethlehem Pike, Ambler, PA 19002
215 654-5000, www.sanmarcopa.com

*S*avona Restaurant has been a bastion of luxury dining in the Philadelphia Main Line since opening in 1997. The culinary team is always on display in Savona's open kitchen ,working on the custom-built Bonnet stove to create Savona's ever-changing menu that is avant-garde yet firmly rooted in the classics.

SAVONA RESTAURANT

The 1,100 bottle wine menu, the largest in Pennsylvania, has multiple 'Best of' Awards of Excellence from Wine Spectator. Additionally, Savona has earned Four Diamonds from AAA and three awards from DiRoNA (Distinguished Restaurants of North America). But even successful businesses must evolve thus Evan Lambert, owner, recently redesigned Savona and incorporate Bar Savona, a casual dining space housed in the front bar area, with second floor dining and a new outdoor patio; all the while preserving the elegant formal dining room and original details that date back to 1762.

PUMPKIN AND LOBSTER SOUP

2 lobsters
1 gallon whole milk
1 cup heavy cream
1 pumpkin
2 tablespoons blended oil
2 shallots, thinly sliced

Pinch of nutmeg
½ cup brandy
Salt and pepper to taste
3 tablespoons whipped cream
½ cup roasted pumpkin seeds

Remove lobster tail and the claws and knuckles. Sauté lobster bodies until bright red. Add milk and heavy cream. Bring to a boil. Reduce heat and simmer 30 minutes; strain and set broth aside.

Cook lobster tails, claws and knuckles in boiling salted water for 6 to 7 minutes. Drain and shock in ice water. Remove meat from shell and roughly chop; set aside.

Wash pumpkin well and cut in half. Scoop out seeds and remove stem. Roughly chop pumpkin.

Heat oil in pan until hot. Add pumpkin and sauté until tender. Add shallot and sauté until translucent. Add nutmeg and deglaze pan with brandy. Add lobster broth and cook for 30 to 45 minutes. Pour soup into a blender and purée until smooth. Strain and season with salt and pepper.

Heat lobster meat in a pan until hot. Reheat soup to desired temperature. Add whipped cream to soup. Ladle soup into individual serving bowls. Top with lobster meat. Garnish with roasted pumpkin seeds.

SERVES 10

THE PICKET POST

Standing as the eastern entrance to Valley Forge, the Picket Post is part of the history of the Revolutionary War. In 1762, John Sturgis built his home on the banks of Gulph Creek which became a place where Washington and his 11,000 men encamped from Dec 13-19, 1777 during which suitable winter quarters and headquarters for the picket line were located. This Gulph Creek traverse, a section through which the British would first have to penetrate if they chased the army further inland, was where Washington set up a picket line under the command of lieutenant colonel Aaron Burr. The picket line extended from Lancaster Pike to the Schuylkill River. Twenty-three years later Burr became the Vice-President of the United States.

Savona Restaurant
100 Old Gulph Road, Gulph Mills, PA 19428
610 520-1200, www.savonarestaurant.com

TIRAMISU

¾ cup egg whites
1 (16 ounce) container
    mascarpone cheese
2 egg yolks
¼ cup sugar

2½ tablespoons cognac
1 package ladyfingers
2 cups brewed espresso
Cocoa powder and shaved
    chocolate for garnish

Whip egg whites until stiff; set aside. Blend mascarpone cheese with egg yolks and sugar. Slowly blend in cognac. Fold cheese mixture into egg whites.

Form alternating layers of cheese mixture and ladyfingers dipped in espresso in individual serving bowls. Sprinkle with cocoa powder and shaved chocolate. Keep refrigerated until serving.

SERVES 8

Scoogi's Classic Italian
738 Bethlehem Pike, Flourtown, PA 19031
215 233-1063, www.scoogis.com

"*Viva* Italia! Scoogi's mission is to bring a bit of our family's Italian culture to you, so that you can celebrate each meal as we do. In our Family, dinnertime was the centerpiece of our lives. I remember great feelings of contentment and gratification at each meal, and an overwhelming feeling of love and security would overcome me. The goal of the restaurant is to make meal time special for you and your family.

SCOOGI'S CLASSIC ITALIAN

I want to bring warmth and love and fresh food to you every day. I want to recreate the connection of the old world meeting the new. I want to recreate the feeling I love. **That's my dream.**"
Robert A Rosato owner and executive chef opened Scoogi's at age 24.

The Shanachie Irish Pub and Restaurant is located directly across from the Ambler Theater in beautiful Ambler, Pennsylvania. The Shanachie features a delicious fusion of Irish and American cuisine served in a relaxing and friendly environment.

SHANACHIE IRISH PUB AND RESTAURANT

The Shanachie has been voted the Philadelphia region's best Irish pub two years in a row. Come see why The Shanachie is truly a great Irish-American pub!

POTATO LEEK SOUP

2 sticks butter
1 stalk celery, chopped
3 bunches leeks, chopped
3 white onions, diced
12 Idaho potatoes, chopped
12 Yukon Gold potatoes, chopped

1 quart heavy cream
2 cups chicken broth (optional)
3 tablespoons kosher salt
1 tablespoon black pepper
Chopped scallion for garnish

Melt butter in a large pot or kettle. Add celery, leek and onion with a little water. Cover and simmer until softened. Add all potato and enough water to reach top of potato. Bring to a boil, stirring frequently.

Add cream and broth. Season with salt and pepper. Using a hand held immersion blender, blend until smooth. Garnish with scallion.

SERVES 20 TO 24

Shanachie Irish Pub and Restaurant
111 East Butler Avenue, Ambler, PA 19002
215 283-4887, www.shanachiepub.com

DARK CHOCOLATE RUM TRUFFLES

Ganache Centers

1⅛ cups heavy cream

14 ounces dark chocolate, finely chopped

2 tablespoons unsalted butter, softened

1-2 tablespoons dark rum of choice (optional)

Coating

20 ounces 64% dark chocolate, finely chopped

Unsweetened cocoa powder

Ganache

For the ganache, bring cream to a gentle boil over medium heat. Remove from heat and let rest for 2 minutes. Pour hot cream over chocolate and let stand for 30 seconds to allow the chocolate to melt. In a circular motion starting from the center of the bowl, stir chocolate in the center until it is a creamy, pudding-like consistency. Continue to stir/ from the center out until the entire mixture becomes a beautiful, shiny and creamy ganache. Stir in butter, then rum. Pour ganache into a flat baking dish. Cover and refrigerate 3 hours or until firm enough to scoop, or let stand overnight at a cool room temperature.

Using a 1 inch scoop, form ganache into rounds and roll between palms of hands into smooth balls. (Vinyl gloves work well for this procedure.)

Coating

To prepare coating, melt chocolate in the microwave on medium power for 2 minutes; stir. Microwave in about 5 second increments on 50 percent power, stirring, until just melted and smooth. Place some cocoa powder in a flat dish. For each truffle, spread a small amount of melted chocolate in the palm of your hand and roll the ganache ball in chocolate until coated. (Again, gloves work well for this.) Roll truffle in cocoa powder until coated. If chocolate thickens while working, microwave on medium power for a few seconds at a time to maintain a good working temperature.

Store truffles at a cool room temperature in an airtight container and enjoy within 1 week; or refrigerate and eat within 2 weeks. Bring to room temperature before enjoying for maximum flavor.

YIELDS ABOUT 55 TRUFFLES

Use the highest possible grade of chocolate you can find.

The Painted Truffle by Sciascia
215 996-0606, www.thepaintedtruffle.com

Since 2001, Tom Sciascia has been creating chocolate as an expression of art. Based on the uncompromising passion that sharing great chocolate makes people happy, Tom and Loren created The Painted Truffle. With fresh cream infusions, chocolate made from the earth's finest cocoa beans, 100% all natural ingredients from around the world, each truffle is impeccably handmade. Cloaked in chocolate, each truffle is truly a work of art with a unique personality.

THE PAINTED TRUFFLE

Tom is constantly refining each recipe with great love and attention to detail. He carefully selects each ingredient to go into the final confection resulting in rich, complex flavors. Philadelphia Style Magazine says, "These sublime gems are sure to make your knees wobbly" and Main Line Today magazine named The Painted Truffle "Best Handmade Chocolates 2009."

PEPPER AND HERB CRUSTED RACK OF LAMB WITH RED WINE LAMB JUS

1 (1½ pound) rack of lamb
2 large cloves garlic, minced and mixed with a touch of salt

Oil for sautéing

Lamb Rub

1 tablespoon fresh or dried rosemary
1 tablespoon fresh or dried parsley

1 tablespoon fresh or dried thyme
1 teaspoon kosher salt
1 teaspoon cracked black pepper
1 teaspoon fresh or dried lavender

Sauce

Red wine, brandy or water
Salt and pepper to taste

Butter

Trim lamb, leaving the rib bones as long as possible. Leave about ¼ inch of fat on the outside of the rack. Cut in a criss-cross manner through the fat; do not cut into the meat. Rub minced garlic all over lamb.

If using fresh herbs, chop by hand with a chef's knife; if using dried herbs, use a coffee grinder and grind until fine. Combine all rub ingredients. Rub mixture all over lamb. Allow rack to stand for 1 to 2 hours at room temperature; this will give a nicer crust.

When ready to cook, preheat oven to 400 degrees. Heat oil in a heavy skillet. Add lamb to skillet and brown on all sides until seared and uniform in color. Place skillet in oven for 20 minutes. Remove lamb from skillet to a cutting board and let rest in a warm place.

Place hot skillet over heat and add red wine, brandy or water. With a wooden spoon, deglaze and scrape up bits in skillet. This is the base for a sauce. Continue to cook until sauce reduces. Add more liquid as needed and season with salt and pepper to taste. Stir in butter.

To serve, cut rack of lamb along bones. Serve with sauce on the side.

SERVES 2

CARROT AND GINGER SOUP

1 tablespoon canola oil, or other
   mild oil
1 large onion, chopped
3 cloves garlic, chopped
1 inch fresh ginger, peeled and
   chopped
3 tablespoons sugar

1 tablespoon salt
1 teaspoon curry powder
6-8 carrots, sliced
48 ounces vegetable or chicken
   broth
2 cups water

Heat oil in a medium saucepan. Add onion and garlic and sauté until lightly golden. Add ginger, sugar, salt and curry and sauté 3 to 5 minutes longer, stirring occasionally. Add carrot, broth and water. Bring to a boil. Reduce heat and simmer 30 minutes or until carrot is tender. Cool and purée in a blender or food processor until smooth and creamy.

S E R V E S   4   T O   6

JOSEPH'S HOUSE GRANOLA

1 cup orange juice concentrate
1 cup firmly packed brown sugar
2 tablespoons vegetable oil
4 cups dry oats
1 cup shredded coconut
½ cup walnuts
½ cup pecans

½ cup macadamia nuts
½ teaspoon cinnamon
½ cup craisins
½ cup golden raisins
Cooking spray, any neutral oil/fat
   to grease baking tray

Heat orange juice concentrate, brown sugar and vegetables oil in saucepan until mixture comes to a boil. Pour this mixture over the oats, coconut, nuts and cinnamon; stir to combine. Spread out on a large greased baking sheet and bake at 325 degrees for 10 minutes. When time is up add the craisins and golden raisins, bake for 12 more minutes. Remove from oven, let cool and dry on the baking sheet for 1 hour.

S E R V E S   4   T O   6

Zakes Café began as a bakery in the East Falls section of Philadelphia. In 1995, we moved to our present location, a charming Victorian house in Fort Washington, Pennsylvania.

ZAKES CAKES AND CAFÉ

The Café now serves breakfast, lunch, dinner and Sunday brunch. We are open 7 days a week. Zakes is known for freshly prepared, great tasting food "made from scratch." Zakes is a local favorite and a well known secret for faculty, parents and students of Germantown Academy.

Zakes Cakes & Café
444 Bethlehem Pike, Fort Washington, PA
19034 215 644-0991, www.zakescafe.com

The *Patriots' Bounty* Committee expresses its heartfelt appreciation to the families and friends of Germantown Academy who shared recipes enjoyed by their families and friends throughout the years! As Germantown Academy celebrates its traditions of 250 years, the art of preserving old-time recipes, submitted by members of our own GA family, for generations to come is very appealing. Your enthusiasm, taste buds and support are treasured and contribute profoundly to the success of the *Patriots' Bounty*.

Additionally, a special thanks goes out to the many TASTERS and volunteers. We could not have printed the bounty of delicious dishes without you!

Aldamlouji, Theresa
Altman, Larry
Ampomah, Karen
Andress, Lori
Aronow, Jamie
Austin, Bonnie
Badami, Heather
Ballay, Nan
Beltz, Rosemarie
Bender, Wendy
Berger, Liz
Biggs-Smith, Alice
Black, Cathy
Bohr, Karin
Blood, Anne
Bradley, Joan Korth
Brandeis, Wendi
Brooke, Cat
Butler, Lisa
Casey, Ann
Chamberlain, Pamela
Champlin, Tabb
Chiccarine, Teresa
Coates, George
Colen, Mazie

Conn, Harriet
Connor, Linda
Corliss, Kathleen
Crane, Holly
Culligan, Kim
Curtis, Charlene
Dalsemer, Kelly
Daulerio, Glenda
Davis, June
Dawe, Virginia
Dean, Charlotte
DeLucca, Carol
Di Donato, Pamela
Dovey, Betty
Doyle, Diane
Dreier, Donna
Duncan, Alaiya
Elefante, Amanda
Elefante, Tony
Epstein, Sandy
Fikioris, Melissa
Fitzgerald, Lesley
Foley, Heather
Foreman, Karin
Franchetti, Anita

Frangakis, Sophia Papadakes
Frost, Stephanie
Galloway, Christy
Galloway, Denise
Gambone, Kirsten
Gambone, Kelly
Garbose, Lynne
Garrett, Jill Binswagner
Gavigan, Jennifer
Gill, Michelle
Gobora, Jennifer
Godick, Andrea
Goodman, Judi
Goodwin, Sara
Gowing, Sara
Grant, Betty
Graziano, Marisa
Griswold, Lori
Hall, Diane
Hall, Maria
Harobin, Becky
Harris, Denise
Harrity, Brian
Haugen, Janet
Haugen, Kevin

Haynie, Karen

Henry, Kris

Hess, Barbara

Hibbits, Christine

Hillman, Jocelyn

Hotte, Jill

Israel, Janet

Jacobs, Carolyn

Jones, Jeanie

Jones, Nancy

Jordan, Samantha MacGregor

Kaltman, Robert

Kaufman, Liz

Kiley, Brooke

Kiley, Maria

Komitzky, Diane

Koons, Cheryl

Korman, Laura

Korth, Joan

Kramp, Marcy

Lamont, SallyJo

Lasdon, Cari

Leone, Carol

Levin, Caren

Logan, Linda

Lorraine, Janet

Lovitz, Ginny

Machikas, Patrice

Markovitz, Robin

Mauro, Linda

McCune, Susan

McDade, Chris

McKenna, Christy

Melley, Diane

Menno, Virginia

Moore, Julie

Morris, Kim

Morris, Kristen

Oberkircher, Kathy

Obrecht, Donna

O'Brien, Polly

Palmer, Stacy

Perlmutter, Ellen

Petras, Myra

Piszek, Beth

Press, Bruce

Reilly, Chris

Rink, Julie Girone

Robertson, Courtney

Robins, Linda

Roman, Aina

Roman, Nicole

Ross, Emily

Roth, Lisa

Sammak, Gerrie

Schell, Joanne

Schlesinger, Kathy

Schwartz, Sheila

Schwartz, Tara Karr

Scordis, Frances

Seybert, Sussi

Shirakawa, Jennifer

Shuler, Jane

Sible, Violet

Signorello, Catherine Bown

Silow, Deenie

Silver, Deborah

Singer, Mary

Skelly, Maureen

Sloane, Kim Flannery

Smith, Cindy

Smolyn, Chris

Specter, Madeline Lamm

Stack, Jennifer

Stack, Kelli

Stack, Laurel

Stambaugh, Michele

Steffens, Livvy

Steffens, Wendie

Sullivan, Suzanne

Tanner, Kathy

Tappen, Kathy

Thistle, Pam Rosser

Topping, Rebecca

Towne, Shawn

Trucksess, Denise

Viola, Karen

Vit, Kathie

Wagner, Emily

Watson, Maryann

Weber, Linda

Weeks, Susan

Wellington ,Peg

Wellington, Tyler

Westrum, Debbie

Westrum, Katie

Westrum, Meg

Williams, Karen

Wood, Michelle

Wroten, Charles

Wysocki, Geri

A sincere thank you to all of those who gave their time and talent to this exciting community cookbook.

Virginia Allenson

Tony Birch

Julia Blumenreich

Gregory Bodison

Jodi Bohr

Barbara Buckley 1760

Kellen Flannery Canavan '71

Sherrea Chadwin 1760

William Cooper

Joe Cotillo

Deena Cross '90

Karen Curry

Charlene Curtis

Bob Davis

Charlotte Dean

Martin Dean

Betsy Walton Duryea '75

Brooke Evans

Kathy Farris

Melissa Fikioris

Bridget Flynn

Lynne Garbose

Jessica Grisafi

Greg Guim

Al Hagdorn

Joy Holmes

Jill Hotte

Richard House

Carolyn Korman Jacobs '80

Cara Jones

Peggy Jones 1760

Woodie Jones '48

Neil Jordan

Dina Katz

Mike Kelly

Deb Kennedy

Bill Korhammer

Charlie Landgrebe

Elly Lawlor

Karl Little

Rose Loher

Graham Martin

Peter McVeigh 1760

Craig Newberger 1760

Gill Newbery

Russell Noble

Ellen Perlmutter

Joseph Pizzino

Nina Pruitt

Dainis Roman

Emily Rubinfield 1760

Nicole Riter

Susan Sarshik

Audrey Schnur

Cannie Shafer

Richard Schellhas

Dick Shoulberg 1760

Nina Smith

John Stipa

Jason Straub

Tom Taft

Kellianne Toland

Roderick Thomas

Cheryl Tornetta

Shawn Towne

Bob Wambold

Brooke Watson

Dave Wentzel

Kurt Wetzel '88

Sara Wolf 1760

Kathy Wyszomierski 1760

A

Absolutely Fabulous Marinade. 186
Absolutely No Work Chicken! 171
Adela's Heavenly Angel Hair 101
Alfredo Sauce 119
All Purpose Basting Recipe. 187
Aloo Gobhi Vegetable 202
Alphabetia Shrimp Florentine 160
Amazing Fusilli with Lemon and Arugula 99
Amish Cole Slaw 91

APPETIZERS *(see also Dips and Spreads)*
    Ann's Clam Pie 10
    Armenian Sausages/Luleh Kabob 21
    Artichoke Nibbles. 14
    Bacon Cheddar Smash-Ups 29
    BBQ Scallops 11
    Beef and Broccoli Wontons 27
    Brie and Apple Appetizers 21
    Carol's Miniature Quiches 18
    Cheesy Spinach Squares 20
    Chicken and Spinach Cakes 276
    Chicken Satay with Spicy Peanut Sauce 26
    Chilled Spiced Shrimp 11
    Cocktail Asparagus 15
    Cocktail Jalapeños 30
    Cocktail Pizzas. 27
    Crabmeat Cocktail 9
    Falafel 15
    Flour Tortillas 22
    Fresh Fishcakes 9
    Fried Ravioli 17
    Game Day Wings 25
    Helen Justice's Rosemary Nuts. 12
    Herbed Goat Cheese Tarts with
       Caramelized Onions 19
    Maryland Crab Cakes. 10
    Mexican Meatballs 24
    Mopsy's Cheese Ball 20
    Pan Fried Spring Rolls 13
    Patriots' Party Cocktail Meatballs 23
    Pepperoni Canapés. 23
    Shrimp Pizza Wedges. 12
    Shrimp Rémoulade 28
    Southern Hush Puppies. 14
    Stuffed Mushrooms 16
    The Kast's Bacon Hors D'oeuvre 19
    Wild Mushroom Pizza. 17
    Wonton Baskets. 28

APPLES
    Apple Bacon Pork. 137
    Apple Noodle Kugel 211
    Apple Pie Cake 254
    Apple Pie with Crumb Topping 248

    Apples Stuffed with Dried Fruits 212
    Apple Streusel Coffee Cake 49
    Apple Walnut Pie 246
    Autumn Chicken 176
    Brie and Apple Appetizers 21
    Butternut Squash and Heirloom Apple Soup 78
    Charlene's Composed Salad 81
    Chicken Waldorf Salad 87
    Cranberry-Apple Pie 249
    Cranberry Relish. 210
    Favorite Apple Pie 247
    GA vs. PC Cross Country Apples. 64
    Healthy Roasted Butternut Squash Soup 77
    Jackson Peak Spiked Apple Crisp 235
    Jewish Apple Cake 259
    Katie's Favorite Apple Cake 48
    KC's Rockhill Salad 281
    Pannekoeken (German Pancake). 53
    Peach Apple Sauce (for Chicken or Pork) 186
    Portabello Buffalo Burgers with Celery Apple Slaw. . . 149
    Quick Baked Apple Crunch 234
    Raw "Oatmeal" 65
    Rough Apple Cake 258
    Sarah's Salad 82
    Sautéed Apples 53
    Uncle Jake's Apple Brown Betty 237

APRICOTS
    Apricot Couscous 146
    Curry Sautéed Chicken with Sweet and Hot Apricots . 166
    Elegant Apricot Sweet Potatoes 204
    Lamb Tagine with Apricot Couscous 146
Armenian Rice Pilaf 206
Armenian Sausages/Luleh Kabob 21
Arroz con Pollo 175

ARTICHOKES
    Artichoke Nibbles. 14
    Cauliflower Vichyssoise 76
    Franchetti Family Chicken Salad 88
    Hot Chicken Salad 181
    Roasted Jerusalem Artichokes 76
    Salad Made by Many 86
    Spinach and Artichoke Dip. 33
    Summer Pasta Salad 89
    Ultimate Creamed Dried Beef 63
Arugula Sauce. 152

ASPARAGUS
    Asparagus Linguini 99
    Asparagus Soup. 75
    Cocktail Asparagus 15
    McLean Hall Stuffed Chicken. 182
    Pollo Jarrettown and Spinach Fettuccine 280
    Roasted Asparagus with Goat Cheese and Bacon . . . 200
    Sandy's Asparagus 201
    Spring Pasta Salad 90

Aunt Ashly and Uncle Dan's Caesar Dressing 83
Aunt Clare's Homemade Chocolate Cake. 266
Aunt Dona's Shrimp Dinner 157
Aunt Gill's Holiday Cranberry Chicken. 174
Aunt Martha's Carrot Cake 261
Autumn Butterscotch Pumpkin Cake 270
Autumn Chicken 176

AVOCADOS
    Avocado, Tomato, Cilantro Salsa
        (for Grilled Seafood or Steak) 185
    Avocado-Tomato Garnish 158
    Cold Avocado Soup 80
    Franchetti Family Chicken Salad 88
    Guacamole 32
    Mango-Avocado Chutney (for Fish) 188
    Salad Made by Many 86
    Salsa de Casa Cody 32

B
Bacon Cheddar Smash-Ups 29
Baked Breakfast 58
Baked Brie with Pesto and Sun-Dried Tomatoes 16
Baked Cauliflower 199
Baked Goat Cheese with
    Caramelized Onion, Garlic and Figs 272
Baked Macaroni and Cheese 115
Baked Macaroni and Cheese with
    Crunchy Crouton Topping 113
Baked Vidalia Onion Dip 34
Baklava 228
Balsamic Sugar Beans 189

BANANAS
    Banana Chocolate Chip Muffins 42
    Chocolate Banana Pancakes 50
    Griswolds' Banana Bread 36
    Not Just Banana Bread 37
    Raw "Oatmeal" 65
    Spiced Fresh Fruit Salad 93
    Strawberry-Banana-Blueberry Bread 35
Barbara's Chicken Divan 179
Barbecue Sauce 140, 142
Barley Casserole 210
BBQ Beef 127
BBQ Scallops 11

BEANS AND PEAS
    Adela's Heavenly Angel Hair 101
    Arroz con Pollo 175
    Balsamic Sugar Beans 189
    Black Bean and Rice Salad 91
    Black Bean Salsa 31
    Blue Bell Inn Lentil Salad 273
    Calico Beans 134
    Chickpea (Chole) Curry 190

Chili and Angel Hair Pasta 134
Creole Spice Soup 67
Crockpot Chicken Chili 182
Falafel 15
Fried Bean Sprout Salad 190
Greek Lentil Soup 72
Green Bean and Potato Salad 189
Hearty Michigan Bean and Sausage Soup 70
Hummus 15
Italian Green Beans 191
Minestra (Escarole and Bean Soup) 70
Minestrone Soup 73
Sarah's Salad 82
Sausage and Bean Casserole 143
Snow Pea Salad 83
Stephen's Venison Chili 150
Summer Pasta Salad 89
Sweet Potato, White Bean and Pepper Tian 203
Turkey and Black Bean Chili 133
Uncle Laurent's French Bean Salad 190
Veal Marsala 147
Vegetarian Chili 71
White Bean, Pasta and
    Sun-Dried Tomato Soup 69
White Bean Salad 87

BEEF
    Armenian Sausages/Luleh Kabob 21
    BBQ Beef 127
    Beef and Broccoli Wontons 27
    Beef Fillet with Rosemary 123
    Beef Stew in a Slow Cooker 128
    Beef Stroganoff 125
    Bracciole (Meatballs and Sausage
        in Tomato Sauce for Pasta) 118
    Calico Beans 134
    Chili and Angel Hair Pasta 134
    Classic Lasagne 106
    Coconut Marinade 188
    Creole Spice Soup 67
    Crockpot Lasagna 109
    Easy Steak Diane 125
    Grandmom's Barbecue Beef 126
    Grandmother's Meatballs and Sauce 116
    Hamburger Casserole 129
    Heart-Warming Beef Stew 128
    Hearty Michigan Bean and Sausage Soup 70
    Italian Meat Lasagna 107
    Kathleen's Hearty Meat Sauce 117
    Korean Beef Shish Kabobs 126
    Low-Fat Mediterranean Meatballs 130
    Meat Loaf with Mushroom Sauce 132
    Mexican Meatballs 24
    Mimi's Brisket 127
    Mini Meat Loaves 131

Mom's Favorite Top Round Roast 124
Nannie's Meatloaf. 131
Patriots' Party Cocktail Meatballs 23
Reuben Dip 32
Reuben Quiche 62
Steak Au Poivre 123
Steak Teriyaki 124
Sweet and Sour Meatballs 129
Ultimate Creamed Dried Beef 63
Betty Silow's Hamentashen (Filled Pastry) . . 232
Bibbie's Lace Cookies 224
Biscotti with Candied Orange and Pecans 231

BLACK BEAN (see Beans and Peas)
Blintze Soufflé 56
Blue Bell Inn Lentil Salad 273

BLUEBERRIES
Blueberry Buckle 236
Blueberry/Lemon Pound Cake 251
Blueberry Muffins 40
Brynne's Blueberry Buckle 50
Chilled Blueberry Soup 80
Energy Boost Bars 66
Fresh Blueberry Pie 246
Lemon Mousse Fruit Tart 253
Strawberry-Banana-Blueberry Bread. 35
Trifle 242
Bluefish in Gin 154
Bok Choy Salad 84
Braciole (Meatballs and Sausage
  in Tomato Sauce for Pasta) 118
Braising Liquid 140

BREADS AND MUFFINS
Banana Chocolate Chip Muffins 42
Blueberry Muffins 40
Carol's Carrot Cake Muffins 43
Challah Bread 39
Chiles and Cheese Cornbread 54
Chocolate Chip Kamish Bread 36
Coffee Cake 47
Cranberry Orange Scones 45
Dried Fruit Cream Scones 44
Dr. J's Sweet Plum Bread 38
Flour Tortillas 22
Food Processor Pie Crust. 268
Grandma's Spoonbread 54
Grandmom McGeehan's Scones. 44
Griswolds' Banana Bread 36
Lemon Bread 38
Not Just Banana Bread 37
Orange Marmalade Muffins 41
Pumpkin Bread Perfection 35
Pumpkin Chip Muffins 42
Southern Hush Puppies. 14
Sticky Buns 46

Strawberry-Banana-Blueberry Bread. 35
Sweet Potato Mini Muffins 40
Zucchini Bread 37
BREAKFAST AND BRUNCH
Apple Streusel Coffee Cake 49
Baked Breakfast. 58
Blintze Soufflé. 56
Breakfast Casserole. 58
Brynne's Blueberry Buckle 50
Chocolate Banana Pancakes 50
Chocolate Chip Pancakes 52
Cinnamon French Toast Bake 56
Coffee Cake. 47
Crème Brûlee French Toast 55
Crêpes 53
Crustless Zucchini Quiche 60
Egg Poof. 58
Energy Boost Bars 66
Garlic Cheese Grits 64
GA vs. PC Cross Country Apples. 64
Granola 65
Hash Brown Egg Bake 59
Jeff's Wonderful Waffles 51
Joseph's House Granola 291
Katie's Favorite Apple Cake 48
Leek and Mushroom Frittata 57
Mango Lassi (Yogurt and Mango Shake) 65
Mare's Fried Matzoh 57
Melanie Omelette. 284
Miss Ellie's Breakfast Casserole 58
Mom's Egg Casserole. 58
Netherlands' Cheese Pie 61
Orange Brunch Pancakes 51
Pannekoeken (German Pancake). 53
Peanut Butter Smoothie 65
Potato Crust Broccoli Quiche 60
Pumpkin Seed Trail Mix. 66
Quick Quiche Lorraine 60
Raw "Oatmeal" 65
Reuben Quiche 62
Sautéed Apples 53
Spinach Quiche 59
Sticky Buns 46
Swedish Pancakes. 49
Texas Bacon 58
Texas Egg Casserole 58
The Best Middle School Advisory Breakfast. . . 58
Tomato Crab Quiche 61
Triplet Fruit Smoothie. 64
Tropical Fruit Smoothie. 64
Ultimate Creamed Dried Beef 63
Whole Wheat Buttermilk Pancakes 52
Bridget's Pork Tenderloin. 274
Brie and Apple Appetizers 21

BROCCOLI

Barbara's Chicken Divan 179
Beef and Broccoli Wontons 27
Broccoli Cheese Casserole 193
Broccoli Salad 86
Broccoli Slaw 193
Chicken Difrancois 179
Comfort Chicken 178
Crunchy Romaine Toss 83
Kindergarten Vegetable Soup 72
Mom's Broccoli Casserole 194
Potato Crust Broccoli Quiche 60
Rotini with Broccoli 98
Summer Pasta Salad 89
Brynne's Blueberry Buckle 50
Buckley Martin Chicken 180

BUFFALO Burgers with
Celery Apple Slaw, Portabello 149
Buffalo Chicken Dip 24

BUTTERNUT SQUASH (see Squash)
Butter Sauce 123

C

CABBAGE

Amish Cole Slaw 91
Cole Slaw 142
Fish Tacos 163
Pan Fried Spring Rolls 13

CAKES (see Desserts)
Calico Beans 134
Candied Orange Peel 231
Candy Cane Pie 267

CANDY (see Desserts)
Carol's Carrot Cake Muffins 43
Carol's Miniature Quiches 18

CARROTS

Aunt Martha's Carrot Cake 261
Carol's Carrot Cake Muffins 43
Carrot and Ginger Soup 291
Carrot Soufflé 199
Easterns Carrot and Pineapple Cake . . . 260

CASSEROLES

Alphabetia Shrimp Florentine 160
Baked Breakfast 58
Baked Cauliflower 199
Baked Macaroni and Cheese 115
Baked Macaroni and Cheese
with Crunchy Crouton Topping 113
Barbara's Chicken Divan 179
Barley Casserole 210
Breakfast Casserole 58
Broccoli Cheese Casserole 193
Buckley Martin Chicken 180

Carrot Soufflé 199
Cauliflower and Tomatoes Au Gratin . . . 199
Chicken Difrancois 179
Chicken Marbella 174
Chicken or Turkey Tetrazzini for a Crowd . . . 98
Chicken Tetrazzini 97
Comfort Chicken 178
Dad's Macaroni and Cheese 116
Dinner Party Chicken Paprika 170
Ecuardorian Humita (Corn Casserole) . . . 198
Egg Poof 58
Eileen's Spinach Soufflé 198
Elegant Apricot Sweet Potatoes 204
Gourmet Mac 'N Cheese 113
Grandma Bowes Macaroni and Cheese . . . 112
Hamburger Casserole 129
Hash Brown Egg Bake 59
"Have a Party" Potatoes 204
Hearty Homemade Ham Macaroni and Cheese . . . 115
Hot Chicken Salad 181
Kyle Smith's Mac 'N Cheese 112
Lobster Macaroni and Cheese 114
Miss Ellie's Breakfast Casserole 58
Mom's Broccoli Casserole 194
Mom's Egg Casserole 58
Netherlands' Cheese Pie 61
Patio Potatoes 205
Pineapple Stuffing 212
Red Book Casserole 178
Sausage and Bean Casserole 143
Scalloped Potatoes with Fennel 206
Summer Squash Casserole 195
Sweet Potato Casserole 201
Sweet Potato, White Bean and Pepper Tian . . . 203
Ten Minute Tortellini à la Erb
with Sausage and Cream 103
Texas Egg Casserole 58
The Best Middle School Advisory Breakfast . . . 58
Three Cheese Pasta 103

CAULIFLOWER

Aloo Gobhi Vegetable 202
Baked Cauliflower 199
Cauliflower and Tomatoes Au Gratin . . . 199
Cauliflower Vichyssoise 76

CEREALS AND GRAINS (see also Rice)

Apricot Couscous 146
Barley Casserole 210
Bibbie's Lace Cookies 224
Couscous 144
Egg Poof 58
Energy Boost Bars 66
Florentine Crispy Cookies 225
Garlic Cheese Grits 64
Granola 65

Joseph's House Granola 291
Low-Fat Mediterranean Meatballs. 130
Mushroom Barley Soup. 71
Opulent Oatmeal Cookies 222
Orange Brunch Pancakes. 51
Patio Potatoes. 205
Raw "Oatmeal" 65
Challah Bread 39
Champagne Risotto 122
Charlene's Composed Salad 81

CHEESE
Baked Brie with Pesto and Sun-Dried Tomatoes 16
Baked Goat Cheese with
    Caramelized Onion, Garlic and Figs 272
Baked Macaroni and Cheese. 115
Baked Macaroni and Cheese
    with Crunchy Crouton Topping 113
Brie and Apple Appetizers 21
Broccoli Cheese Casserole 193
Cheddar Chicken Chowder 68
Cheese Torte 18
Cheesy Spinach Squares 20
Chiles and Cheese Cornbread 54
Classic Lasagne 106
Classic Swiss Fondue 34
Cocktail Jalapeños 30
Dad's Macaroni and Cheese 116
Garlic Cheese Grits 64
Gin Cheese 25
Gourmet Mac 'N Cheese. 113
Grandma Bowes Macaroni and Cheese 112
Hash Brown Egg Bake 59
Hearty Homemade Ham Macaroni and Cheese 115
Herbed Goat Cheese Tarts
    with Caramelized Onions 19
Homestyle Baked Ziti 111
Hot Swiss Bacon Dip 31
I Can't Believe It's Vegetarian Lasagna 108
Italian Meat Lasagna 107
Kyle Smith's Mac 'N Cheese 112
Lobster Macaroni and Cheese 114
Mopsy's Cheese Ball 20
Netherlands' Cheese Pie 61
Oyster and Brie Cheese Soup 73
Ricotta Cookies 224
Rigatoni with Spinach and Feta Cheese. 100
Roasted Asparagus with Goat Cheese and Bacon . . . 200
Salad Made by Many 86
Southern Hush Puppies. 14
Spinach and Cheese Stuffed Tomatoes 191
Three Cheese Pasta. 103
Whole Wheat Pasta with Brie and Fresh Tomatoes. . . 97
Wonton Baskets. 28

CHEESECAKES (see Desserts)

CHERRIES
Opulent Oatmeal Cookies 222
Pumpkin Seed Trail Mix. 66
CHICKEN (see Poultry)
Chickpea (Chole) Curry 190
Chilean Sea Bass with Spinach, Pine Nuts and Shallots . . 155
Chiles and Cheese Cornbread 54
CHILI
Chili and Angel Hair Pasta 134
Crockpot Chicken Chili 182
Stephen's Venison Chili 150
Turkey and Black Bean Chili 133
Vegetarian Chili 71
Chilled Blueberry Soup 80
Chilled Spiced Shrimp 11
CHOCOLATE (see also Desserts)
Aunt Clare's Homemade Chocolate Cake 266
Banana Chocolate Chip Muffins 42
Chocolate Banana Pancakes 50
Chocolate Chip Cheesecake 256
Chocolate Chip Kamish Bread 36
Chocolate Chip Pancakes 52
Chocolate Iced Checkerboard Brownies
    (Grandma Zick's Marble Brownies) 219
Chocolate Pots de Crème 241
Crumble Bars 214
Dark Chocolate Rum Truffles 289
Decadent Chocolate Brownies. 218
Derby Pie 267
Dirt 235
Easy Chocolate Chip Cake 266
Fabulous Hot Fudge Sauce 239
Grammie's Marshmallow Fudge 240
Kahlúa Cake 263
Linda's Peanut Butter Squares 215
Mama Jacobs' Chocolate Chip
    (Caramel Surprise) Cups 245
Norma's Treats 243
One-Bowl Brownies. 219
Opulent Oatmeal Cookies 222
Oreo Ice Cream Explosion 262
Patriots' Dinner Party Mocha Roll 244
Pumpkin Chip Muffins 42
Red Velvet Cake. 264
Robert's Rocky Road Brownies 218
Rocky Mountain Chip Cookies 223
Saltine Chocolate Toffee Treat 230
Seven Layer Bars 213
S'mores Bars. 215
Snickers Bar Pie 266
Soft Batch Chocolate Chip Cookies 220
Sour Cream Double Chocolate Cake 267
Cinnamon French Toast Bake 56

CLAMS *(see Seafood)*
Classic Chicken Marinade 186
Classic Lasagne 106
Classic Swiss Fondue 34
Coach Shoulberg's Favorite Cheesecake 255
Cocktail Asparagus 15
Cocktail Jalapeños 30
Cocktail Pizzas 27

COCONUT
   Coconut Marinade 188
   Granola 65
   Irish Potatoes 229
   Joseph's House Granola 291
   Seven Layer Bars 213
Coffee Cake 47
Cold Avocado Soup 80
Cole Slaw 142
Comfort Chicken 178
Company Chicken 180

CONDIMENTS AND SAUCES
   Absolutely Fabulous Marinade 186
   Alfredo Sauce 119
   All Purpose Basting Recipe 187
   Arugula Sauce 152
   Avocado, Tomato, Cilantro Salsa
     (for Grilled Seafood or Steak) 185
   Avocado-Tomato Garnish 158
   Barbecue Sauce 140, 142
   Braising Liquid 140
   Butter Sauce 123
   Classic Chicken Marinade 186
   Coconut Marinade 188
   Coriander Sauce (for Chicken) 185
   Cranberry Relish 210
   Dill Sauce 151
   Dipping Sauce 13
   Dry Rub 142
   Dry Rub and Ribs 140
   Fish Taco Sauce 163
   Fresh Tomato and Caper Fish Sauce 156
   Hawaiian Marinade (for Chicken or Steak) 184
   Lamb Rub 290
   Lemon Caper Mayonnaise 10
   Lemon-Lime Brown Sugar Marinade (for Chicken) . . . 184
   London Broil Marinade 187
   Mango-Avocado Chutney (for Fish) 188
   Mango Chutney 156
   Memorable Marinade 187
   Mint Sauce 144
   Mom's Marinade (for Grilled Fish or Chicken) 185
   Mustard Vinaigrette 153
   Peach Apple Sauce (for Chicken or Pork) 186
   Pesto II 120
   Pesto Sauce I 120

   Roasted Pepper Vinaigrette 197
   Salsa 163
   Seafood Parmesan Sauce (for Fish) 188
   Secret Recipe Seafood Sauce 161
   Spaghetti Sauce Marinara 119
   Spicy Caramelized Pecans 81
   Spicy Peanut Sauce 26
   Steak Marinade 187
   Sunday Football Vodka Sauce 121
   Sun-Dried Tomato Pesto 90
   Tartar Sauce 163
   Tomato-Mango Salsa for Grilled Scallops 162
   Vinaigrette 271

COOKIES AND BARS *(see Desserts)*

CORN
   Black Bean Salsa 31
   Cheddar Chicken Chowder 68
   Ecuardorian Humita (Corn Casserole) 198
   Grilled Corn on the Cob 196
   Hot Corn Queso 22
   Peg's Louisiana Shrimp and Corn Chowder 74
   Southern Hush Puppies 14
   Tomato Corn Pie 192
Couscous 144

CRAB *(see Seafood)*

CRANBERRY *(Fruit and Sauce)*
   Aunt Gill's Holiday Cranberry Chicken 174
   Butternut Squash with
     Wild Rice and Cranberries 194
   Cranberry-Apple Pie 249
   Cranberry Orange Scones 45
   Cranberry Pudding 233
   Cranberry Relish 210
   Cranberry Roast Pork 138
   Energy Boost Bars 66
   KC's Rockhill Salad 281
   Pearls and Rubies 209
   Pumpkin Seed Trail Mix 66
Cream Cheese Icing 43, 260
Creamed Spinach 198
Creamy Potato Salad 89
Crème Brûlée 275
Crème Brûlee French Toast 55
Creole Spice Soup 67
Crêpes 53
Crockpot Chicken Chili 182
Crockpot Lasagna 109
Crumble Bars 214
Crunchy Romaine Toss 83
Crustless Zucchini Quiche 60
Cucumber Raita 84
Curry Sautéed Chicken with
   Sweet and Hot Apricots 166

D

Dad's Macaroni and Cheese 116
Dark Chocolate Rum Truffles 289
Decadent Butterscotch Pudding 234
Decadent Chocolate Brownies 218
Delicious Grapes 238

DESSERTS

Cakes

Apple Pie Cake 254
Aunt Clare's Homemade Chocolate Cake 266
Aunt Martha's Carrot Cake 261
Autumn Butterscotch Pumpkin Cake 270
Blueberry/Lemon Pound Cake 251
Dr. Samuel Osbourn's (Beloved!)
    Camp Susquehannock Pound Cake 258
Dulce de Leche Cake (Pastel de Cuatro Leches) . . . 269
Easterns Carrot and Pineapple Cake 260
Easy Chocolate Chip Cake 266
Jewish Apple Cake 259
Kahlúa Cake 263
Lemon Cupcakes with Orange Glaze 250
Mama Jacobs' Best Ever Butter Cake 263
Mrs. McClure's Great Moist Cake 265
Pribitkin Fresh Pear Cake 254
Rakowsky Zucchini Cakes 265
Red Velvet Cake 264
Rough Apple Cake 258
Sour Cream Double Chocolate Cake 267

Candy

Candied Orange Peel 231
Dark Chocolate Rum Truffles 289
Grammie's Marshmallow Fudge 240
Mama Jacobs' Chocolate Chip
    (Caramel Surprise) Cups 245
Norma's Treats 243

Cheesecakes

Apple Brandy Cheesecake 257
Chocolate Chip Cheesecake 256
Coach Shoulberg's Favorite Cheesecake 255

Cookies and Bars 226

Baklava 228
Bibbie's Lace Cookies 224
Biscotti with Candied Orange and Pecans 231
Chocolate Iced Checkerboard Brownies (
    Grandma Zick's Marble Brownies) 219
Crumble Bars 214
Decadent Chocolate Brownies 218
Dr. J's Famous Vanilla Cookies 225
Everyone's Favorite Sugar Cookie 220
Fannie's Poppyseed Cookies 229
Florentine Crispy Cookies 225
Icebox Cookies 230
Irish Potatoes 229

Linda's Peanut Butter Squares 215
Nana's Gingerbread Christmas Cookies 221
One-Bowl Brownies 219
Opulent Oatmeal Cookies 222
Pecan Pie Bars 213
Pumpkin Streusel Squares 216
Raspberry Bars 214
Ricotta Cookies 224
Robert's Rocky Road Brownies 218
Rocky Mountain Chip Cookies 223
Saltine Chocolate Toffee Treat 230
Seven Layer Bars 213
S'mores Bars 215
Soft Batch Chocolate Chip Cookies 220
Spice Cookies 272
Supreme Lemon Squares 217
Viscoti Italian Cookies 227

Frozen Desserts

Candy Cane Pie 267
Oreo Ice Cream Explosion 262
Peanut Butter Dream Pie 262
Snickers Bar Pie 266

Icing

Cream Cheese Icing 43, 260

Pies and Tarts

Apple Pie with Crumb Topping 248
Apple Walnut Pie 246
Candy Cane Pie 267
Cranberry-Apple Pie 249
Derby Pie 267
Favorite Apple Pie 247
Food Processor Pie Crust 268
Fresh Blueberry Pie 246
Lemon Mousse Fruit Tart 253
Lemon Sponge Pie 252
Peanut Butter Dream Pie 262
Snickers Bar Pie 266
Sweet Potato Pie 270
The Best Key Lime Pie 250

Puddings and Desserts

Betty Silow's Hamentashen (Filled Pastry) 232
Blueberry Buckle 236
Chocolate Pots de Crème 241
Cranberry Pudding 233
Crème Brûlée 275
Decadent Butterscotch Pudding 234
Delicious Grapes 238
Dirt 235
Fabulous Hot Fudge Sauce 239
Georgia Peach Cobbler 239
Jackson Peak Spiked Apple Crisp 235
Lemon Walnut Dessert 241
Meadow Glen Lemon Trifle 243
Oreo Ice Cream Explosion 262

Patriots' Dinner Party Mocha Roll 244
Peach Cheese Cobbler 238
Peach Clafouti 240
Prune-Plum Filling 232
Quick Baked Apple Crunch 234
Rice Pudding 233
Tiramisu 287
Trifle 242
Uncle Jake's Apple Brown Betty 237
Dill Sauce 151
Dinner Party Chicken Paprika 170

DIPS AND SPREADS
Baked Brie with Pesto and
   Sun-Dried Tomatoes 16
Baked Vidalia Onion Dip 34
Black Bean Salsa 31
Buffalo Chicken Dip 24
Cheese Torte 18
Classic Swiss Fondue 34
Dipping Sauce 13
Gin Cheese 25
Greek Salad Salsa 30
Guacamole 32
Hot Corn Queso 22
Hot Crab Dip 282
Hot Swiss Bacon Dip 31
Hummus 15
Kachumber 85
Mango Salsa 33
Mexican Layer Dip 30
Reuben Dip 32
Salsa 163
Salsa de Casa Cody 32
Scarborough Fair Dip 29
Sequoia's Salmon Spread 33
Spinach and Artichoke Dip 33
Dirt 235
Dried Fruit Cream Scones 44
Dr. J's Famous Vanilla Cookies 225
Dr. J's Sweet Plum Bread 38
Dr. Samuel Osbourn's (Beloved!)
   Camp Susquehannock Pound Cake 258
Dry Rub 142
Dry Rub and Ribs 140
Dulce de Leche Cake (Pastel de Cuatro Leches) 269

E
Easterns Carrot and Pineapple Cake 260
Easy Chocolate Chip Cake 266
Easy Steak Diane 125
Ecuardorian Humita (Corn Casserole) 198

EGGPLANT
Grilled Eggplant 202
I Can't Believe It's Vegetarian Lasagna 108

EGGS (see Breakfast and Brunch)
Eileen's Spinach Soufflé 198
Elegant Apricot Sweet Potatoes 204
ENCHILADAS, Chicken 183
Energy Boost Bars 66
ESCAROLE and Bean Soup, Minestra 70
Everyone's Favorite Sugar Cookie 220

F
Fabulous Hot Fudge Sauce 239
Falafel 15
Fall Dinner Party Stuffed Pork Loin 136
Fannie's Poppyseed Cookies 229
Favorite Apple Pie 247
Fettuccine with Shrimp Maggiore 100
Field Day Chicken 171
FISH (see also Seafood)
Bluefish in Gin 154
Chilean Sea Bass with Spinach,
   Pine Nuts and Shallots 155
Coconut Marinade 188
Fish Tacos 163
Fresh Fishcakes 9
Grilled Island Fish Burgers 163
Harvey Cedars Bluefish 154
Hawaiian Fish Stew 162
Marvelous Mahi Mahi with Cucumber Sauce 153
Mustard-Herb Crusted Salmon with Arugula Sauce . . 152
Panko Encrusted Fish 153
Parents' Committee Pecan Flounder 155
Patriot Fish Fillets in Wine 154
Poached Salmon with Yogurt Dill Sauce 151
Roast Rock Cod or Striped Bass with
   Fennel and Beurre Blanc 278
Salmon in Papillote 151
Salmon with Miso-Soy Sauce 152
Seafood Parmesan Sauce (for Fish) 188
Sequoia's Salmon Spread 33
Simple Swordfish 151
Tuna Steaks with Mango Chutney 156
Flavorful Veal Stew 146
Florentine Crispy Cookies 225
Flour Tortillas 22
Food Processor Pie Crust 268
Franchetti Family Chicken Salad 88
Fresh Blueberry Pie 246
Fresh Fishcakes 9
Fresh Tomato and Caper Fish Sauce 156
Fried Bean Sprout Salad 190
Fried Ravioli 17
Fried Soft Shell Crabs 157
FROZEN DESSERTS (see Desserts)

FRUITS *(see also individual listings)*
Apples Stuffed with Dried Fruits 212
Baked Goat Cheese with
   Caramelized Onion, Garlic and Figs 272
Betty Silow's Hamentashen (Filled Pastry) 232
Delicious Grapes 238
Dried Fruit Cream Scones 44
Trifle 242
Triplet Fruit Smoothie 64
Tropical Fruit Smoothie 64

G
Game Day Wings 25
Garlic Cheese Grits 64
GA vs. PC Cross Country Apples 64
Gazpacho 79
Georgia Peach Cobbler 239
German Potato Salad 94
Gin Cheese 25
Gingered Pear Chicken with Walnuts 169
Goodman Gazpacho 79
Gourmet Mac 'N Cheese 113
Graham's Graduation Tortellini Salad 90
Grammie's Marshmallow Fudge 240
Grandma Bowes Macaroni and Cheese 112
Grandma's Spoonbread 54
Grandmom McGeehan's Scones 44
Grandmom's Barbecue Beef 126
Grandmother's Meatballs and Sauce 116
Grandmother's Turkey Meatloaf 133
Granola 65
Greek Lentil Soup 72
Greek Potato 205
Greek Salad Salsa 30
Greek Shrimp Scampi 159
Greek Style Shrimp with Penne 105
Green Bean and Potato Salad 189
GRILLING RECIPES
Bridget's Pork Tenderloin 274
Grilled Corn on the Cob 196
Grilled Eggplant 202
Grilled Island Fish Burgers 163
Grilled Leg of Lamb 145
Harvey Cedars Bluefish 154
Korean Beef Shish Kabobs 126
Lemon-Lime Brown Sugar Marinade
   (for Chicken) 184
Marinated Pork Tenderloin 135
Mom's Marinade (for Grilled Fish or Chicken) 185
Simple Swordfish 151
Steak Teriyaki 124
Tuna Steaks with Mango Chutney 156
Tuscan Chicken 172
Tuscan-Style Spare Ribs 143

Griswolds' Banana Bread 36
Guacamole 32

H
Hamburger Casserole 129
Harvey Cedars Bluefish 154
Hash Brown Egg Bake 59
"Have a Party" Potatoes 204
Hawaiian Fish Stew 162
Hawaiian Marinade (for Chicken or Steak) 184
Healthy Roasted Butternut Squash Soup 77
Heart-Warming Beef Stew 128
Hearty Homemade Ham Macaroni and Cheese 115
Hearty Michigan Bean and Sausage Soup 70
Helen Justice's Rosemary Nut 12
Herbed Goat Cheese Tarts with Caramelized Onions . . . 19
Homestyle Baked Ziti 111
Hot Chicken Salad 181
Hot Corn Queso 22
Hot Crab Dip 282
Hot Swiss Bacon Dip 31
Hummus 15

I
I Can't Believe It's Vegetarian Lasagna 108
Icebox Cookies 230
ICING *(see Desserts)*
Irish Potatoes 229
Italian Green Beans 191
Italian Meat Lasagna 107

J
Jackson Peak Spiked Apple Crisp 235
Jeera Rice 208
Jeff's Wonderful Waffles 51
Jewish Apple Cake 259
Joseph's House Granola 291
Joy's Chicken Rosemary 165

K
Kachumber 85
Kahlúa Cake 263
Kathleen's Hearty Meat Sauce 117
Katie's Favorite Apple Cake 48
KC's Rockhill Salad 281
Kevin's Amazing Pulled Pig 142
Kindergarten Vegetable Soup 72
Korean Beef Shish Kabobs 126
KUGELS
Apple Noodle Kugel 211
Sylvia's Garlic Kugel 211
Kyle Smith's Mac 'N Cheese 112

L

LAMB
- Armenian Sausages/Luleh Kabob 21
- Grilled Leg of Lamb. 145
- Lamb Tagine with Apricot Couscous 146
- Pepper and Herb Crusted Rack of Lamb
  with Red Wine Lamb Jus 290
- Rack of Lamb Persille 145
- Rack of Lamb with Mint Sauce and Couscous 144

LASAGNA
- Classic Lasagne 106
- Crockpot Lasagna. 109
- I Can't Believe It's Vegetarian Lasagna 108
- Italian Meat Lasagna 107
- Spinach and Chicken Alfredo Lasagna 110
- Leek and Mushroom Frittata 57

LEMON
- Blueberry/Lemon Pound Cake. 251
- Lemon Bread 38
- Lemon Caper Mayonnaise 10
- Lemon Cupcakes with Orange Glaze 250
- Lemon Garlic Chicken 172
- Lemon-Lime Brown Sugar Marinade (for Chicken) . . . 184
- Lemon Mousse Fruit Tart 253
- Lemon Sponge Pie 252
- Lemon Veal 148
- Lemon Walnut Dessert 241
- Meadow Glen Lemon Trifle 243
- Preserved Lemons 146
- Supreme Lemon Squares 217
- White Wine and Lemon Herbed Chicken Legs 168

LIME Pie, The Best Key 250
Linda's Peanut Butter Squares 215

LOBSTER (see Seafood)
London Broil Marinade 187
Low-Fat Mediterranean Meatballs 130

M

Mama Jacobs' Best Ever Butter Cake 263
Mama Jacobs' Chocolate Chip (Caramel Surprise) Cups . . 245
Mandarin Orange Salad 93

MANGOES
- Mango-Avocado Chutney (for Fish) 188
- Mango Chutney. 156
- Mango Lassi (Yogurt and Mango Shake) 65
- Mango Salsa. 33
- Strawberry and Mango Salad 92
- Tomato-Mango Salsa for Grilled Scallops. 162
- Tropical Fruit Smoothie. 64

Mare's Fried Matzoh 57
Marinated Pork Tenderloin 135
Marvelous Mahi Mahi with Cucumber Sauce 153
Marvelous Molasses Cookies 226

Maryland Crab Cakes. 10
McLean Hall Stuffed Chicken 182
Meadow Glen Lemon Trifle 243

MEATLOAF
- Grandmother's Turkey Meatloaf 133
- Meat Loaf with Mushroom Sauce 132
- Mini Meat Loaves 131
- Nannie's Meatloaf. 131

Melanie Omelette 289
Memorable Marinade 187
Mexican Layer Dip 30
Mexican Meatballs 24
Mimi's Brisket 127
Minestra (Escarole and Bean Soup) 70
Minestrone Soup 73
Mint Sauce. 144
Miss Ellie's Breakfast Casserole 58
Mom's Broccoli Casserole 194
Mom's Egg Casserole 58
Mom's Favorite Top Round Roast 124
Mom's Marinade (for Grilled Fish or Chicken). 185
Mom's Pixie Salad Dressing 89
Mopsy's Cheese Ball 20
Mrs. McClure's Great Moist Cake 265
Mrs. P's Secret Sea Scallops,
  from the kitchen of Mrs. Paul 161

MUFFINS (see Breads and Muffins)

MUSHROOMS
- Chicken or Turkey Tetrazzini for a Crowd 98
- Leek and Mushroom Frittata 57
- Meat Loaf with Mushroom Sauce 132
- Miriam's Portabello Mushroom Chicken. 173
- Mushroom Barley Soup. 71
- Portabello Mushrooms Stuffed with Wild Rice 197
- Stuffed Mushrooms 16
- Wild Mushroom Pizza 17

MUSSELS (see Seafood)
Mustard-Herb Crusted Salmon with Arugula Sauce . . . 152
Mustard Vinaigrette. 153
My Son's Favorite Post-Football Practice Dinner 183

N

Nana's Gingerbread Christmas Cookies. 221
Nancy's Seafood Fancy 161
Nannie's Meatloaf. 131
Netherlands' Cheese Pie 61
Never Fail Rice 208
Norma's Treats 243
Not Just Banana Bread. 37

NUTS
- Apples Stuffed with Dried Fruits 212
- Apple Walnut Pie 246
- Baklava. 228

Biscotti with Candied Orange and Pecans 231
Bok Choy Salad 84
Chocolate Iced Checkerboard Brownies
   (Grandma Zick's Marble Brownies) 219
Energy Boost Bars 66
Granola 65
Helen Justice's Rosemary Nuts. 12
Icebox Cookies 230
Joseph's House Granola 291
Lemon Walnut Dessert 241
Parents' Committee Pecan Flounder 155
Pecan Pie Bars. 213
Seven Layer Bars 213
Spicy Caramelized Pecans 81
Squash and Cashew Soup 77

O

One-Bowl Brownies. 219
Opulent Oatmeal Cookies 222
ORANGE (*Fruit and Juice*)
   Biscotti with Candied Orange and Pecans 231
   Candied Orange Peel 231
   Cranberry Orange Scones 45
   Mandarin Orange Salad 93
   Orange Brunch Pancakes. 51
   Orange Marmalade Muffins 41
   Sarah's Salad 82
   Spiced Fresh Fruit Salad 93
   Triplet Fruit Smoothie. 64
Oreo Ice Cream Explosion 262
Oriental Spare Ribs 143
Orzo Feta Salad. 85
Oven Roasted Parmesan Vegetables 200
OYSTERS (*see Seafood*)

P

Pan Fried Spring Rolls 13
Panko Encrusted Fish. 153
Pannekoeken (German Pancake). 53
Parents' Committee Pecan Flounder 155
PASTA
   Adela's Heavenly Angel Hair 101
   Amazing Fusilli with Lemon and Arugula 99
   Apple Noodle Kugel 211
   Armenian Rice Pilaf 206
   Asparagus Linguini 99
   Baked Macaroni and Cheese 115
   Baked Macaroni and Cheese with
      Crunchy Crouton Topping. 113
   Bok Choy Salad 84
   Bracciole (Meatballs and Sausage
      in Tomato Sauce for Pasta) 118
   Broccoli Salad 86
   Buckley Martin Chicken. 180

Cheese Tortellini Soup 68
Chicken Napolitano. 96
Chicken or Turkey Tetrazzini for a Crowd 98
Chicken Tetrazzini 97
Chicken with Fresh Herbs and Tomatoes on Linguini . 95
Chili and Angel Hair Pasta 134
Classic Lasagne 106
Crockpot Lasagna. 109
Crunchy Romaine Toss 83
Dad's Macaroni and Cheese 116
Fettuccine with Shrimp Maggiore 100
Fried Ravioli 17
Gourmet Mac 'N Cheese. 113
Graham's Graduation Tortellini Salad 90
Grandma Bowes Macaroni and Cheese 112
Grandmother's Meatballs and Sauce 116
Greek Style Shrimp with Penne 105
Hamburger Casserole 129
Heart-Warming Beef Stew 128
Hearty Homemade Ham Macaroni and Cheese . . . 115
Homestyle Baked Ziti 111
I Can't Believe It's Vegetarian Lasagna 108
Italian Meat Lasagna 107
Kathleen's Hearty Meat Sauce 117
Kyle Smith's Mac 'N Cheese 112
Lobster Macaroni and Cheese 114
Orzo Feta Salad. 85
Penne and Chicken Dijon 96
Pollo Jarrettown and Spinach Fettuccine 280
Quick and Healthy Chicken in Wine Sauce 173
Rigatoni with Spinach and Feta Cheese. 100
Rotini with Broccoli 98
Scallops Wolfeboro 162
Shrimp Scampi with Linguini 104
Spinach and Chicken Alfredo Lasagna 110
Spring Pasta Salad 90
Stuffed Shells 111
Summer Pasta Salad 89
Sylvia's Garlic Kugel 211
Ten Minute Tortellini à la Erb with
   Sausage and Cream 103
Thai Sesame Noodle Salad. 82
Three Cheese Pasta. 103
Tortellini with Creamy Herb Sauce 102
White Bean, Pasta and Sun-Dried Tomato Soup . . . 69
Whole Wheat Pasta with Brie and Fresh Tomatoes. . 97
Patio Potatoes. 205
Patriot Fish Fillets in Wine 154
Patriots' Dinner Party Mocha Roll 244
Patriots' Golden Chicken. 168
Patriots' Party Cocktail Meatballs 23
PEACHES
   Georgia Peach Cobbler 239
   Peach Apple Sauce (for Chicken or Pork) 186

Peach Cheese Cobbler 238
Peach Clafouti 240
PEANUT BUTTER
Linda's Peanut Butter Squares 215
Peanut Butter Dream Pie 262
Peanut Butter Smoothie 65
Pearls and Rubies 209
PEARS
Gingered Pear Chicken with Walnuts . . . 169
Pribitkin Fresh Pear Cake 254
Pumpkin Pear Soup 75
PEAS *(see Beans and Peas)*
Pecan Pie Bars 213
Peg's Louisiana Shrimp and Corn Chowder . . 74
Penne and Chicken Dijon 96
Pepper and Herb Crusted
Rack of Lamb with Red Wine Lamb Jus 290
Pepperoni Canapés 23
Pesto II 120
Pesto Sauce I 120
Philly Roast Pork Sandwiches 139
PIES AND TARTS *(see Desserts)*
PINEAPPLE
Carol's Carrot Cake Muffins 43
Cranberry Relish 210
Easterns Carrot and Pineapple Cake 260
Pineapple Stuffing 212
Spiced Fresh Fruit Salad 93
PIZZA
Cocktail Pizzas 27
Shrimp Pizza Wedges 12
Wild Mushroom Pizza 17
PLANTAINS, Spanish Green 210
Poached Salmon with Yogurt Dill Sauce . . 151
Pollo Jarrettown and Spinach Fettuccine . . . 280
Pollo San Marco 285
PORK
Apple Bacon Pork 137
Bacon Cheddar Smash-Ups 29
BBQ Scallops 11
Bracciole (Meatballs and Sausage
in Tomato Sauce for Pasta) 118
Breakfast Casserole 58
Bridget's Pork Tenderloin 274
Calico Beans 134
Cocktail Pizzas 27
Cranberry Roast Pork 138
Fall Dinner Party Stuffed Pork Loin 136
Hearty Homemade Ham Macaroni and Cheese . . . 115
Hot Swiss Bacon Dip 31
Kathleen's Hearty Meat Sauce 117
Kevin's Amazing Pulled Pig 142
Marinated Pork Tenderloin 135

Meat Loaf with Mushroom Sauce 132
Miss Ellie's Breakfast Casserole 58
Oriental Spare Ribs 143
Patriots' Party Cocktail Meatballs 23
Pepperoni Canapés 23
Philly Roast Pork Sandwiches 139
Pork Barbecue 138
Roasted Asparagus with Goat Cheese and Bacon . . . 200
Russ's Baby-Backs with
Coffee-Bourbon Barbecue Sauce 140
Salad Made by Many 86
Sausage and Bean Casserole 143
Sweet and Sour Meatballs 129
Ten Minute Tortellini à la Erb
with Sausage and Cream 103
Texas Bacon 58
Texas Egg Casserole 58
The Kast's Bacon Hors D'oeuvre 19
Tuscan-Style Spare Ribs 143
Wonton Baskets 28
Portabello Buffalo Burgers with Celery Apple Slaw . . . 149
Portabello Mushrooms Stuffed with Wild Rice . . . 197
POTATOES
Beef Stew in a Slow Cooker 128
Creamy Potato Salad 89
Creole Spice Soup 67
Fresh Fishcakes 9
German Potato Salad 94
Greek Potato 205
Green Bean and Potato Salad 189
Hash Brown Egg Bake 59
"Have a Party" Potatoes 204
Patio Potatoes 205
Potato Crust Broccoli Quiche 60
Potato Leek Soup 288
Potato, Tomato, Zucchini Galette 205
Refrigerator Mashed Potatoes 206
Scalloped Potatoes with Fennel 206
POULTRY
Chicken
Absolutely No Work Chicken! 171
Arroz con Pollo 175
Aunt Gill's Holiday Cranberry Chicken . . . 174
Autumn Chicken 176
Barbara's Chicken Divan 179
Buckley Martin Chicken 180
Buffalo Chicken Dip 24
Cheddar Chicken Chowder 68
Chicken and Spinach Cakes 276
Chicken Difrancois 179
Chicken Enchiladas 183
Chicken Marbella 174
Chicken Napolitano 96
Chicken or Turkey Tetrazzini for a Crowd 98

Chicken Satay with Spicy Peanut Sauce 26
Chicken Tetrazzini. 97
Chicken Waldorf Salad 87
Chicken with Fresh Herbs and
   Tomatoes on Linguini 95
Chicken Ziggy. 177
Comfort Chicken 178
Company Chicken 180
Crockpot Chicken Chili. 182
Curry Sautéed Chicken
   with Sweet and Hot Apricots 166
Dinner Party Chicken Paprika 170
Field Day Chicken. 171
Franchetti Family Chicken Salad 88
Game Day Wings 25
Gingered Pear Chicken with Walnuts 169
Hawaiian Marinade (for Chicken or Steak). 184
Hot Chicken Salad 181
Joy's Chicken Rosemary 165
Lemon Garlic Chicken 172
Lemon-Lime Brown Sugar Marinade (for Chicken) . . 184
McLean Hall Stuffed Chicken 182
Miriam's Portabello Mushroom Chicken. 173
My Son's Favorite Post-Football Practice Dinner . . . 183
Patriots' Golden Chicken. 168
Penne and Chicken Dijon. 96
Pollo Jarrettown and Spinach Fettuccine 280
Pollo San Marco 285
Potts Chicken Crunch. 181
Quick and Healthy Chicken in Wine Sauce 173
Red Book Casserole 178
Salad Made by Many 86
Spinach and Chicken Alfredo Lasagna 110
Tuscan Chicken 172
Under the Blue Moon Sesame Pecan Chicken 167
Unlucky Chicken. 180
White Wine and Lemon Herbed Chicken Legs 168
   Turkey
Chicken or Turkey Tetrazzini for a Crowd 98
Crockpot Lasagna. 109
Grandmother's Turkey Meatloaf 133
Meat Loaf with Mushroom Sauce 132
Salad Made by Many 86
Turkey and Black Bean Chili 133
Preserved Lemons 146
Pribitkin Fresh Pear Cake. 254
Prune-Plum Filling 232

PUDDINGS AND DESSERTS (*see Desserts*)
Pulao Rice 207

PUMPKIN
Autumn Butterscotch Pumpkin Cake 270
Pumpkin and Lobster Soup 286
Pumpkin Bread Perfection 35
Pumpkin Chip Muffins 42

Pumpkin Pear Soup. 75
Pumpkin Seed Trail Mix. 66
Pumpkin Streusel Squares 216

Q
QUICHE (*see Breakfast and Brunch*)
Quick and Healthy Chicken in Wine Sauce 173
Quick Baked Apple Crunch 234

R
Rack of Lamb Persille 145
Rakowsky Zucchini Cakes. 265
RASPBERRIES
Lemon Mousse Fruit Tart 253
Raspberry Bars 214
Trifle 242
Tropical Fruit Smoothie. 64
Raw "Oatmeal" 65
Red Book Casserole 178
Red Velvet Cake. 264
Refrigerator Mashed Potatoes 206
Reuben Dip 32
Reuben Quiche 62
RICE
Armenian Rice Pilaf 206
Arroz con Pollo 175
Aunt Dona's Shrimp Dinner 157
Black Bean and Rice Salad 91
Butternut Squash Risotto. 122
Butternut Squash with Wild Rice and Cranberries . . . 194
Champagne Risotto. 122
Comfort Chicken 178
Fall Dinner Party Stuffed Pork Loin 136
Jeera Rice 208
Mrs. P's Secret Sea Scallops,
   from the kitchen of Mrs. Paul 161
Never Fail Rice 208
Patriots' Golden Chicken. 168
Portabello Mushrooms Stuffed with Wild Rice 197
Pulao Rice 207
Rice Pilaf. 207
Rice Pudding 233
Saffron Steamed Basmati Rice 209
Summer Rice Salad 92
Unlucky Chicken. 180
Ricotta Cookies 224
Rigatoni with Spinach and Feta Cheese. 100
Roasted Asparagus with Goat Cheese and Bacon 200
Roasted Brussels Sprouts
   with Balsamic Bacon and Parmesan 271
Roasted Cherry Tomatoes 191
Roasted Jerusalem Artichokes. 76
Roasted Pepper Vinaigrette 197

Roast Rock Cod or Striped Bass
   with Fennel and Beurre Blanc 278
Roast Venison Loin 150
Robert's Rocky Road Brownies 218
Rocky Mountain Chip Cookies 223
Rotini with Broccoli 98
Rough Apple Cake 258
Russ's Baby-Backs with
   Coffee-Bourbon Barbecue Sauce 140

S
Saffron Steamed Basmati Rice 209
SALAD DRESSINGS
   Aunt Ashly and Uncle Dan's Caesar Dressing 83
   Mom's Pixie Salad Dressing 89
   Roasted Pepper Vinaigrette 197
   Sherry Vinaigrette 81
   Sun-Dried Tomato Pesto 90
   Vinaigrette 271
SALADS
   Amish Cole Slaw 91
   Black Bean and Rice Salad 91
   Blue Bell Inn Lentil Salad 273
   Bok Choy Salad 84
   Broccoli Salad 86
   Broccoli Slaw 193
   Charlene's Composed Salad 81
   Chicken Waldorf Salad 87
   Cole Slaw 142
   Creamy Potato Salad 89
   Crunchy Romaine Toss 83
   Cucumber Raita 84
   Franchetti Family Chicken Salad 88
   Fried Bean Sprout Salad 190
   German Potato Salad 94
   Graham's Graduation Tortellini Salad 90
   Green Bean and Potato Salad 189
   Kachumber 85
   KC's Rockhill Salad 281
   Mandarin Orange Salad 93
   Orzo Feta Salad 85
   Salad Made by Many 86
   Sarah's Salad 82
   Snow Pea Salad 83
   Spiced Fresh Fruit Salad 93
   Spinach and Strawberry Salad 93
   Spring Pasta Salad 90
   Strawberry and Mango Salad 92
   Summer Pasta Salad 89
   Summer Rice Salad 92
   Thai Sesame Noodle Salad 82
   Uncle Laurent's French Bean Salad 190
   White Bean Salad 87
SALMON (*see Fish*)

Salsa 163
Salsa de Casa Cody 32
Saltine Chocolate Toffee Treat 230
SANDWICHES
   BBQ Beef 127
   Grandmom's Barbecue Beef 126
   Grilled Island Fish Burgers 163
   Kevin's Amazing Pulled Pig 142
   Philly Roast Pork Sandwiches 139
   Pork Barbecue 138
   Portabello Buffalo Burgers with Celery Apple Slaw . . 149
Sandy's Asparagus 201
Sarah's Salad 82
SAUCES (*see Condiments and Sauces*)
SAUERKRAUT
   Reuben Dip 32
   Reuben Quiche 62
SAUSAGE (*see Pork*)
Sautéed Apples 53
Scalloped Potatoes with Fennel 206
Scarborough Fair Dip 29
SEAFOOD
   Clams
     Ann's Clam Pie 10
     Sumptuous Seafood Stew 164
   Crab
     Crab Cakes with Avocado-Tomato Garnish 158
     Crabmeat Cocktail 9
     Fried Soft Shell Crabs 157
     Hot Crab Dip 282
     Maryland Crab Cakes 10, 158
     Sumptuous Seafood Stew 164
     Tomato Crab Quiche 61
   Lobster
     Lobster Macaroni and Cheese 114
     Pumpkin and Lobster Soup 286
   Mussels
     Tequila Mussels 156
   Oysters
     Oyster and Brie Cheese Soup 73
   Scallops
     BBQ Scallops 11
     Coconut Marinade 188
     Mrs. P's Secret Sea Scallops,
      from the kitchen of Mrs. Paul 161
     Scallops Wolfeboro 162
     Sumptuous Seafood Stew 164
   Shrimp
     Alphabetia Shrimp Florentine 160
     Aunt Dona's Shrimp Dinner 157
     Chilled Spiced Shrimp 11
     Fettuccine with Shrimp Maggiore 100
     Greek Shrimp Scampi 159
     Greek Style Shrimp with Penne 105

Nancy's Seafood Fancy 161
Peg's Louisiana Shrimp and Corn Chowder 74
Shrimp Pizza Wedges 12
Shrimp Rémoulade 28
Shrimp Scampi with Linguini 104
Sumptuous Seafood Stew 164
Seafood Parmesan Sauce (for Fish) 188
Secret Recipe Seafood Sauce 161
Sequoia's Salmon Spread 33
Seven Layer Bars 213
Simple Swordfish 151

SMOOTHIES
Mango Lassi (Yogurt and Mango Shake) 65
Peanut Butter Smoothie 65
Triplet Fruit Smoothie 64
Tropical Fruit Smoothie 64
S'mores Bars 215
Snickers Bar Pie 266
Snow Pea Salad 83
Soft Batch Chocolate Chip Cookies 220

SOUPS, STEWS AND CHILI
Asparagus Soup 75
Beef Stew in a Slow Cooker 128
Butternut Squash and Heirloom Apple Soup 78
Carrot and Ginger Soup 291
Cauliflower Vichyssoise 76
Cheddar Chicken Chowder 68
Cheese Tortellini Soup 68
Chili and Angel Hair Pasta 134
Chilled Blueberry Soup 80
Cold Avocado Soup 80
Creole Spice Soup 67
Crockpot Chicken Chili 182
Flavorful Veal Stew 146
Gazpacho 79
Goodman Gazpacho 79
Greek Lentil Soup 72
Hawaiian Fish Stew 162
Healthy Roasted Butternut Squash Soup 77
Hearty Michigan Bean and Sausage Soup 70
Kindergarten Vegetable Soup 72
Minestra (Escarole and Bean Soup) 70
Minestrone Soup 73
Mushroom Barley Soup 71
Oyster and Brie Cheese Soup 73
Peg's Louisiana Shrimp and Corn Chowder 74
Potato Leek Soup 288
Pumpkin and Lobster Soup 286
Pumpkin Pear Soup 75
Squash and Cashew Soup 77
Sumptuous Seafood Stew 164
Turkey and Black Bean Chili 133
Vegetarian Chili 71
White Bean, Pasta and Sun-Dried Tomato Soup 69

Sour Cream Double Chocolate Cake 267
Southern Hush Puppies 14
Spaghetti Sauce Marinara 119
Spanish Green Plantains 210
Spice Cookies 272
Spiced Fresh Fruit Salad 93
Spicy Peanut Sauce 26

SPINACH
Alphabetia Shrimp Florentine 160
Cheese Torte 18
Cheese Tortellini Soup 68
Cheesy Spinach Squares 20
Chicken and Spinach Cakes 276
Chilean Sea Bass with
    Spinach, Pine Nuts and Shallots 155
Creamed Spinach 198
Eileen's Spinach Soufflé 198
Field Day Chicken 171
Greek Potato 205
Minestrone Soup 73
Red Book Casserole 178
Rigatoni with Spinach and Feta Cheese 100
Spinach and Artichoke Dip 33
Spinach and Cheese Stuffed Tomatoes 191
Spinach and Chicken Alfredo Lasagna 110
Spinach and Strawberry Salad 93
Spinach Quiche 59
Stuffed Shells 111
Veal Saltimbocca 277
Spring Pasta Salad 90

SQUASH *(see also Zucchini)*
Butternut Squash and Heirloom Apple Soup 78
Butternut Squash Risotto 122
Butternut Squash with Wild Rice and Cranberries . . . 194
Healthy Roasted Butternut Squash Soup 77
Oven Roasted Parmesan Vegetables 200
Squash and Cashew Soup 77
Stuffed Squash 196
Summer Squash Casserole 195
Steak Au Poivre 123
Steak Marinade 187
Steak Teriyaki 124
Stephen's Venison Chili 150
Sticky Buns 46

STRAWBERRIES
Spinach and Strawberry Salad 93
Strawberry and Mango Salad 92
Strawberry-Banana-Blueberry Bread 35
Trifle 242
Stuffed Mushrooms 16
Stuffed Shells 111
Stuffed Squash 196
STUFFING, Pineapple 212
Summer Pasta Salad 89

Summer Rice Salad 92
Summer Squash Casserole 195
Sumptuous Seafood Stew 164
Sunday Football Vodka Sauce 121
Sun-Dried Tomato Pesto 90
Supreme Lemon Squares 217
Swedish Pancakes 49
Sweet and Sour Meatballs 129
SWEET POTATOES
   Elegant Apricot Sweet Potatoes 204
   Sweet Potato Casserole 201
   Sweet Potato Mini Muffins 40
   Sweet Potato Pie 270
   Sweet Potato, White Bean and Pepper Tian . . . 203
Sylvia's Garlic Kugel 211

T
Tartar Sauce 163
Ten Minute Tortellini à la Erb with Sausage and Cream . . 103
Tequila Mussels 156
Texas Bacon 58
Texas Egg Casserole 58
Thai Sesame Noodle Salad 82
The Best Key Lime Pie 250
The Best Middle School Advisory Breakfast 58
The Kast's Bacon Hors D'oeuvre 19
Three Cheese Pasta 103
Tiramisu 287
TOMATOES
   Avocado, Tomato, Cilantro Salsa
     (for Grilled Seafood or Steak) 185
   Avocado-Tomato Garnish 158
   Baked Brie with Pesto and Sun-Dried Tomatoes . . 16
   Cauliflower and Tomatoes Au Gratin 199
   Chicken with Fresh Herbs and Tomatoes on Linguini . 95
   Creole Spice Soup 67
   Fresh Tomato and Caper Fish Sauce 156
   I Can't Believe It's Vegetarian Lasagna 108
   Peg's Louisiana Shrimp and Corn Chowder . . . 74
   Potato, Tomato, Zucchini Galette 205
   Rigatoni with Spinach and Feta Cheese 100
   Roasted Cherry Tomatoes 191
   Salsa 163
   Salsa de Casa Cody 32
   Scarborough Fair Dip 29
   Spinach and Cheese Stuffed Tomatoes 191
   Sumptuous Seafood Stew 164
   Sun-Dried Tomato Pesto 90
   Tomato Corn Pie 192
   Tomato-Mango Salsa for Grilled Scallops 162
   Tomato Pie 192
   White Bean, Pasta and Sun-Dried Tomato Soup . . 69
Tortellini with Creamy Herb Sauce 102
Trifle 242
Triplet Fruit Smoothie 64

Tropical Fruit Smoothie 64
Tuna Steaks with Mango Chutney 156
TURKEY *(see Poultry)*
Tuscan Chicken 172
Tuscan-Style Spare Ribs 143
U
Ultimate Creamed Dried Beef 63
Uncle Jake's Apple Brown Betty 237
Uncle Laurent's French Bean Salad 190
Under the Blue Moon Sesame Pecan Chicken 167
Unlucky Chicken 180
V
VEAL
   Flavorful Veal Stew 146
   Lemon Veal 148
   Patriots' Party Cocktail Meatballs 23
   Sweet and Sour Meatballs 129
   Veal Marsala 147
   Veal Saltimbocca 277
VEGETABLES *(see also individual listings)*
   Aloo Gobhi Vegetable 202
   I Can't Believe It's Vegetarian Lasagna 108
   Kindergarten Vegetable Soup 72
   Roasted Brussels Sprouts with
     Balsamic Bacon and Parmesan 271
   Roasted Pepper Vinaigrette 197
   Vegetarian Chili 71
VENISON
   Roast Venison Loin 150
   Stephen's Venison Chili 150
Viscoti Italian Cookies 227
W
White Bean, Pasta and Sun-Dried Tomato Soup . . . 69
White Bean Salad 87
White Wine and Lemon Herbed Chicken Legs 168
Whole Wheat Buttermilk Pancakes 52
Whole Wheat Pasta with Brie and Fresh Tomatoes . . 97
Wild Mushroom Pizza 17
WONTON WRAPPERS
   Beef and Broccoli Wontons 27
   Pan Fried Spring Rolls 13
   Wonton Baskets 28
Z
ZUCCHINI *(see also Squash)*
   Crustless Zucchini Quiche 60
   Hash Brown Egg Bake 59
   Kindergarten Vegetable Soup 72
   Oven Roasted Parmesan Vegetables 200
   Potato, Tomato, Zucchini Galette 205
   Rakowsky Zucchini Cakes 265
   Zucchini Bread 37
   Zucchini Rounds 195

Send order with payment to:

Germantown Academy Parents' Committee
340 Morris Road, Fort Washington, PA 19034
Or order online at www.germantownacademy.net/cookbookorder

Name _____ Phone _____ Email _____

Address _____ City _____ State _____ Zip _____

Credit Card Payment (circle one)   MasterCard   Visa

Credit Card number _____ Expiration Date _____

Name on Card _____ Signature _____

Patriots' Bounty Cookbook
*PA residents add 6% sales tax
*Postage and handling for first book
*Postage and handling for each additional book

Quantity _____ x $30 each   = $ _____
Quantity _____ x $1.80 each = $ _____
                              = $ __11.00__
Quantity _____ x $2 each   = $ _____
Total Enclosed   = $ _____

Please make checks payable to Germantown Academy — Thank you for your order!
Questions? Email cookbook250@germantownacademy.org

Send order with payment to:

Germantown Academy Parents' Committee
340 Morris Road, Fort Washington, PA 19034
Or order online at www.germantownacademy.net/cookbookorder

Name _____ Phone _____ Email _____

Address _____ City _____ State _____ Zip _____

Credit Card Payment (circle one)   MasterCard   Visa

Credit Card number _____ Expiration Date _____

Name on Card _____ Signature _____

Patriots' Bounty Cookbook
*PA residents add 6% sales tax
*Postage and handling for first book
*Postage and handling for each additional book

Quantity _____ x $30 each   = $ _____
Quantity _____ x $1.80 each = $ _____
                              = $ __11.00__
Quantity _____ x $2 each   = $ _____
Total Enclosed   = $ _____

Please make checks payable to Germantown Academy — Thank you for your order!
Questions? Email cookbook250@germantownacademy.org